W9-CFE-566

DPOOL VOL. 3: THE GOOD, THE BAD AND THE UGLY. Contains material originally published in magazine form as DEADPOOL #13-19. Third printing 2015. ISBN# 978-0-7851-6682-5. Published by MARVEL LDWIDE, INC., a subsidiary of MARVEL ENTERTAINMENT, LLC. OFFICE OF PUBLICATION: 135 West 50th Street, New York, NY 10020. Copyright © 2013 MARVEL No similarity between any of the names, characters, ons, and/or institutions in this magazine with those of any living or dead person or institution is intended, and any such similarity which may exist is purely coincidental. **Printed in Canada.** ALAN FINE, President, el Entertainment; DAN BUCKLEY, President, TV, Publishing and Brand Management; JOE QUESADA, Chief Creative Officer; TOM BREVOORT, SVP of Publishing; DAVID BOGART, SVP of Operations & Procurement, shing; C.B. CEBULSKI, VP of International Development & Brand Management; DAVID GABRIEL, SVP Print, Sales & Marketing; JIM O'KEEFE, VP of Operations & Logistics; DAN CARR, Executive Director of Publishing nology; SUSAN CRESPI, Editorial Operations Manager; ALEX MORALES, Publishing Operations Manager; STAN LEE, Chairman Emeritus. For information regarding advertising in Marvel Comics or on Marvel.com, se contact Jonathan Rheingold, VP of Custom Solutions & Ad Sales, at jrheingold@marvel.com. For Marvel subscription inquiries, please call 800-217-9158. **Manufactured between 8/26/15 and 9/28/15 by** SCO PRINTERS, SCOTT, QC, CANADA.

DEADPOOL

WRITERS
GERRY DUGGAN & BRIAN POSEHN

ARTISTS
SCOTT KOBLISH (#13-14) & DECLAN SHALVEY (#15-19)

COLORISTS
VAL STAPLES (#13-14) & JORDIE BELLAIRE (#15-19)

COVER ART
KRIS ANKA (#13-14) AND DECLAN SHALVEY & JORDIE BELLAIRE (#15-19)

LETTERER
VC'S JOE SABINO

EDITOR
JORDAN D. WHITE

DEADPOOL CREATED BY ROB LIEFELD & FABIAN NICIEZA

Collection Editor: Jennifer Grünwald • Assistant Editor: Sarah Brunstad • Associate Managing Editor: Alex Starbuck
Editor, Special Projects: Mark D. Beazley • Senior Editor, Special Projects: Jeff Youngquist
SVP Print, Sales & Marketing: David Gabriel • Book Design: Jeff Powell

Editor in Chief: Axel Alonso • Chief Creative Officer: Joe Quesada • Publisher: Dan Buckley • Executive Producer: Alan Fine

Talkin' jive
& takin' lives.

DEADPOOL, POWER MAN AND IRON FIST

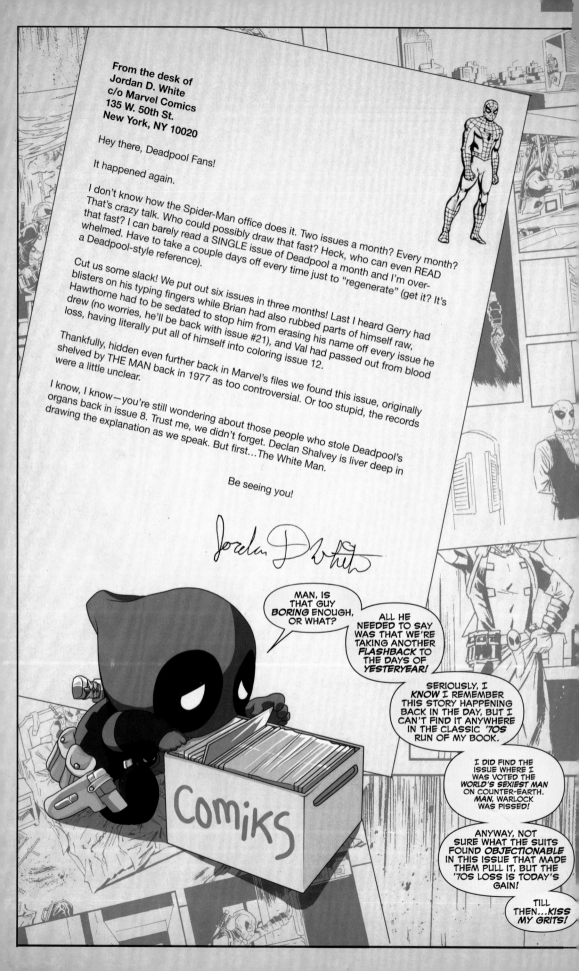

From the desk of
Jordan D. White
c/o Marvel Comics
135 W. 50th St.
New York, NY 10020

Hey there, Deadpool Fans!

It happened again.

I don't know how the Spider-Man office does it. Two issues a month? Every month? That's crazy talk. Who could possibly draw that fast? Heck, who can even READ that fast? I can barely read a SINGLE issue of Deadpool a month and I'm overwhelmed. Have to take a couple days off every time just to "regenerate" (get it? It's a Deadpool-style reference).

Cut us some slack! We put out six issues in three months! Last I heard Gerry had blisters on his typing fingers while Brian had also rubbed parts of himself raw, Hawthorne had to be sedated to stop him from erasing his name off every issue he drew (no worries, he'll be back with issue #21), and Val had passed out from blood loss, having literally put all of himself into coloring issue 12.

Thankfully, hidden even further back in Marvel's files we found this issue, originally shelved by THE MAN back in 1977 as too controversial. Or too stupid, the records were a little unclear.

I know, I know—you're still wondering about those people who stole Deadpool's organs back in issue 8. Trust me, we didn't forget. Declan Shalvey is liver deep in drawing the explanation as we speak. But first…The White Man.

Be seeing you!

Jordan D White

MAN, IS THAT GUY *BORING* ENOUGH, OR WHAT?
ALL HE NEEDED TO SAY WAS THAT WE'RE TAKING ANOTHER *FLASHBACK* TO THE DAYS OF *YESTERYEAR!*
SERIOUSLY, I *KNOW* I REMEMBER THIS STORY HAPPENING BACK IN THE DAY, BUT I CAN'T FIND IT ANYWHERE IN THE CLASSIC *'70S* RUN OF MY BOOK.
I DID FIND THE ISSUE WHERE I WAS VOTED THE *WORLD'S SEXIEST MAN* ON COUNTER-EARTH. *MAN,* WARLOCK WAS PISSED!
ANYWAY, NOT SURE WHAT THE SUITS FOUND *OBJECTIONABLE* IN THIS ISSUE THAT MADE THEM PULL IT, BUT THE '70S LOSS IS TODAY'S GAIN!
TILL THEN…*KISS MY GRITS!*
COMIKS

UKE CAGE: a child of the streets…DANIEL RAND: a son of the mystic city of K'un-Lun…WADE WILSON: government experiment gone wrong… Three men from different worlds—all reborn with **strength** and **power beyond belief!** And together, no one can stop them!

DEADPOOL, POWER MAN AND IRON FIST

ERRY DUGGAN, BRIAN POSEHN — WRITERS
SCOTT KOBLISH — ARTIST
VAL STAPLES — COLORIST
VC'S JOE SABINO — LETTERER
JORDAN D. WHITE — EDITOR
AXEL ALONSO — EDITOR IN CHIEF
JOE QUESADA — CHIEF CREATIVE OFFICER
DAN BUCKLEY — PUBLISHER
ALAN FINE — EXEC. PRODUCER

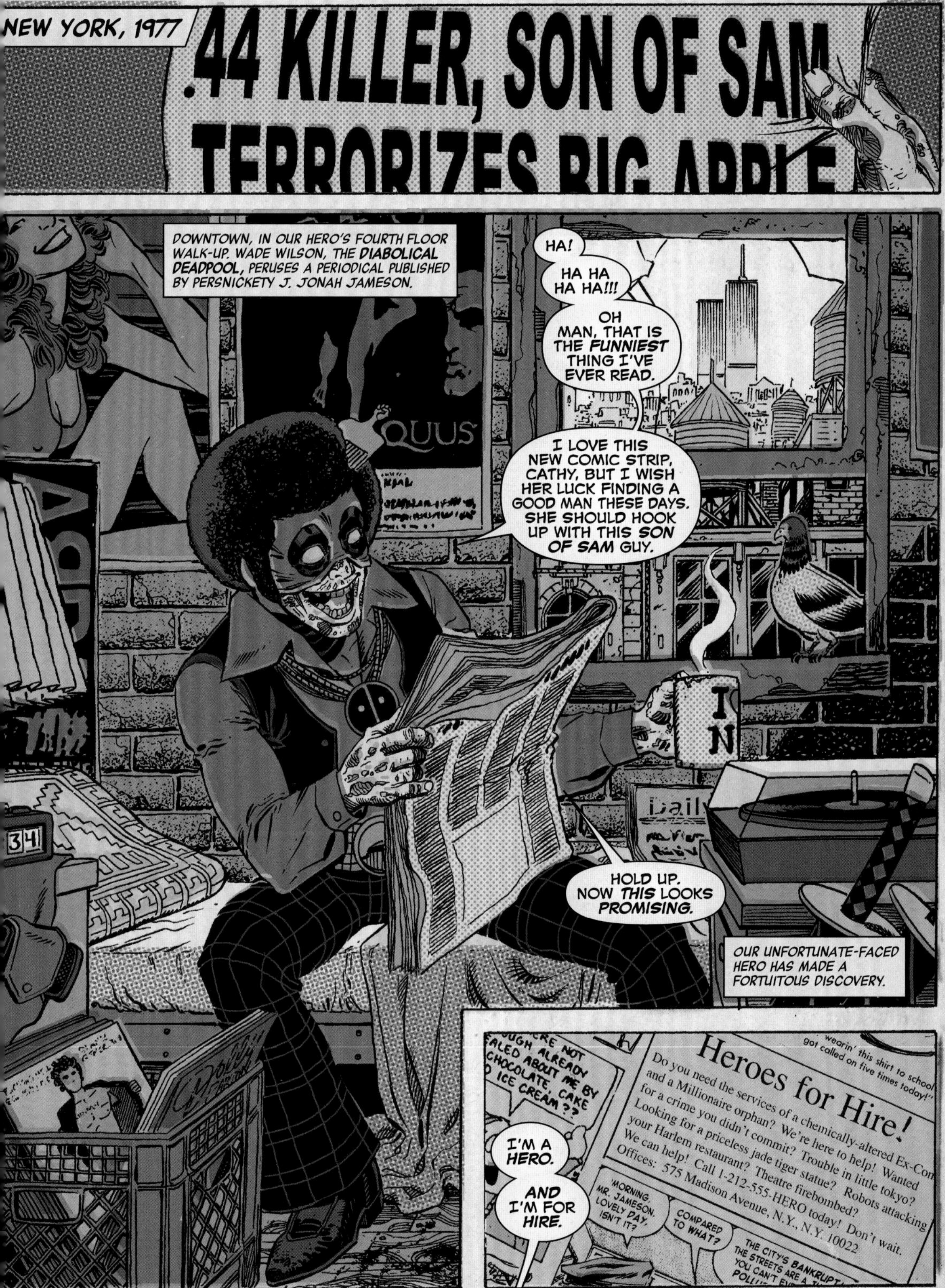

NEW YORK, 1977
.44 KILLER, SON OF SAM
TERRORIZES BIG APPLE
DOWNTOWN, IN OUR HERO'S FOURTH FLOOR WALK-UP. WADE WILSON, THE DIABOLICAL DEADPOOL, PERUSES A PERIODICAL PUBLISHED BY PERSNICKETY J. JONAH JAMESON.
HA!
HA HA HA HA!!!
OH MAN, THAT IS THE FUNNIEST THING I'VE EVER READ.
I LOVE THIS NEW COMIC STRIP, CATHY, BUT I WISH HER LUCK FINDING A GOOD MAN THESE DAYS. SHE SHOULD HOOK UP WITH THIS SON OF SAM GUY.
QUUS
HOLD UP. NOW THIS LOOKS PROMISING.
OUR UNFORTUNATE-FACED HERO HAS MADE A FORTUITOUS DISCOVERY.
Heroes for Hire!
wearin' this shirt to school got called on five times today!"
Do you need the services of a chemically-altered Ex-Con and a Millionaire orphan? We're here to help! Wanted for a crime you didn't commit? Trouble in little tokyo? Looking for a priceless jade tiger statue? Robots attacking your Harlem restaurant? Theatre firebombed? We can help! Call 1-212-555-HERO today! Don't wait. Offices: 575 Madison Avenue, N.Y., N.Y. 10022
FAILED ABOUT ME BY CHOCOLATE, CAKE AND ICE CREAM??
I'M A HERO.
AND I'M FOR HIRE.
MORNING, MR. JAMESON. LOVELY DAY, ISN'T IT?
COMPARED TO WHAT?
THE CITY'S BANKRUPT. THE STREETS ARE A

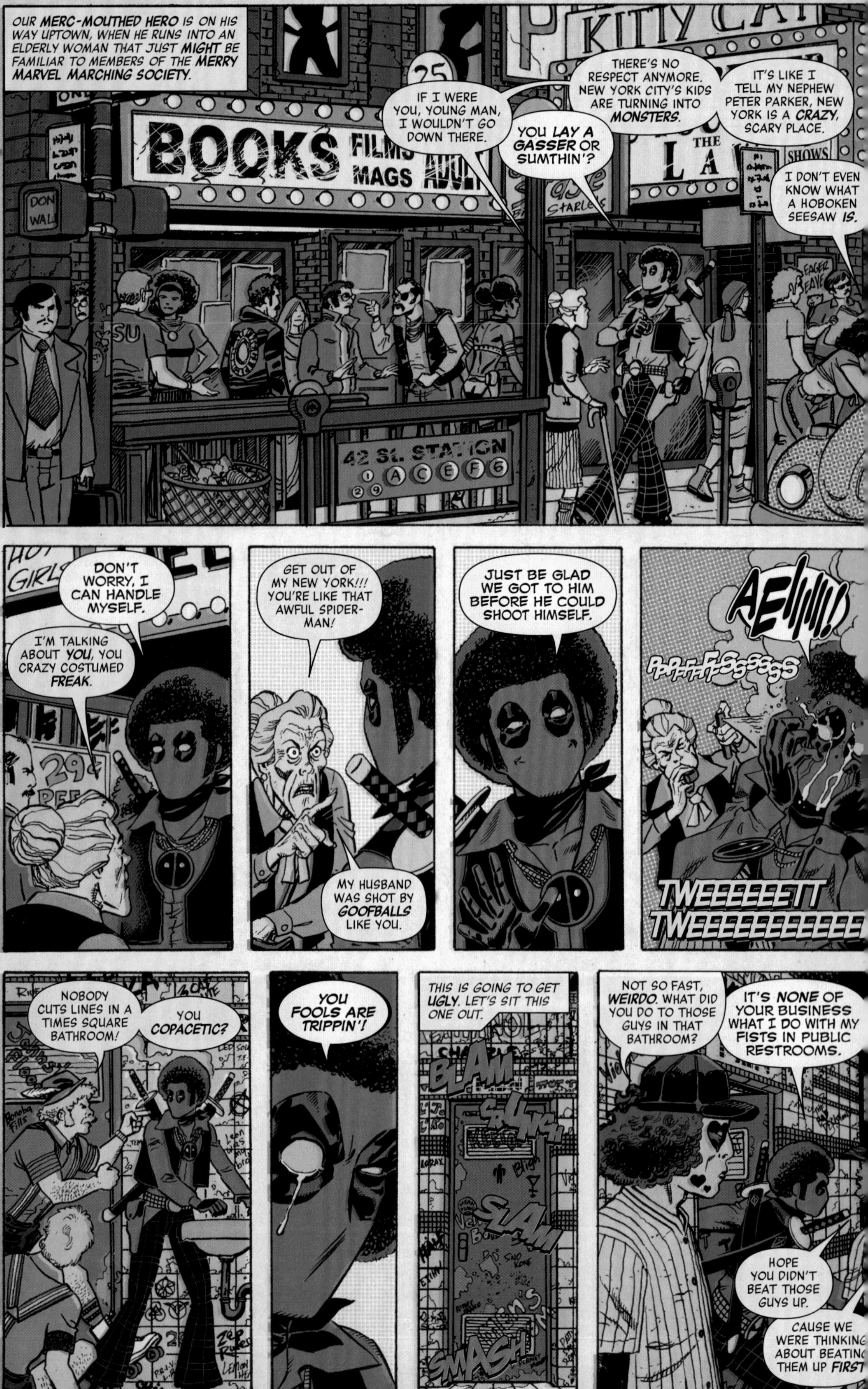
OUR MERC-MOUTHED HERO IS ON HIS WAY UPTOWN, WHEN HE RUNS INTO AN ELDERLY WOMAN THAT JUST MIGHT BE FAMILIAR TO MEMBERS OF THE MERRY MARVEL MARCHING SOCIETY.
KITTY CAT
BOOKS FILMS MAGS ADULT
IF I WERE YOU, YOUNG MAN, I WOULDN'T GO DOWN THERE.
YOU LAY A GASSER OR SUMTHIN'?
THERE'S NO RESPECT ANYMORE. NEW YORK CITY'S KIDS ARE TURNING INTO MONSTERS.
IT'S LIKE I TELL MY NEPHEW PETER PARKER, NEW YORK IS A CRAZY, SCARY PLACE.
I DON'T EVEN KNOW WHAT A HOBOKEN SEESAW IS.
42 St. STATION
DON'T WORRY, I CAN HANDLE MYSELF.
I'M TALKING ABOUT YOU, YOU CRAZY COSTUMED FREAK.
GET OUT OF MY NEW YORK!!! YOU'RE LIKE THAT AWFUL SPIDER-MAN!
MY HUSBAND WAS SHOT BY GOOFBALLS LIKE YOU.
JUST BE GLAD WE GOT TO HIM BEFORE HE COULD SHOOT HIMSELF.
AEIIIII!
PPPPFFSSSSSS
TWEEEEEETT TWEEEEEEEEEEE
NOBODY CUTS LINES IN A TIMES SQUARE BATHROOM!
YOU COPACETIC?
YOU FOOLS ARE TRIPPIN'!
THIS IS GOING TO GET UGLY. LET'S SIT THIS ONE OUT.
BLAM
SPLUNCH
SLAM
SMASH
NOT SO FAST, WEIRDO. WHAT DID YOU DO TO THOSE GUYS IN THAT BATHROOM?
IT'S NONE OF YOUR BUSINESS WHAT I DO WITH MY FISTS IN PUBLIC RESTROOMS.
HOPE YOU DIDN'T BEAT THOSE GUYS UP.
CAUSE WE WERE THINKING ABOUT BEATING THEM UP FIRST

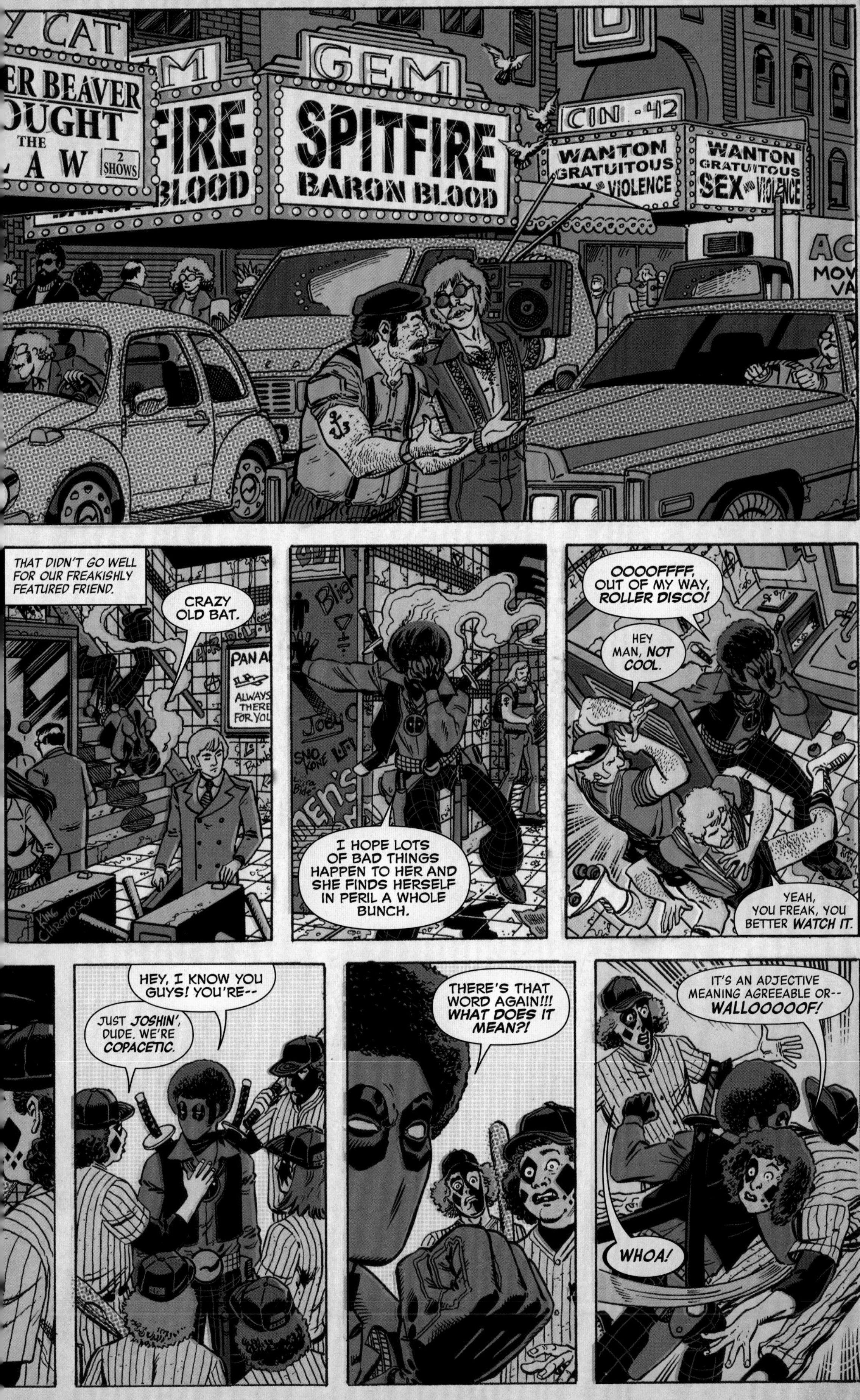

GEM
SPITFIRE
BARON BLOOD
CIN-42
WANTON GRATUITOUS SEX AND VIOLENCE
2 SHOWS
THAT DIDN'T GO WELL FOR OUR FREAKISHLY FEATURED FRIEND.
CRAZY OLD BAT.
PAN AM
ALWAYS THERE FOR YOU
I HOPE LOTS OF BAD THINGS HAPPEN TO HER AND SHE FINDS HERSELF IN PERIL A WHOLE BUNCH.
OOOOFFFF, OUT OF MY WAY, ROLLER DISCO!
HEY MAN, NOT COOL.
YEAH, YOU FREAK, YOU BETTER WATCH IT.
HEY, I KNOW YOU GUYS! YOU'RE--
JUST JOSHIN', DUDE. WE'RE COPACETIC.
THERE'S THAT WORD AGAIN!!! WHAT DOES IT MEAN?!
IT'S AN ADJECTIVE MEANING AGREEABLE OR-- WALLOOOOOF!
WHOA!

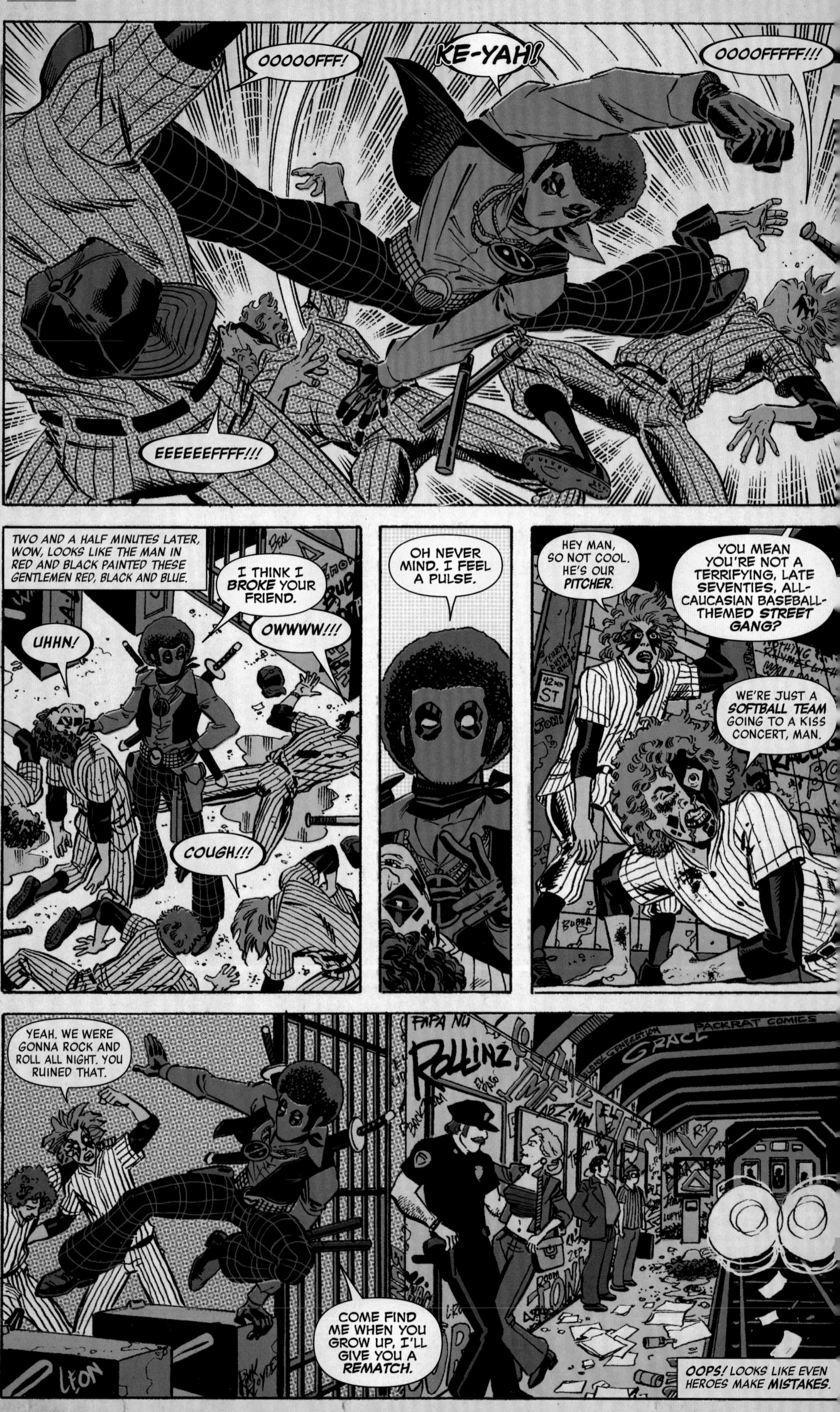
OOOOOFFF!
KE-YAH!
OOOOFFFFF!!!
EEEEEEFFFF!!!
TWO AND A HALF MINUTES LATER, WOW, LOOKS LIKE THE MAN IN RED AND BLACK PAINTED THESE GENTLEMEN RED, BLACK AND BLUE.
I THINK I BROKE YOUR FRIEND.
UHHN!
OWWWW!!!
COUGH!!!
OH NEVER MIND. I FEEL A PULSE.
HEY MAN, SO NOT COOL. HE'S OUR PITCHER.
YOU MEAN YOU'RE NOT A TERRIFYING, LATE SEVENTIES, ALL-CAUCASIAN BASEBALL-THEMED STREET GANG?
WE'RE JUST A SOFTBALL TEAM GOING TO A KISS CONCERT, MAN.
YEAH. WE WERE GONNA ROCK AND ROLL ALL NIGHT. YOU RUINED THAT.
COME FIND ME WHEN YOU GROW UP, I'LL GIVE YOU A REMATCH.
OOPS! LOOKS LIKE EVEN HEROES MAKE MISTAKES.

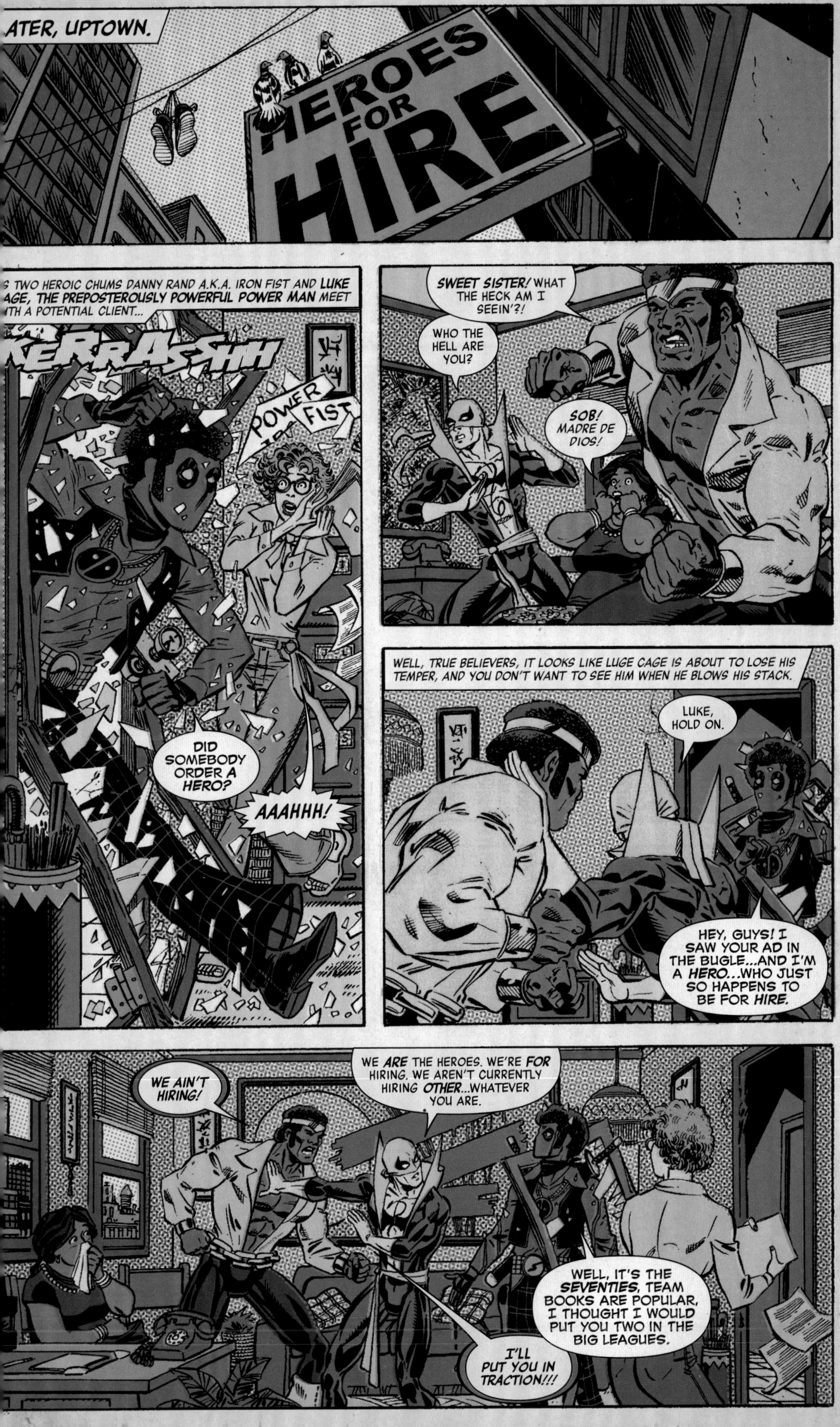
ATER, UPTOWN.
HEROES FOR HIRE
S TWO HEROIC CHUMS DANNY RAND A.K.A. IRON FIST AND LUKE AGE, THE PREPOSTEROUSLY POWERFUL POWER MAN MEET TH A POTENTIAL CLIENT...
KERRASSHH
POWER FIST
DID SOMEBODY ORDER A HERO?
AAAHHH!
SWEET SISTER! WHAT THE HECK AM I SEEIN'?!
WHO THE HELL ARE YOU?
SOB! MADRE DE DIOS!
WELL, TRUE BELIEVERS, IT LOOKS LIKE LUGE CAGE IS ABOUT TO LOSE HIS TEMPER, AND YOU DON'T WANT TO SEE HIM WHEN HE BLOWS HIS STACK.
LUKE, HOLD ON.
HEY, GUYS! I SAW YOUR AD IN THE BUGLE...AND I'M A HERO...WHO JUST SO HAPPENS TO BE FOR HIRE.
WE AIN'T HIRING!
WE ARE THE HEROES. WE'RE FOR HIRING. WE AREN'T CURRENTLY HIRING OTHER...WHATEVER YOU ARE.
WELL, IT'S THE SEVENTIES, TEAM BOOKS ARE POPULAR, I THOUGHT I WOULD PUT YOU TWO IN THE BIG LEAGUES.
I'LL PUT YOU IN TRACTION!!!

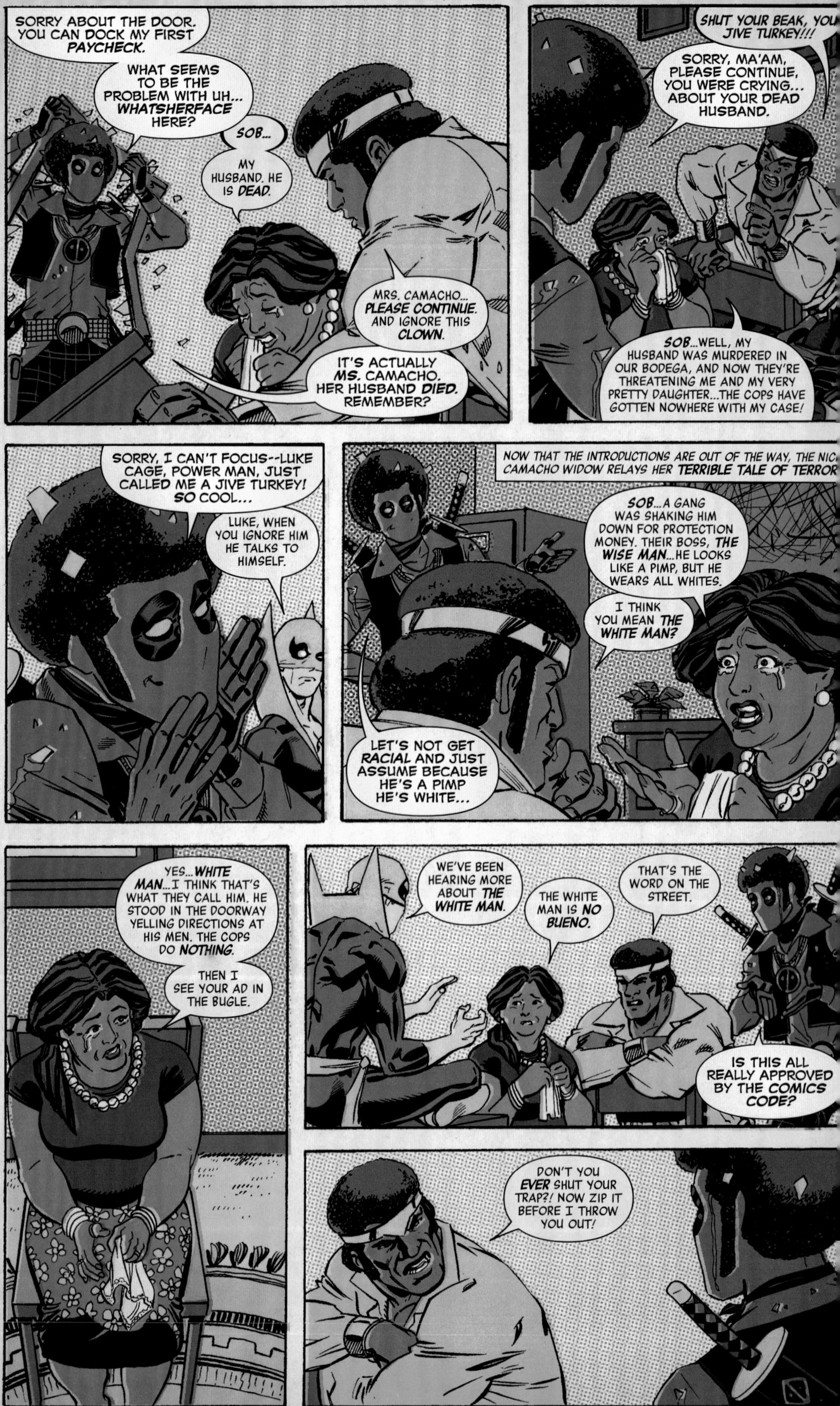
SORRY ABOUT THE DOOR. YOU CAN DOCK MY FIRST PAYCHECK.
WHAT SEEMS TO BE THE PROBLEM WITH UH... WHATSHERFACE HERE?
SOB...
MY HUSBAND. HE IS DEAD.
MRS. CAMACHO... PLEASE CONTINUE. AND IGNORE THIS CLOWN.
IT'S ACTUALLY MS. CAMACHO. HER HUSBAND DIED. REMEMBER?
SHUT YOUR BEAK, YOU JIVE TURKEY!!!
SORRY, MA'AM, PLEASE CONTINUE, YOU WERE CRYING... ABOUT YOUR DEAD HUSBAND.
SOB...WELL, MY HUSBAND WAS MURDERED IN OUR BODEGA, AND NOW THEY'RE THREATENING ME AND MY VERY PRETTY DAUGHTER...THE COPS HAVE GOTTEN NOWHERE WITH MY CASE!
SORRY, I CAN'T FOCUS--LUKE CAGE, POWER MAN, JUST CALLED ME A JIVE TURKEY! SO COOL...
LUKE, WHEN YOU IGNORE HIM HE TALKS TO HIMSELF.
NOW THAT THE INTRODUCTIONS ARE OUT OF THE WAY, THE NIC CAMACHO WIDOW RELAYS HER TERRIBLE TALE OF TERROR
SOB...A GANG WAS SHAKING HIM DOWN FOR PROTECTION MONEY. THEIR BOSS, THE WISE MAN...HE LOOKS LIKE A PIMP, BUT HE WEARS ALL WHITES.
I THINK YOU MEAN THE WHITE MAN?
LET'S NOT GET RACIAL AND JUST ASSUME BECAUSE HE'S A PIMP HE'S WHITE...
YES...WHITE MAN...I THINK THAT'S WHAT THEY CALL HIM. HE STOOD IN THE DOORWAY YELLING DIRECTIONS AT HIS MEN. THE COPS DO NOTHING.
THEN I SEE YOUR AD IN THE BUGLE.
WE'VE BEEN HEARING MORE ABOUT THE WHITE MAN.
THE WHITE MAN IS NO BUENO.
THAT'S THE WORD ON THE STREET.
IS THIS ALL REALLY APPROVED BY THE COMICS CODE?
DON'T YOU EVER SHUT YOUR TRAP?! NOW ZIP IT BEFORE I THROW YOU OUT!

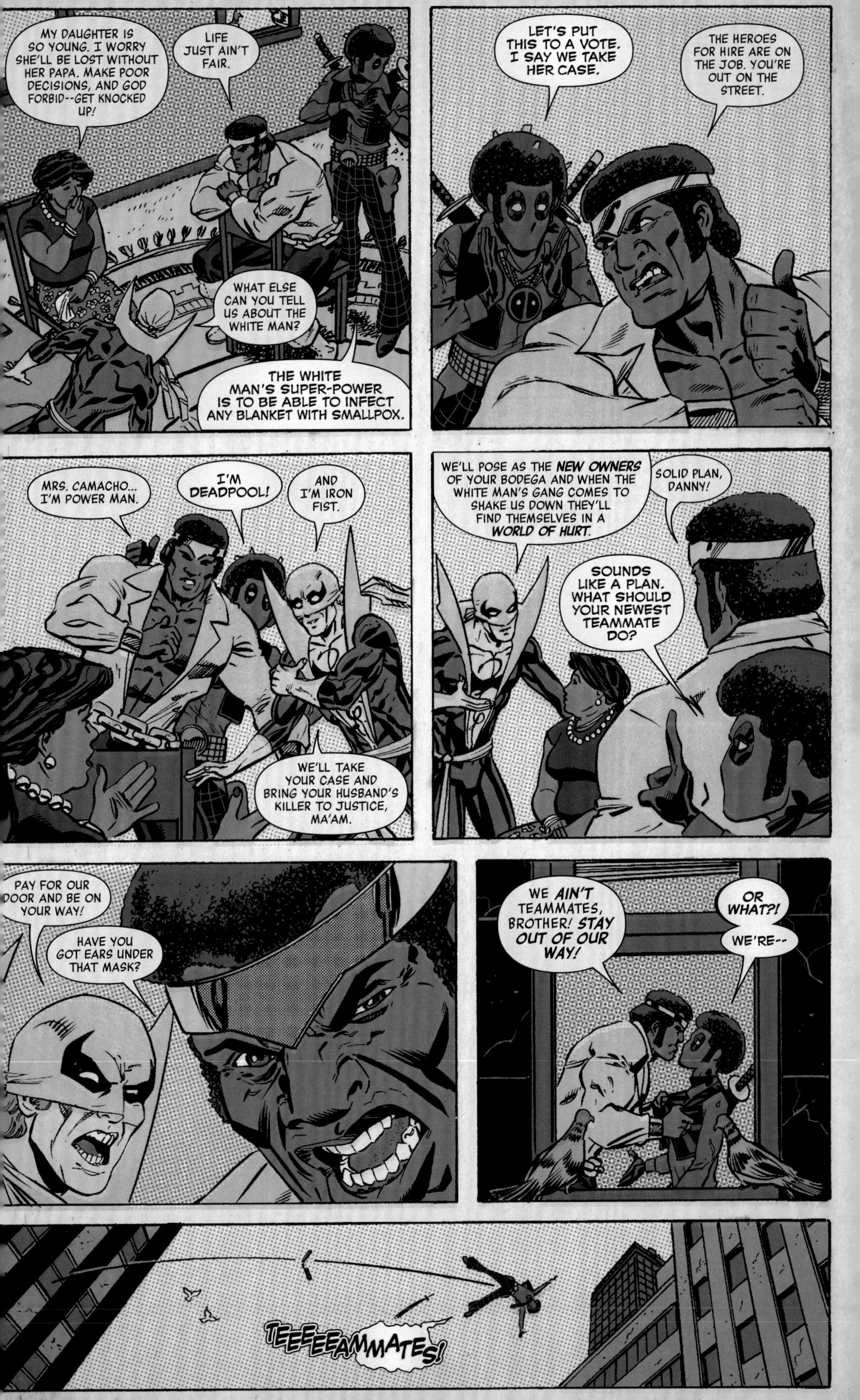
MY DAUGHTER IS SO YOUNG. I WORRY SHE'LL BE LOST WITHOUT HER PAPA. MAKE POOR DECISIONS, AND GOD FORBID--GET KNOCKED UP!
LIFE JUST AIN'T FAIR.
WHAT ELSE CAN YOU TELL US ABOUT THE WHITE MAN?
THE WHITE MAN'S SUPER-POWER IS TO BE ABLE TO INFECT ANY BLANKET WITH SMALLPOX.
LET'S PUT THIS TO A VOTE. I SAY WE TAKE HER CASE.
THE HEROES FOR HIRE ARE ON THE JOB. YOU'RE OUT ON THE STREET.
MRS. CAMACHO... I'M POWER MAN.
I'M DEADPOOL!
AND I'M IRON FIST.
WE'LL TAKE YOUR CASE AND BRING YOUR HUSBAND'S KILLER TO JUSTICE, MA'AM.
WE'LL POSE AS THE NEW OWNERS OF YOUR BODEGA AND WHEN THE WHITE MAN'S GANG COMES TO SHAKE US DOWN THEY'LL FIND THEMSELVES IN A WORLD OF HURT.
SOLID PLAN, DANNY!
SOUNDS LIKE A PLAN. WHAT SHOULD YOUR NEWEST TEAMMATE DO?
PAY FOR OUR DOOR AND BE ON YOUR WAY!
HAVE YOU GOT EARS UNDER THAT MASK?
WE AIN'T TEAMMATES, BROTHER! STAY OUT OF OUR WAY!
OR WHAT?!
WE'RE--
TEEEEEEAMMATES!

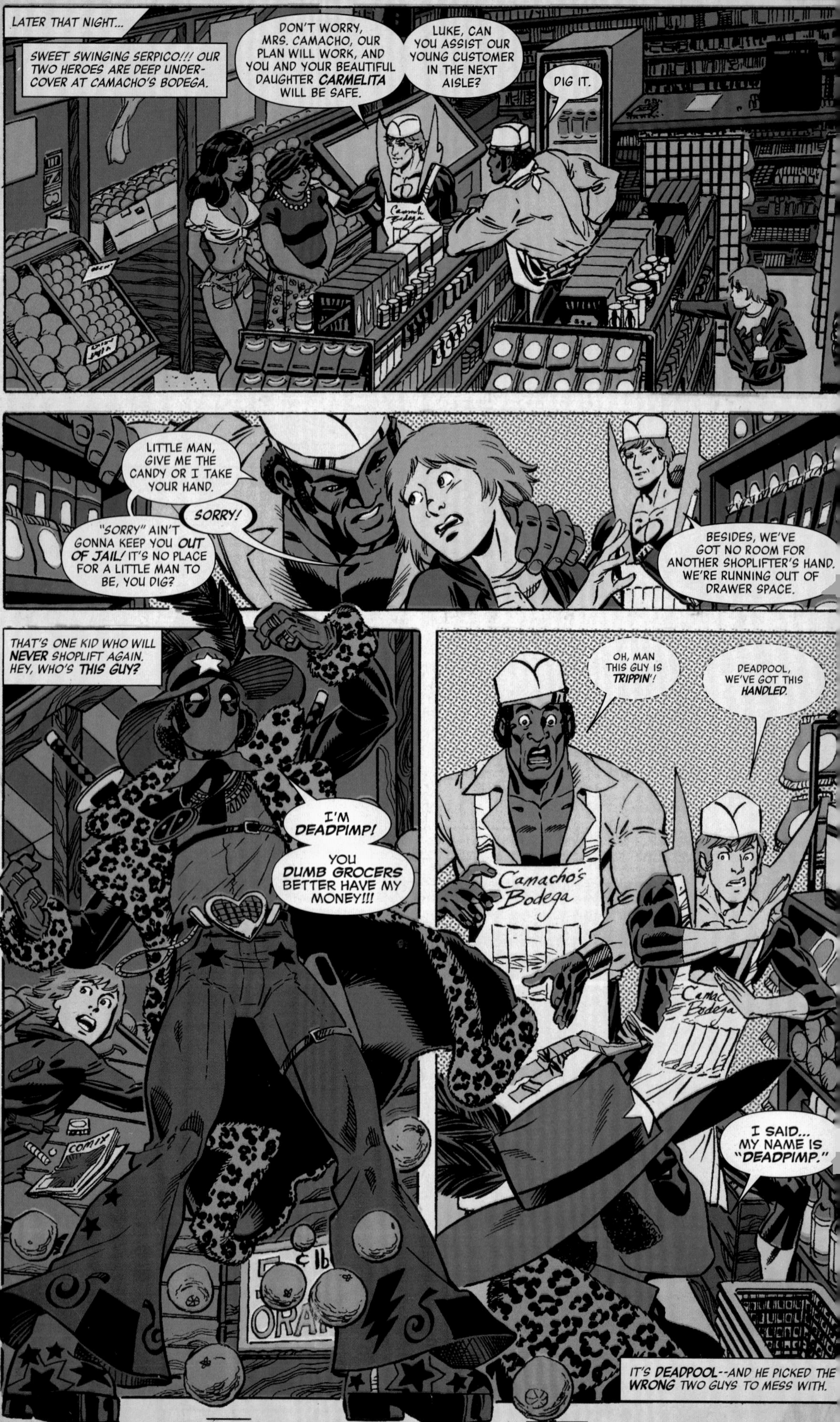
LATER THAT NIGHT...
SWEET SWINGING SERPICO!!! OUR TWO HEROES ARE DEEP UNDER-COVER AT CAMACHO'S BODEGA.
DON'T WORRY, MRS. CAMACHO, OUR PLAN WILL WORK, AND YOU AND YOUR BEAUTIFUL DAUGHTER CARMELITA WILL BE SAFE.
LUKE, CAN YOU ASSIST OUR YOUNG CUSTOMER IN THE NEXT AISLE?
DIG IT.
LITTLE MAN, GIVE ME THE CANDY OR I TAKE YOUR HAND.
SORRY!
"SORRY" AIN'T GONNA KEEP YOU OUT OF JAIL! IT'S NO PLACE FOR A LITTLE MAN TO BE, YOU DIG?
BESIDES, WE'VE GOT NO ROOM FOR ANOTHER SHOPLIFTER'S HAND. WE'RE RUNNING OUT OF DRAWER SPACE.
THAT'S ONE KID WHO WILL NEVER SHOPLIFT AGAIN. HEY, WHO'S THIS GUY?
I'M DEADPIMP!
YOU DUMB GROCERS BETTER HAVE MY MONEY!!!
OH, MAN THIS GUY IS TRIPPIN'!
DEADPOOL, WE'VE GOT THIS HANDLED.
Camacho's Bodega
I SAID... MY NAME IS "DEADPIMP."
IT'S DEADPOOL--AND HE PICKED THE WRONG TWO GUYS TO MESS WITH.

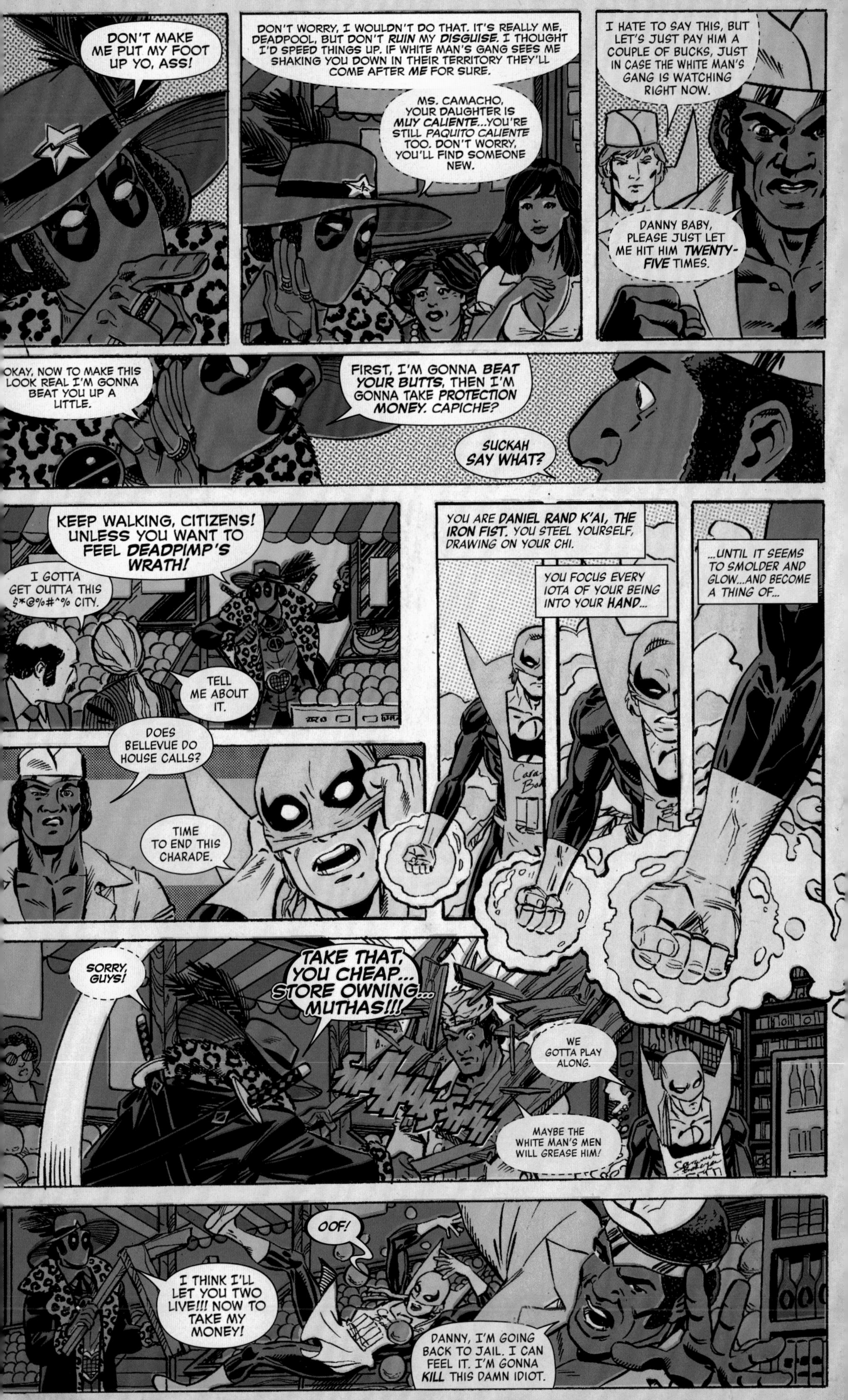
DON'T MAKE ME PUT MY FOOT UP YO, ASS!
DON'T WORRY, I WOULDN'T DO THAT. IT'S REALLY ME, DEADPOOL, BUT DON'T RUIN MY DISGUISE. I THOUGHT I'D SPEED THINGS UP. IF WHITE MAN'S GANG SEES ME SHAKING YOU DOWN IN THEIR TERRITORY THEY'LL COME AFTER ME FOR SURE.
MS. CAMACHO, YOUR DAUGHTER IS MUY CALIENTE...YOU'RE STILL PAQUITO CALIENTE TOO. DON'T WORRY, YOU'LL FIND SOMEONE NEW.
I HATE TO SAY THIS, BUT LET'S JUST PAY HIM A COUPLE OF BUCKS, JUST IN CASE THE WHITE MAN'S GANG IS WATCHING RIGHT NOW.
DANNY BABY, PLEASE JUST LET ME HIT HIM TWENTY-FIVE TIMES.
OKAY, NOW TO MAKE THIS LOOK REAL I'M GONNA BEAT YOU UP A LITTLE.
FIRST, I'M GONNA BEAT YOUR BUTTS, THEN I'M GONNA TAKE PROTECTION MONEY. CAPICHE?
SUCKAH SAY WHAT?
KEEP WALKING, CITIZENS! UNLESS YOU WANT TO FEEL DEADPIMP'S WRATH!
I GOTTA GET OUTTA THIS $*@%#^% CITY.
TELL ME ABOUT IT.
YOU ARE DANIEL RAND K'AI, THE IRON FIST. YOU STEEL YOURSELF, DRAWING ON YOUR CHI.
YOU FOCUS EVERY IOTA OF YOUR BEING INTO YOUR HAND...
...UNTIL IT SEEMS TO SMOLDER AND GLOW...AND BECOME A THING OF...
DOES BELLEVUE DO HOUSE CALLS?
TIME TO END THIS CHARADE.
SORRY, GUYS!
TAKE THAT, YOU CHEAP... STORE OWNING... MUTHAS!!!
WE GOTTA PLAY ALONG.
MAYBE THE WHITE MAN'S MEN WILL GREASE HIM!
OOF!
I THINK I'LL LET YOU TWO LIVE!!! NOW TO TAKE MY MONEY!
DANNY, I'M GOING BACK TO JAIL. I CAN FEEL IT. I'M GONNA KILL THIS DAMN IDIOT.

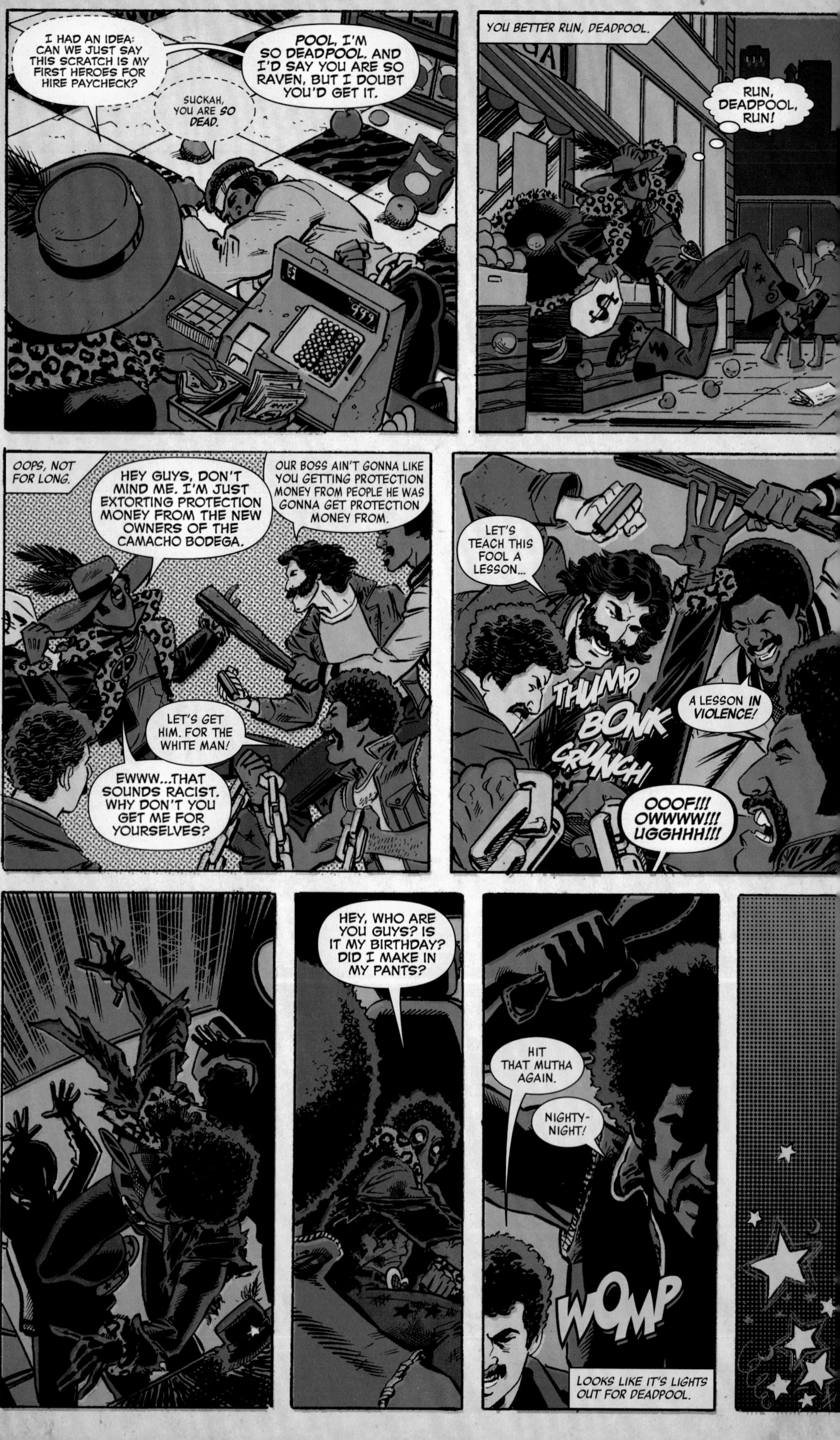
I HAD AN IDEA: CAN WE JUST SAY THIS SCRATCH IS MY FIRST HEROES FOR HIRE PAYCHECK?
POOL, I'M SO DEADPOOL. AND I'D SAY YOU ARE SO RAVEN, BUT I DOUBT YOU'D GET IT.
SUCKAH, YOU ARE SO DEAD.
YOU BETTER RUN, DEADPOOL.
RUN, DEADPOOL, RUN!
OOPS, NOT FOR LONG.
HEY GUYS, DON'T MIND ME. I'M JUST EXTORTING PROTECTION MONEY FROM THE NEW OWNERS OF THE CAMACHO BODEGA.
OUR BOSS AIN'T GONNA LIKE YOU GETTING PROTECTION MONEY FROM PEOPLE HE WAS GONNA GET PROTECTION MONEY FROM.
LET'S GET HIM. FOR THE WHITE MAN!
EWWW...THAT SOUNDS RACIST. WHY DON'T YOU GET ME FOR YOURSELVES?
LET'S TEACH THIS FOOL A LESSON...
THUMP
BONK
CRUNCH
A LESSON IN VIOLENCE!
OOOF!!! OWWWW!!! UGGHHH!!!
HEY, WHO ARE YOU GUYS? IS IT MY BIRTHDAY? DID I MAKE IN MY PANTS?
HIT THAT MUTHA AGAIN.
NIGHTY-NIGHT!
WOMP
LOOKS LIKE IT'S LIGHTS OUT FOR DEADPOOL.

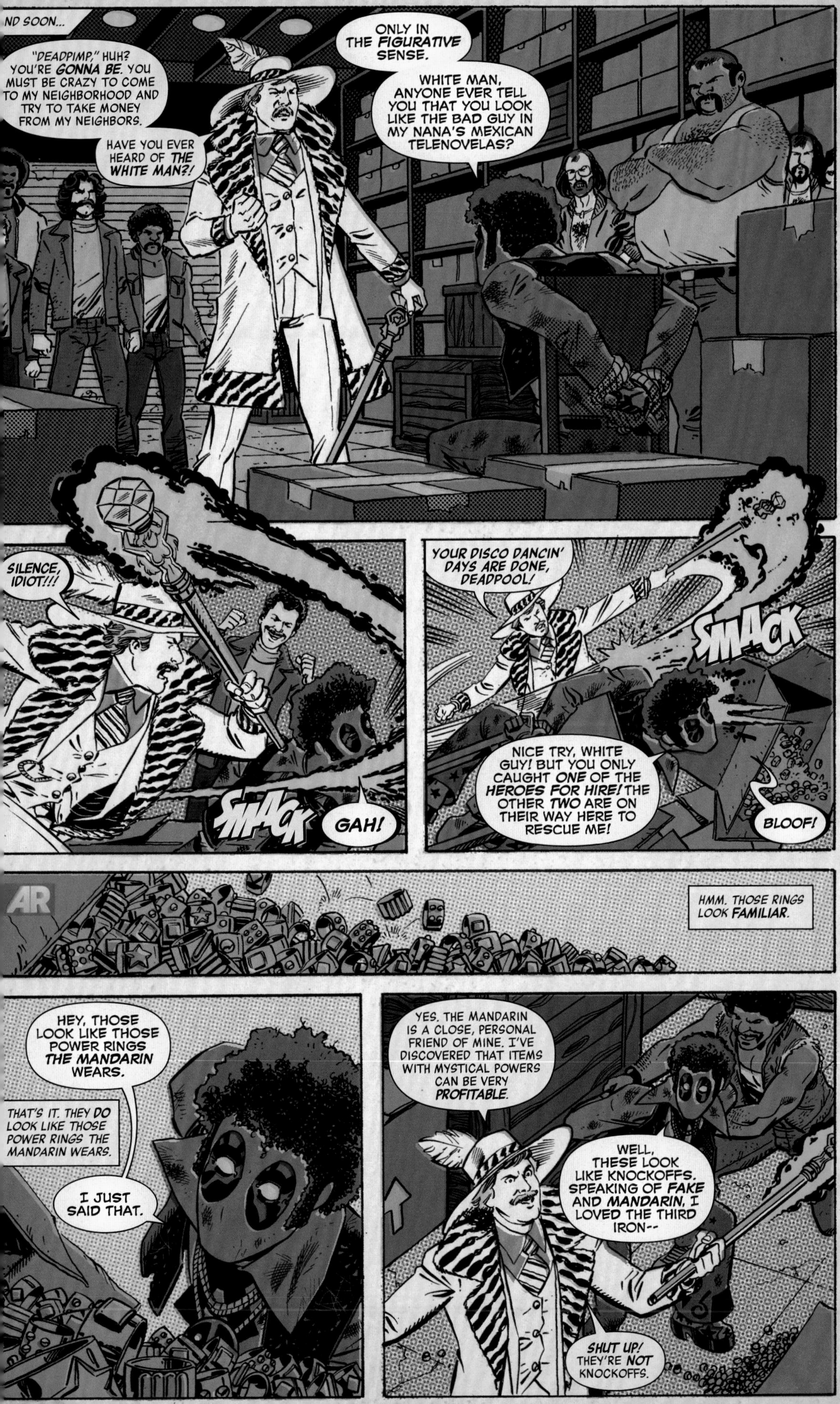
ND SOON...
"DEADPIMP," HUH? YOU'RE GONNA BE. YOU MUST BE CRAZY TO COME TO MY NEIGHBORHOOD AND TRY TO TAKE MONEY FROM MY NEIGHBORS.
HAVE YOU EVER HEARD OF THE WHITE MAN?!
ONLY IN THE FIGURATIVE SENSE.
WHITE MAN, ANYONE EVER TELL YOU THAT YOU LOOK LIKE THE BAD GUY IN MY NANA'S MEXICAN TELENOVELAS?
SILENCE, IDIOT!!!
SMACK
GAH!
YOUR DISCO DANCIN' DAYS ARE DONE, DEADPOOL!
SMACK
NICE TRY, WHITE GUY! BUT YOU ONLY CAUGHT ONE OF THE HEROES FOR HIRE! THE OTHER TWO ARE ON THEIR WAY HERE TO RESCUE ME!
BLOOF!
HMM. THOSE RINGS LOOK FAMILIAR.
HEY, THOSE LOOK LIKE THOSE POWER RINGS THE MANDARIN WEARS.
THAT'S IT. THEY DO LOOK LIKE THOSE POWER RINGS THE MANDARIN WEARS.
I JUST SAID THAT.
YES. THE MANDARIN IS A CLOSE, PERSONAL FRIEND OF MINE. I'VE DISCOVERED THAT ITEMS WITH MYSTICAL POWERS CAN BE VERY PROFITABLE.
WELL, THESE LOOK LIKE KNOCKOFFS. SPEAKING OF FAKE AND MANDARIN, I LOVED THE THIRD IRON--
SHUT UP! THEY'RE NOT KNOCKOFFS.

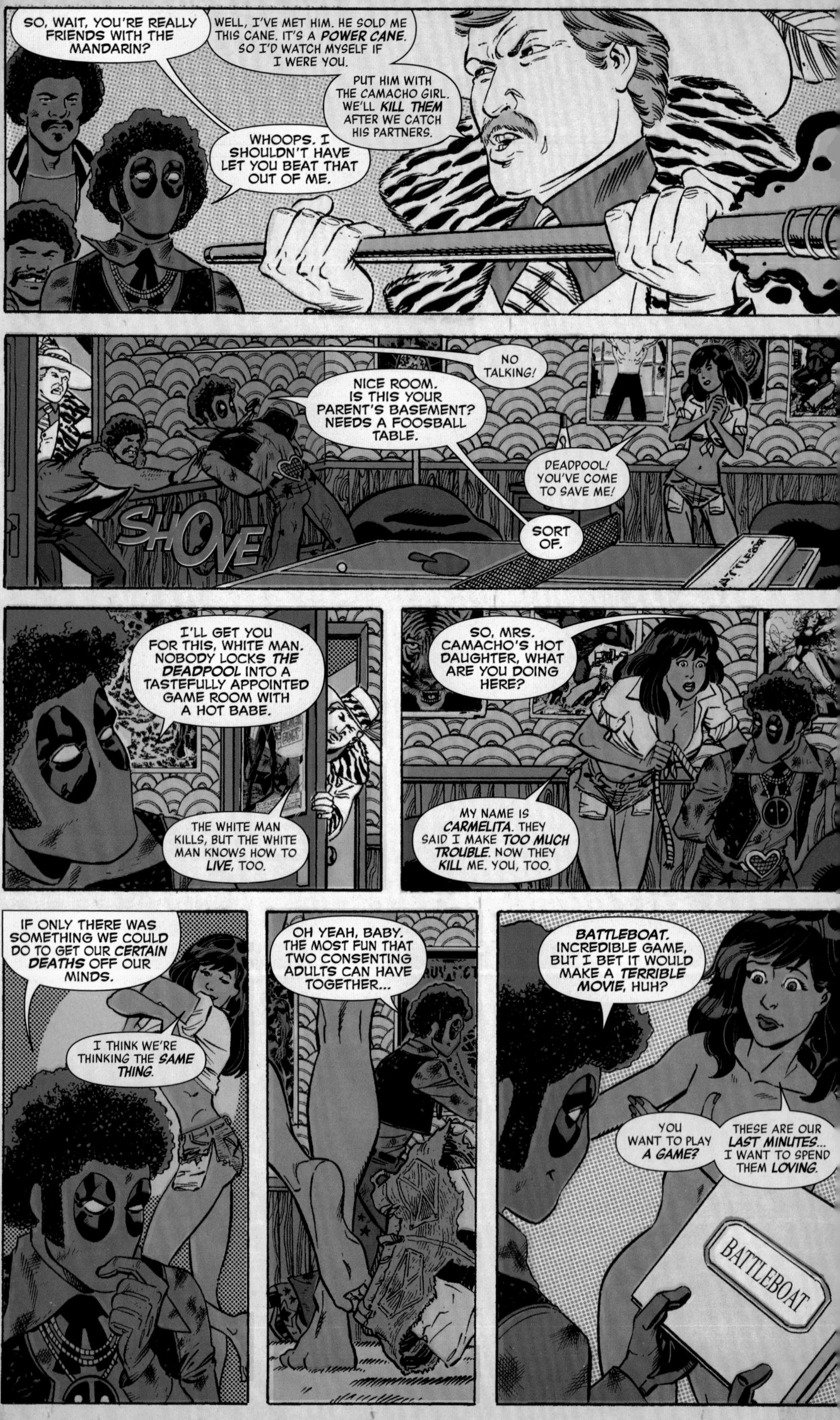

SO, WAIT, YOU'RE REALLY FRIENDS WITH THE MANDARIN?
WELL, I'VE MET HIM. HE SOLD ME THIS CANE. IT'S A POWER CANE. SO I'D WATCH MYSELF IF I WERE YOU.
PUT HIM WITH THE CAMACHO GIRL. WE'LL KILL THEM AFTER WE CATCH HIS PARTNERS.
WHOOPS. I SHOULDN'T HAVE LET YOU BEAT THAT OUT OF ME.
NO TALKING!
NICE ROOM. IS THIS YOUR PARENT'S BASEMENT? NEEDS A FOOSBALL TABLE.
SHOVE
DEADPOOL! YOU'VE COME TO SAVE ME!
SORT OF.
I'LL GET YOU FOR THIS, WHITE MAN. NOBODY LOCKS THE DEADPOOL INTO A TASTEFULLY APPOINTED GAME ROOM WITH A HOT BABE.
THE WHITE MAN KILLS, BUT THE WHITE MAN KNOWS HOW TO LIVE, TOO.
SO, MRS. CAMACHO'S HOT DAUGHTER, WHAT ARE YOU DOING HERE?
MY NAME IS CARMELITA. THEY SAID I MAKE TOO MUCH TROUBLE. NOW THEY KILL ME. YOU, TOO.
IF ONLY THERE WAS SOMETHING WE COULD DO TO GET OUR CERTAIN DEATHS OFF OUR MINDS.
I THINK WE'RE THINKING THE SAME THING.
OH YEAH, BABY. THE MOST FUN THAT TWO CONSENTING ADULTS CAN HAVE TOGETHER...
BATTLEBOAT. INCREDIBLE GAME, BUT I BET IT WOULD MAKE A TERRIBLE MOVIE, HUH?
YOU WANT TO PLAY A GAME?
THESE ARE OUR LAST MINUTES... I WANT TO SPEND THEM LOVING.
BATTLEBOAT

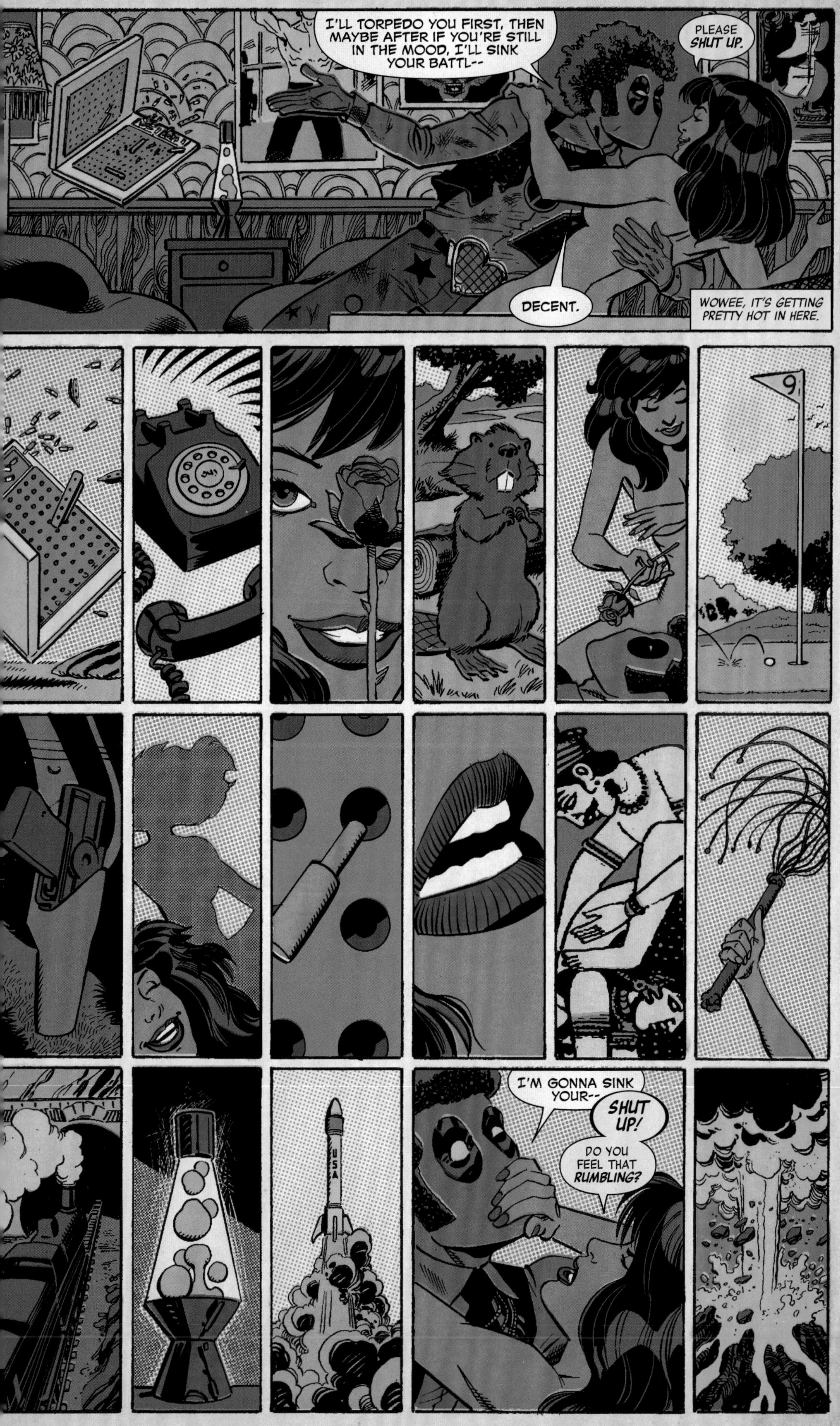
I'LL TORPEDO YOU FIRST, THEN MAYBE AFTER IF YOU'RE STILL IN THE MOOD, I'LL SINK YOUR BATTL--
PLEASE SHUT UP.
DECENT.
WOWEE, IT'S GETTING PRETTY HOT IN HERE.
I'M GONNA SINK YOUR--
SHUT UP!
DO YOU FEEL THAT RUMBLING?

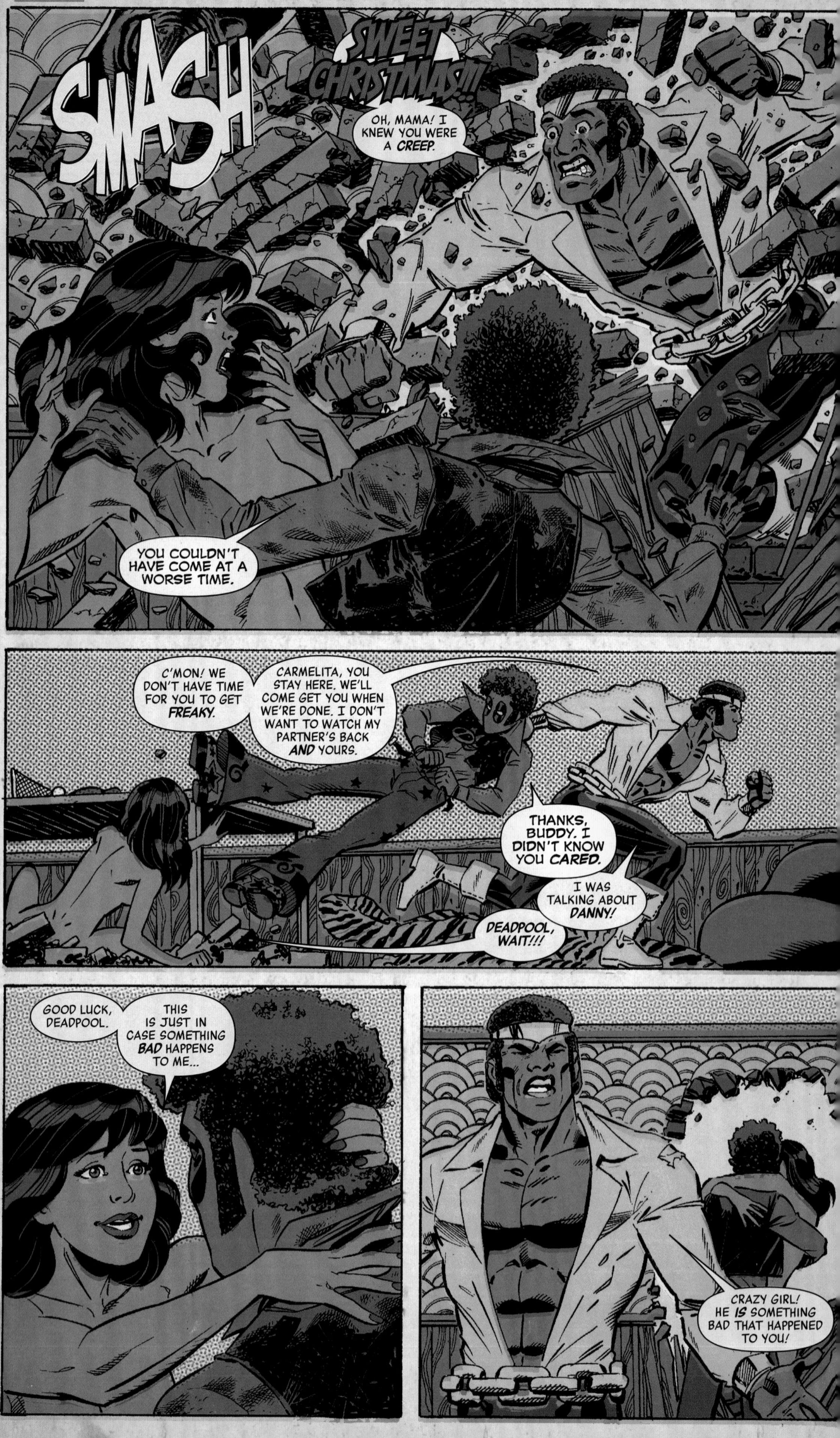
SWASH
SWEET CHRISTMAS!!!
OH, MAMA! I KNEW YOU WERE A CREEP.
YOU COULDN'T HAVE COME AT A WORSE TIME.
C'MON! WE DON'T HAVE TIME FOR YOU TO GET FREAKY.
CARMELITA, YOU STAY HERE. WE'LL COME GET YOU WHEN WE'RE DONE. I DON'T WANT TO WATCH MY PARTNER'S BACK AND YOURS.
THANKS, BUDDY. I DIDN'T KNOW YOU CARED.
I WAS TALKING ABOUT DANNY!
DEADPOOL, WAIT!!!
GOOD LUCK, DEADPOOL.
THIS IS JUST IN CASE SOMETHING BAD HAPPENS TO ME...
CRAZY GIRL! HE IS SOMETHING BAD THAT HAPPENED TO YOU!

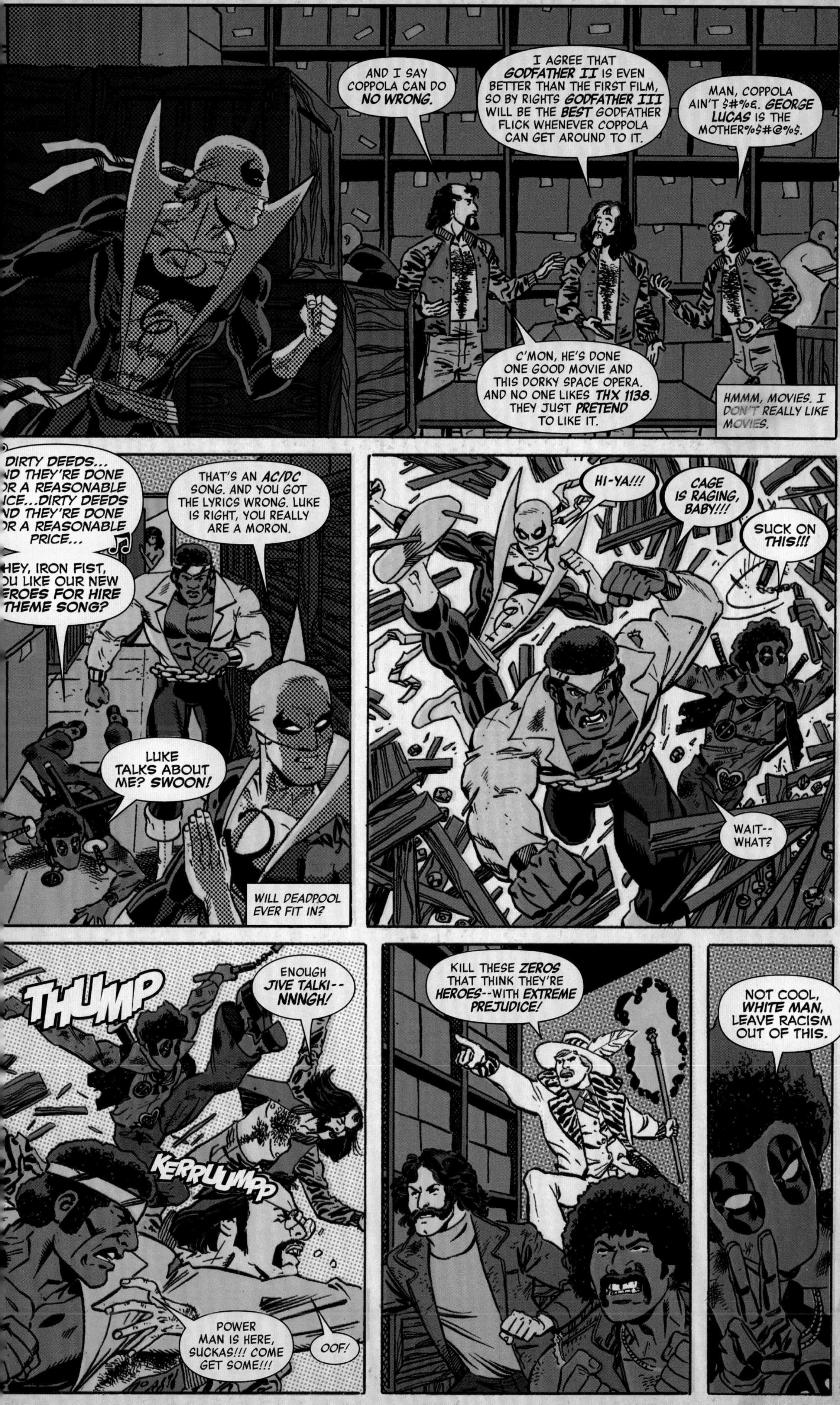
AND I SAY COPPOLA CAN DO NO WRONG.
I AGREE THAT GODFATHER II IS EVEN BETTER THAN THE FIRST FILM, SO BY RIGHTS GODFATHER III WILL BE THE BEST GODFATHER FLICK WHENEVER COPPOLA CAN GET AROUND TO IT.
MAN, COPPOLA AIN'T $#%€. GEORGE LUCAS IS THE MOTHER%$#@%$.
C'MON, HE'S DONE ONE GOOD MOVIE AND THIS DORKY SPACE OPERA. AND NO ONE LIKES THX 1138. THEY JUST PRETEND TO LIKE IT.
HMMM, MOVIES. I DON'T REALLY LIKE MOVIES.
DIRTY DEEDS... ND THEY'RE DONE R A REASONABLE ICE...DIRTY DEEDS ND THEY'RE DONE R A REASONABLE PRICE...
HEY, IRON FIST, OU LIKE OUR NEW EROES FOR HIRE THEME SONG?
THAT'S AN AC/DC SONG. AND YOU GOT THE LYRICS WRONG. LUKE IS RIGHT, YOU REALLY ARE A MORON.
LUKE TALKS ABOUT ME? SWOON!
WILL DEADPOOL EVER FIT IN?
HI-YA!!!
CAGE IS RAGING, BABY!!!
SUCK ON THIS!!!
WAIT-- WHAT?
THUMP
ENOUGH JIVE TALKI-- NNNGH!
KERRUUMPP
POWER MAN IS HERE, SUCKAS!!! COME GET SOME!!!
OOF!
KILL THESE ZEROS THAT THINK THEY'RE HEROES--WITH EXTREME PREJUDICE!
NOT COOL, WHITE MAN. LEAVE RACISM OUT OF THIS.

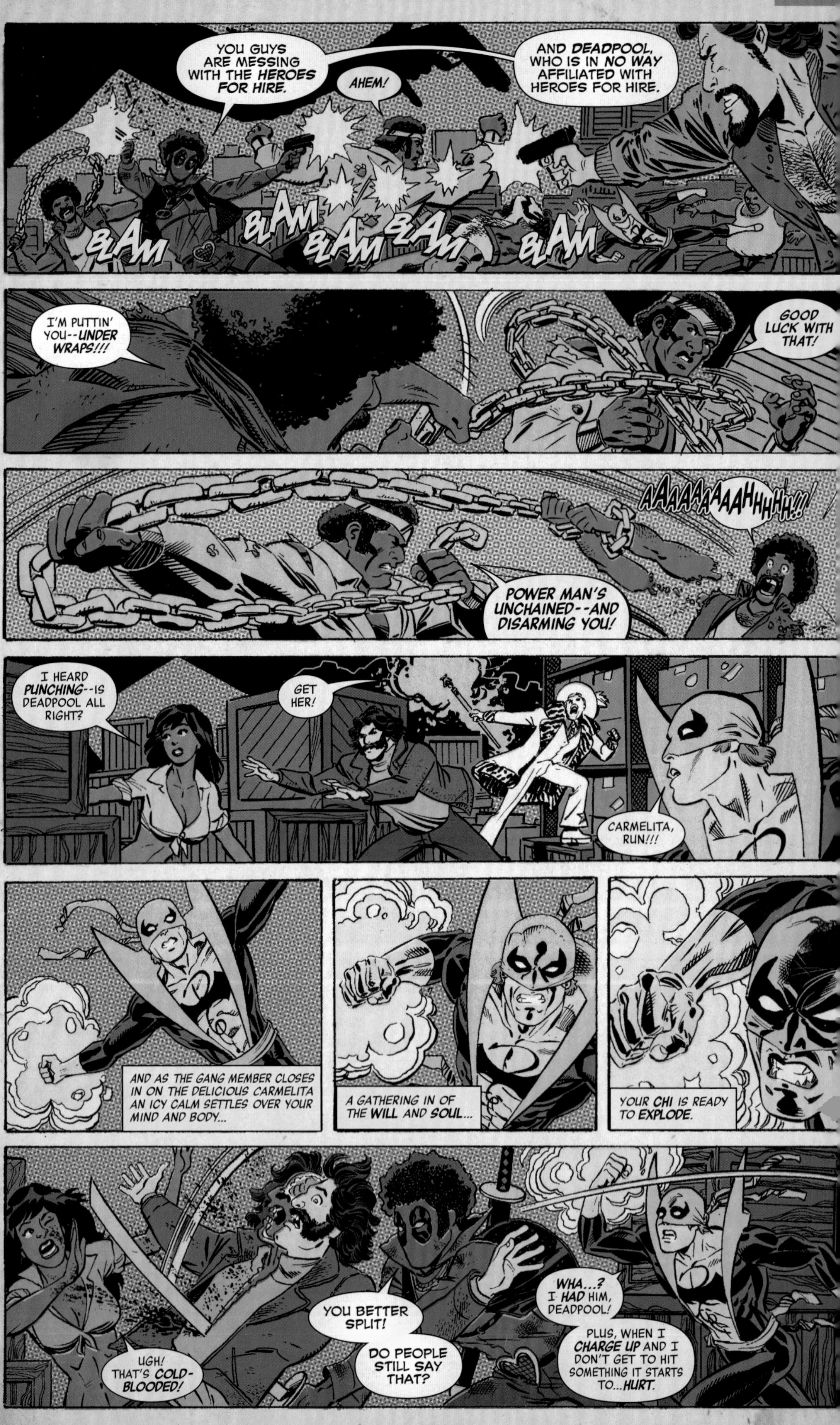
YOU GUYS ARE MESSING WITH THE HEROES FOR HIRE.
AHEM!
AND DEADPOOL, WHO IS IN NO WAY AFFILIATED WITH HEROES FOR HIRE.
BLAM BLAM BLAM BLAM BLAM
I'M PUTTIN' YOU--UNDER WRAPS!!!
GOOD LUCK WITH THAT!
AAAAAAAAHHHHH!!!
POWER MAN'S UNCHAINED--AND DISARMING YOU!
I HEARD PUNCHING--IS DEADPOOL ALL RIGHT?
GET HER!
CARMELITA, RUN!!!
AND AS THE GANG MEMBER CLOSES IN ON THE DELICIOUS CARMELITA AN ICY CALM SETTLES OVER YOUR MIND AND BODY...
A GATHERING IN OF THE WILL AND SOUL...
YOUR CHI IS READY TO EXPLODE.
UGH! THAT'S COLD-BLOODED!
YOU BETTER SPLIT!
DO PEOPLE STILL SAY THAT?
WHA...? I HAD HIM, DEADPOOL!
PLUS, WHEN I CHARGE UP AND I DON'T GET TO HIT SOMETHING IT STARTS TO...HURT.

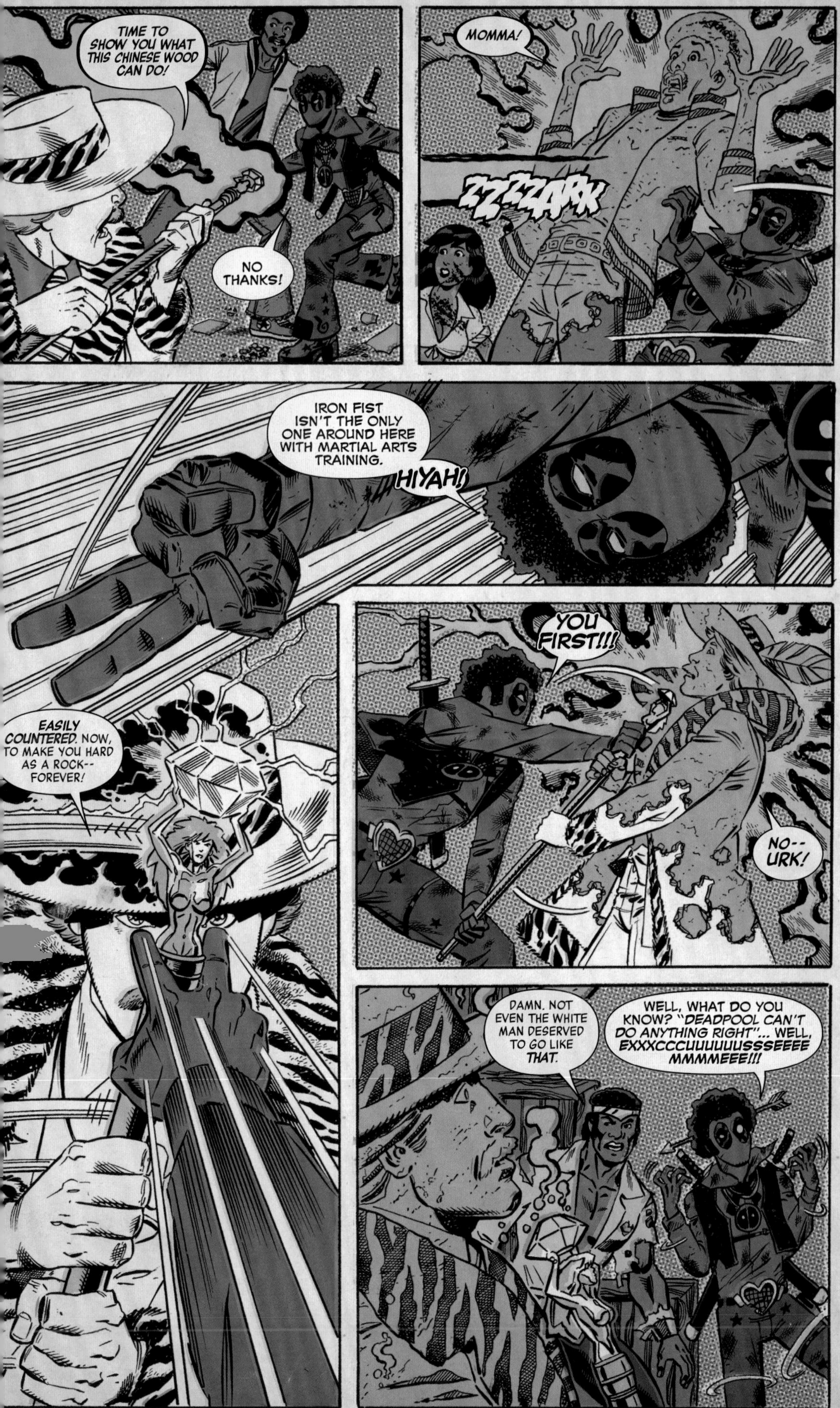
TIME TO SHOW YOU WHAT THIS CHINESE WOOD CAN DO!
NO THANKS!
MOMMA!
ZZZZZARK
IRON FIST ISN'T THE ONLY ONE AROUND HERE WITH MARTIAL ARTS TRAINING.
HIYAH!
EASILY COUNTERED. NOW, TO MAKE YOU HARD AS A ROCK-- FOREVER!
YOU FIRST!!!
NO-- URK!
DAMN. NOT EVEN THE WHITE MAN DESERVED TO GO LIKE THAT.
WELL, WHAT DO YOU KNOW? "DEADPOOL CAN'T DO ANYTHING RIGHT"... WELL, EXXXCCCUUUUUUSSSEEEE MMMMEEE!!!

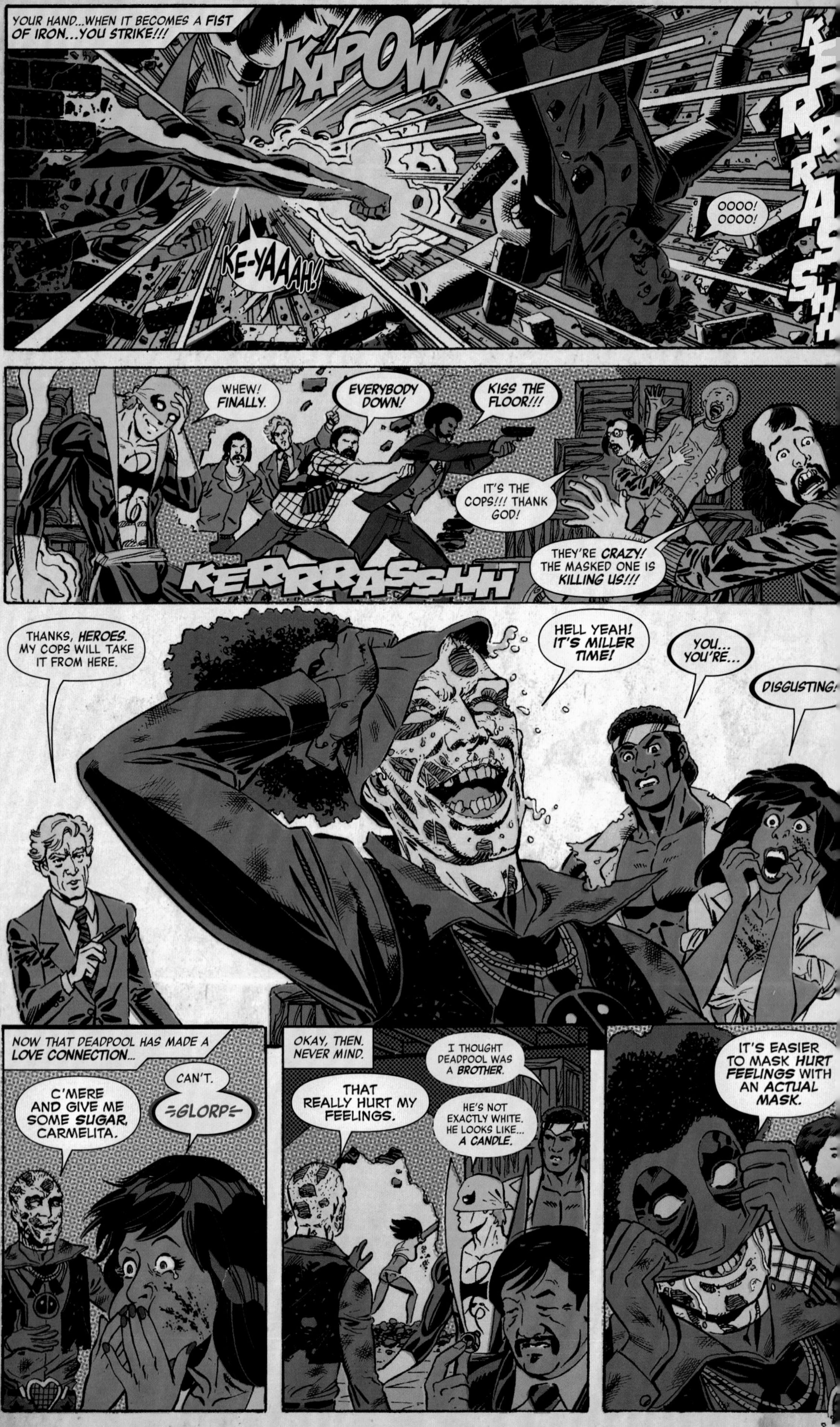

YOUR HAND...WHEN IT BECOMES A FIST OF IRON...YOU STRIKE!!!
KAPOW
KERRRASHH
OOOO! OOOO!
KE-YAAAH!
WHEW! FINALLY.
EVERYBODY DOWN!
KISS THE FLOOR!!!
IT'S THE COPS!!! THANK GOD!
THEY'RE CRAZY! THE MASKED ONE IS KILLING US!!!
KERRRASSHH
THANKS, HEROES. MY COPS WILL TAKE IT FROM HERE.
HELL YEAH! IT'S MILLER TIME!
YOU... YOU'RE...
DISGUSTING!
NOW THAT DEADPOOL HAS MADE A LOVE CONNECTION...
C'MERE AND GIVE ME SOME SUGAR, CARMELITA.
CAN'T.
GLORP
OKAY, THEN. NEVER MIND.
THAT REALLY HURT MY FEELINGS.
I THOUGHT DEADPOOL WAS A BROTHER.
HE'S NOT EXACTLY WHITE. HE LOOKS LIKE... A CANDLE.
IT'S EASIER TO MASK HURT FEELINGS WITH AN ACTUAL MASK.

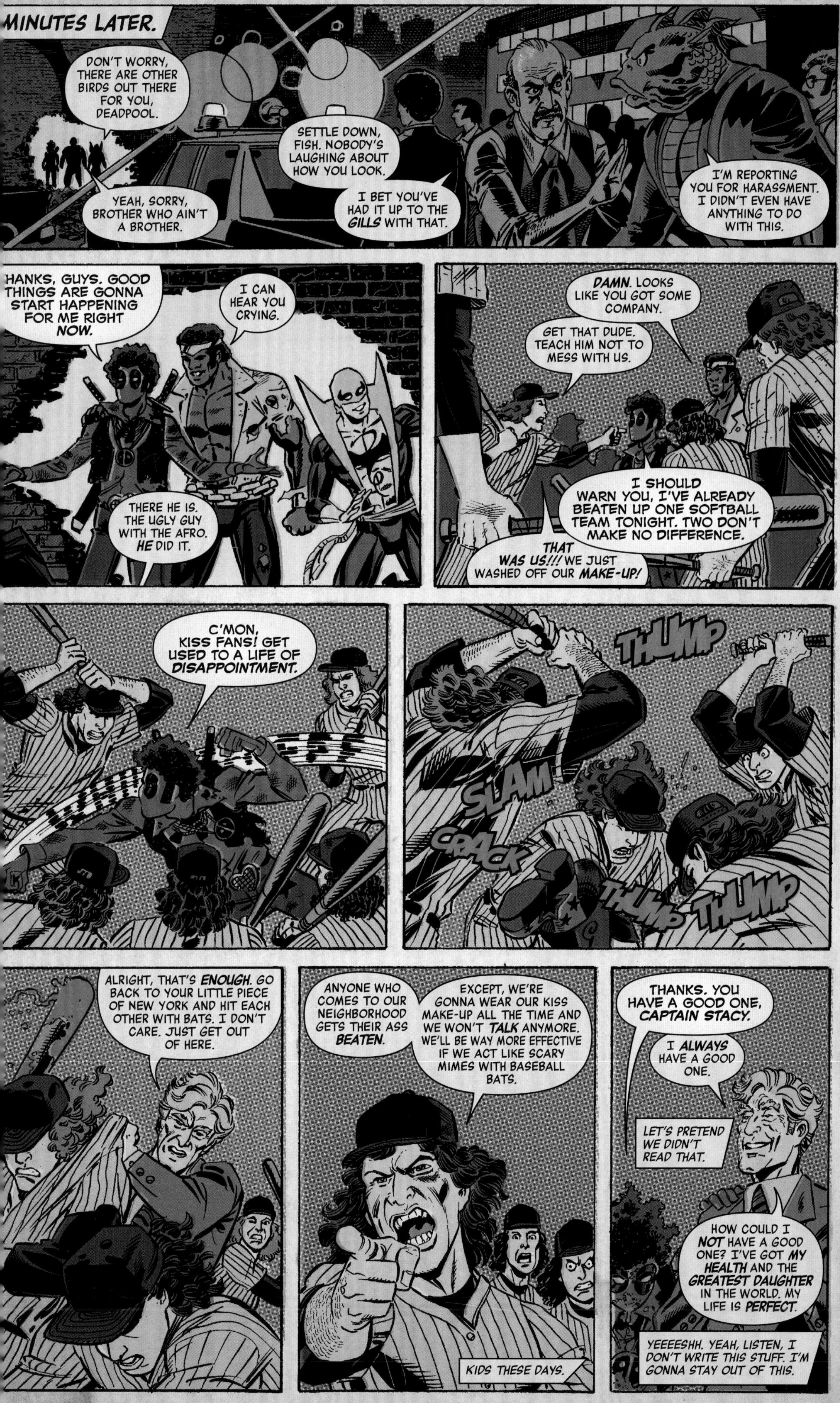
MINUTES LATER.
DON'T WORRY, THERE ARE OTHER BIRDS OUT THERE FOR YOU, DEADPOOL.
YEAH, SORRY, BROTHER WHO AIN'T A BROTHER.
SETTLE DOWN, FISH. NOBODY'S LAUGHING ABOUT HOW YOU LOOK.
I BET YOU'VE HAD IT UP TO THE GILLS WITH THAT.
I'M REPORTING YOU FOR HARASSMENT. I DIDN'T EVEN HAVE ANYTHING TO DO WITH THIS.
HANKS, GUYS. GOOD THINGS ARE GONNA START HAPPENING FOR ME RIGHT NOW.
I CAN HEAR YOU CRYING.
THERE HE IS. THE UGLY GUY WITH THE AFRO. HE DID IT.
DAMN. LOOKS LIKE YOU GOT SOME COMPANY.
GET THAT DUDE. TEACH HIM NOT TO MESS WITH US.
I SHOULD WARN YOU, I'VE ALREADY BEATEN UP ONE SOFTBALL TEAM TONIGHT. TWO DON'T MAKE NO DIFFERENCE.
THAT WAS US!!! WE JUST WASHED OFF OUR MAKE-UP!
C'MON, KISS FANS! GET USED TO A LIFE OF DISAPPOINTMENT.
THUMP
SLAM
CRACK
THUMP THUMP
ALRIGHT, THAT'S ENOUGH. GO BACK TO YOUR LITTLE PIECE OF NEW YORK AND HIT EACH OTHER WITH BATS. I DON'T CARE. JUST GET OUT OF HERE.
ANYONE WHO COMES TO OUR NEIGHBORHOOD GETS THEIR ASS BEATEN.
EXCEPT, WE'RE GONNA WEAR OUR KISS MAKE-UP ALL THE TIME AND WE WON'T TALK ANYMORE. WE'LL BE WAY MORE EFFECTIVE IF WE ACT LIKE SCARY MIMES WITH BASEBALL BATS.
KIDS THESE DAYS.
THANKS. YOU HAVE A GOOD ONE, CAPTAIN STACY.
I ALWAYS HAVE A GOOD ONE.
LET'S PRETEND WE DIDN'T READ THAT.
HOW COULD I NOT HAVE A GOOD ONE? I'VE GOT MY HEALTH AND THE GREATEST DAUGHTER IN THE WORLD. MY LIFE IS PERFECT.
YEEEESHH. YEAH, LISTEN, I DON'T WRITE THIS STUFF. I'M GONNA STAY OUT OF THIS.

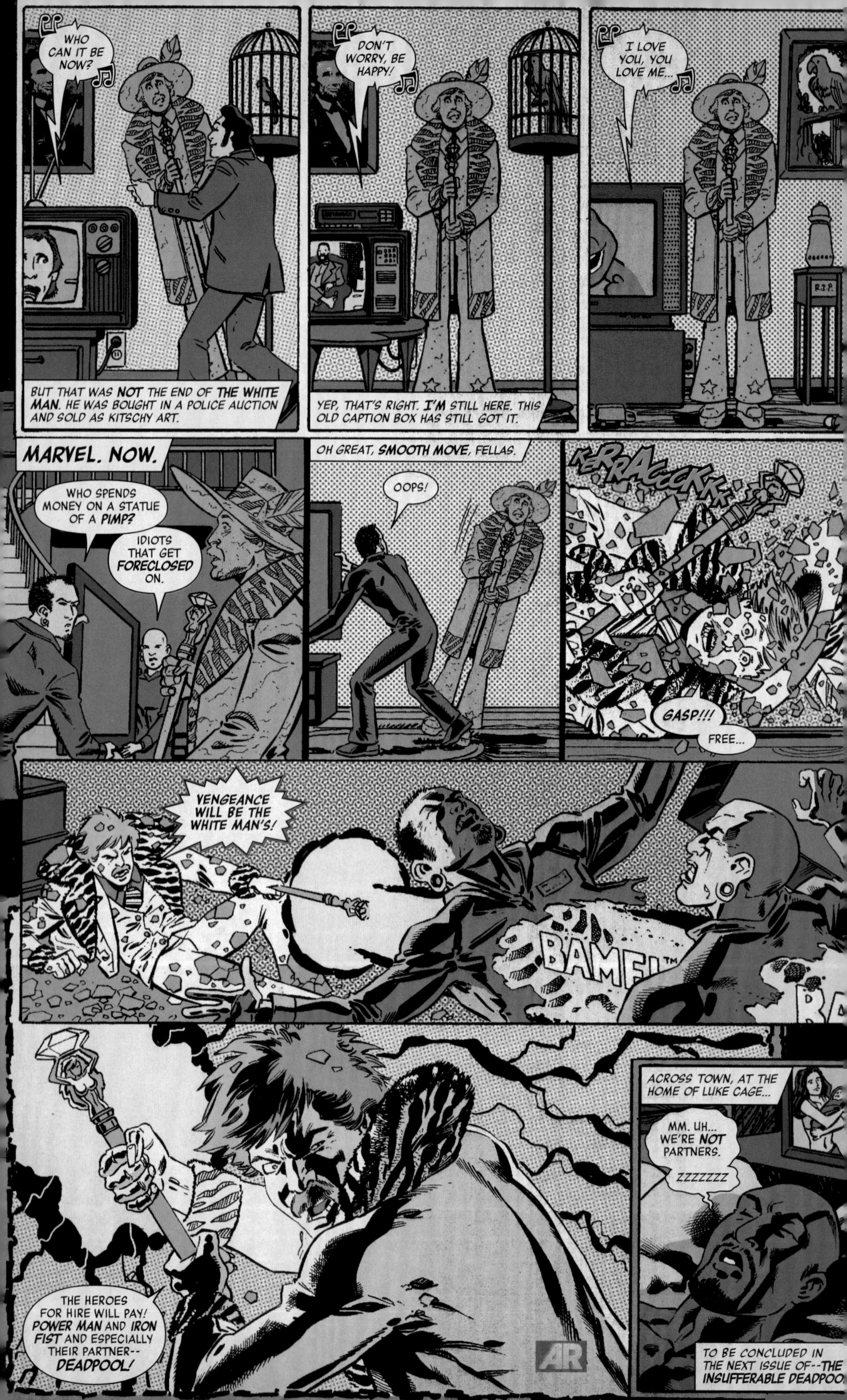

WHO CAN IT BE NOW?
BUT THAT WAS NOT THE END OF THE WHITE MAN. HE WAS BOUGHT IN A POLICE AUCTION AND SOLD AS KITSCHY ART.
DON'T WORRY, BE HAPPY!
YEP, THAT'S RIGHT. I'M STILL HERE. THIS OLD CAPTION BOX HAS STILL GOT IT.
I LOVE YOU, YOU LOVE ME...
R.I.P.
MARVEL. NOW.
WHO SPENDS MONEY ON A STATUE OF A PIMP?
IDIOTS THAT GET FORECLOSED ON.
OH GREAT, SMOOTH MOVE, FELLAS.
OOPS!
KERRACCKK
GASP!!!
FREE...
VENGEANCE WILL BE THE WHITE MAN'S!
BAMF!!™
THE HEROES FOR HIRE WILL PAY! POWER MAN AND IRON FIST AND ESPECIALLY THEIR PARTNER-- DEADPOOL!
ACROSS TOWN, AT THE HOME OF LUKE CAGE...
MM. UH... WE'RE NOT PARTNERS.
ZZZZZZZ
TO BE CONCLUDED IN THE NEXT ISSUE OF--THE INSUFFERABLE DEADPOO

14

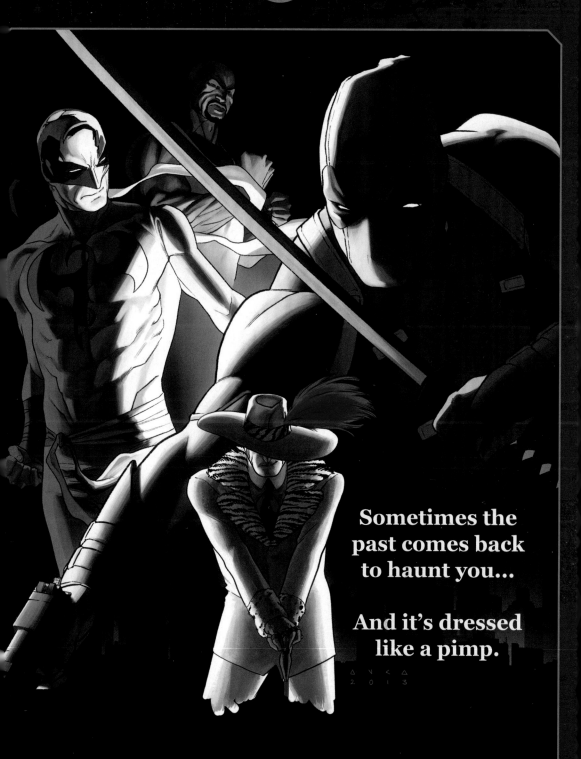

Sometimes the
past comes back
to haunt you...

And it's dressed
like a pimp.

THE WHITE MAN COMETH

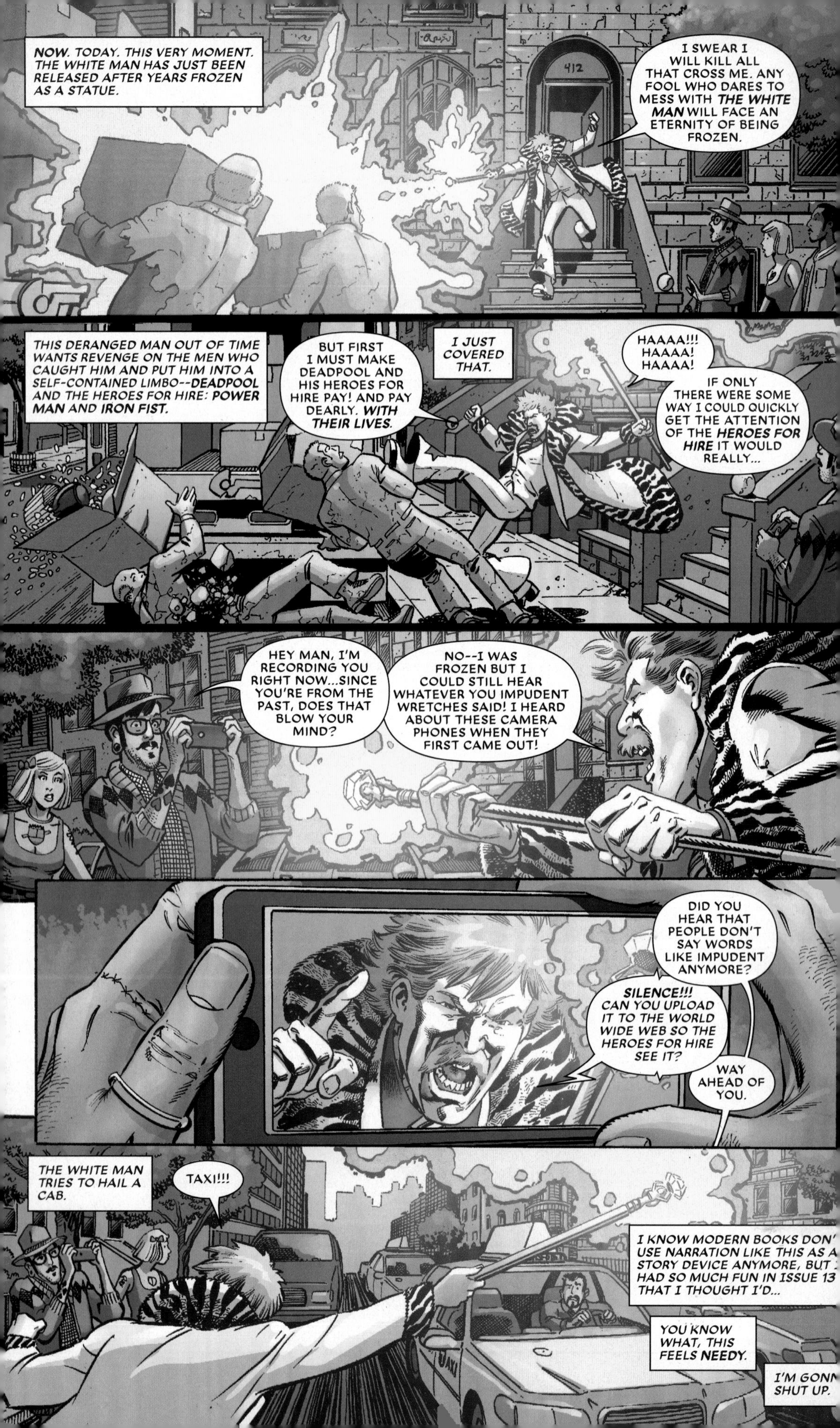
NOW. TODAY. THIS VERY MOMENT. THE WHITE MAN HAS JUST BEEN RELEASED AFTER YEARS FROZEN AS A STATUE.
I SWEAR I WILL KILL ALL THAT CROSS ME. ANY FOOL WHO DARES TO MESS WITH THE WHITE MAN WILL FACE AN ETERNITY OF BEING FROZEN.
412
THIS DERANGED MAN OUT OF TIME WANTS REVENGE ON THE MEN WHO CAUGHT HIM AND PUT HIM INTO A SELF-CONTAINED LIMBO--DEADPOOL AND THE HEROES FOR HIRE: POWER MAN AND IRON FIST.
BUT FIRST I MUST MAKE DEADPOOL AND HIS HEROES FOR HIRE PAY! AND PAY DEARLY. WITH THEIR LIVES.
I JUST COVERED THAT.
HAAAA!!! HAAAA! HAAAA!
IF ONLY THERE WERE SOME WAY I COULD QUICKLY GET THE ATTENTION OF THE HEROES FOR HIRE IT WOULD REALLY...
HEY MAN, I'M RECORDING YOU RIGHT NOW...SINCE YOU'RE FROM THE PAST, DOES THAT BLOW YOUR MIND?
NO--I WAS FROZEN BUT I COULD STILL HEAR WHATEVER YOU IMPUDENT WRETCHES SAID! I HEARD ABOUT THESE CAMERA PHONES WHEN THEY FIRST CAME OUT!
DID YOU HEAR THAT PEOPLE DON'T SAY WORDS LIKE IMPUDENT ANYMORE?
SILENCE!!! CAN YOU UPLOAD IT TO THE WORLD WIDE WEB SO THE HEROES FOR HIRE SEE IT?
WAY AHEAD OF YOU.
THE WHITE MAN TRIES TO HAIL A CAB.
TAXI!!!
I KNOW MODERN BOOKS DON' USE NARRATION LIKE THIS AS A STORY DEVICE ANYMORE, BUT HAD SO MUCH FUN IN ISSUE 13 THAT I THOUGHT I'D...
YOU KNOW WHAT, THIS FEELS NEEDY.
I'M GONN SHUT UP.
TAXI

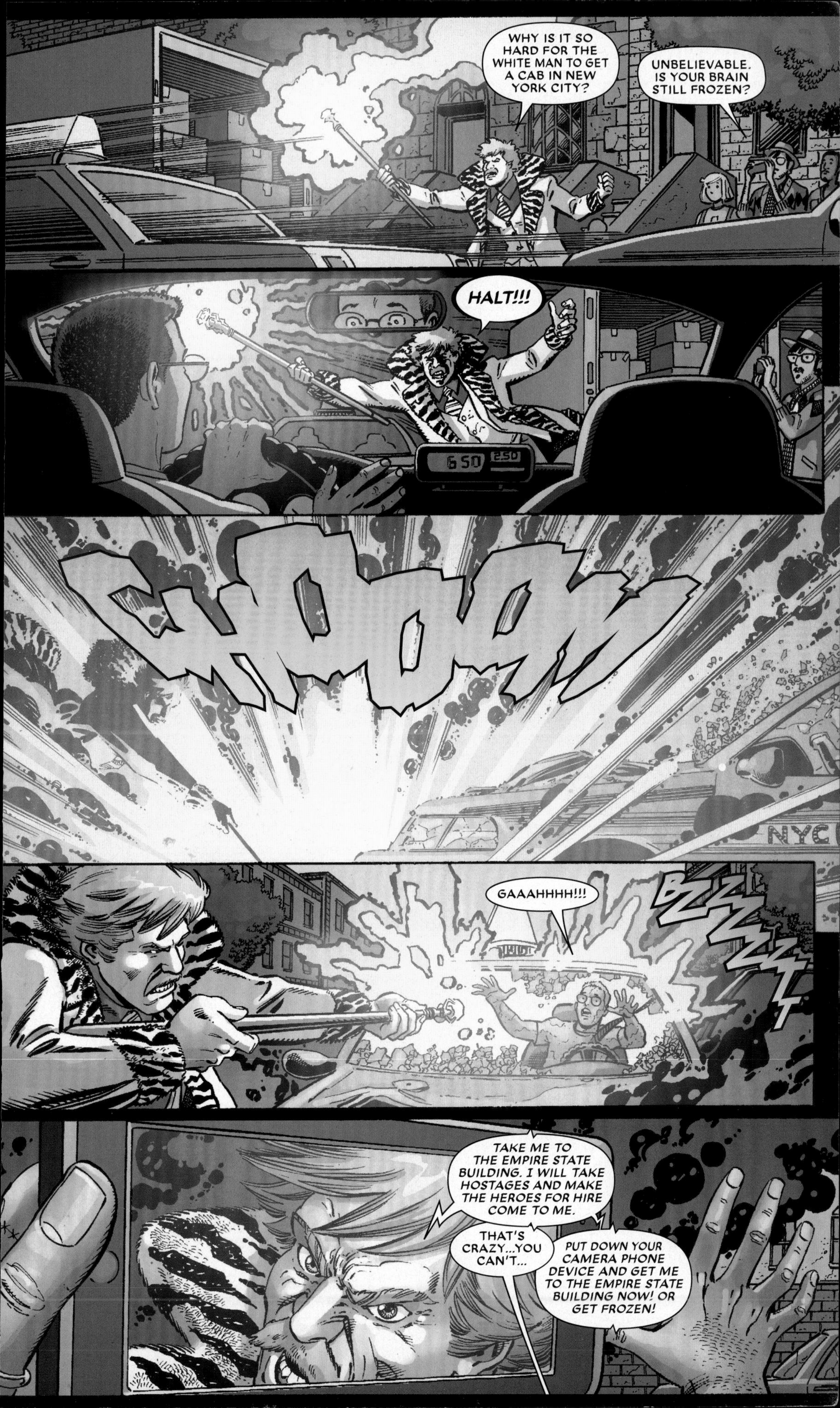

WHY IS IT SO HARD FOR THE WHITE MAN TO GET A CAB IN NEW YORK CITY?
UNBELIEVABLE. IS YOUR BRAIN STILL FROZEN?
HALT!!!
650
2.50
WHOOM
NYC
GAAAHHHH!!!
BZZZZZT
TAKE ME TO THE EMPIRE STATE BUILDING. I WILL TAKE HOSTAGES AND MAKE THE HEROES FOR HIRE COME TO ME.
THAT'S CRAZY...YOU CAN'T...
PUT DOWN YOUR CAMERA PHONE DEVICE AND GET ME TO THE EMPIRE STATE BUILDING NOW! OR GET FROZEN!

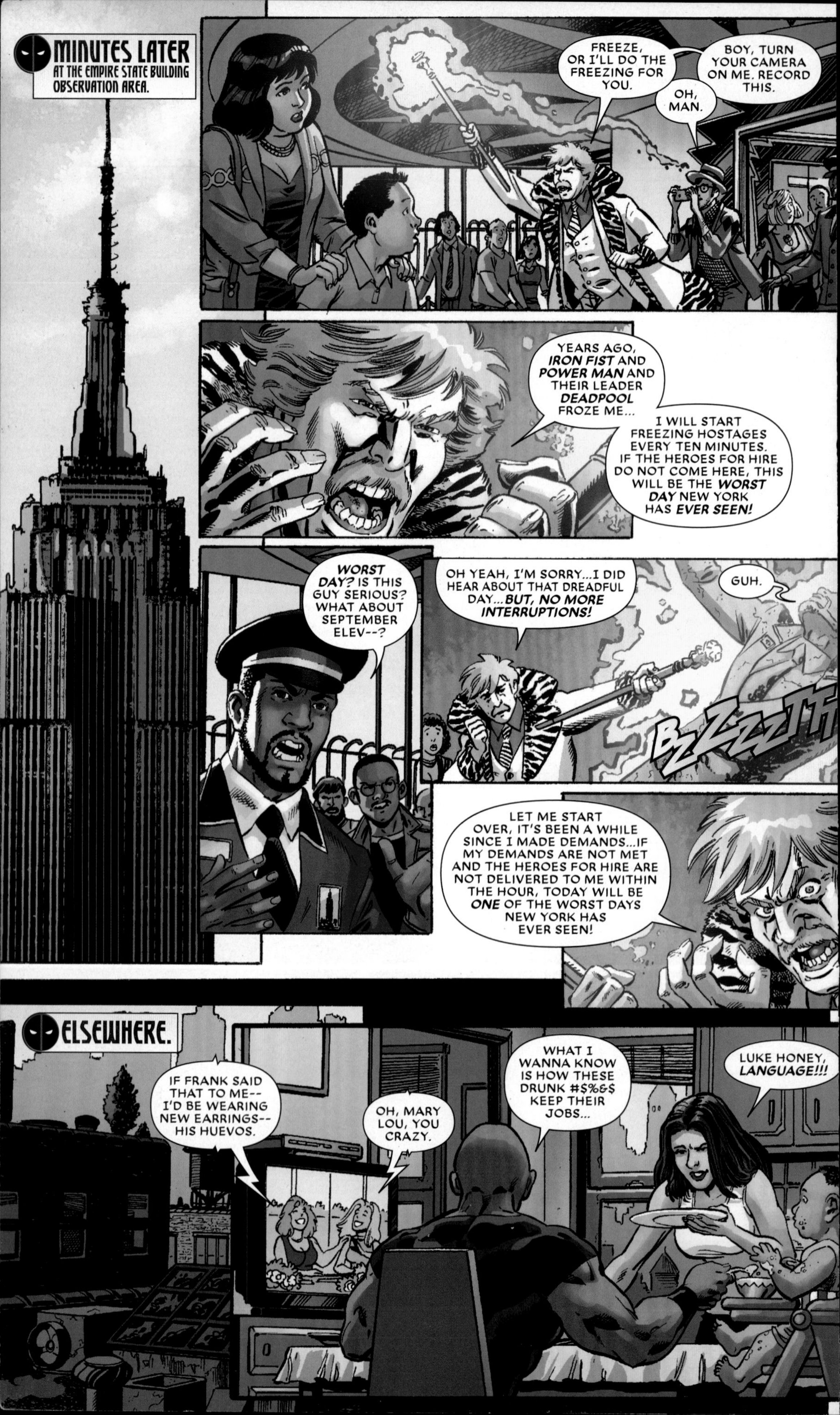
MINUTES LATER
AT THE EMPIRE STATE BUILDING OBSERVATION AREA.
FREEZE, OR I'LL DO THE FREEZING FOR YOU.
OH, MAN.
BOY, TURN YOUR CAMERA ON ME. RECORD THIS.
YEARS AGO, IRON FIST AND POWER MAN AND THEIR LEADER DEADPOOL FROZE ME...
I WILL START FREEZING HOSTAGES EVERY TEN MINUTES. IF THE HEROES FOR HIRE DO NOT COME HERE, THIS WILL BE THE WORST DAY NEW YORK HAS EVER SEEN!
WORST DAY? IS THIS GUY SERIOUS? WHAT ABOUT SEPTEMBER ELEV--?
OH YEAH, I'M SORRY...I DID HEAR ABOUT THAT DREADFUL DAY...BUT, NO MORE INTERRUPTIONS!
GUH.
BZZZZTH
LET ME START OVER, IT'S BEEN A WHILE SINCE I MADE DEMANDS...IF MY DEMANDS ARE NOT MET AND THE HEROES FOR HIRE ARE NOT DELIVERED TO ME WITHIN THE HOUR, TODAY WILL BE ONE OF THE WORST DAYS NEW YORK HAS EVER SEEN!
ELSEWHERE.
IF FRANK SAID THAT TO ME-- I'D BE WEARING NEW EARRINGS-- HIS HUEVOS.
OH, MARY LOU, YOU CRAZY.
WHAT I WANNA KNOW IS HOW THESE DRUNK #$%&$ KEEP THEIR JOBS...
LUKE HONEY, LANGUAGE!!!

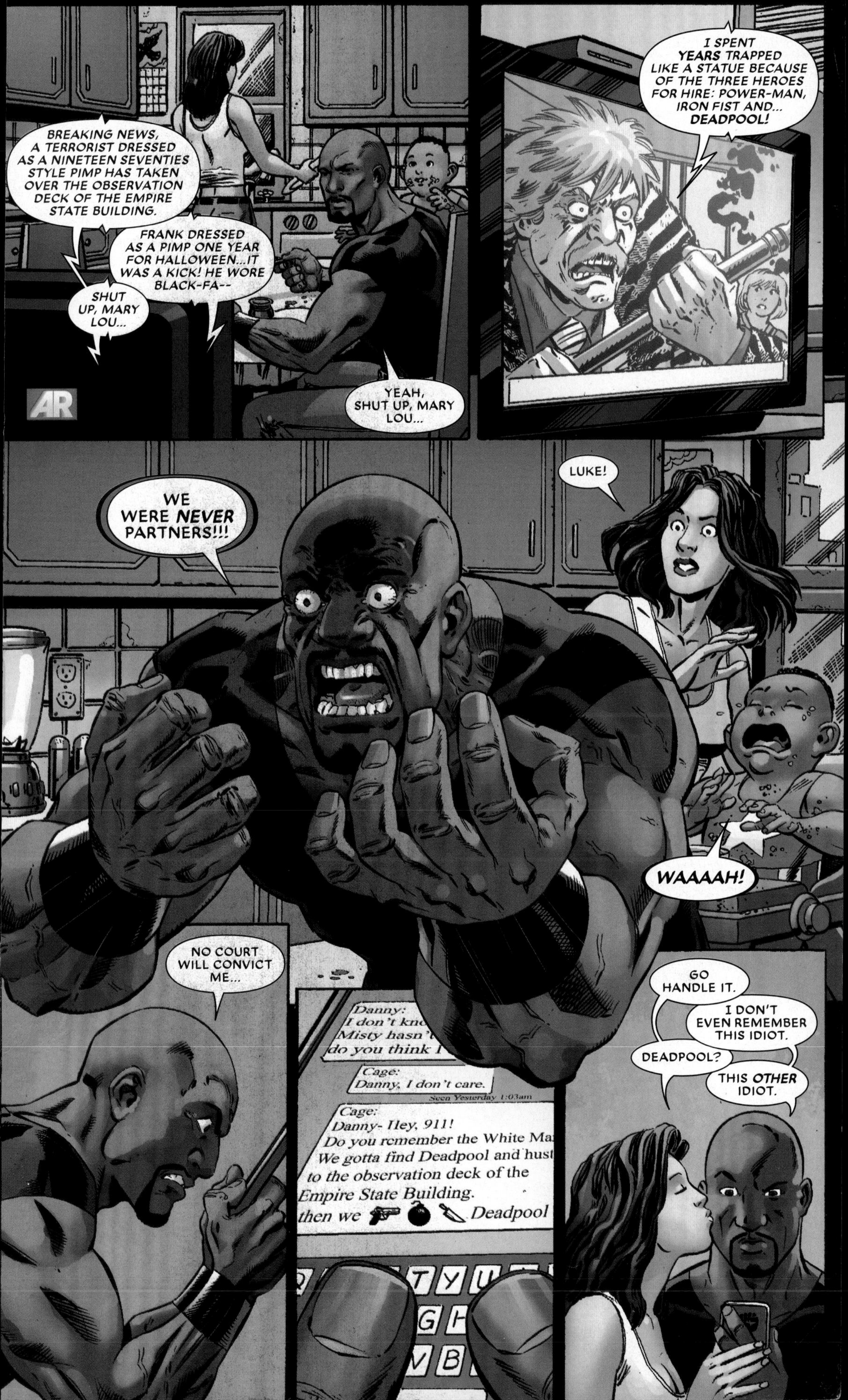

BREAKING NEWS, A TERRORIST DRESSED AS A NINETEEN SEVENTIES STYLE PIMP HAS TAKEN OVER THE OBSERVATION DECK OF THE EMPIRE STATE BUILDING.
FRANK DRESSED AS A PIMP ONE YEAR FOR HALLOWEEN...IT WAS A KICK! HE WORE BLACK-FA--
SHUT UP, MARY LOU...
YEAH, SHUT UP, MARY LOU...
I SPENT YEARS TRAPPED LIKE A STATUE BECAUSE OF THE THREE HEROES FOR HIRE: POWER-MAN, IRON FIST AND... DEADPOOL!
WE WERE NEVER PARTNERS!!!
LUKE!
WAAAAH!
NO COURT WILL CONVICT ME...
Danny:
I don't kn
Misty hasn'
do you think I
Cage:
Danny, I don't care.
Seen Yesterday 1:03am
Cage:
Danny- Hey, 911!
Do you remember the White Ma
We gotta find Deadpool and hust
to the observation deck of the
Empire State Building.
then we Deadpool
GO HANDLE IT.
I DON'T EVEN REMEMBER THIS IDIOT.
DEADPOOL?
THIS OTHER IDIOT.

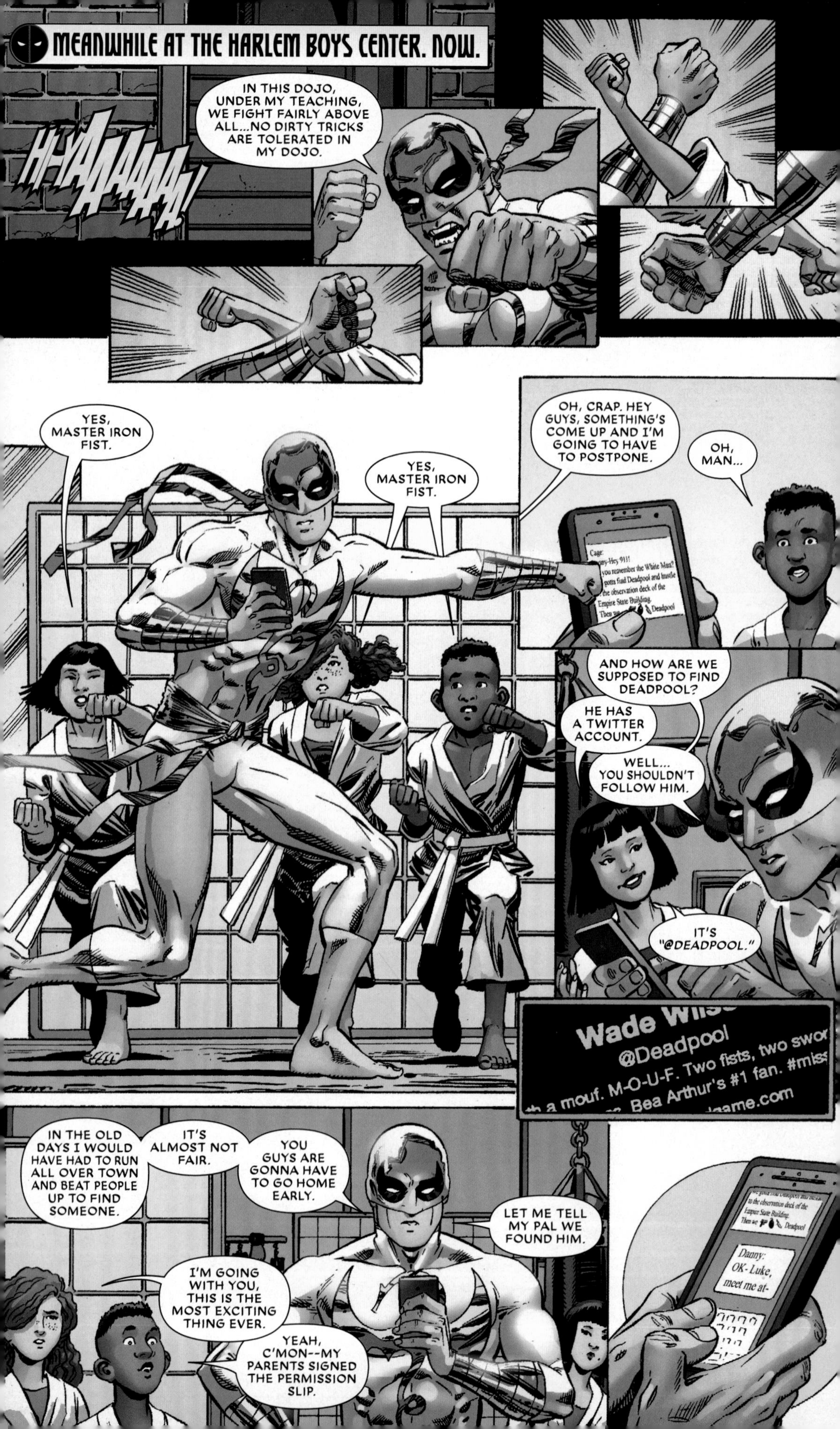
MEANWHILE AT THE HARLEM BOYS CENTER. NOW.
HI-YAAAAAA!
IN THIS DOJO, UNDER MY TEACHING, WE FIGHT FAIRLY ABOVE ALL...NO DIRTY TRICKS ARE TOLERATED IN MY DOJO.
YES, MASTER IRON FIST.
YES, MASTER IRON FIST.
OH, CRAP. HEY GUYS, SOMETHING'S COME UP AND I'M GOING TO HAVE TO POSTPONE.
OH, MAN...
Cage:
you remember the White Man?
the observation deck of the
Empire State Building.
Deadpool
AND HOW ARE WE SUPPOSED TO FIND DEADPOOL?
HE HAS A TWITTER ACCOUNT.
WELL... YOU SHOULDN'T FOLLOW HIM.
IT'S "@DEADPOOL."
Wade Wils
@Deadpool
a mouf. M-O-U-F. Two fists, two swor
Bea Arthur's #1 fan.
IN THE OLD DAYS I WOULD HAVE HAD TO RUN ALL OVER TOWN AND BEAT PEOPLE UP TO FIND SOMEONE.
IT'S ALMOST NOT FAIR.
YOU GUYS ARE GONNA HAVE TO GO HOME EARLY.
LET ME TELL MY PAL WE FOUND HIM.
I'M GOING WITH YOU, THIS IS THE MOST EXCITING THING EVER.
YEAH, C'MON--MY PARENTS SIGNED THE PERMISSION SLIP.
Empire State Building.
Deadpool
Danny:
OK- Luke,
meet me at-

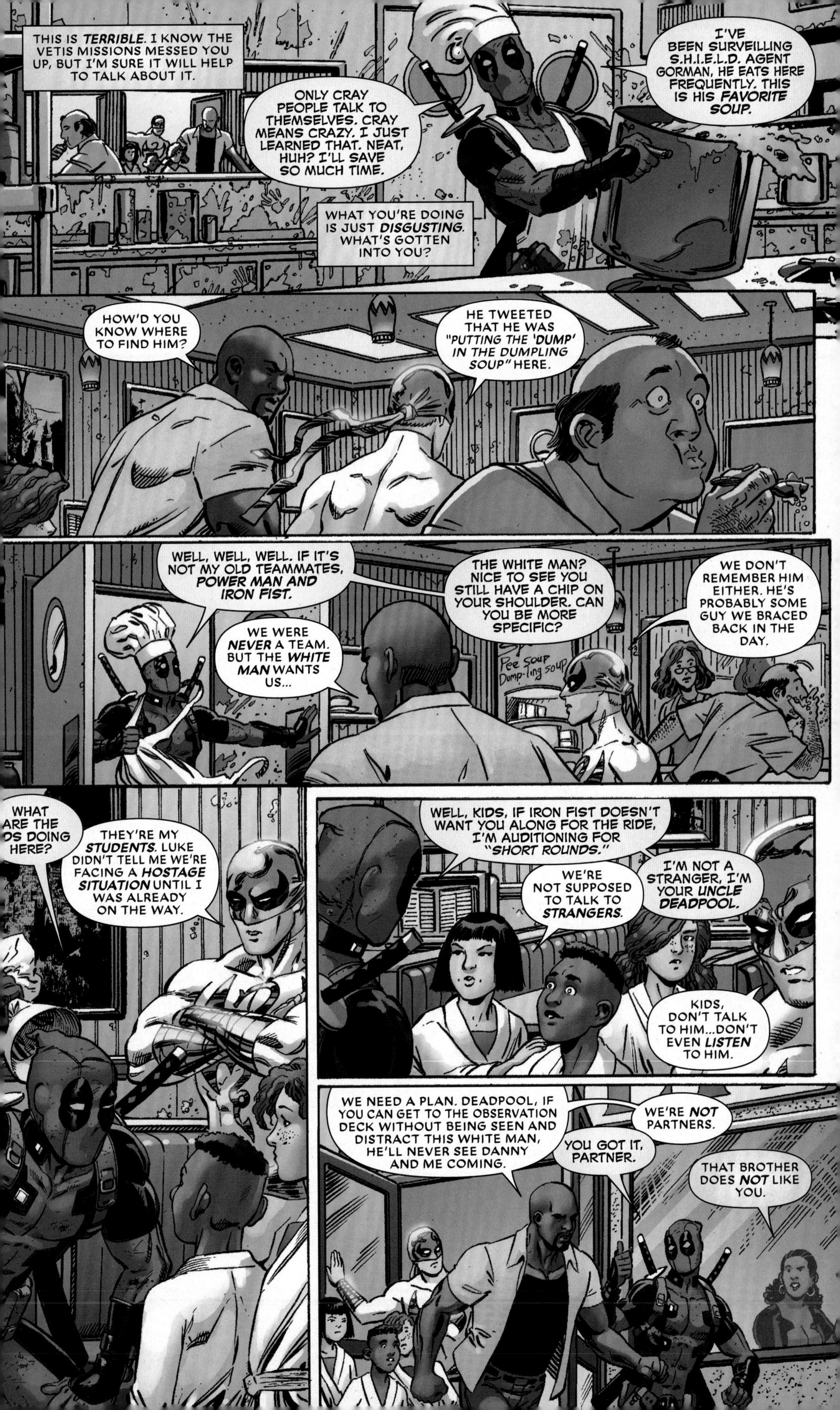

THIS IS *TERRIBLE*. I KNOW THE VETIS MISSIONS MESSED YOU UP, BUT I'M SURE IT WILL HELP TO TALK ABOUT IT.
ONLY CRAY PEOPLE TALK TO THEMSELVES. CRAY MEANS CRAZY. I JUST LEARNED THAT. NEAT, HUH? I'LL SAVE SO MUCH TIME.
I'VE BEEN SURVEILLING S.H.I.E.L.D. AGENT GORMAN, HE EATS HERE FREQUENTLY. THIS IS HIS *FAVORITE SOUP.*
WHAT YOU'RE DOING IS JUST *DISGUSTING*. WHAT'S GOTTEN INTO YOU?
HOW'D YOU KNOW WHERE TO FIND HIM?
HE TWEETED THAT HE WAS *"PUTTING THE 'DUMP' IN THE DUMPLING SOUP"* HERE.
WELL, WELL, WELL. IF IT'S NOT MY OLD TEAMMATES, *POWER MAN AND IRON FIST.*
WE WERE *NEVER* A TEAM. BUT THE *WHITE MAN* WANTS US...
THE WHITE MAN? NICE TO SEE YOU STILL HAVE A CHIP ON YOUR SHOULDER. CAN YOU BE MORE SPECIFIC?
WE DON'T REMEMBER HIM EITHER. HE'S PROBABLY SOME GUY WE BRACED BACK IN THE DAY.
Pee soup
Dump-ling soup
WHAT ARE THE DS DOING HERE?
THEY'RE MY *STUDENTS*. LUKE DIDN'T TELL ME WE'RE FACING A *HOSTAGE SITUATION* UNTIL I WAS ALREADY ON THE WAY.
WELL, KIDS, IF IRON FIST DOESN'T WANT YOU ALONG FOR THE RIDE, I'M AUDITIONING FOR *"SHORT ROUNDS."*
WE'RE NOT SUPPOSED TO TALK TO *STRANGERS*.
I'M NOT A STRANGER, I'M YOUR *UNCLE DEADPOOL.*
KIDS, DON'T TALK TO HIM...DON'T EVEN *LISTEN* TO HIM.
WE NEED A PLAN. DEADPOOL, IF YOU CAN GET TO THE OBSERVATION DECK WITHOUT BEING SEEN AND DISTRACT THIS WHITE MAN, HE'LL NEVER SEE DANNY AND ME COMING.
YOU GOT IT, PARTNER.
WE'RE *NOT* PARTNERS.
THAT BROTHER DOES *NOT* LIKE YOU.

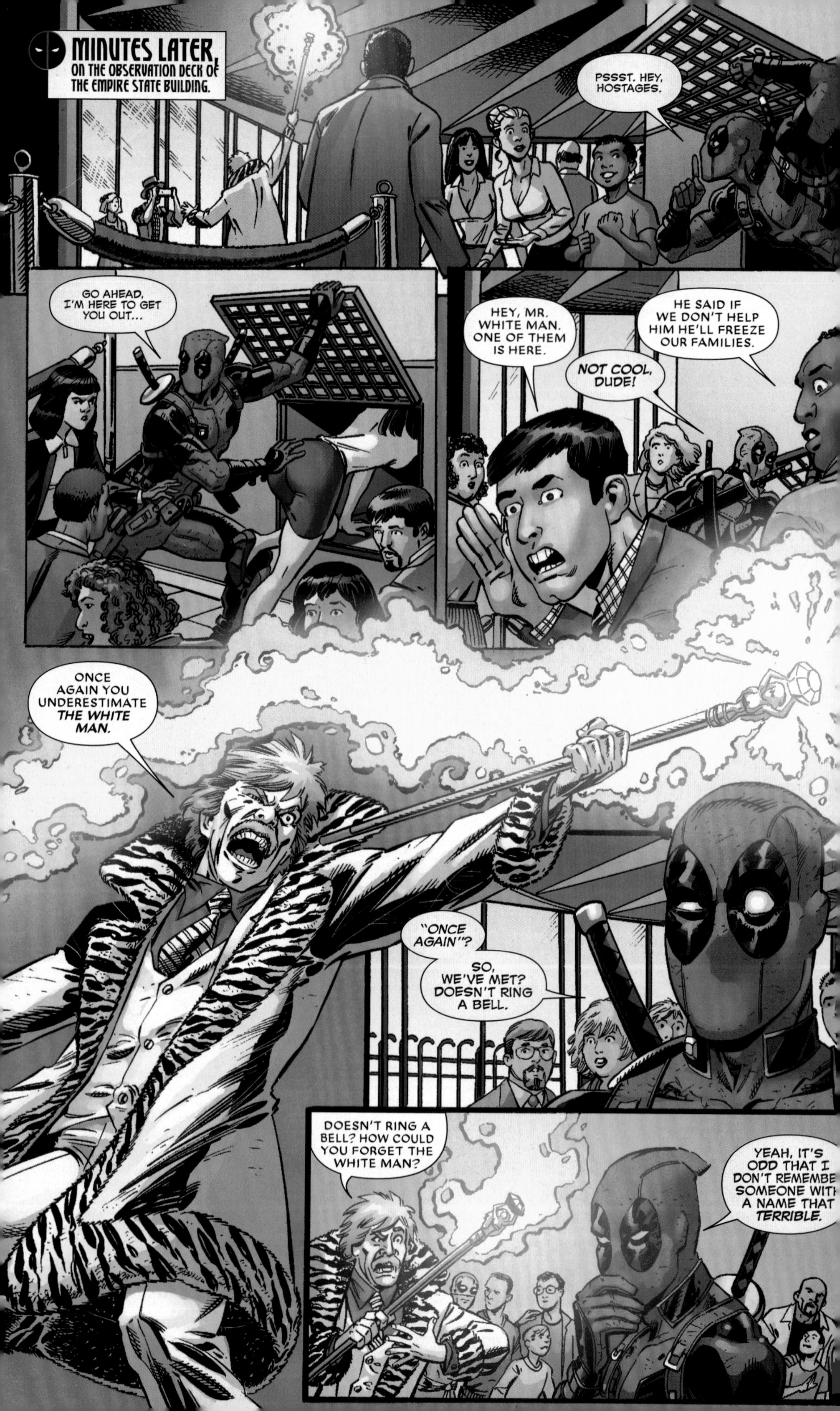
MINUTES LATER, ON THE OBSERVATION DECK OF THE EMPIRE STATE BUILDING.
PSSST. HEY, HOSTAGES.
GO AHEAD, I'M HERE TO GET YOU OUT...
HEY, MR. WHITE MAN. ONE OF THEM IS HERE.
NOT COOL, DUDE!
HE SAID IF WE DON'T HELP HIM HE'LL FREEZE OUR FAMILIES.
ONCE AGAIN YOU UNDERESTIMATE THE WHITE MAN.
"ONCE AGAIN"?
SO, WE'VE MET? DOESN'T RING A BELL.
DOESN'T RING A BELL? HOW COULD YOU FORGET THE WHITE MAN?
YEAH, IT'S ODD THAT I DON'T REMEMBE SOMEONE WIT A NAME THAT TERRIBLE.

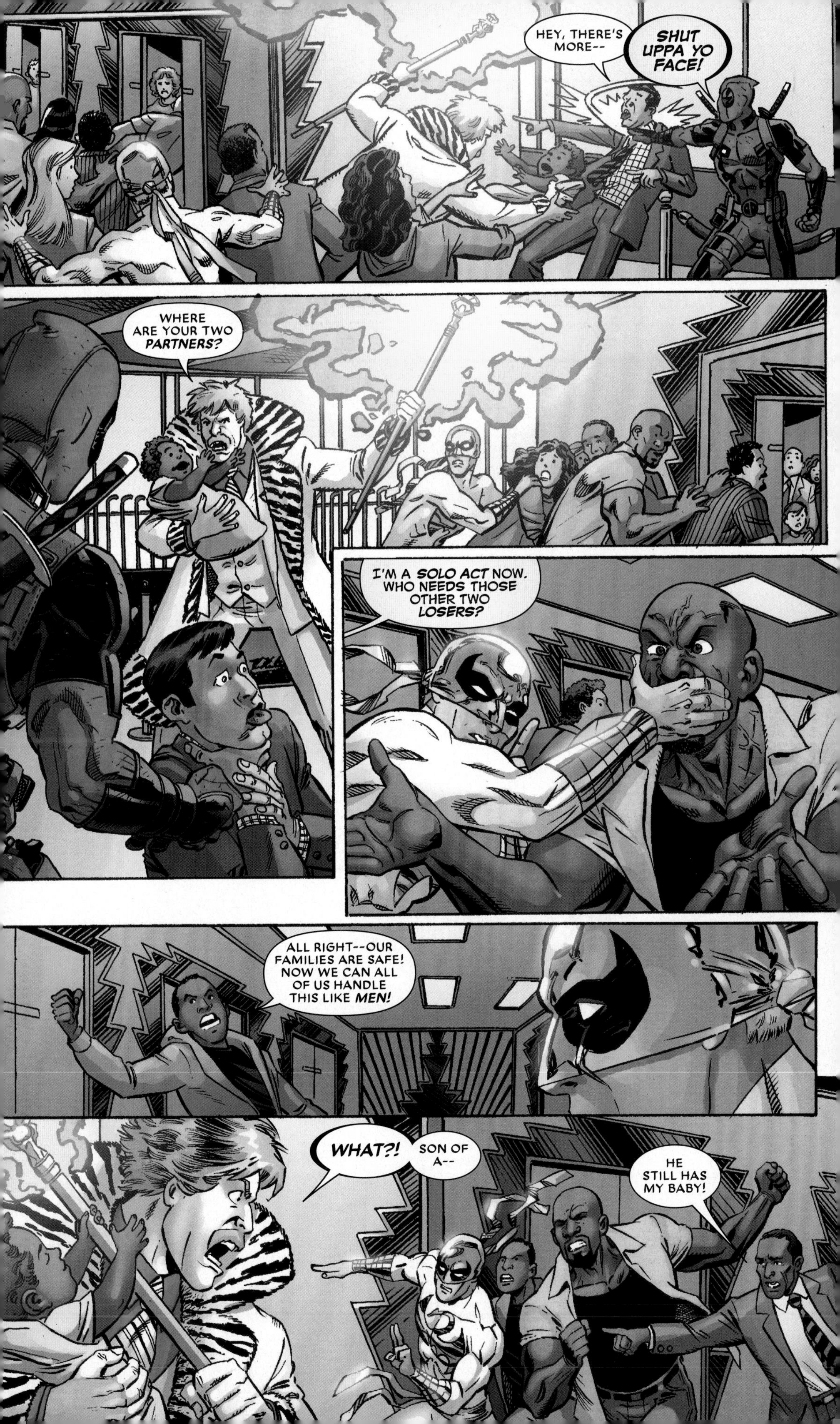
HEY, THERE'S MORE--
SHUT UPPA YO FACE!
WHERE ARE YOUR TWO PARTNERS?
I'M A SOLO ACT NOW. WHO NEEDS THOSE OTHER TWO LOSERS?
ALL RIGHT--OUR FAMILIES ARE SAFE! NOW WE CAN ALL OF US HANDLE THIS LIKE MEN!
WHAT?!
SON OF A--
HE STILL HAS MY BABY!

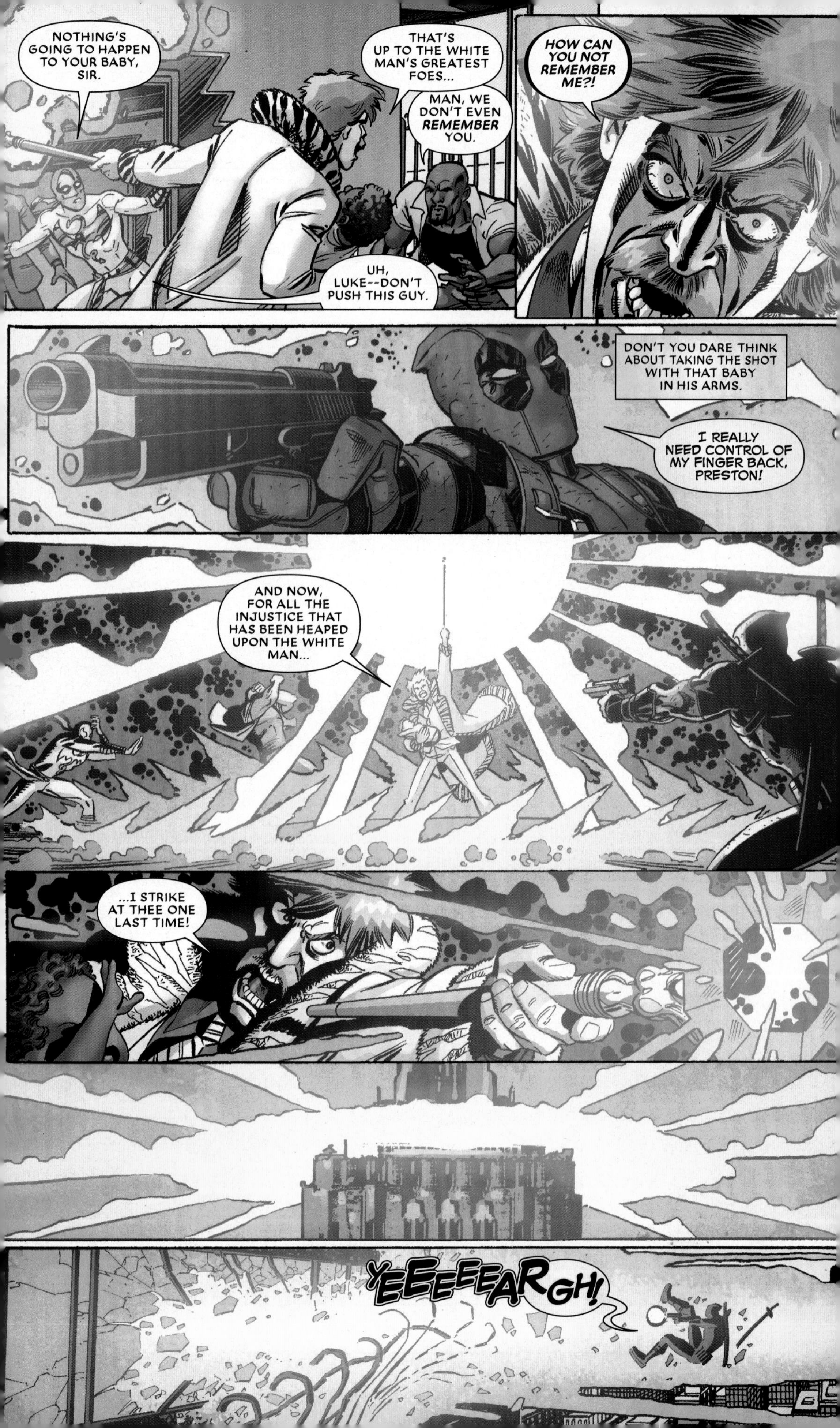
NOTHING'S GOING TO HAPPEN TO YOUR BABY, SIR.
THAT'S UP TO THE WHITE MAN'S GREATEST FOES...
MAN, WE DON'T EVEN REMEMBER YOU.
UH, LUKE--DON'T PUSH THIS GUY.
HOW CAN YOU NOT REMEMBER ME?!
DON'T YOU DARE THINK ABOUT TAKING THE SHOT WITH THAT BABY IN HIS ARMS.
I REALLY NEED CONTROL OF MY FINGER BACK, PRESTON!
AND NOW, FOR ALL THE INJUSTICE THAT HAS BEEN HEAPED UPON THE WHITE MAN...
...I STRIKE AT THEE ONE LAST TIME!
YEEEEEEARGH!

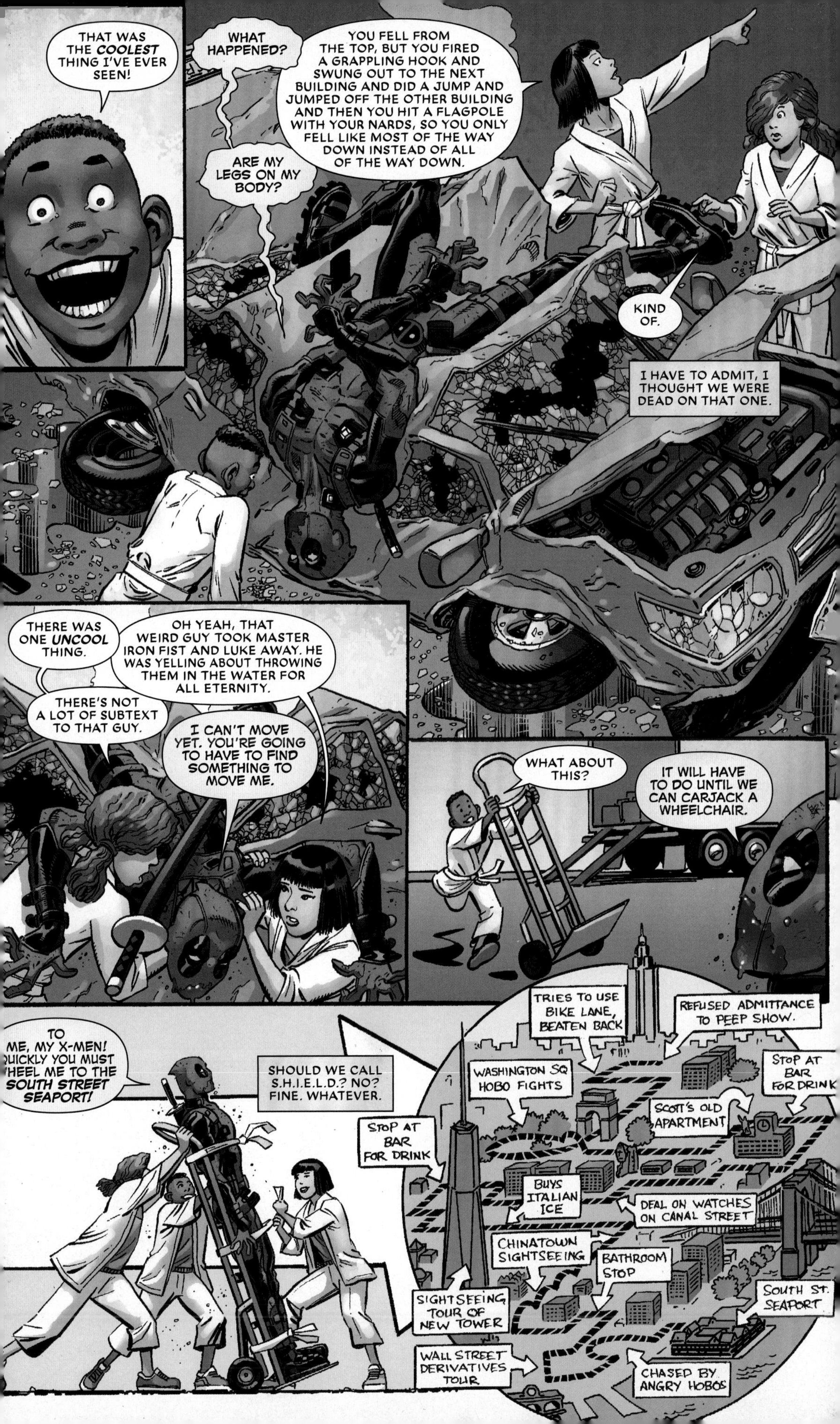

THAT WAS THE COOLEST THING I'VE EVER SEEN!
WHAT HAPPENED?
YOU FELL FROM THE TOP, BUT YOU FIRED A GRAPPLING HOOK AND SWUNG OUT TO THE NEXT BUILDING AND DID A JUMP AND JUMPED OFF THE OTHER BUILDING AND THEN YOU HIT A FLAGPOLE WITH YOUR NARDS, SO YOU ONLY FELL LIKE MOST OF THE WAY DOWN INSTEAD OF ALL OF THE WAY DOWN.
ARE MY LEGS ON MY BODY?
KIND OF.
I HAVE TO ADMIT, I THOUGHT WE WERE DEAD ON THAT ONE.
THERE WAS ONE UNCOOL THING.
OH YEAH, THAT WEIRD GUY TOOK MASTER IRON FIST AND LUKE AWAY. HE WAS YELLING ABOUT THROWING THEM IN THE WATER FOR ALL ETERNITY.
THERE'S NOT A LOT OF SUBTEXT TO THAT GUY.
I CAN'T MOVE YET. YOU'RE GOING TO HAVE TO FIND SOMETHING TO MOVE ME.
WHAT ABOUT THIS?
IT WILL HAVE TO DO UNTIL WE CAN CARJACK A WHEELCHAIR.
TO ME, MY X-MEN! UICKLY YOU MUST HEEL ME TO THE SOUTH STREET SEAPORT!
SHOULD WE CALL S.H.I.E.L.D.? NO? FINE. WHATEVER.
TRIES TO USE BIKE LANE, BEATEN BACK
REFUSED ADMITTANCE TO PEEP SHOW.
WASHINGTON SQ HOBO FIGHTS
STOP AT BAR FOR DRINK
SCOTT'S OLD APARTMENT
STOP AT BAR FOR DRINK
BUYS ITALIAN ICE
DEAL ON WATCHES ON CANAL STREET
CHINATOWN SIGHTSEEING
BATHROOM STOP
SIGHTSEEING TOUR OF NEW TOWER
SOUTH ST. SEAPORT
WALL STREET DERIVATIVES TOUR
CHASED BY ANGRY HOBOS

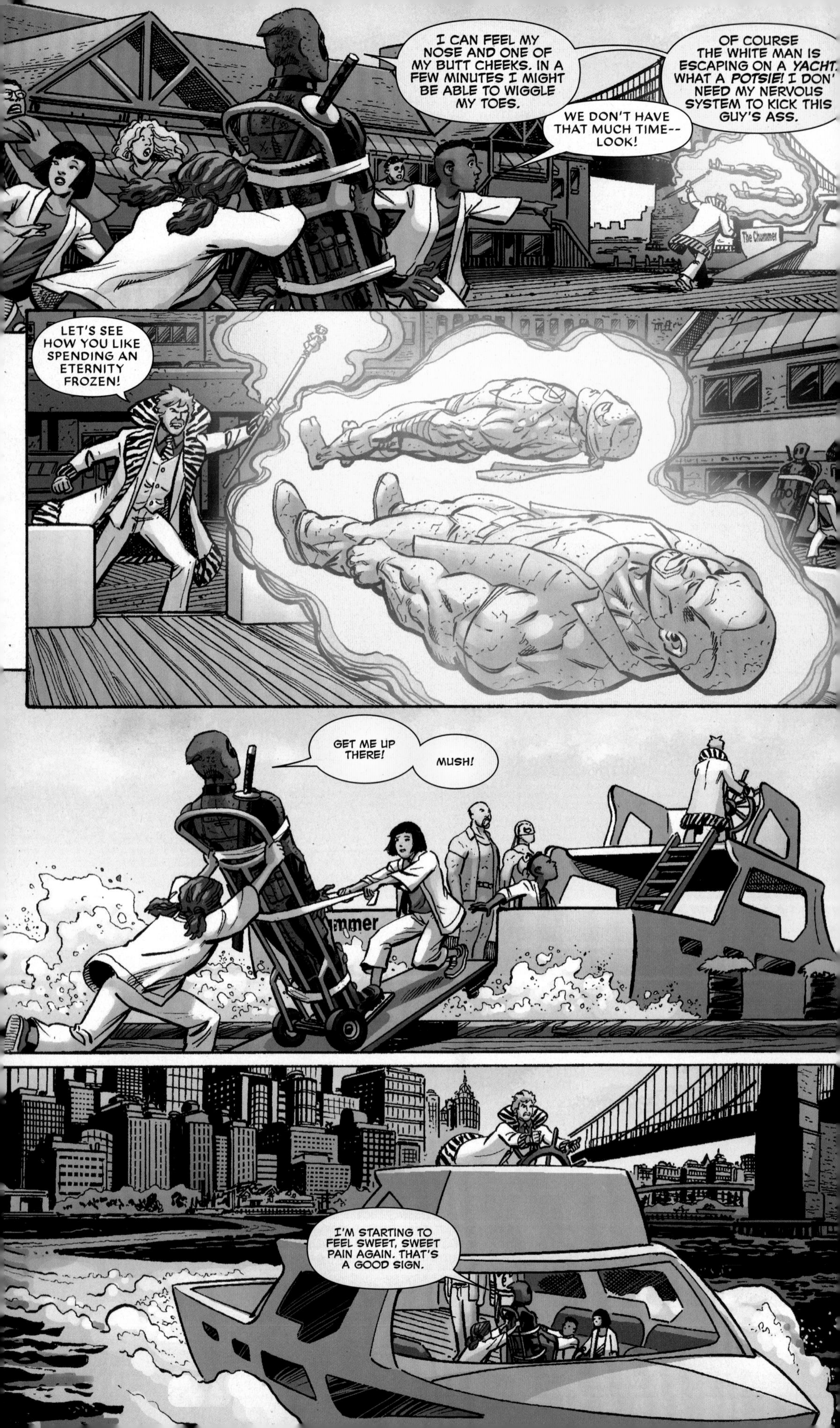
I CAN FEEL MY NOSE AND ONE OF MY BUTT CHEEKS. IN A FEW MINUTES I MIGHT BE ABLE TO WIGGLE MY TOES.
OF COURSE THE WHITE MAN IS ESCAPING ON A *YACHT*. WHAT A *POTSIE!* I DON' NEED MY NERVOUS SYSTEM TO KICK THIS GUY'S ASS.
WE DON'T HAVE THAT MUCH TIME-- LOOK!
The Chummer
LET'S SEE HOW YOU LIKE SPENDING AN ETERNITY FROZEN!
GET ME UP THERE!
MUSH!
I'M STARTING TO FEEL SWEET, SWEET PAIN AGAIN. THAT'S A GOOD SIGN.

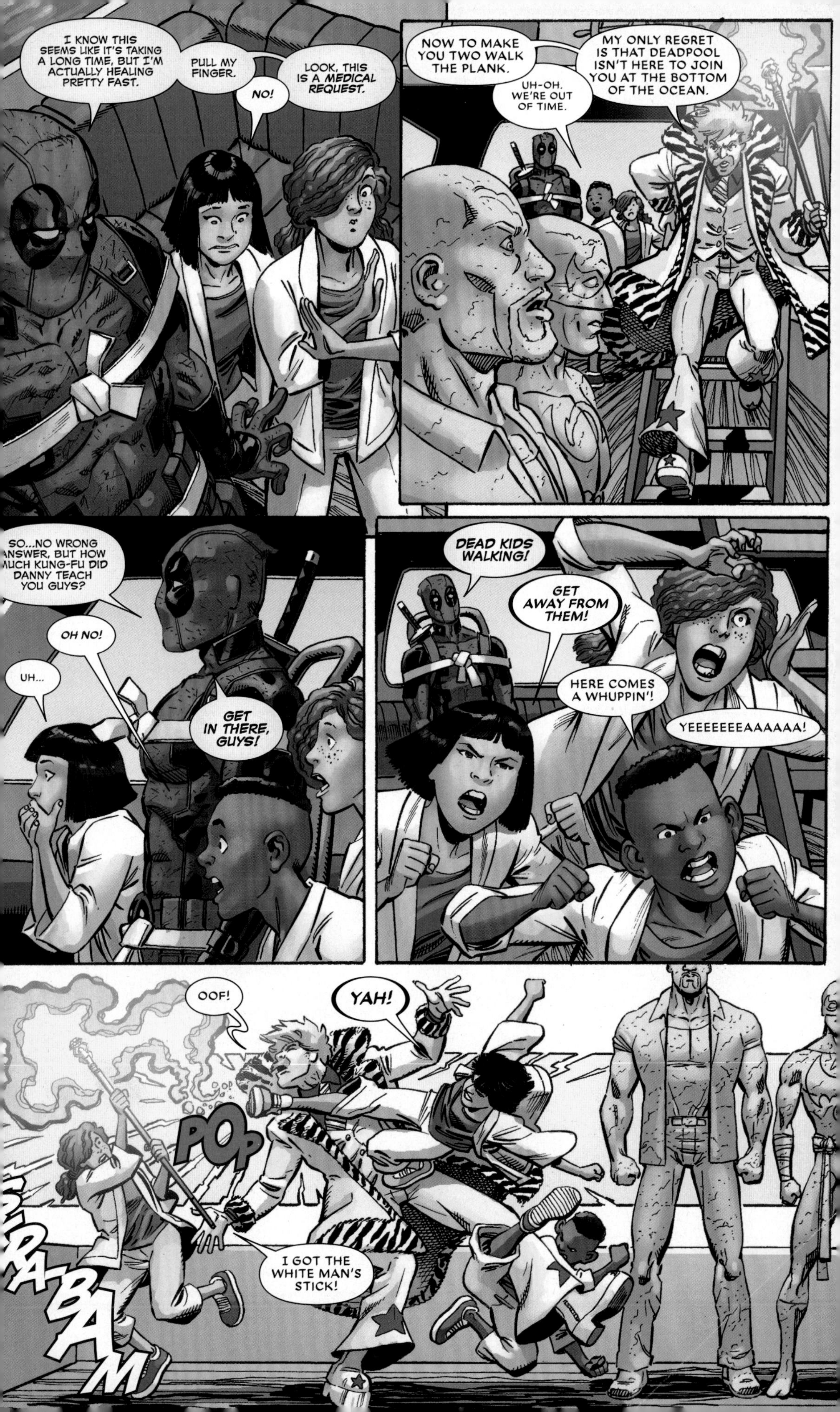
I KNOW THIS SEEMS LIKE IT'S TAKING A LONG TIME, BUT I'M ACTUALLY HEALING PRETTY FAST.
PULL MY FINGER.
NO!
LOOK, THIS IS A MEDICAL REQUEST.
NOW TO MAKE YOU TWO WALK THE PLANK.
MY ONLY REGRET IS THAT DEADPOOL ISN'T HERE TO JOIN YOU AT THE BOTTOM OF THE OCEAN.
UH-OH. WE'RE OUT OF TIME.
SO...NO WRONG ANSWER, BUT HOW MUCH KUNG-FU DID DANNY TEACH YOU GUYS?
OH NO!
UH...
GET IN THERE, GUYS!
DEAD KIDS WALKING!
GET AWAY FROM THEM!
HERE COMES A WHUPPIN'!
YEEEEEEEAAAAAA!
OOF!
YAH!
POP
SPADABAM
I GOT THE WHITE MAN'S STICK!

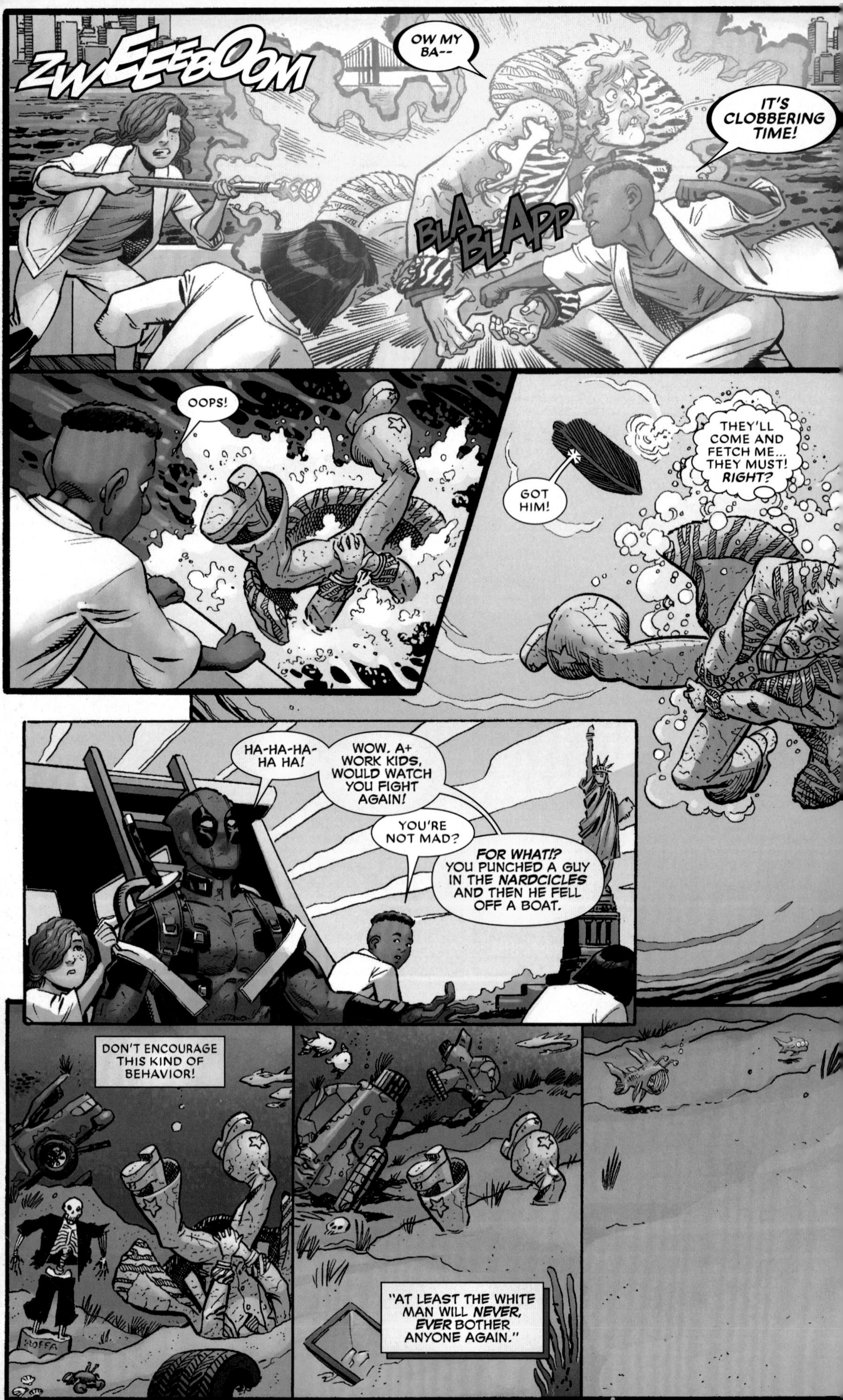
ZWEEEBOOM
OW MY BA--
IT'S CLOBBERING TIME!
BLA BLAPP
OOPS!
GOT HIM!
THEY'LL COME AND FETCH ME... THEY MUST! RIGHT?
HA-HA-HA-HA HA!
WOW. A+ WORK KIDS. WOULD WATCH YOU FIGHT AGAIN!
YOU'RE NOT MAD?
FOR WHAT!? YOU PUNCHED A GUY IN THE NARDCICLES AND THEN HE FELL OFF A BOAT.
DON'T ENCOURAGE THIS KIND OF BEHAVIOR!
HOFFA
"AT LEAST THE WHITE MAN WILL NEVER, EVER BOTHER ANYONE AGAIN."

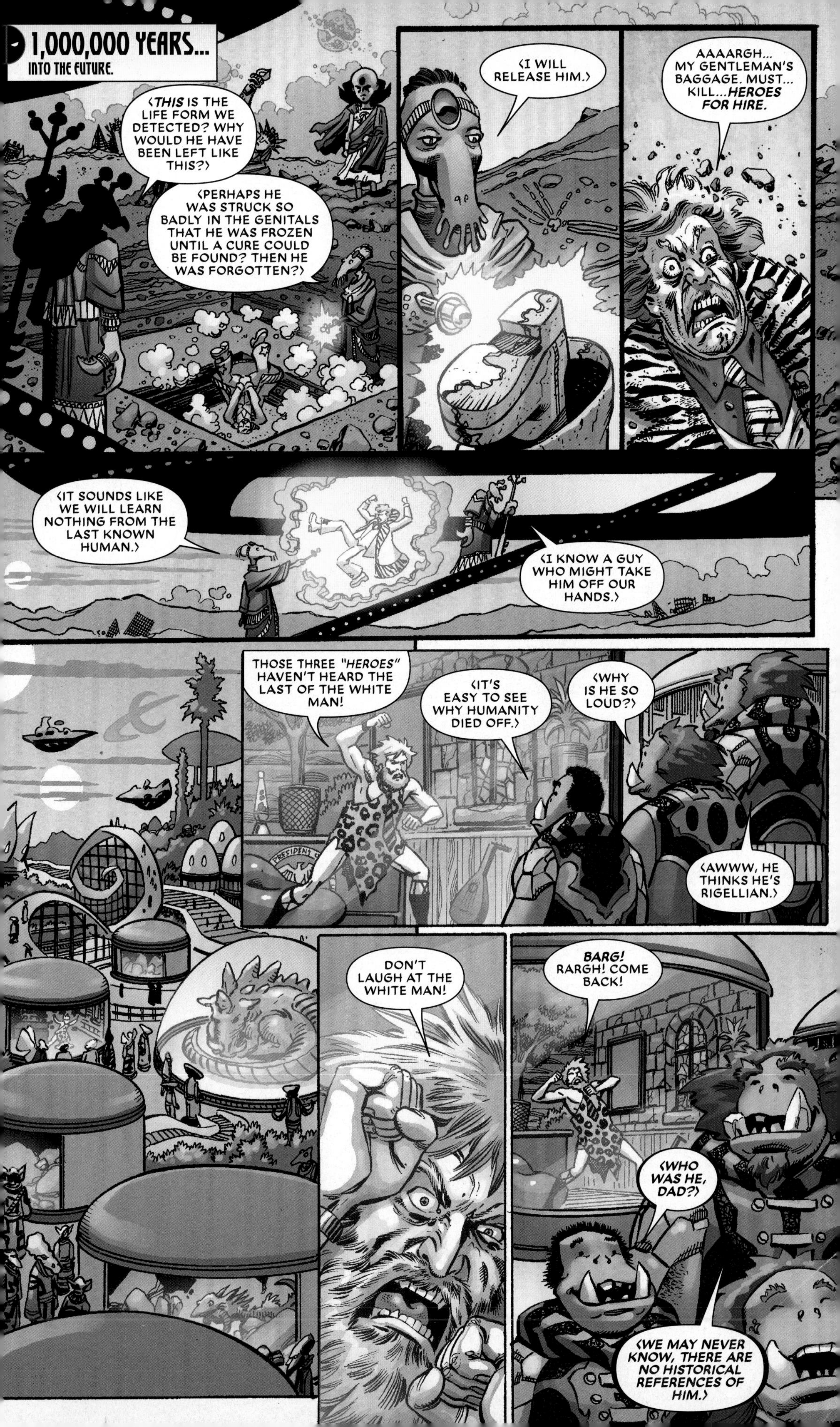
1,000,000 YEARS...
INTO THE FUTURE.
‹THIS IS THE LIFE FORM WE DETECTED? WHY WOULD HE HAVE BEEN LEFT LIKE THIS?›
‹PERHAPS HE WAS STRUCK SO BADLY IN THE GENITALS THAT HE WAS FROZEN UNTIL A CURE COULD BE FOUND? THEN HE WAS FORGOTTEN?›
‹I WILL RELEASE HIM.›
AAAARGH... MY GENTLEMAN'S BAGGAGE. MUST... KILL...HEROES FOR HIRE.
‹IT SOUNDS LIKE WE WILL LEARN NOTHING FROM THE LAST KNOWN HUMAN.›
‹I KNOW A GUY WHO MIGHT TAKE HIM OFF OUR HANDS.›
THOSE THREE "HEROES" HAVEN'T HEARD THE LAST OF THE WHITE MAN!
‹IT'S EASY TO SEE WHY HUMANITY DIED OFF.›
‹WHY IS HE SO LOUD?›
‹AWWW, HE THINKS HE'S RIGELLIAN.›
DON'T LAUGH AT THE WHITE MAN!
BARG! RARGH! COME BACK!
‹WHO WAS HE, DAD?›
‹WE MAY NEVER KNOW, THERE ARE NO HISTORICAL REFERENCES OF HIM.›

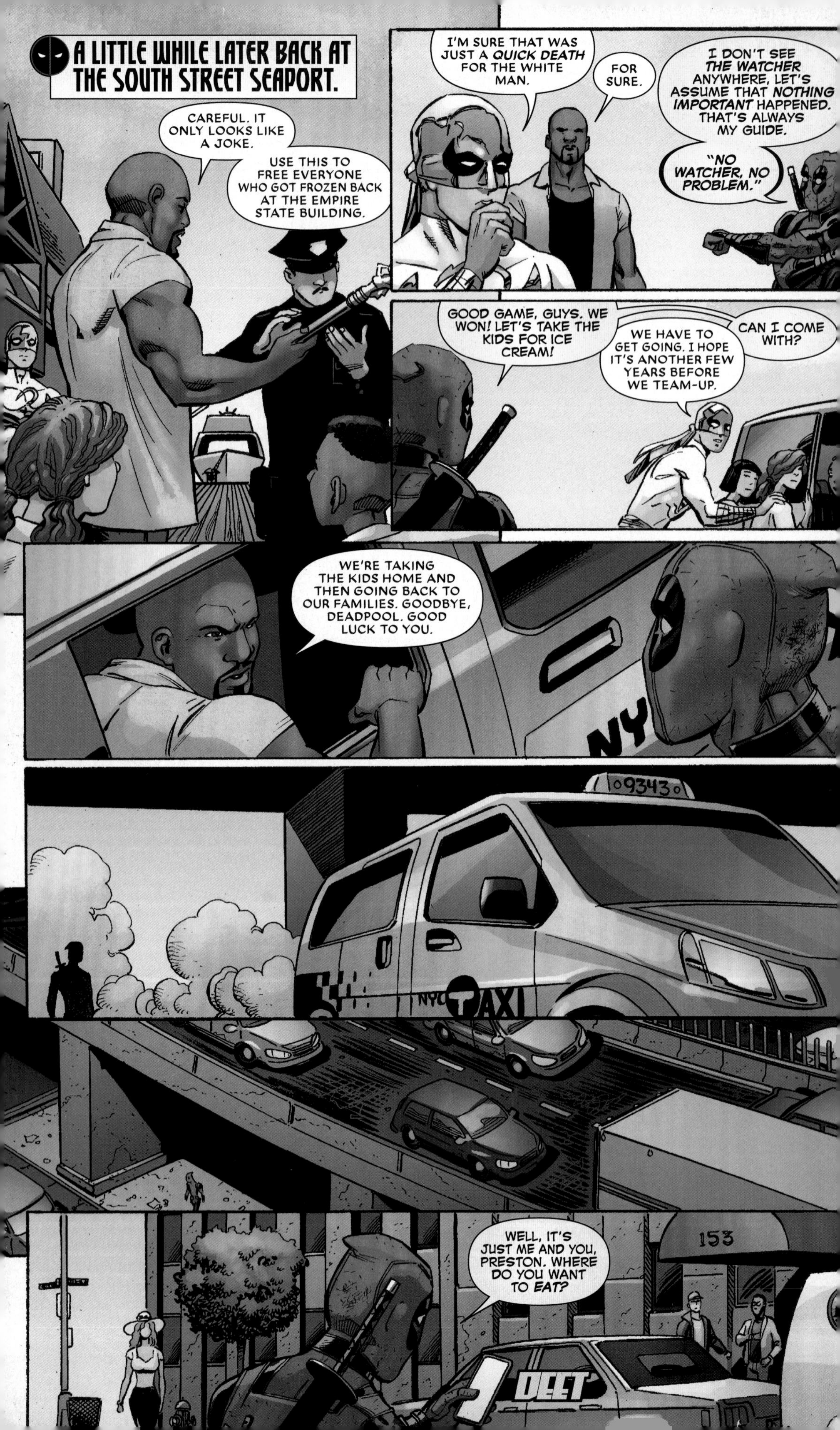
A LITTLE WHILE LATER BACK AT THE SOUTH STREET SEAPORT.
CAREFUL. IT ONLY LOOKS LIKE A JOKE.
USE THIS TO FREE EVERYONE WHO GOT FROZEN BACK AT THE EMPIRE STATE BUILDING.
I'M SURE THAT WAS JUST A QUICK DEATH FOR THE WHITE MAN.
FOR SURE.
I DON'T SEE THE WATCHER ANYWHERE, LET'S ASSUME THAT NOTHING IMPORTANT HAPPENED. THAT'S ALWAYS MY GUIDE.
"NO WATCHER, NO PROBLEM."
GOOD GAME, GUYS. WE WON! LET'S TAKE THE KIDS FOR ICE CREAM!
CAN I COME WITH?
WE HAVE TO GET GOING. I HOPE IT'S ANOTHER FEW YEARS BEFORE WE TEAM-UP.
WE'RE TAKING THE KIDS HOME AND THEN GOING BACK TO OUR FAMILIES. GOODBYE, DEADPOOL. GOOD LUCK TO YOU.
NY
9343
NYC TAXI
153
WELL, IT'S JUST ME AND YOU, PRESTON. WHERE DO YOU WANT TO EAT?

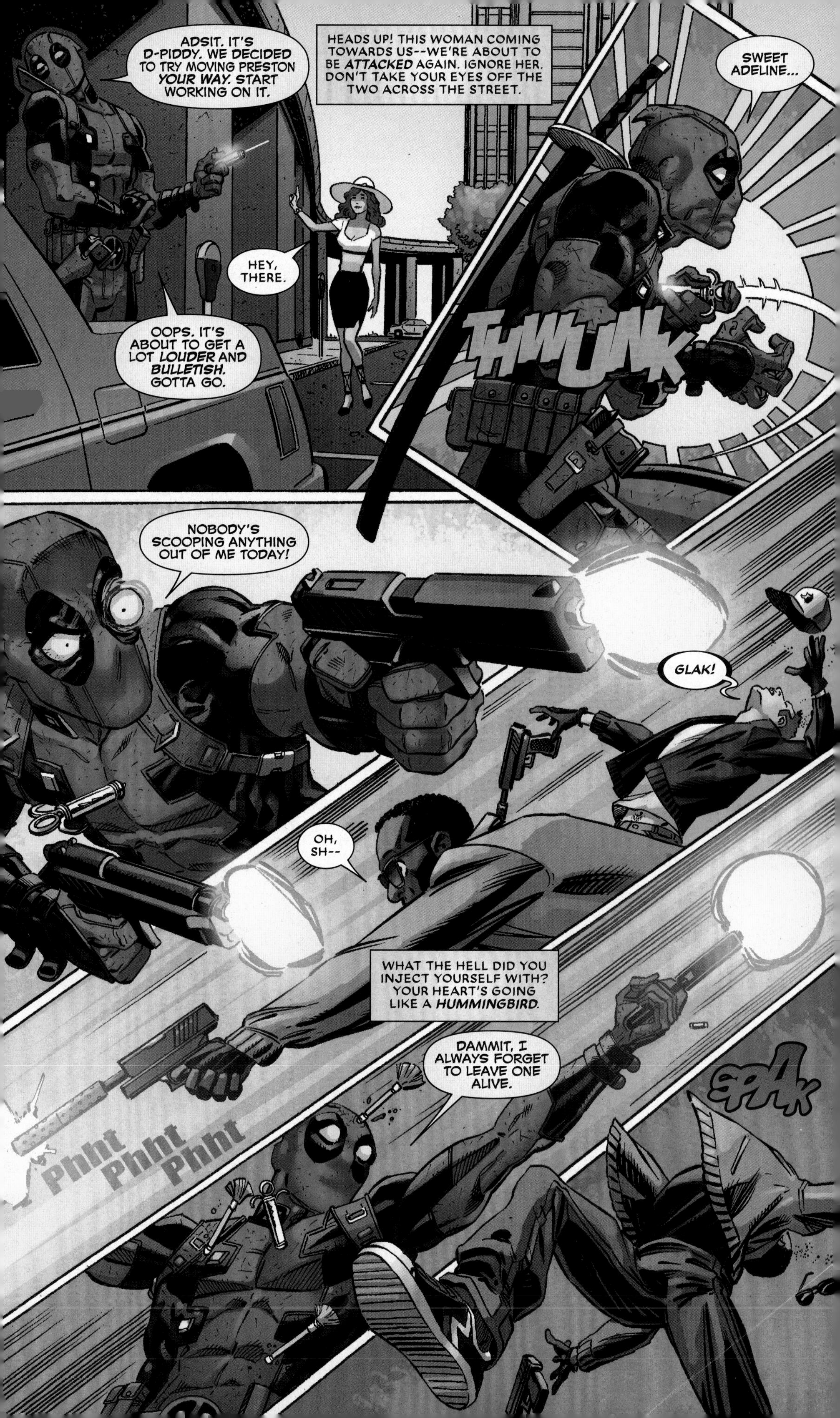
ADSIT. IT'S D-PIDDY. WE DECIDED TO TRY MOVING PRESTON YOUR WAY. START WORKING ON IT.
HEADS UP! THIS WOMAN COMING TOWARDS US--WE'RE ABOUT TO BE ATTACKED AGAIN. IGNORE HER. DON'T TAKE YOUR EYES OFF THE TWO ACROSS THE STREET.
HEY, THERE.
OOPS. IT'S ABOUT TO GET A LOT LOUDER AND BULLETISH. GOTTA GO.
SWEET ADELINE...
THWUNK
NOBODY'S SCOOPING ANYTHING OUT OF ME TODAY!
GLAK!
OH, SH--
WHAT THE HELL DID YOU INJECT YOURSELF WITH? YOUR HEART'S GOING LIKE A HUMMINGBIRD.
DAMMIT, I ALWAYS FORGET TO LEAVE ONE ALIVE.
SPAK
Phht Phht Phht

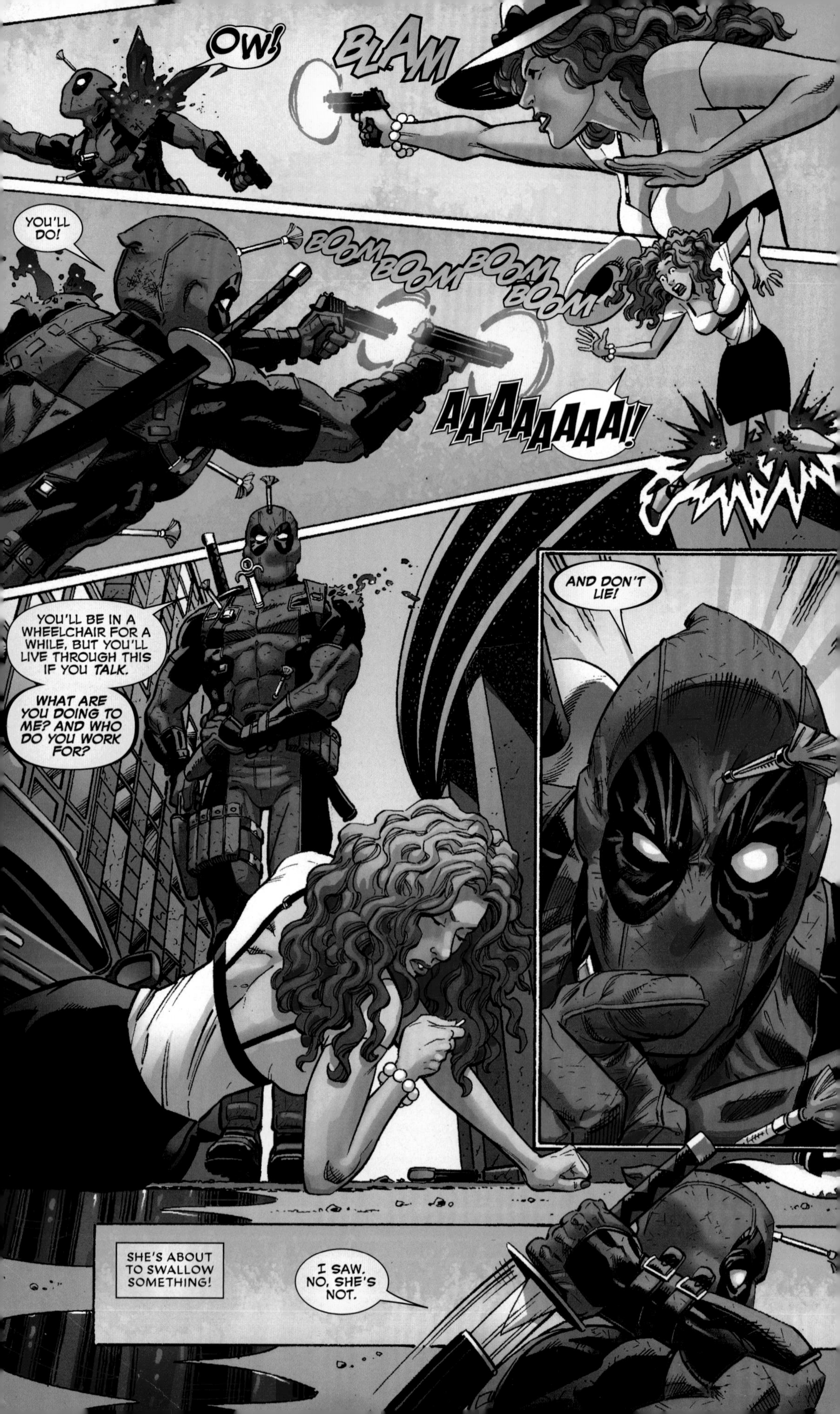
OW!
BLAM
YOU'LL DO!
BOOM BOOM BOOM BOOM
AAAAAAAAI!
YOU'LL BE IN A WHEELCHAIR FOR A WHILE, BUT YOU'LL LIVE THROUGH THIS IF YOU TALK.
WHAT ARE YOU DOING TO ME? AND WHO DO YOU WORK FOR?
AND DON'T LIE!
SHE'S ABOUT TO SWALLOW SOMETHING!
I SAW. NO, SHE'S NOT.

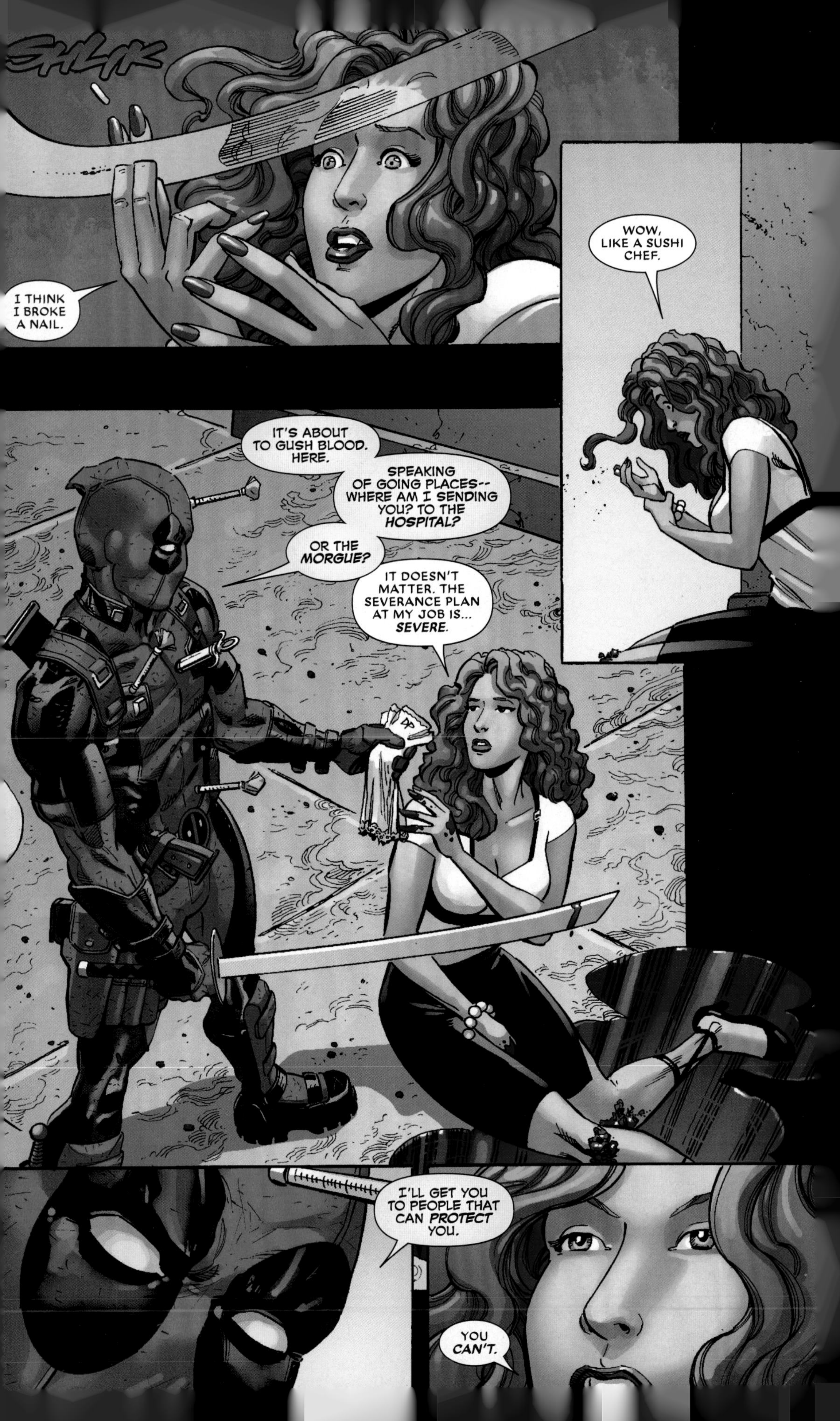
SHLIK
I THINK I BROKE A NAIL.
WOW, LIKE A SUSHI CHEF.
IT'S ABOUT TO GUSH BLOOD. HERE.
SPEAKING OF GOING PLACES-- WHERE AM I SENDING YOU? TO THE HOSPITAL?
OR THE MORGUE?
IT DOESN'T MATTER. THE SEVERANCE PLAN AT MY JOB IS... SEVERE.
I'LL GET YOU TO PEOPLE THAT CAN PROTECT YOU.
YOU CAN'T.

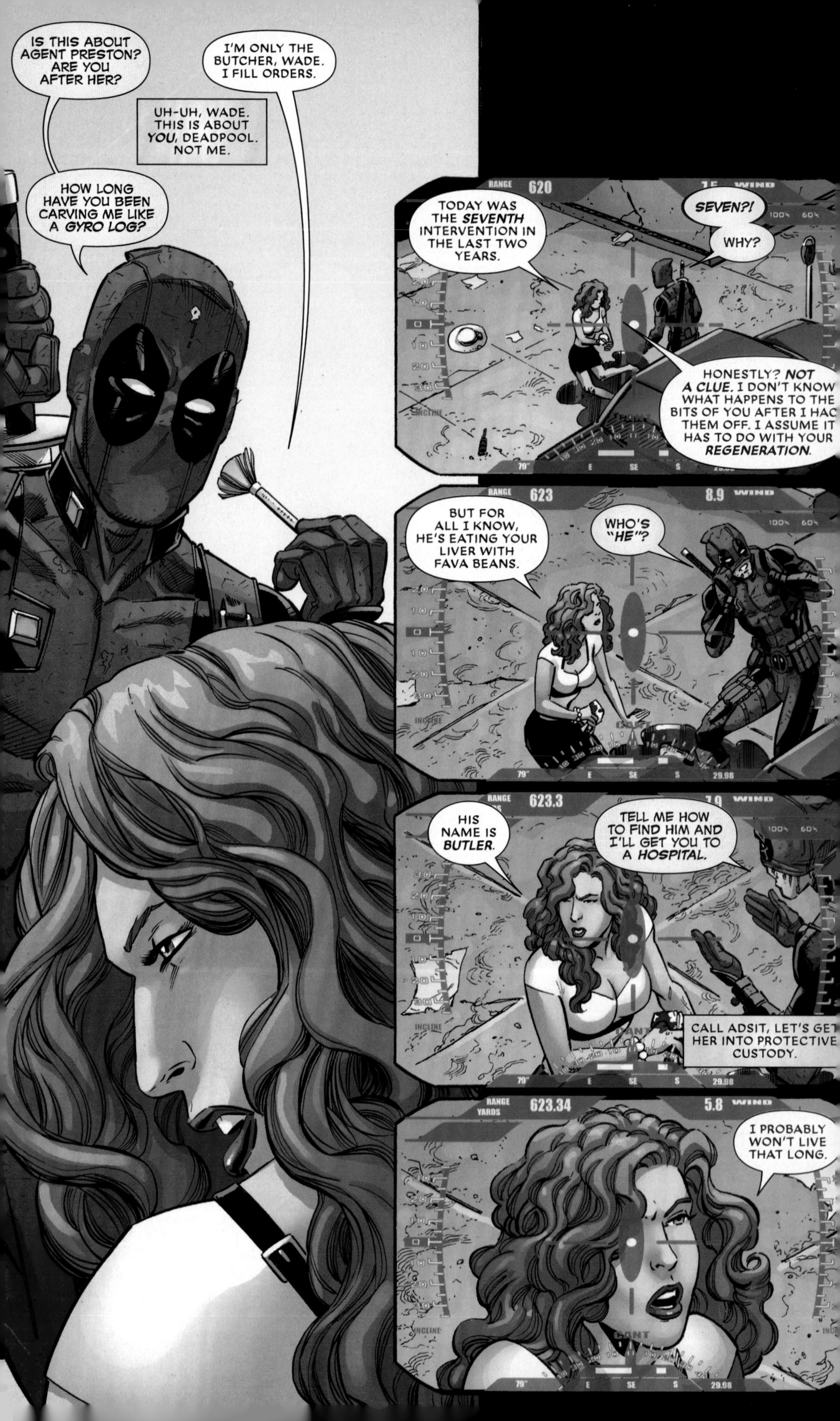
IS THIS ABOUT AGENT PRESTON? ARE YOU AFTER HER?
UH-UH, WADE. THIS IS ABOUT YOU, DEADPOOL. NOT ME.
HOW LONG HAVE YOU BEEN CARVING ME LIKE A GYRO LOG?
I'M ONLY THE BUTCHER, WADE. I FILL ORDERS.
RANGE 620
WIND
TODAY WAS THE SEVENTH INTERVENTION IN THE LAST TWO YEARS.
SEVEN?!
WHY?
HONESTLY? NOT A CLUE. I DON'T KNOW WHAT HAPPENS TO THE BITS OF YOU AFTER I HAC THEM OFF. I ASSUME IT HAS TO DO WITH YOUR REGENERATION.
RANGE 623
8.9 WIND
BUT FOR ALL I KNOW, HE'S EATING YOUR LIVER WITH FAVA BEANS.
WHO'S "HE"?
RANGE 623.3
WIND
HIS NAME IS BUTLER.
TELL ME HOW TO FIND HIM AND I'LL GET YOU TO A HOSPITAL.
CALL ADSIT, LET'S GET HER INTO PROTECTIVE CUSTODY.
RANGE YARDS 623.34
5.8 WIND
I PROBABLY WON'T LIVE THAT LONG.

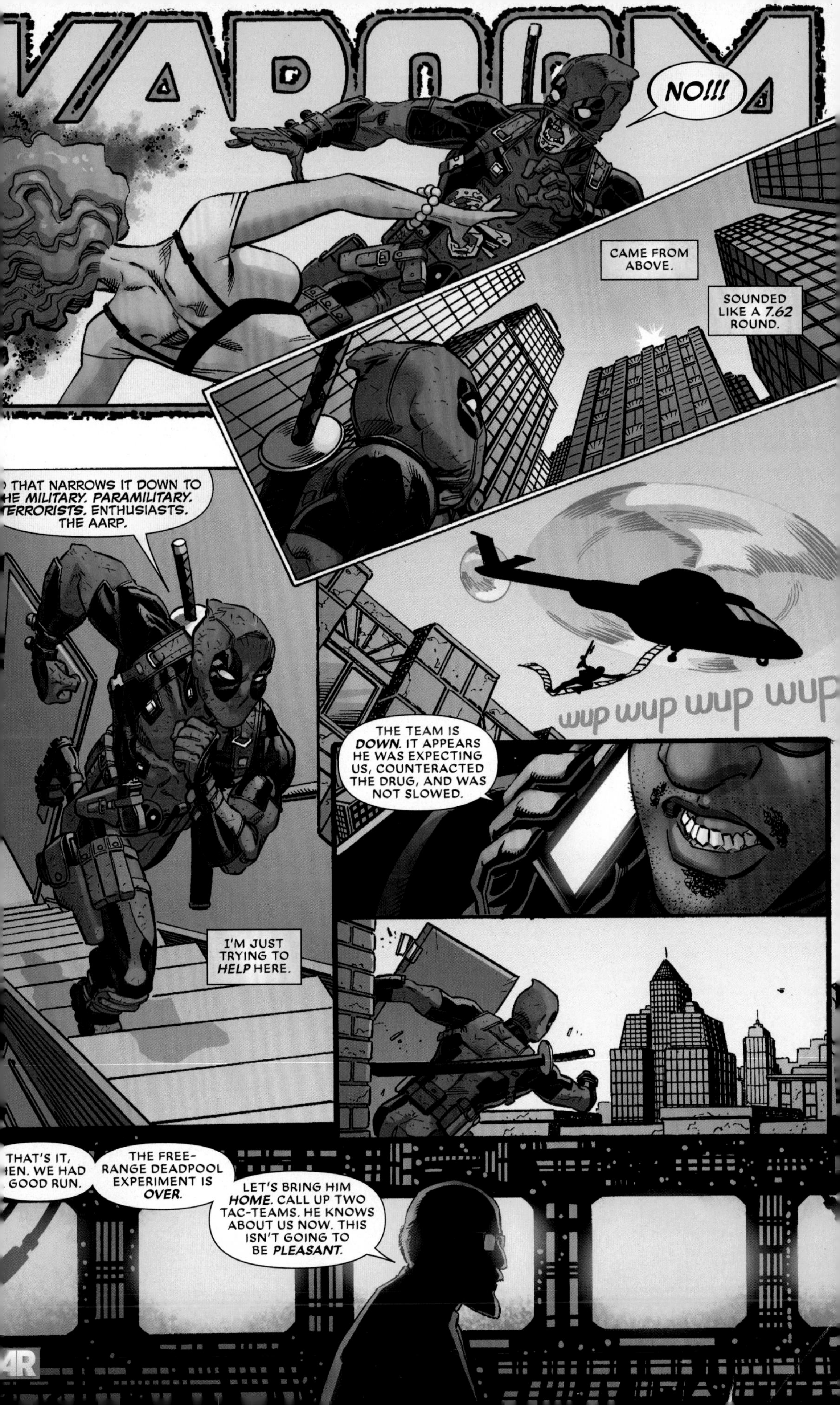
VADOOM
NO!!!
CAME FROM ABOVE.
SOUNDED LIKE A 7.62 ROUND.
THAT NARROWS IT DOWN TO HE MILITARY. PARAMILITARY. TERRORISTS. ENTHUSIASTS. THE AARP.
wup wup wup wup
THE TEAM IS DOWN. IT APPEARS HE WAS EXPECTING US, COUNTERACTED THE DRUG, AND WAS NOT SLOWED.
I'M JUST TRYING TO HELP HERE.
THAT'S IT, HEN. WE HAD GOOD RUN.
THE FREE-RANGE DEADPOOL EXPERIMENT IS OVER.
LET'S BRING HIM HOME. CALL UP TWO TAC-TEAMS. HE KNOWS ABOUT US NOW. THIS ISN'T GOING TO BE PLEASANT.

15

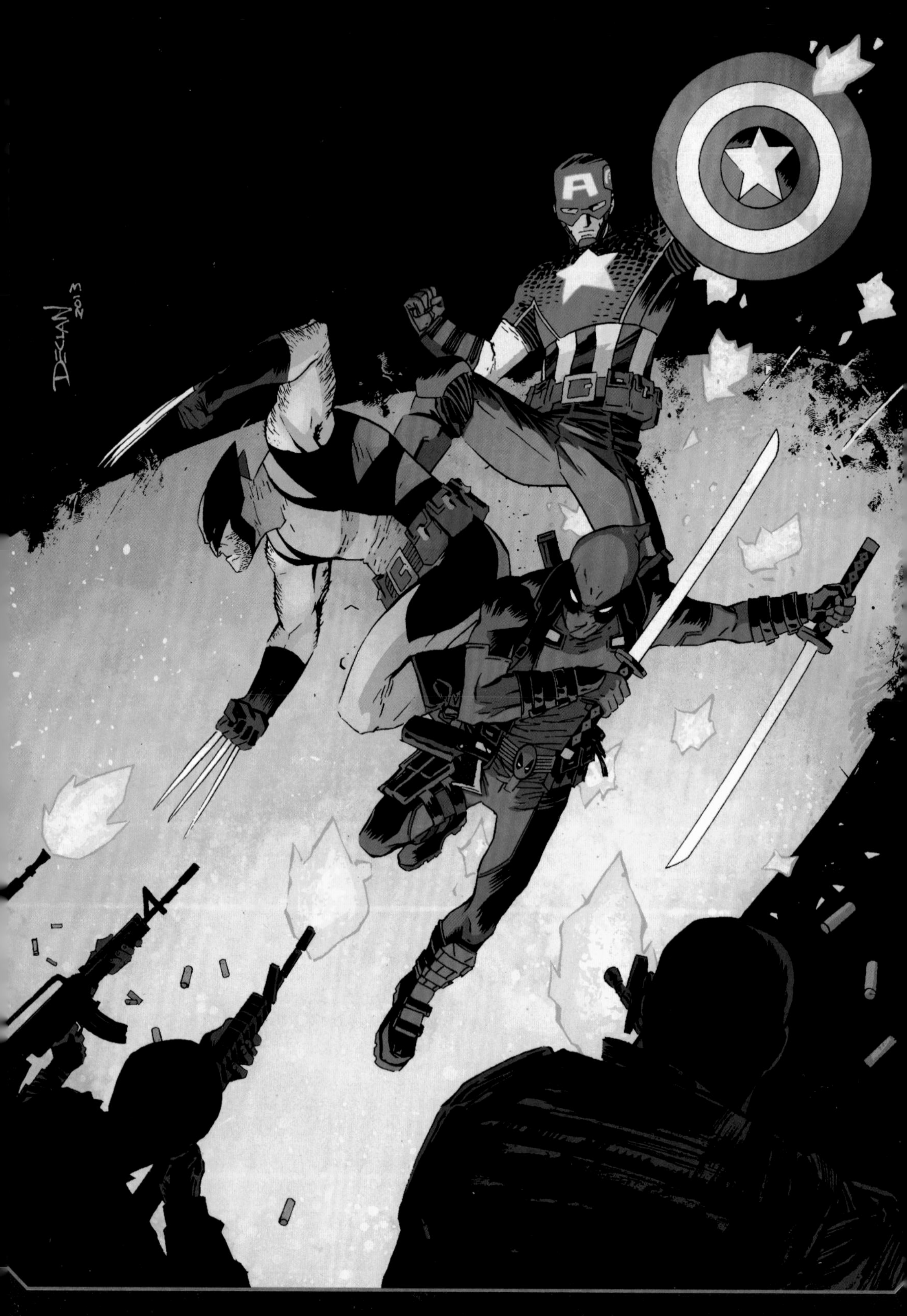

THE GOOD, THE BAD AND THE UGLY PART ONE

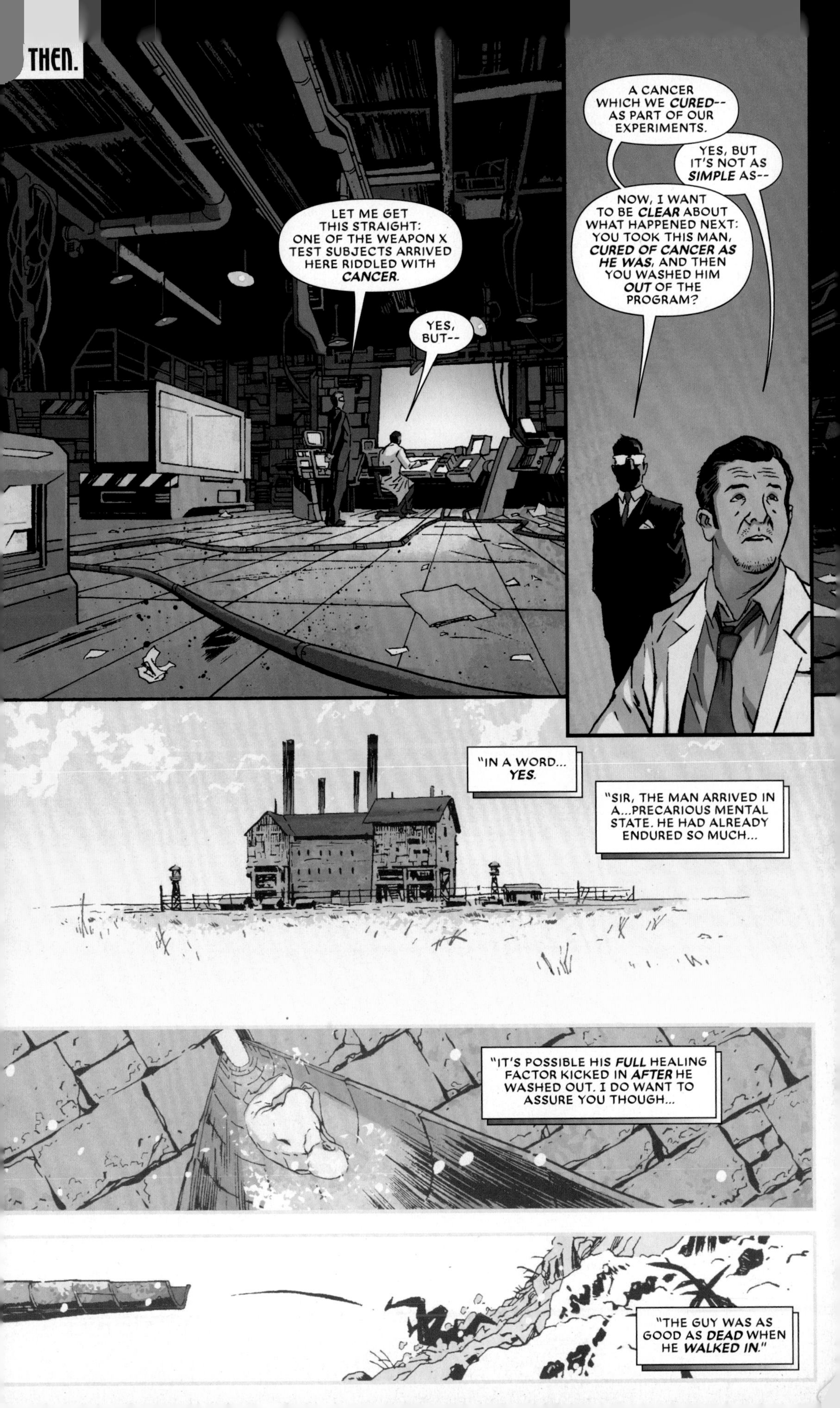
THEN.
LET ME GET THIS STRAIGHT: ONE OF THE WEAPON X TEST SUBJECTS ARRIVED HERE RIDDLED WITH CANCER.
YES, BUT--
A CANCER WHICH WE CURED-- AS PART OF OUR EXPERIMENTS.
YES, BUT IT'S NOT AS SIMPLE AS--
NOW, I WANT TO BE CLEAR ABOUT WHAT HAPPENED NEXT: YOU TOOK THIS MAN, CURED OF CANCER AS HE WAS, AND THEN YOU WASHED HIM OUT OF THE PROGRAM?
"IN A WORD... YES.
"SIR, THE MAN ARRIVED IN A...PRECARIOUS MENTAL STATE. HE HAD ALREADY ENDURED SO MUCH...
"IT'S POSSIBLE HIS FULL HEALING FACTOR KICKED IN AFTER HE WASHED OUT. I DO WANT TO ASSURE YOU THOUGH...
"THE GUY WAS AS GOOD AS DEAD WHEN HE WALKED IN."

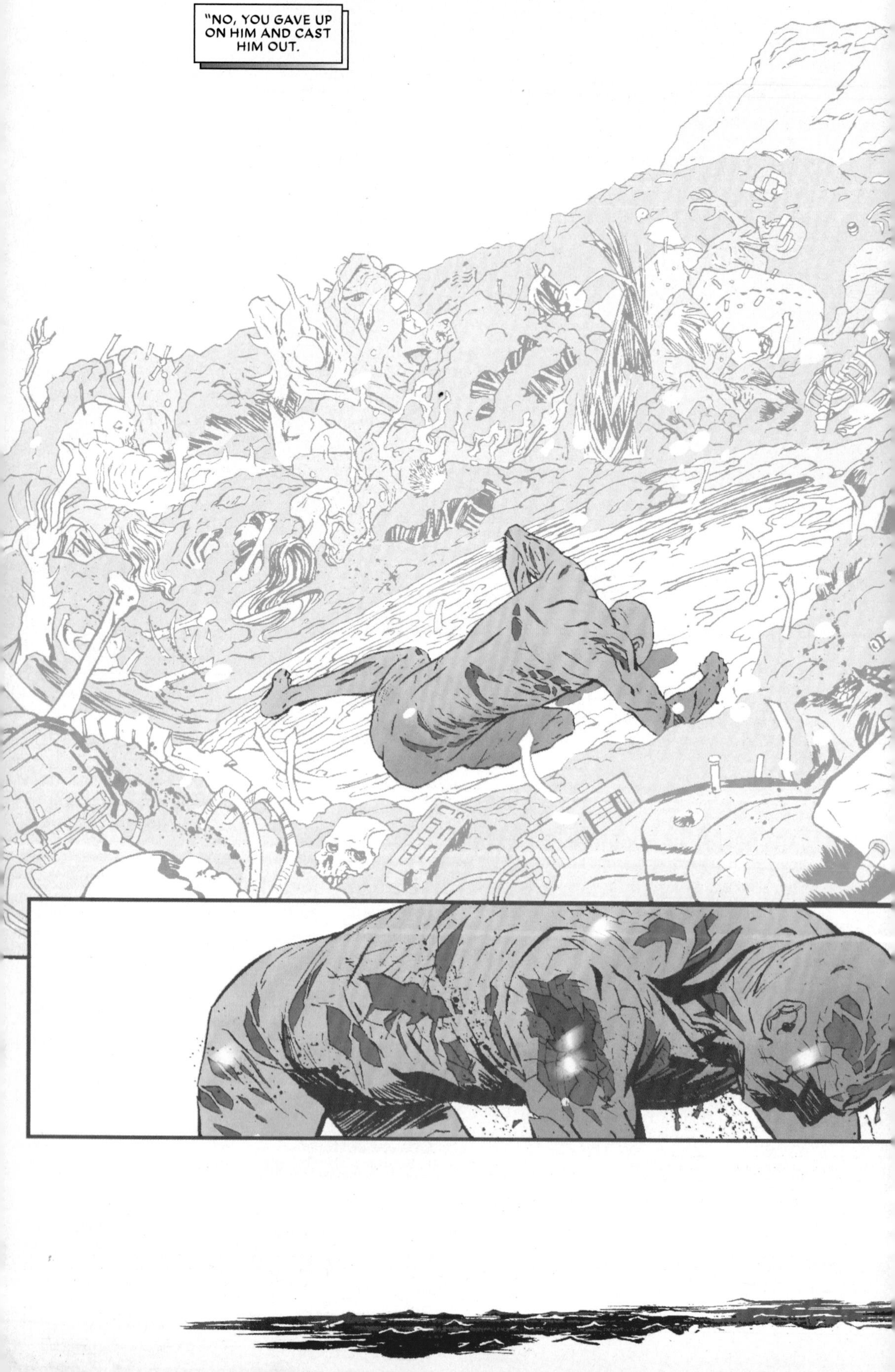
"NO, YOU GAVE UP ON HIM AND CAST HIM OUT.

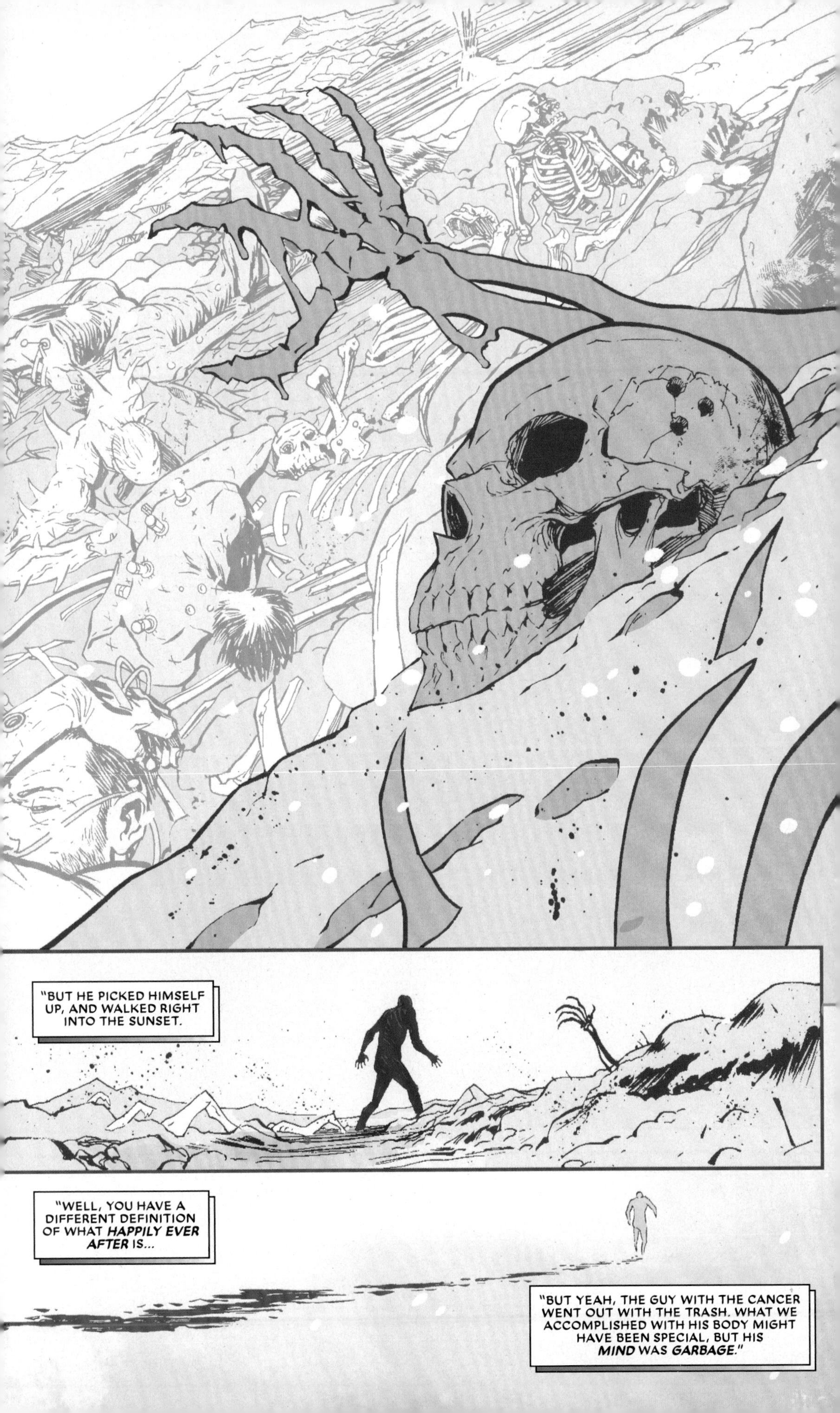
"BUT HE PICKED HIMSELF UP, AND WALKED RIGHT INTO THE SUNSET.
"WELL, YOU HAVE A DIFFERENT DEFINITION OF WHAT *HAPPILY EVER AFTER* IS...
"BUT YEAH, THE GUY WITH THE CANCER WENT OUT WITH THE TRASH. WHAT WE ACCOMPLISHED WITH HIS BODY MIGHT HAVE BEEN SPECIAL, BUT HIS *MIND* WAS *GARBAGE*."

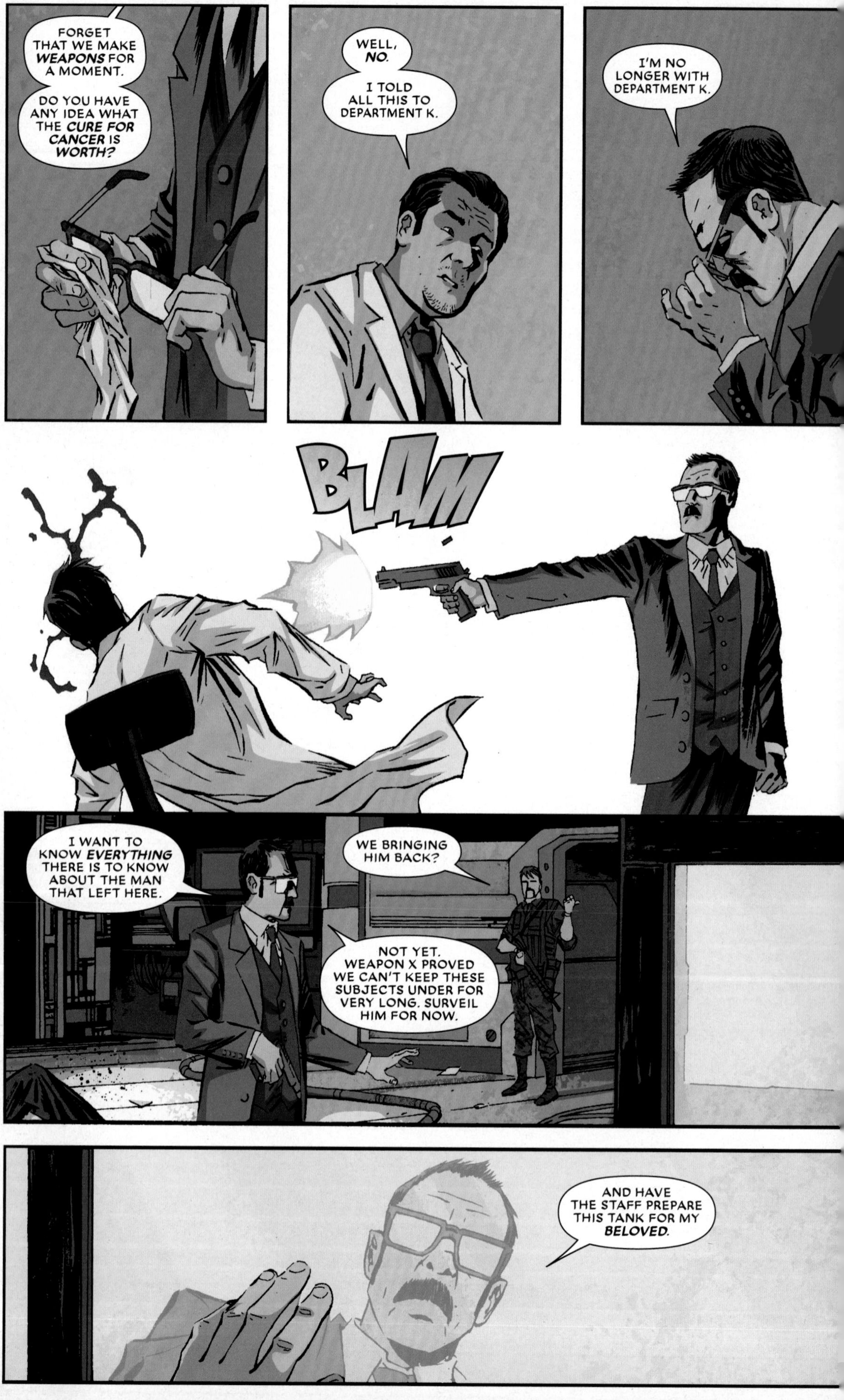
FORGET THAT WE MAKE WEAPONS FOR A MOMENT.
DO YOU HAVE ANY IDEA WHAT THE CURE FOR CANCER IS WORTH?
WELL, NO.
I TOLD ALL THIS TO DEPARTMENT K.
I'M NO LONGER WITH DEPARTMENT K.
BLAM
I WANT TO KNOW EVERYTHING THERE IS TO KNOW ABOUT THE MAN THAT LEFT HERE.
WE BRINGING HIM BACK?
NOT YET. WEAPON X PROVED WE CAN'T KEEP THESE SUBJECTS UNDER FOR VERY LONG. SURVEIL HIM FOR NOW.
AND HAVE THE STAFF PREPARE THIS TANK FOR MY BELOVED.

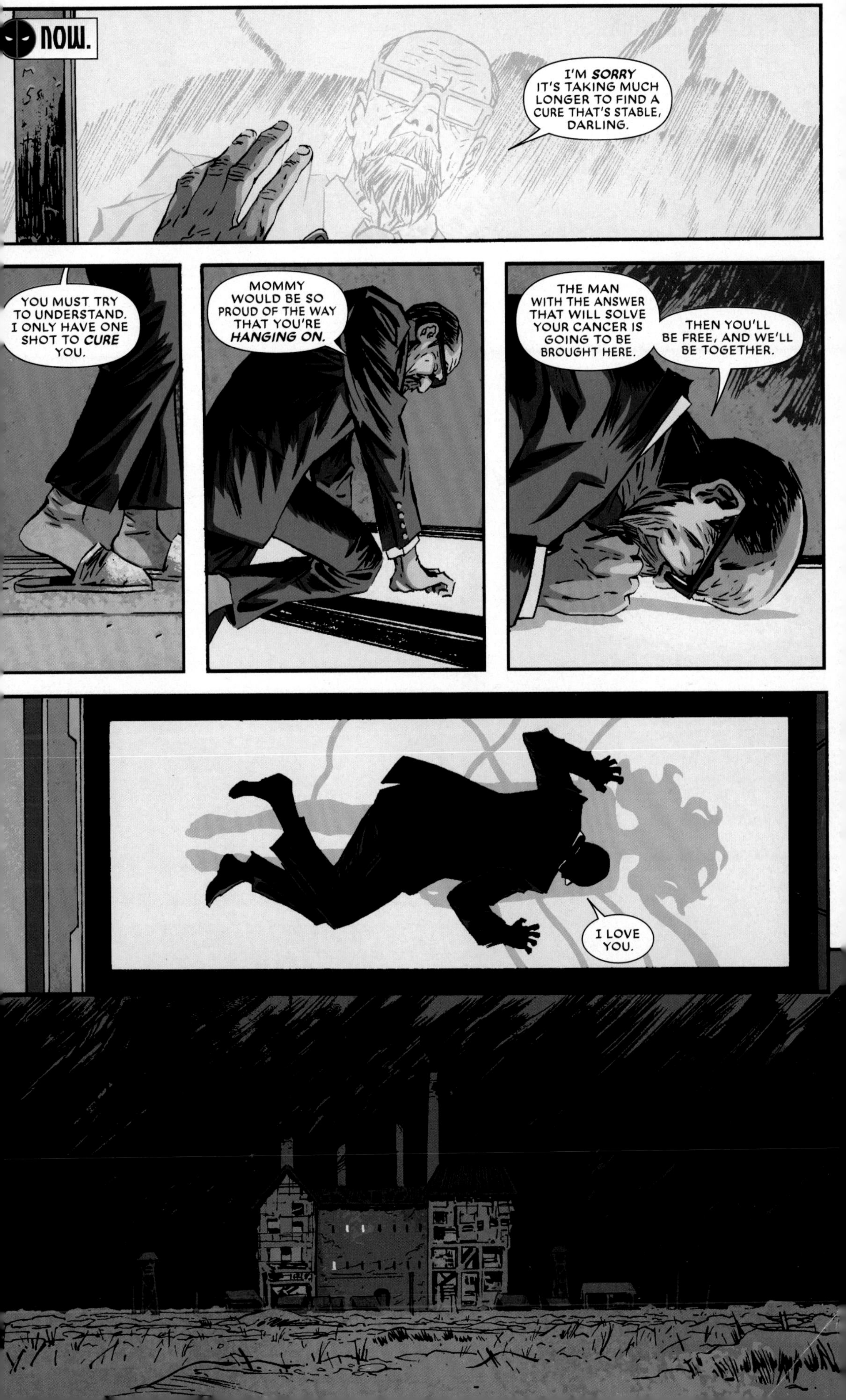
NOW.
I'M SORRY IT'S TAKING MUCH LONGER TO FIND A CURE THAT'S STABLE, DARLING.
YOU MUST TRY TO UNDERSTAND. I ONLY HAVE ONE SHOT TO CURE YOU.
MOMMY WOULD BE SO PROUD OF THE WAY THAT YOU'RE HANGING ON.
THE MAN WITH THE ANSWER THAT WILL SOLVE YOUR CANCER IS GOING TO BE BROUGHT HERE.
THEN YOU'LL BE FREE, AND WE'LL BE TOGETHER.
I LOVE YOU.

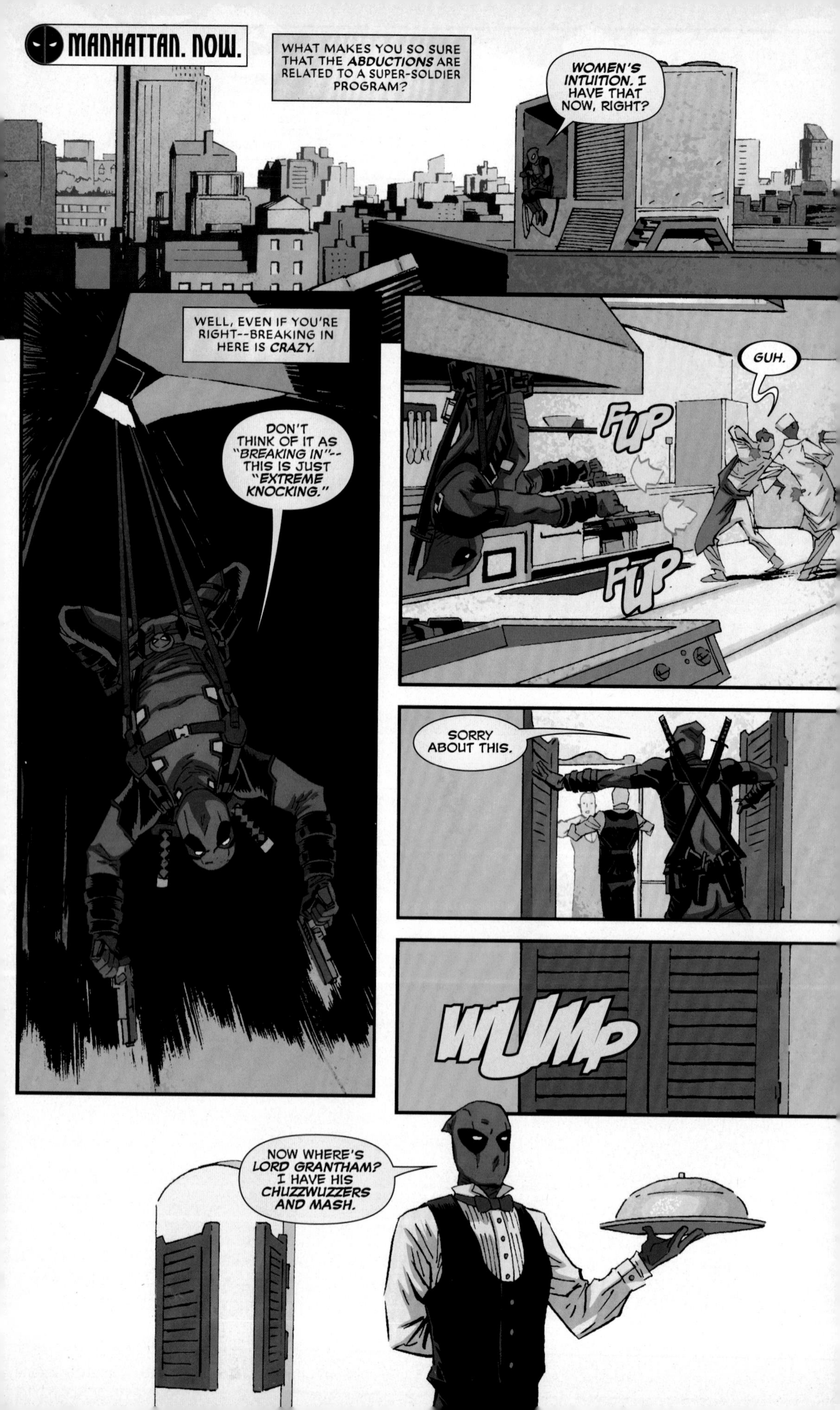
MANHATTAN. NOW.
WHAT MAKES YOU SO SURE THAT THE ABDUCTIONS ARE RELATED TO A SUPER-SOLDIER PROGRAM?
WOMEN'S INTUITION. I HAVE THAT NOW, RIGHT?
WELL, EVEN IF YOU'RE RIGHT--BREAKING IN HERE IS CRAZY.
DON'T THINK OF IT AS "BREAKING IN"-- THIS IS JUST "EXTREME KNOCKING."
FUP
FUP
GUH.
SORRY ABOUT THIS.
WUMP
NOW WHERE'S LORD GRANTHAM? I HAVE HIS CHUZZWUZZERS AND MASH.

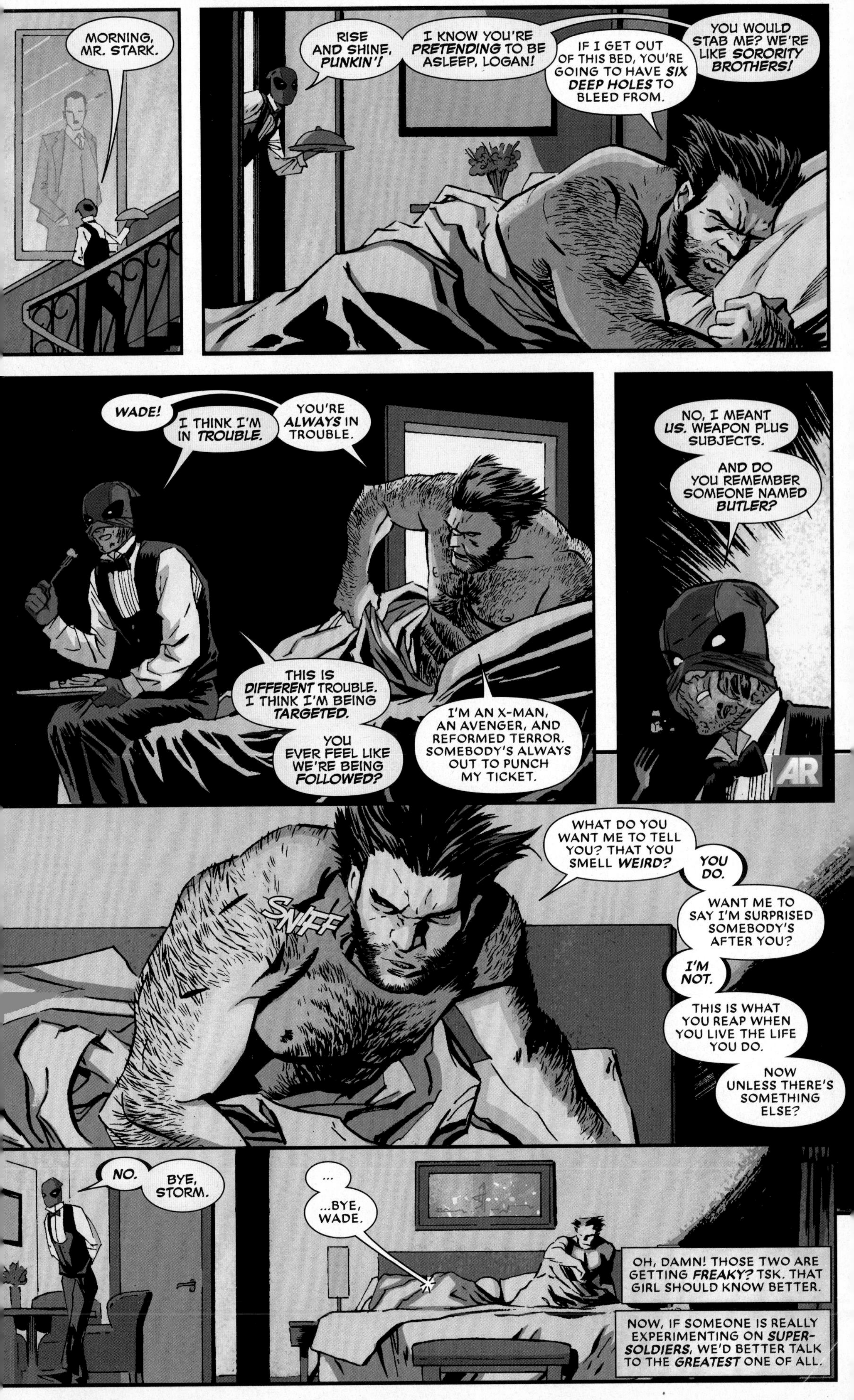
MORNING, MR. STARK.
RISE AND SHINE, PUNKIN'!
I KNOW YOU'RE PRETENDING TO BE ASLEEP, LOGAN!
IF I GET OUT OF THIS BED, YOU'RE GOING TO HAVE SIX DEEP HOLES TO BLEED FROM.
YOU WOULD STAB ME? WE'RE LIKE SORORITY BROTHERS!
WADE!
I THINK I'M IN TROUBLE.
YOU'RE ALWAYS IN TROUBLE.
THIS IS DIFFERENT TROUBLE. I THINK I'M BEING TARGETED.
YOU EVER FEEL LIKE WE'RE BEING FOLLOWED?
I'M AN X-MAN, AN AVENGER, AND REFORMED TERROR. SOMEBODY'S ALWAYS OUT TO PUNCH MY TICKET.
NO, I MEANT US. WEAPON PLUS SUBJECTS.
AND DO YOU REMEMBER SOMEONE NAMED BUTLER?
AR
SNIFF
WHAT DO YOU WANT ME TO TELL YOU? THAT YOU SMELL WEIRD?
YOU DO.
WANT ME TO SAY I'M SURPRISED SOMEBODY'S AFTER YOU?
I'M NOT.
THIS IS WHAT YOU REAP WHEN YOU LIVE THE LIFE YOU DO.
NOW UNLESS THERE'S SOMETHING ELSE?
NO.
BYE, STORM.
...
...BYE, WADE.
OH, DAMN! THOSE TWO ARE GETTING FREAKY? TSK. THAT GIRL SHOULD KNOW BETTER.
NOW, IF SOMEONE IS REALLY EXPERIMENTING ON SUPER-SOLDIERS, WE'D BETTER TALK TO THE GREATEST ONE OF ALL.

A FEW HOURS LATER AT S.H.I.E.L.D. OPERATION "HAMMER-N-ANVIL."
SURRENDER NOW, AND MAYBE YOU'LL BE ALLOWED TO LIVE.
AEEEEIIIII!
POK
SKLUNCH
CAPTAIN AMERICA, A MOMENT OF YOUR TIME?
I'M MORE THAN A LITTLE BUSY, DEADPOOL.
I'LL GET RIGHT TO THE POINT: I'VE BEEN THE SUBJECT OF SOME MEDICAL EXPERIMENTS.
I THINK IT'S BEEN HAPPENING FOR A WHILE, BUT I MANAGED TO STOP THE LAST ONE BEFORE THEY KNOCKED ME OUT.
WHAT DOES THIS HAVE TO DO WITH ME?
WE THOUGHT, I THOUGHT, IF SOMEONE'S EXPERIMENTING ON SUPER-SOLDIERS, YOU MIGHT HAVE CROSSED PATHS WITH THEM.
I'M TERRIFIED.
YOU ARE?
YES, I CAN ACTUALLY FOLLOW THE LOGIC OF YOU COMING TO ME. BUT I HAVE BAD NEWS: I DON'T KNOW ANYTHING. NONE OF THE INTELLIGENCE BRIEFINGS I RECEIVE HAVE MENTIONED ABDUCTIONS OR EXPERIMENTS. I'LL ASK UNCLE SAM.
I ASSUME YOU ALREADY SPOKE TO LOGAN. WHAT DID HE SAY?
ON "THREE," ONE, TWO...
FWABOOM
THE USUAL: "YOU'RE CRAZY." "GET OUT OF MY BED. TAKE OFF THE BUTLER'S SUIT." BLAH. BLAH.
I'D LIKE TO MAKE A SUGGESTION IF I MAY...
PLEASE DO! YOU'RE LIKE THE TONY ROBBINS OF SUPER HEROES. THE GUIDANCE COUNSELOR WE ALL WANT.

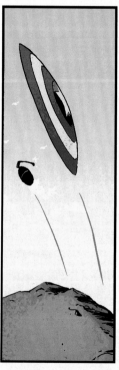

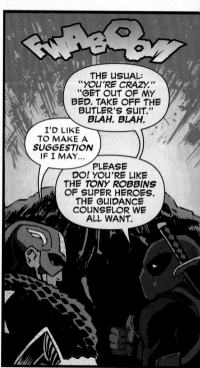

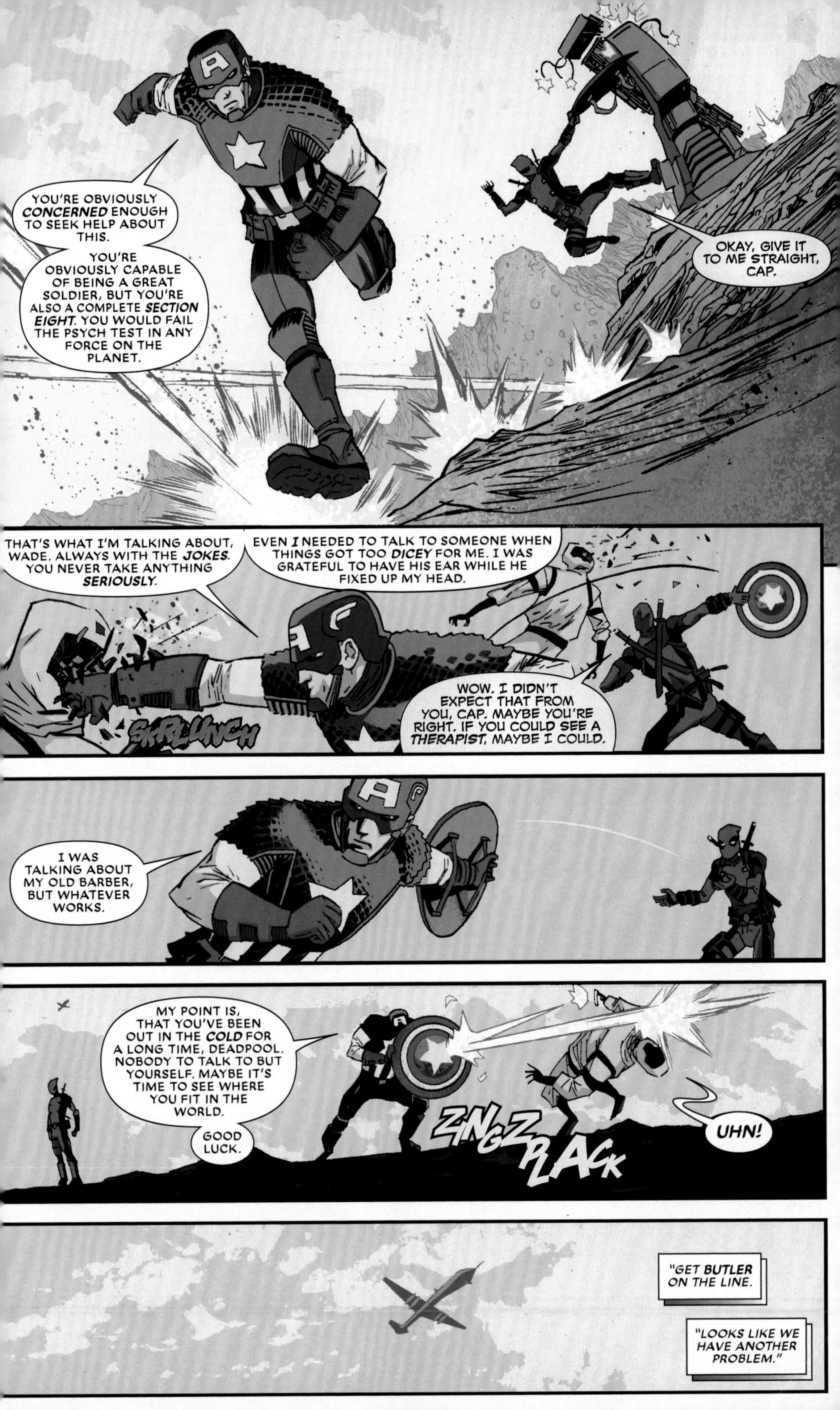
YOU'RE OBVIOUSLY CONCERNED ENOUGH TO SEEK HELP ABOUT THIS.
YOU'RE OBVIOUSLY CAPABLE OF BEING A GREAT SOLDIER, BUT YOU'RE ALSO A COMPLETE SECTION EIGHT. YOU WOULD FAIL THE PSYCH TEST IN ANY FORCE ON THE PLANET.
OKAY, GIVE IT TO ME STRAIGHT, CAP.
THAT'S WHAT I'M TALKING ABOUT, WADE. ALWAYS WITH THE JOKES. YOU NEVER TAKE ANYTHING SERIOUSLY.
EVEN I NEEDED TO TALK TO SOMEONE WHEN THINGS GOT TOO DICEY FOR ME. I WAS GRATEFUL TO HAVE HIS EAR WHILE HE FIXED UP MY HEAD.
SKRLUNCH
WOW. I DIDN'T EXPECT THAT FROM YOU, CAP. MAYBE YOU'RE RIGHT. IF YOU COULD SEE A THERAPIST, MAYBE I COULD.
I WAS TALKING ABOUT MY OLD BARBER, BUT WHATEVER WORKS.
MY POINT IS, THAT YOU'VE BEEN OUT IN THE COLD FOR A LONG TIME, DEADPOOL. NOBODY TO TALK TO BUT YOURSELF. MAYBE IT'S TIME TO SEE WHERE YOU FIT IN THE WORLD.
GOOD LUCK.
ZINGZ
PLACK
UHN!
"GET BUTLER ON THE LINE.
"LOOKS LIKE WE HAVE ANOTHER PROBLEM."

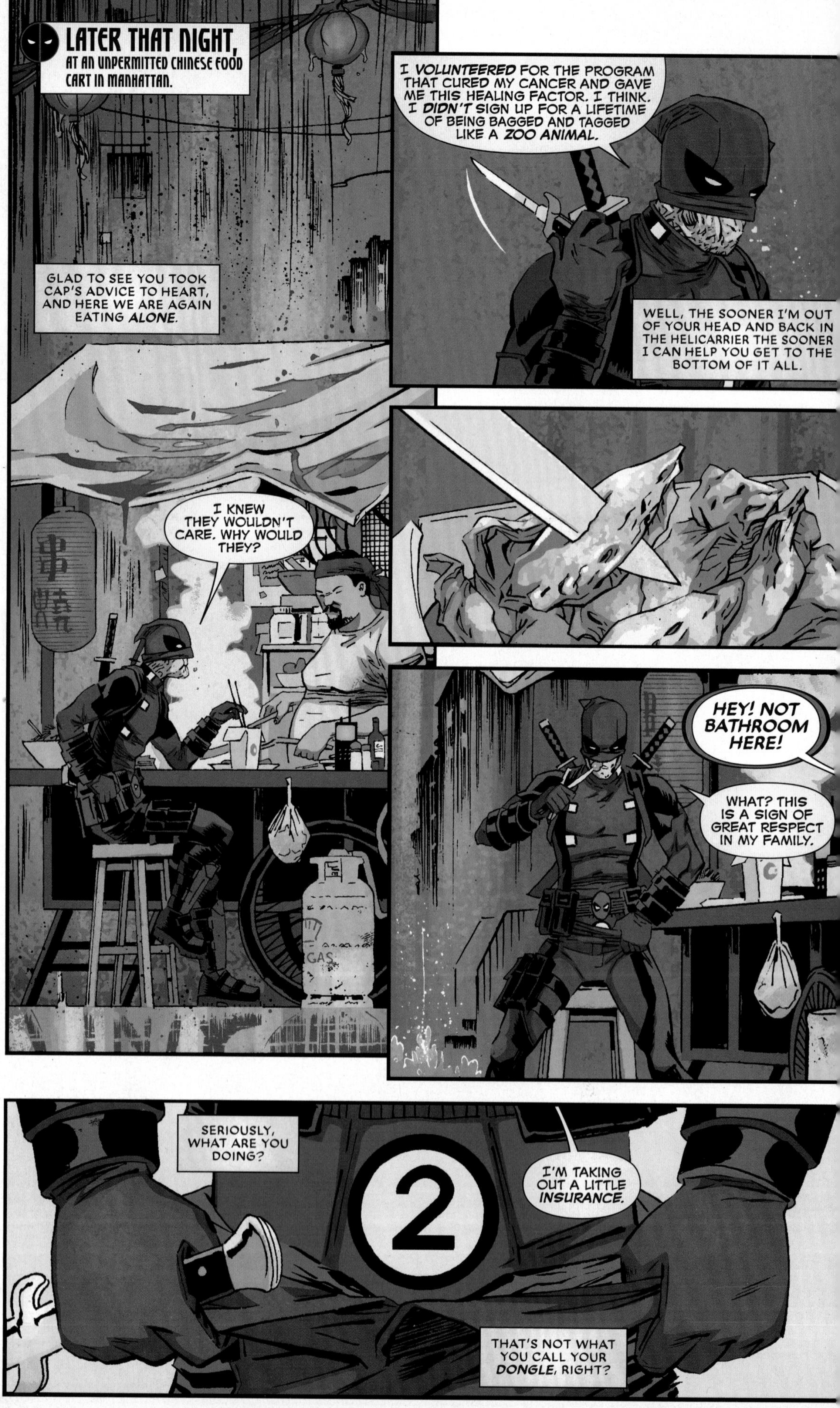
LATER THAT NIGHT,
AT AN UNPERMITTED CHINESE FOOD CART IN MANHATTAN.
GLAD TO SEE YOU TOOK CAP'S ADVICE TO HEART, AND HERE WE ARE AGAIN EATING ALONE.
I KNEW THEY WOULDN'T CARE. WHY WOULD THEY?
I VOLUNTEERED FOR THE PROGRAM THAT CURED MY CANCER AND GAVE ME THIS HEALING FACTOR. I THINK. I DIDN'T SIGN UP FOR A LIFETIME OF BEING BAGGED AND TAGGED LIKE A ZOO ANIMAL.
WELL, THE SOONER I'M OUT OF YOUR HEAD AND BACK IN THE HELICARRIER THE SOONER I CAN HELP YOU GET TO THE BOTTOM OF IT ALL.
HEY! NOT BATHROOM HERE!
WHAT? THIS IS A SIGN OF GREAT RESPECT IN MY FAMILY.
SERIOUSLY, WHAT ARE YOU DOING?
I'M TAKING OUT A LITTLE INSURANCE.
2
THAT'S NOT WHAT YOU CALL YOUR DONGLE, RIGHT?

OW!

WHOEVER MY ABDUCTORS ARE--THEY KNOW I KNOW NOW.

THE GAME'S NOT THE SAME. THEY WON'T COME AT ME WITH THEIR LITTLE TEAMS AGAIN.

SWK

THWOK

THEY'LL COME STRONG. MY FIRST PLAN IS TO KILL THEM ALL, BUT IF I FAIL I WANT TO HAVE AN ACE UP MY TROUSERS.

OFFICER RUTHERFORD, WHAT IS YOUR STATUS?

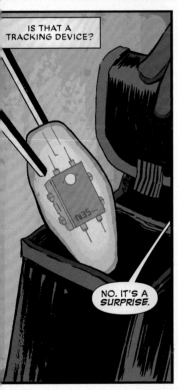

IS THAT A TRACKING DEVICE?

N35...

NO. IT'S A SURPRISE.

IN YOU GO, MY LITTLE FRIEND.

I CHANGED MY MIND, I DON'T WANT TO KNOW WHAT THAT IS.

IT'S ANT-MAN IN A CONDOM.

TOK

I SAID I DIDN'T WANT TO KNOW!

BE ADVISED: THE CORONER IS WRAPPING UP AT 91 MORNINGSIDE. THE RESIDENCE IS BEING SEALED.

LET'S GO, PRESTON. OUR ROOM IS READY!

I REALLY DON'T WANT TO SPEND ANOTHER NIGHT IN ONE OF THOSE PLACES...

WHAT ARE YOU TALKING ABOUT? THIS IS WAY BETTER THAN STAYING AT A NICE, DRY, WARM ROOM AT EITHER THE AVENGERS MANSION OR XAVIER'S DUMP, RIGHT?

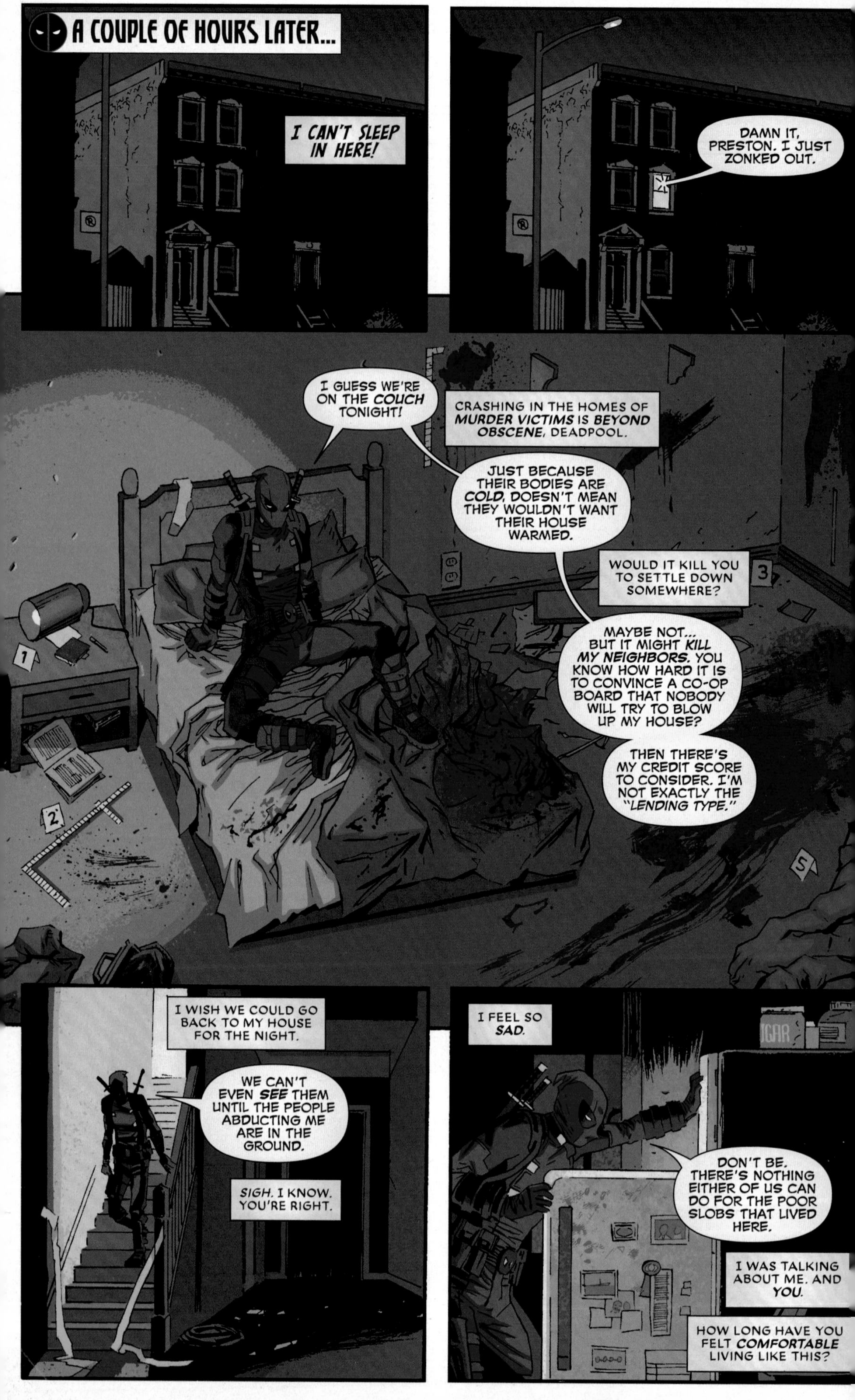

A COUPLE OF HOURS LATER...
I CAN'T SLEEP IN HERE!
DAMN IT, PRESTON. I JUST ZONKED OUT.
I GUESS WE'RE ON THE COUCH TONIGHT!
CRASHING IN THE HOMES OF MURDER VICTIMS IS BEYOND OBSCENE, DEADPOOL.
JUST BECAUSE THEIR BODIES ARE COLD, DOESN'T MEAN THEY WOULDN'T WANT THEIR HOUSE WARMED.
WOULD IT KILL YOU TO SETTLE DOWN SOMEWHERE?
MAYBE NOT... BUT IT MIGHT KILL MY NEIGHBORS. YOU KNOW HOW HARD IT IS TO CONVINCE A CO-OP BOARD THAT NOBODY WILL TRY TO BLOW UP MY HOUSE?
THEN THERE'S MY CREDIT SCORE TO CONSIDER. I'M NOT EXACTLY THE "LENDING TYPE."
I WISH WE COULD GO BACK TO MY HOUSE FOR THE NIGHT.
WE CAN'T EVEN SEE THEM UNTIL THE PEOPLE ABDUCTING ME ARE IN THE GROUND.
SIGH. I KNOW. YOU'RE RIGHT.
I FEEL SO SAD.
DON'T BE. THERE'S NOTHING EITHER OF US CAN DO FOR THE POOR SLOBS THAT LIVED HERE.
I WAS TALKING ABOUT ME. AND YOU.
HOW LONG HAVE YOU FELT COMFORTABLE LIVING LIKE THIS?

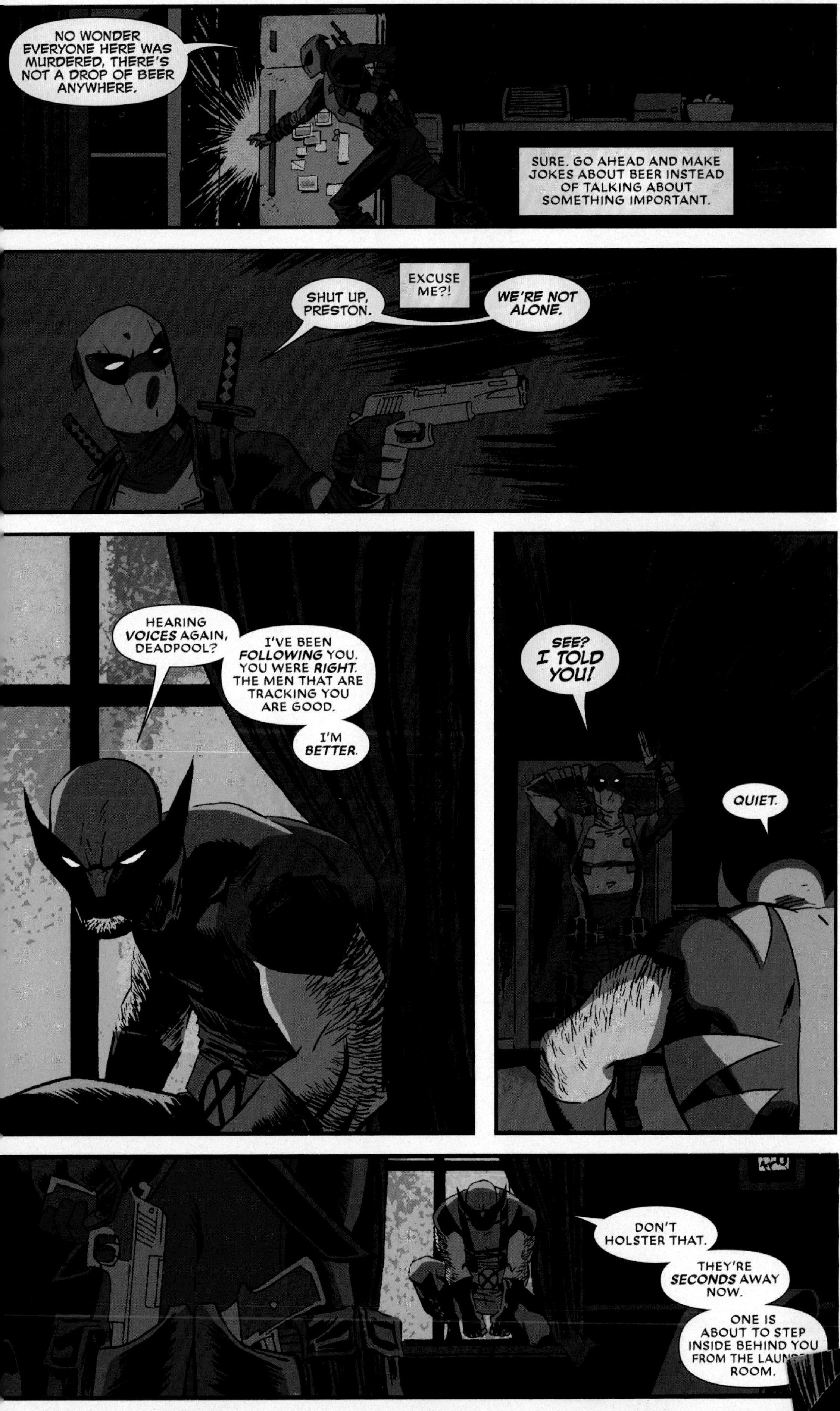
NO WONDER EVERYONE HERE WAS MURDERED, THERE'S NOT A DROP OF BEER ANYWHERE.
SURE. GO AHEAD AND MAKE JOKES ABOUT BEER INSTEAD OF TALKING ABOUT SOMETHING IMPORTANT.
SHUT UP, PRESTON.
EXCUSE ME?!
WE'RE NOT ALONE.
HEARING VOICES AGAIN, DEADPOOL?
I'VE BEEN FOLLOWING YOU. YOU WERE RIGHT. THE MEN THAT ARE TRACKING YOU ARE GOOD.
I'M BETTER.
SEE? I TOLD YOU!
QUIET.
DON'T HOLSTER THAT.
THEY'RE SECONDS AWAY NOW.
ONE IS ABOUT TO STEP INSIDE BEHIND YOU FROM THE LAUN
ROOM.

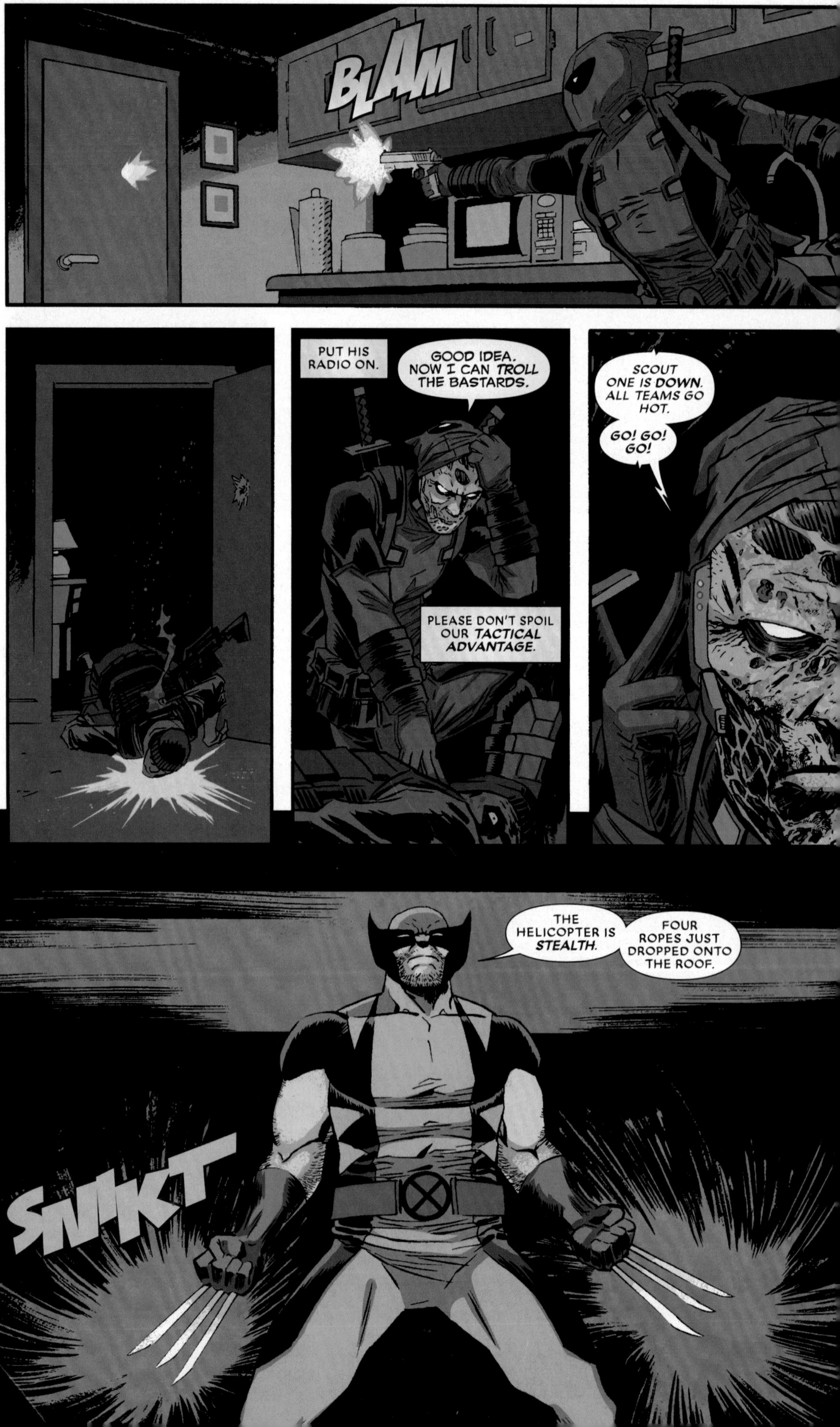
BLAM
PUT HIS RADIO ON.
GOOD IDEA. NOW I CAN TROLL THE BASTARDS.
PLEASE DON'T SPOIL OUR TACTICAL ADVANTAGE.
SCOUT ONE IS DOWN. ALL TEAMS GO HOT.
GO! GO! GO!
THE HELICOPTER IS STEALTH.
FOUR ROPES JUST DROPPED ONTO THE ROOF.
SNIKT

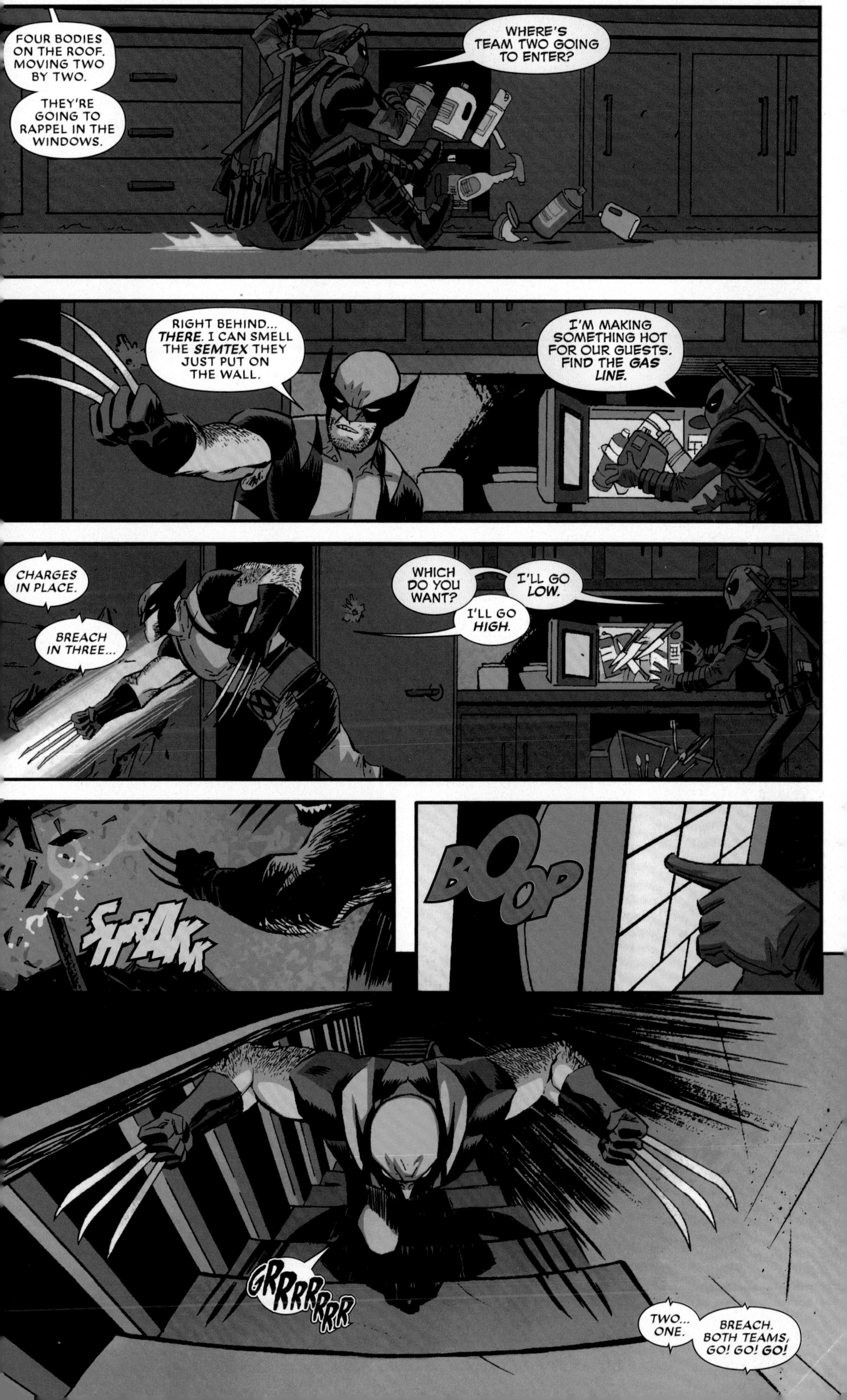
FOUR BODIES ON THE ROOF. MOVING TWO BY TWO.
THEY'RE GOING TO RAPPEL IN THE WINDOWS.
WHERE'S TEAM TWO GOING TO ENTER?
RIGHT BEHIND... THERE. I CAN SMELL THE SEMTEX THEY JUST PUT ON THE WALL.
I'M MAKING SOMETHING HOT FOR OUR GUESTS. FIND THE GAS LINE.
CHARGES IN PLACE.
BREACH IN THREE...
WHICH DO YOU WANT?
I'LL GO LOW.
I'LL GO HIGH.
SHRAKK
BOOP
GRRRRRRR
TWO... ONE.
BREACH. BOTH TEAMS, GO! GO! GO!

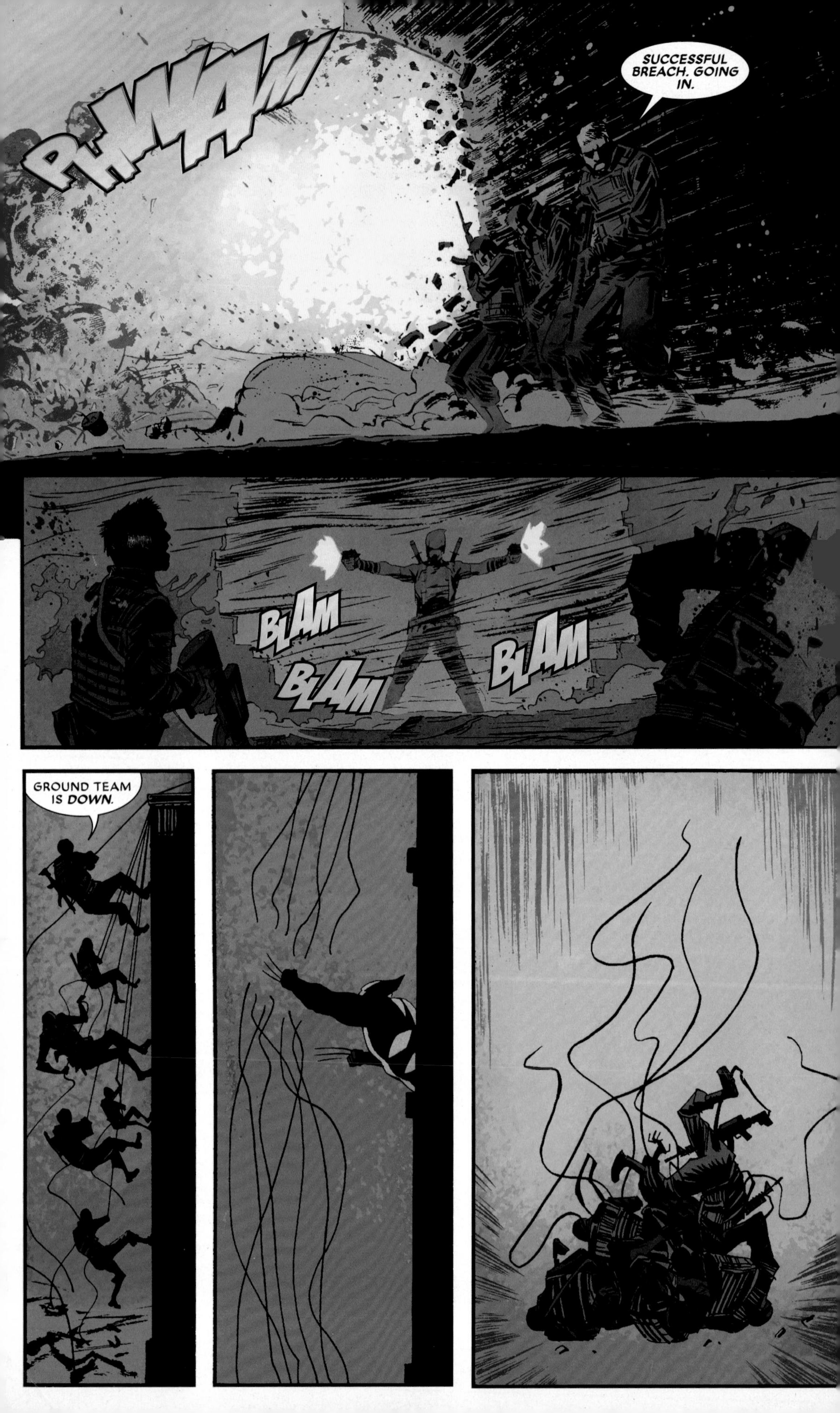
PHWAM
SUCCESSFUL BREACH. GOING IN.
BLAM
BLAM
BLAM
GROUND TEAM IS DOWN.

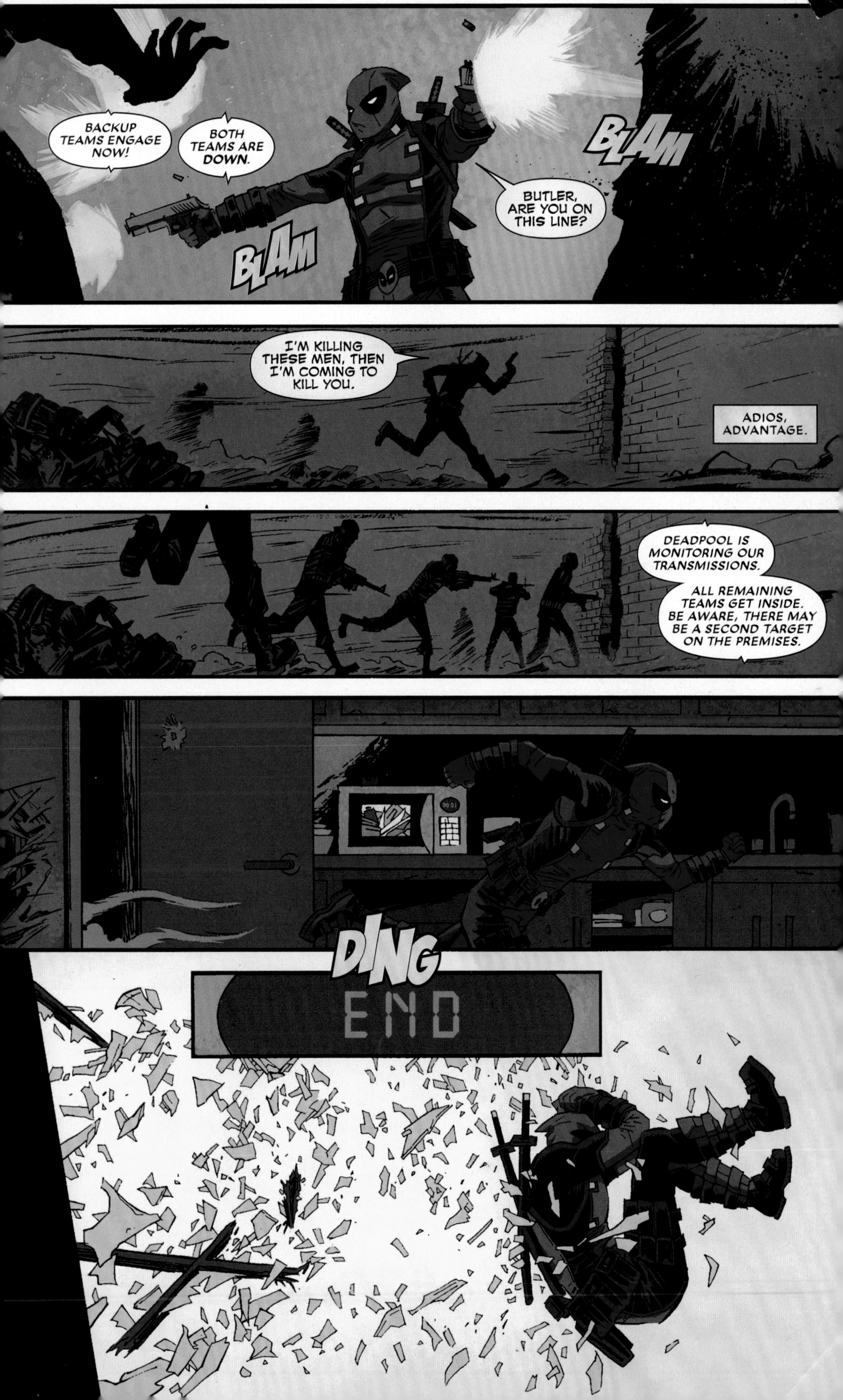

BACKUP TEAMS ENGAGE NOW!
BOTH TEAMS ARE DOWN.
BLAM
BUTLER, ARE YOU ON THIS LINE?
BLAM
I'M KILLING THESE MEN, THEN I'M COMING TO KILL YOU.
ADIOS, ADVANTAGE.
DEADPOOL IS MONITORING OUR TRANSMISSIONS.
ALL REMAINING TEAMS GET INSIDE. BE AWARE, THERE MAY BE A SECOND TARGET ON THE PREMISES.
DING
END

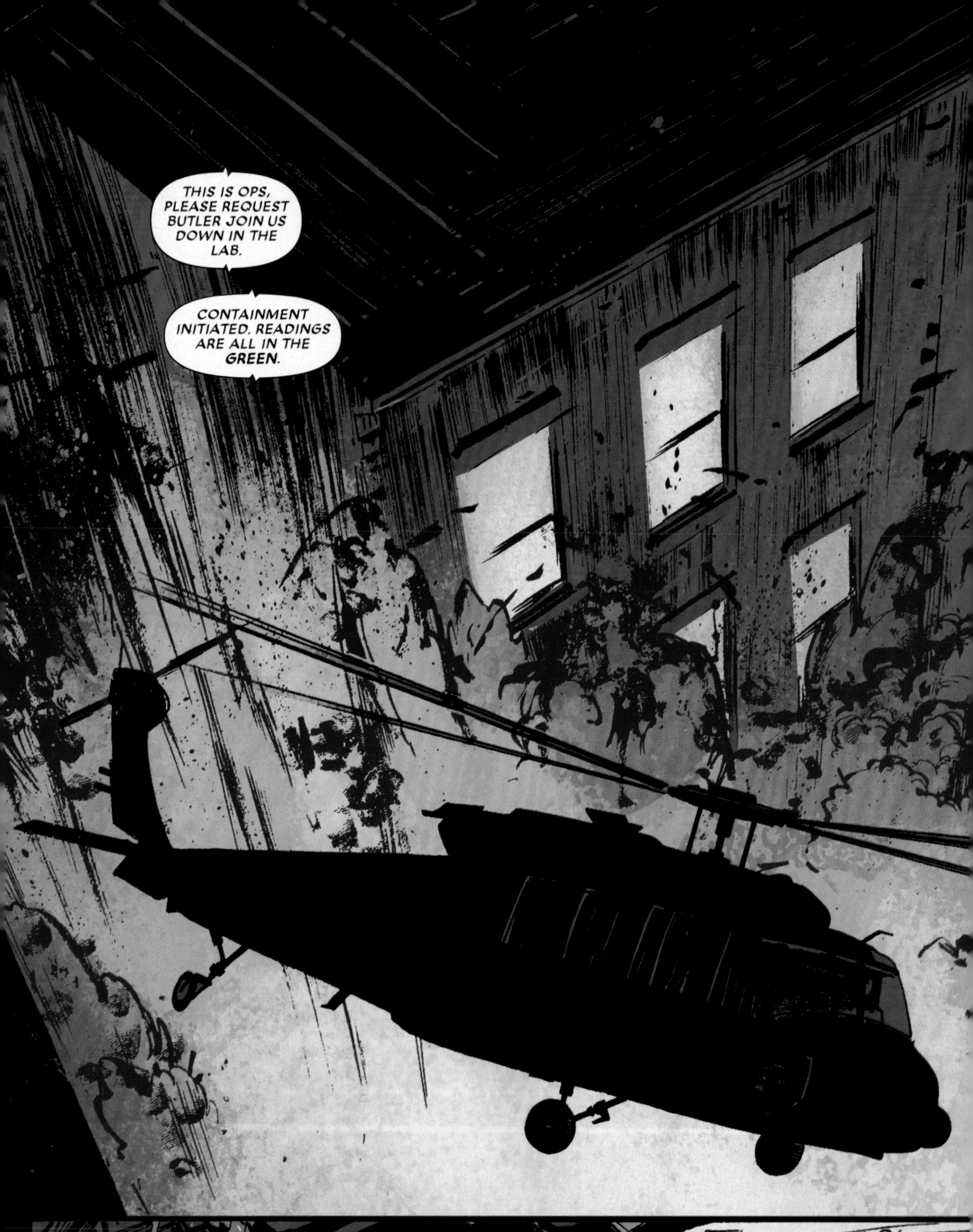
THIS IS OPS, PLEASE REQUEST BUTLER JOIN US DOWN IN THE LAB.
CONTAINMENT INITIATED. READINGS ARE ALL IN THE GREEN.

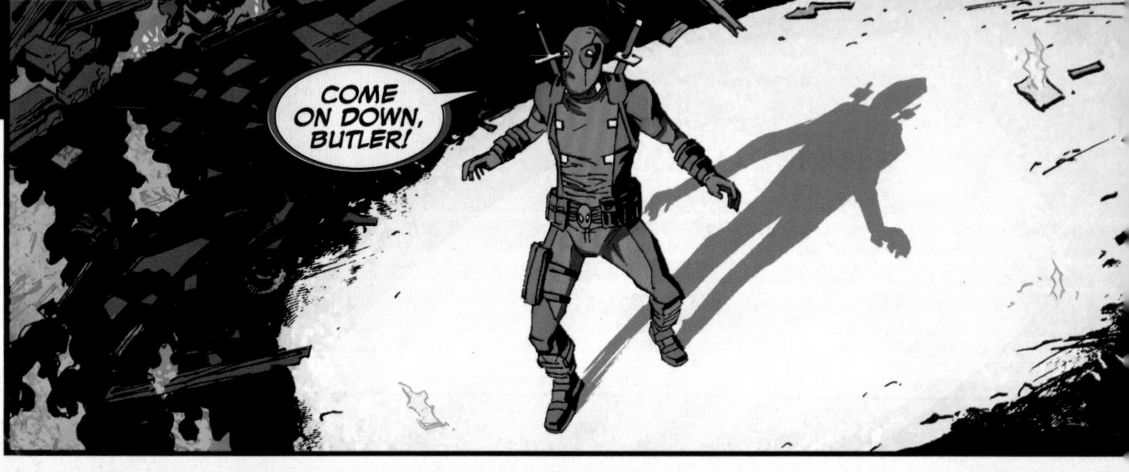
COME ON DOWN, BUTLER!

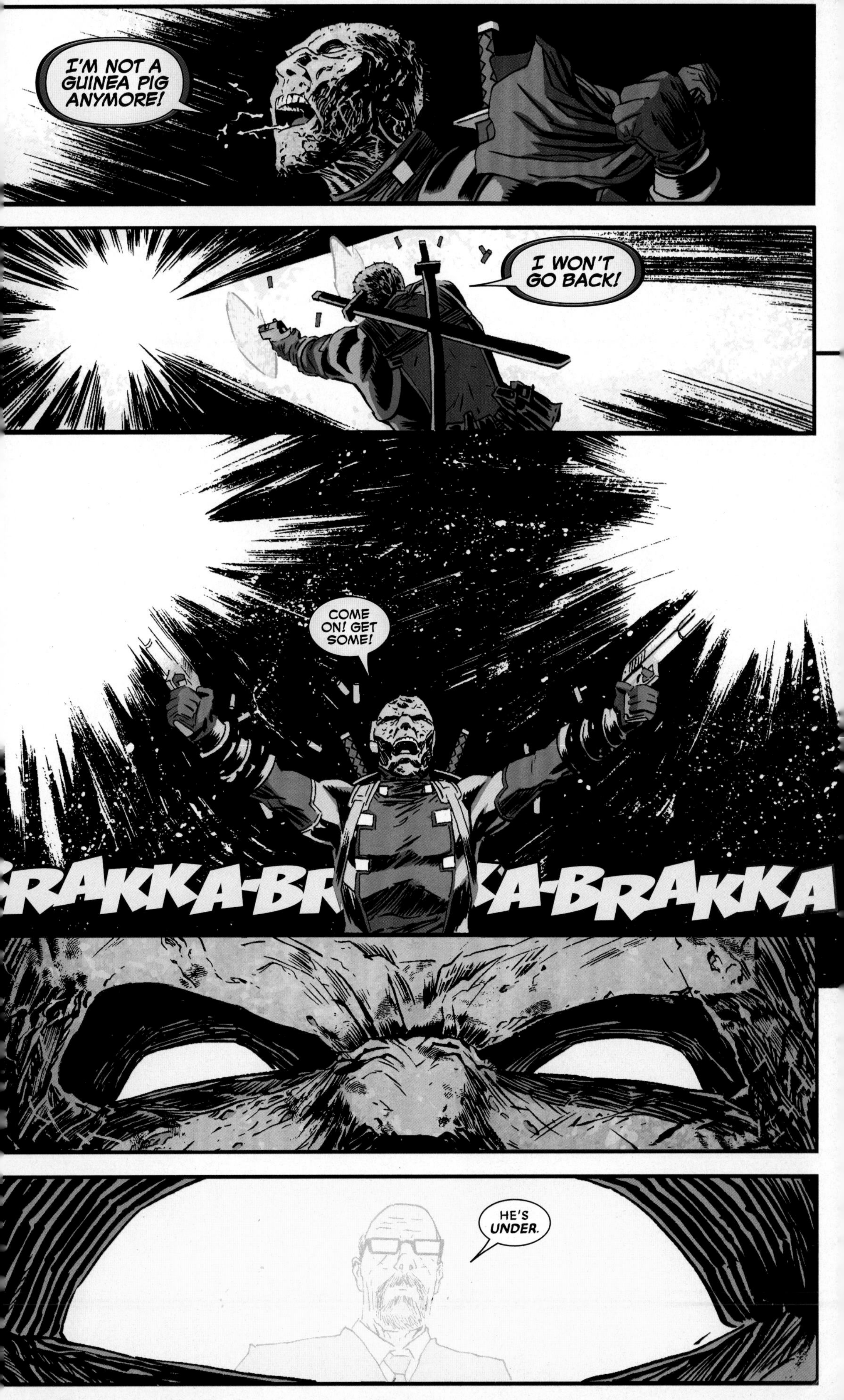
I'M NOT A GUINEA PIG ANYMORE!
I WON'T GO BACK!
COME ON! GET SOME!
RAKKA-BR KA-BRAKKA
HE'S UNDER.

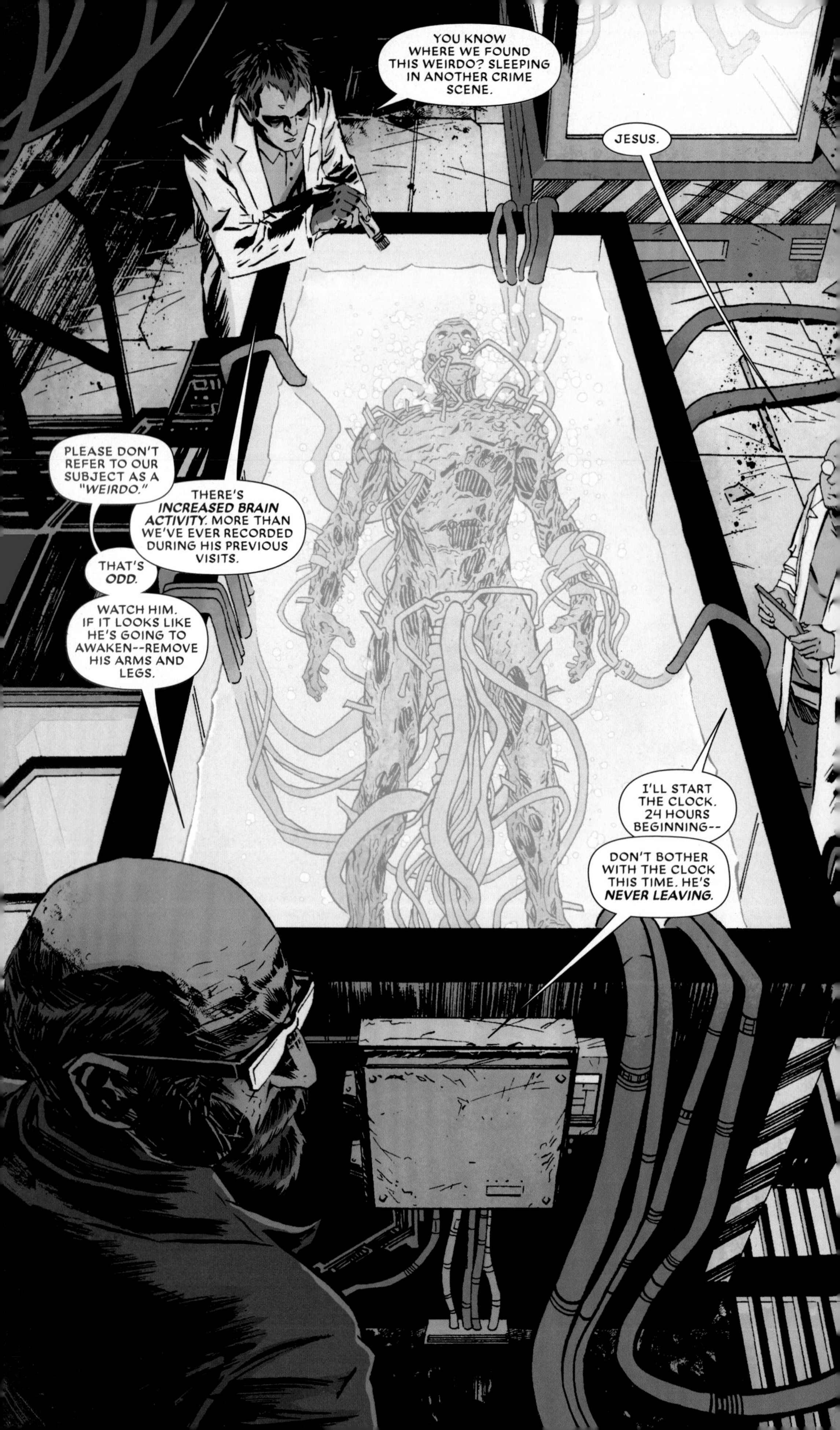

YOU KNOW WHERE WE FOUND THIS WEIRDO? SLEEPING IN ANOTHER CRIME SCENE.
JESUS.
PLEASE DON'T REFER TO OUR SUBJECT AS A "*WEIRDO*."
THERE'S ***INCREASED BRAIN ACTIVITY***. MORE THAN WE'VE EVER RECORDED DURING HIS PREVIOUS VISITS.
THAT'S ***ODD***.
WATCH HIM. IF IT LOOKS LIKE HE'S GOING TO AWAKEN--REMOVE HIS ARMS AND LEGS.
I'LL START THE CLOCK. 24 HOURS BEGINNING--
DON'T BOTHER WITH THE CLOCK THIS TIME. HE'S ***NEVER LEAVING***.

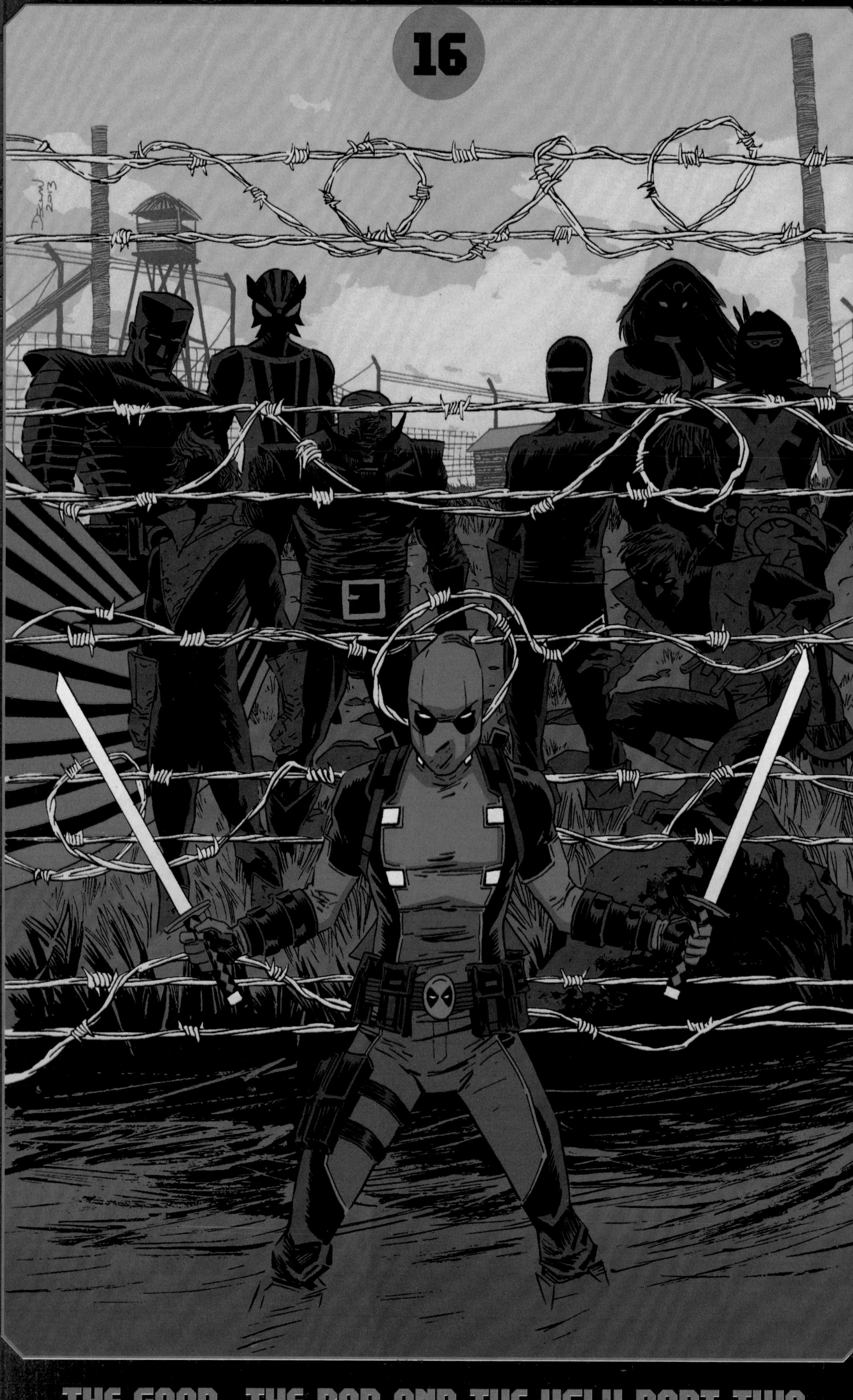
16

THE GOOD, THE BAD AND THE UGLY PART TWO

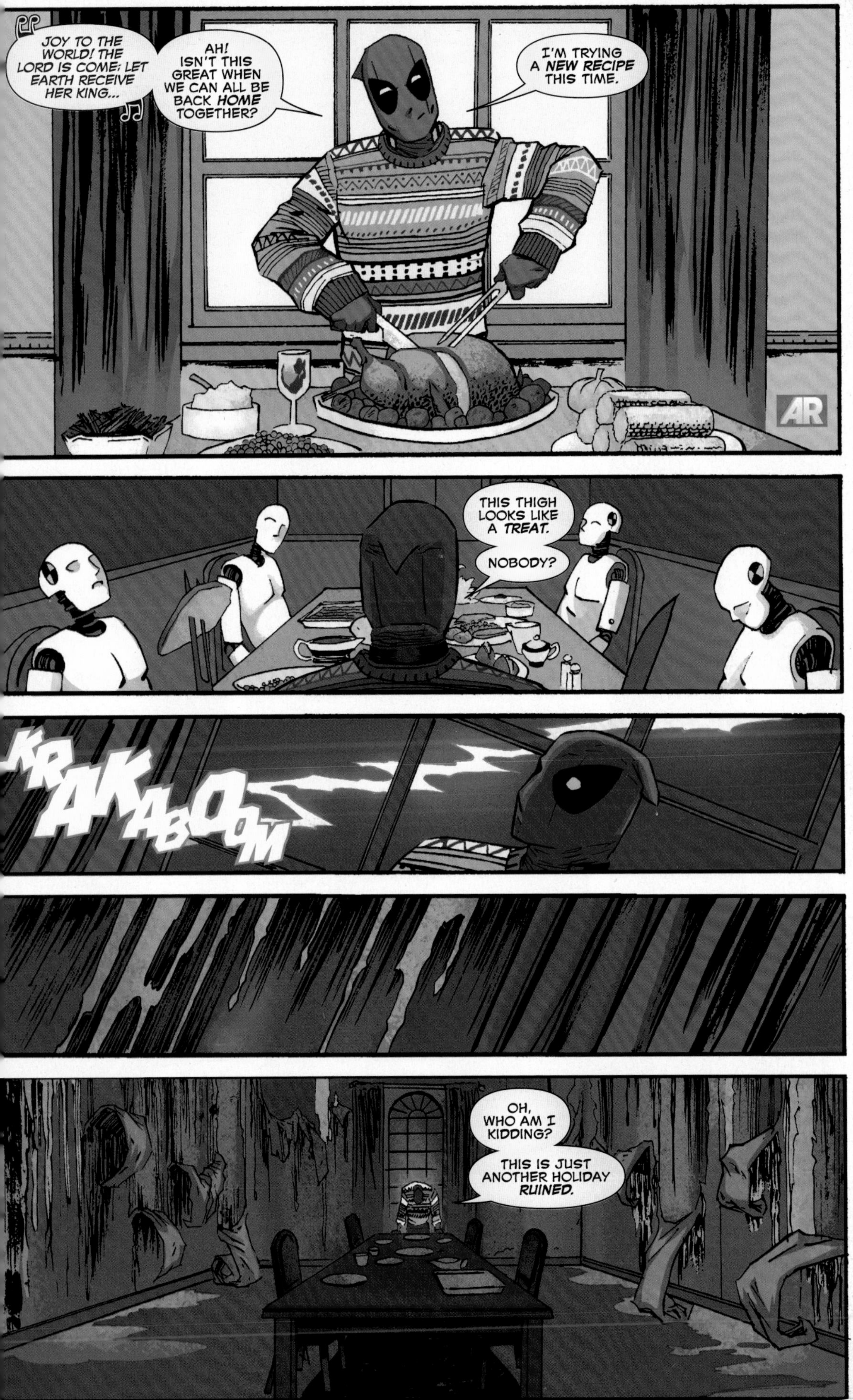
JOY TO THE WORLD! THE LORD IS COME; LET EARTH RECEIVE HER KING...
AH! ISN'T THIS GREAT WHEN WE CAN ALL BE BACK HOME TOGETHER?
I'M TRYING A NEW RECIPE THIS TIME.
AR
THIS THIGH LOOKS LIKE A TREAT.
NOBODY?
KRAKABOOM
OH, WHO AM I KIDDING?
THIS IS JUST ANOTHER HOLIDAY RUINED.

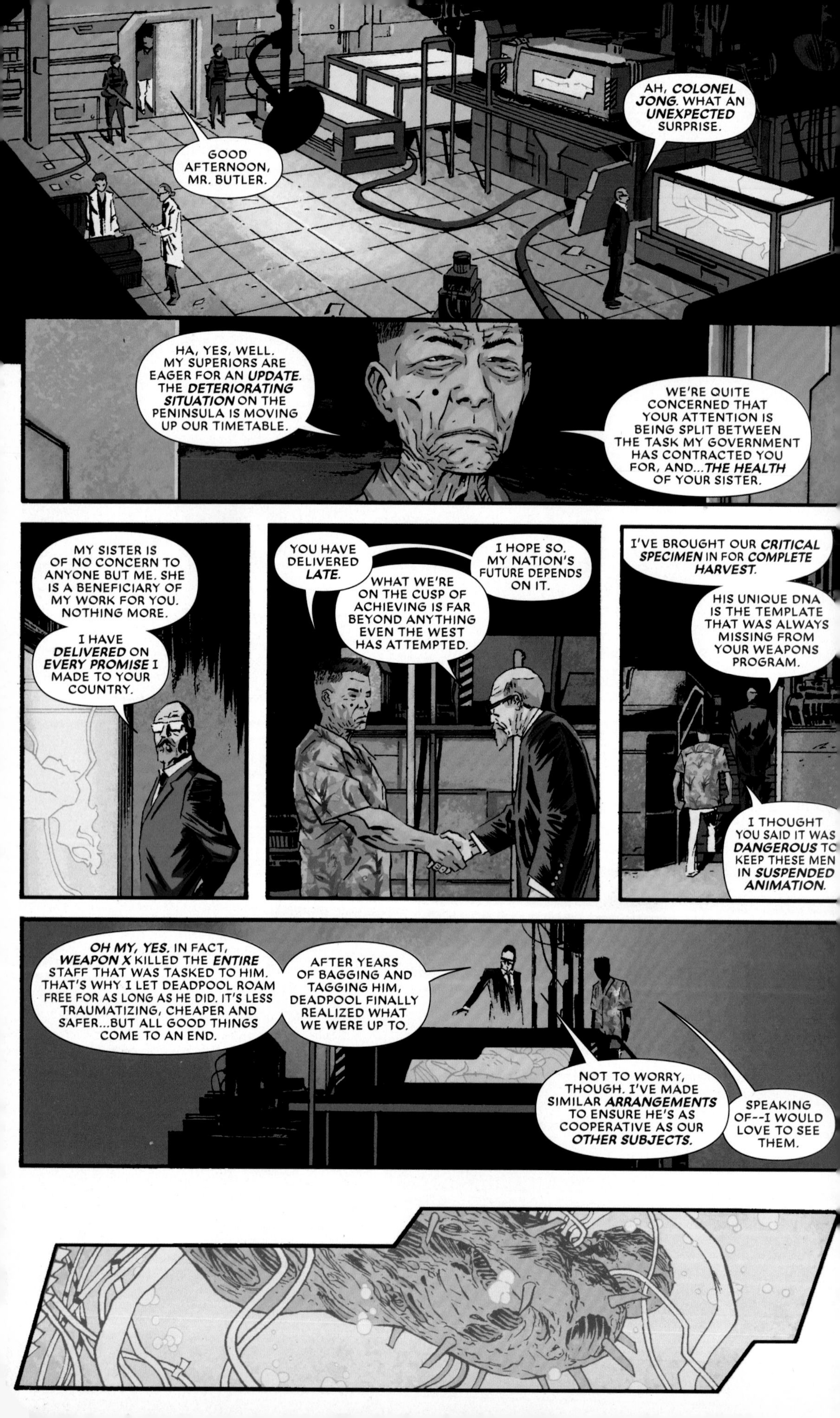
GOOD AFTERNOON, MR. BUTLER.
AH, COLONEL JONG. WHAT AN UNEXPECTED SURPRISE.
HA, YES, WELL. MY SUPERIORS ARE EAGER FOR AN UPDATE. THE DETERIORATING SITUATION ON THE PENINSULA IS MOVING UP OUR TIMETABLE.
WE'RE QUITE CONCERNED THAT YOUR ATTENTION IS BEING SPLIT BETWEEN THE TASK MY GOVERNMENT HAS CONTRACTED YOU FOR, AND...THE HEALTH OF YOUR SISTER.
MY SISTER IS OF NO CONCERN TO ANYONE BUT ME. SHE IS A BENEFICIARY OF MY WORK FOR YOU. NOTHING MORE.
I HAVE DELIVERED ON EVERY PROMISE I MADE TO YOUR COUNTRY.
YOU HAVE DELIVERED LATE.
WHAT WE'RE ON THE CUSP OF ACHIEVING IS FAR BEYOND ANYTHING EVEN THE WEST HAS ATTEMPTED.
I HOPE SO. MY NATION'S FUTURE DEPENDS ON IT.
I'VE BROUGHT OUR CRITICAL SPECIMEN IN FOR COMPLETE HARVEST.
HIS UNIQUE DNA IS THE TEMPLATE THAT WAS ALWAYS MISSING FROM YOUR WEAPONS PROGRAM.
I THOUGHT YOU SAID IT WAS DANGEROUS TO KEEP THESE MEN IN SUSPENDED ANIMATION.
OH MY, YES. IN FACT, WEAPON X KILLED THE ENTIRE STAFF THAT WAS TASKED TO HIM. THAT'S WHY I LET DEADPOOL ROAM FREE FOR AS LONG AS HE DID. IT'S LESS TRAUMATIZING, CHEAPER AND SAFER...BUT ALL GOOD THINGS COME TO AN END.
AFTER YEARS OF BAGGING AND TAGGING HIM, DEADPOOL FINALLY REALIZED WHAT WE WERE UP TO.
NOT TO WORRY, THOUGH. I'VE MADE SIMILAR ARRANGEMENTS TO ENSURE HE'S AS COOPERATIVE AS OUR OTHER SUBJECTS.
SPEAKING OF--I WOULD LOVE TO SEE THEM.

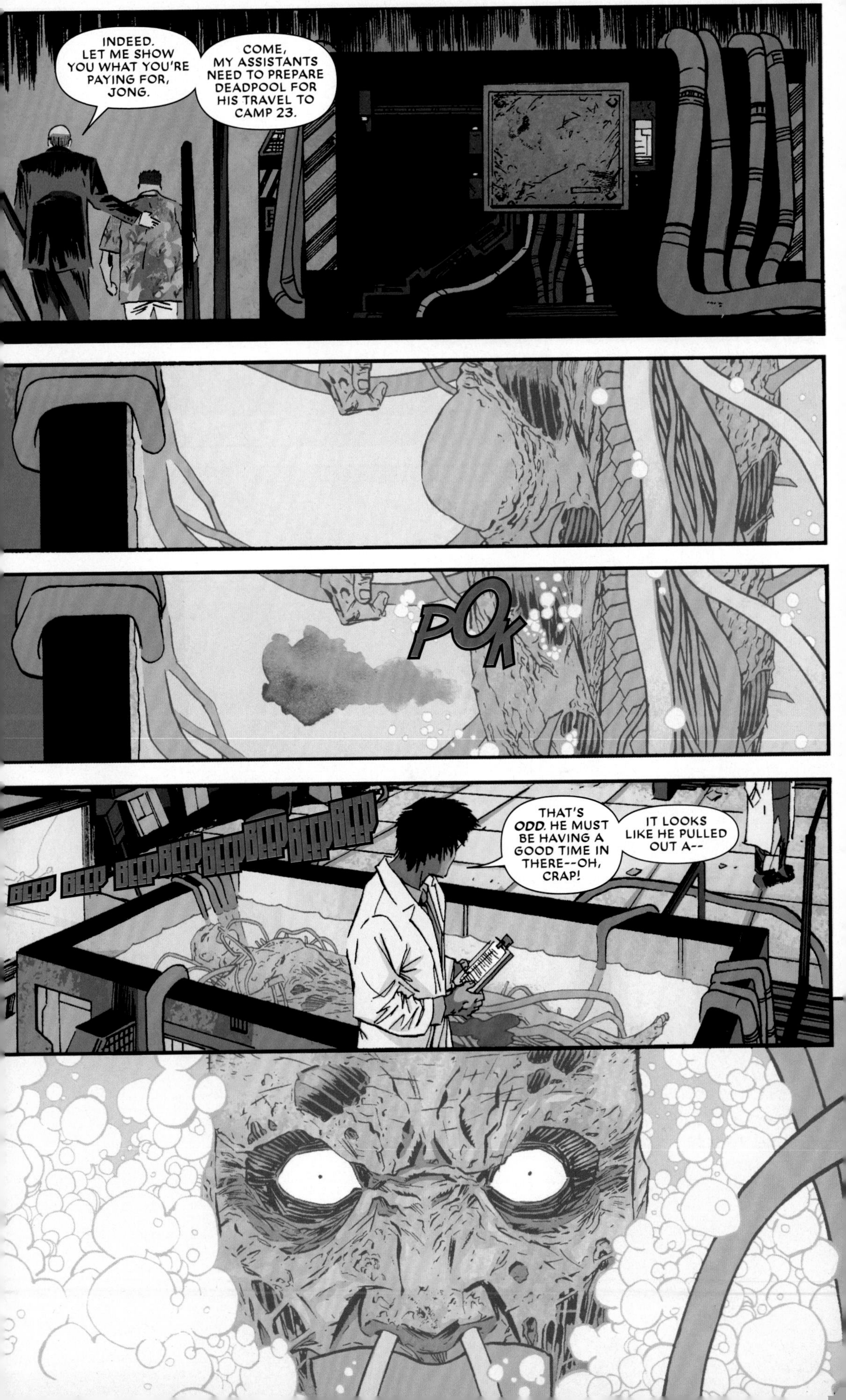
INDEED. LET ME SHOW YOU WHAT YOU'RE PAYING FOR, JONG.
COME, MY ASSISTANTS NEED TO PREPARE DEADPOOL FOR HIS TRAVEL TO CAMP 23.
POK
BEEP BEEP BEEP BEEP BEEP BEEP BEEP BEEP
THAT'S ODD. HE MUST BE HAVING A GOOD TIME IN THERE--OH, CRAP!
IT LOOKS LIKE HE PULLED OUT A--

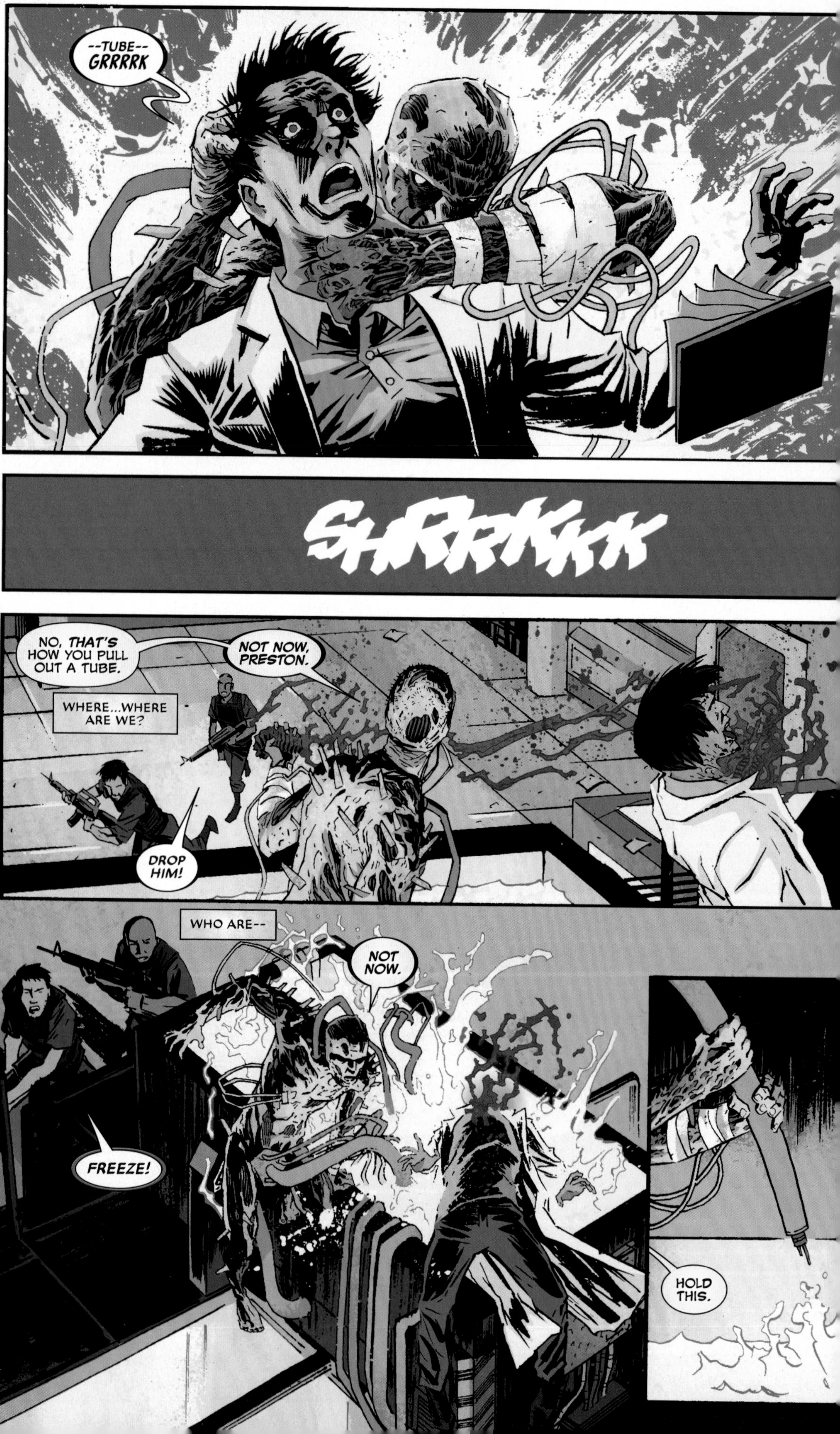
--TUBE--
GRRRRK
SHRRKKK
NO, THAT'S HOW YOU PULL OUT A TUBE.
NOT NOW, PRESTON.
WHERE...WHERE ARE WE?
DROP HIM!
WHO ARE--
NOT NOW.
FREEZE!
HOLD THIS.

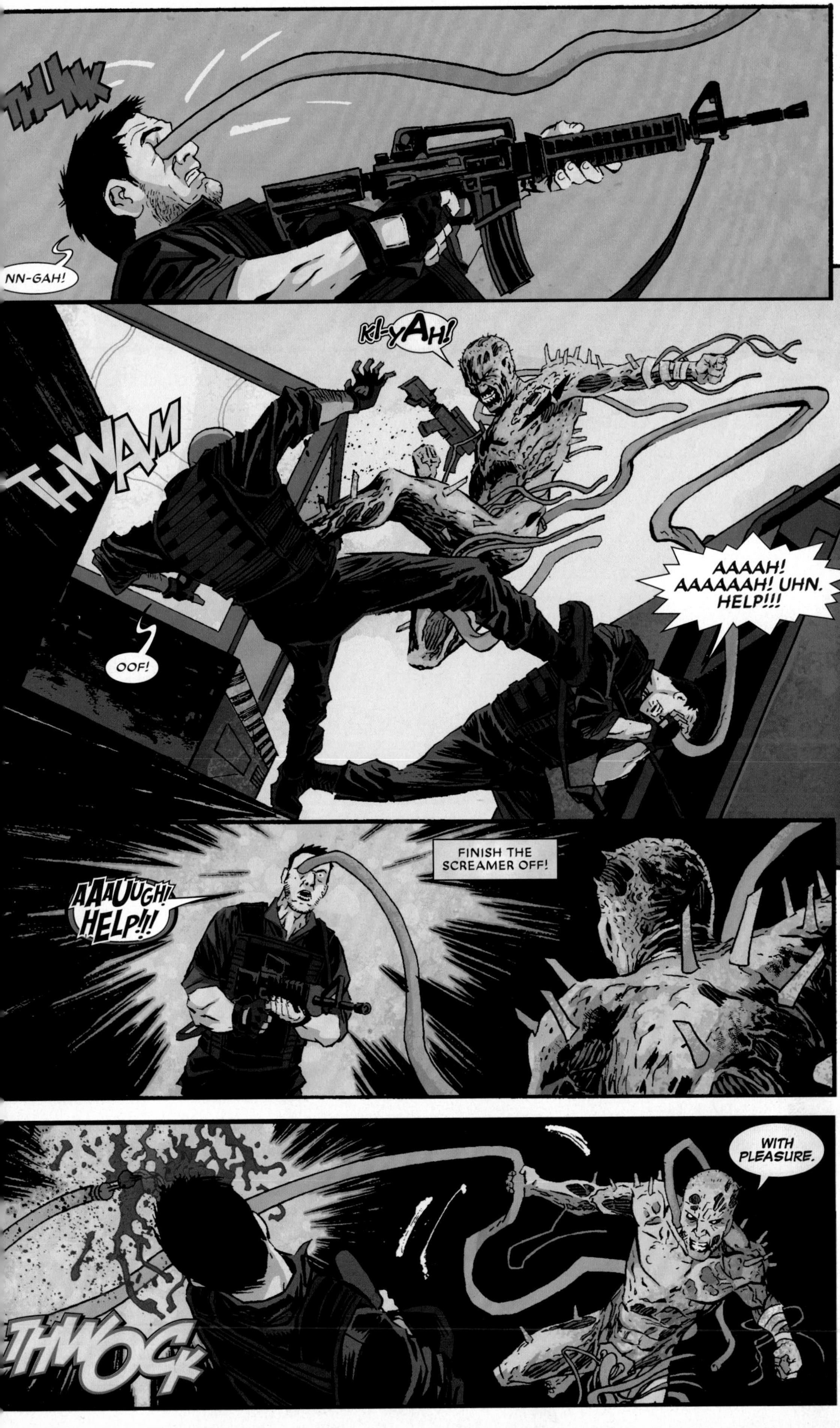
THUNK
NN-GAH!
KI-YAH!
THWAM
AAAAH! AAAAAAH! UHN. HELP!!!
OOF!
FINISH THE SCREAMER OFF!
AAAUUGH! HELP!!!
WITH PLEASURE.
THWOCK

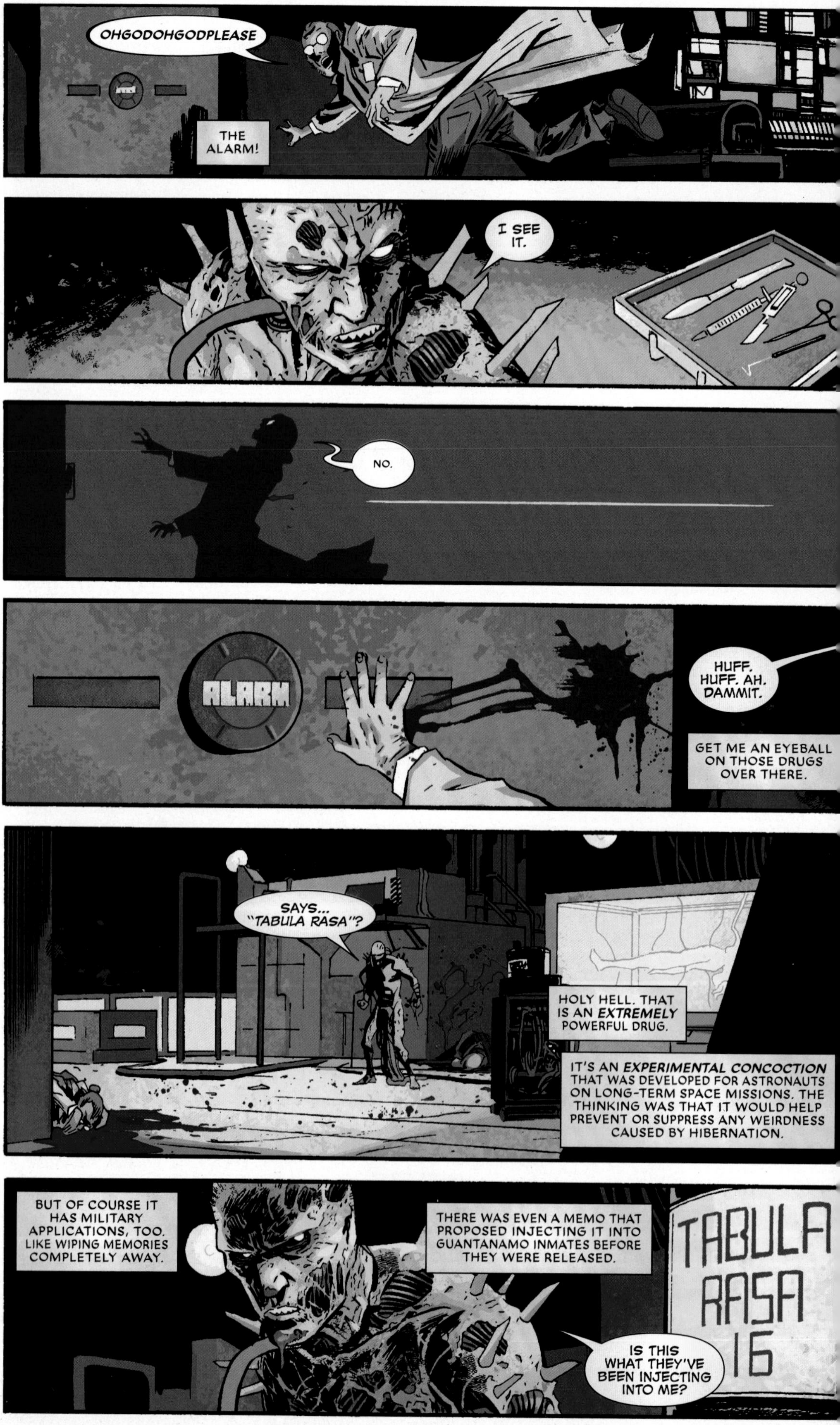
OHGODOHGODPLEASE
THE ALARM!
I SEE IT.
NO.
ALARM
HUFF. HUFF. AH. DAMMIT.
GET ME AN EYEBALL ON THOSE DRUGS OVER THERE.
SAYS... "TABULA RASA"?
HOLY HELL. THAT IS AN *EXTREMELY* POWERFUL DRUG.
IT'S AN *EXPERIMENTAL CONCOCTION* THAT WAS DEVELOPED FOR ASTRONAUTS ON LONG-TERM SPACE MISSIONS. THE THINKING WAS THAT IT WOULD HELP PREVENT OR SUPPRESS ANY WEIRDNESS CAUSED BY HIBERNATION.
BUT OF COURSE IT HAS MILITARY APPLICATIONS, TOO. LIKE WIPING MEMORIES COMPLETELY AWAY.
THERE WAS EVEN A MEMO THAT PROPOSED INJECTING IT INTO GUANTANAMO INMATES BEFORE THEY WERE RELEASED.
TABULA RASA 16
IS THIS WHAT THEY'VE BEEN INJECTING INTO ME?

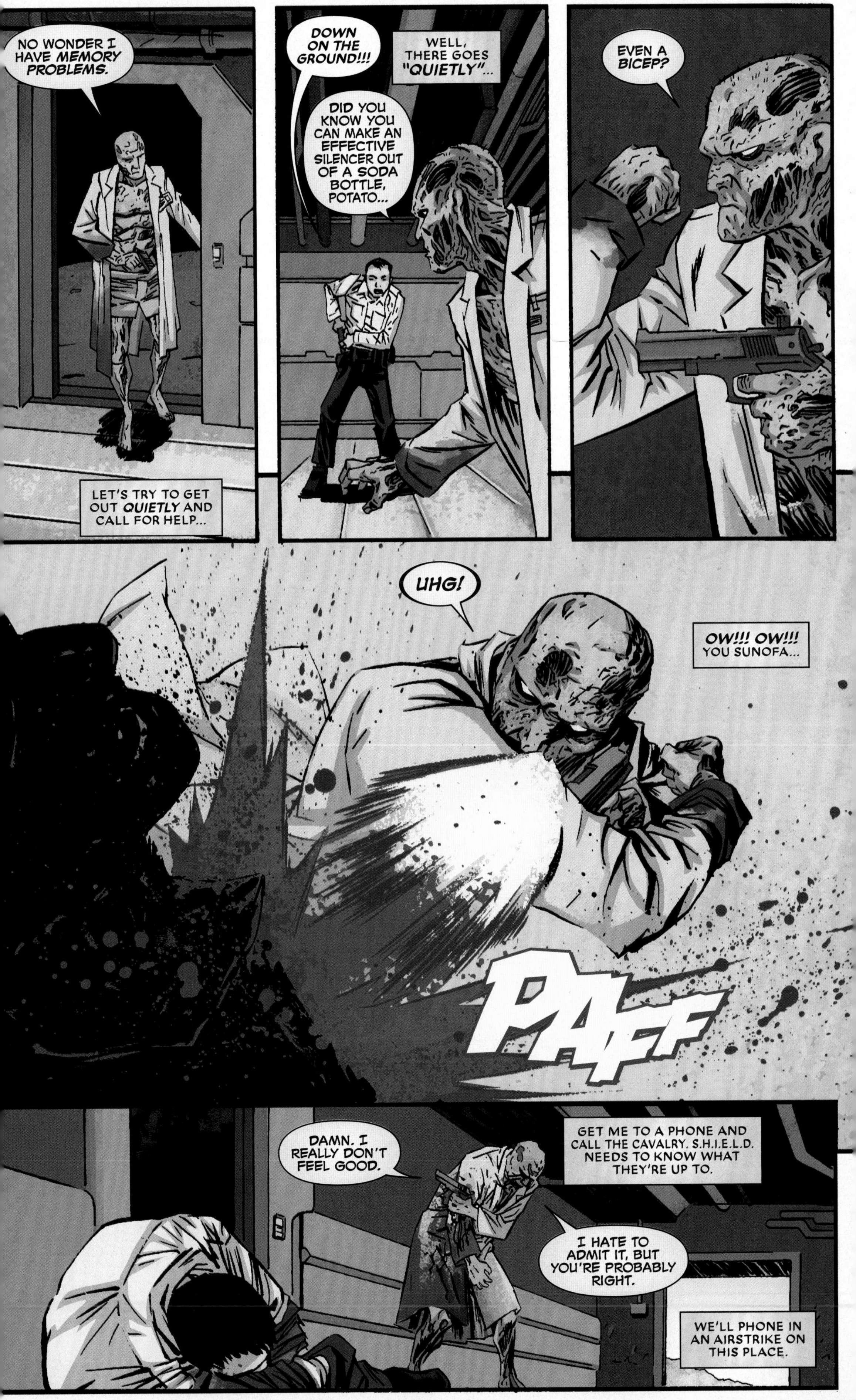
NO WONDER I HAVE MEMORY PROBLEMS.
LET'S TRY TO GET OUT QUIETLY AND CALL FOR HELP...
DOWN ON THE GROUND!!!
WELL, THERE GOES "QUIETLY"...
DID YOU KNOW YOU CAN MAKE AN EFFECTIVE SILENCER OUT OF A SODA BOTTLE, POTATO...
EVEN A BICEP?
UHG!
OW!!! OW!!! YOU SUNOFA...
PAFF
DAMN. I REALLY DON'T FEEL GOOD.
GET ME TO A PHONE AND CALL THE CAVALRY. S.H.I.E.L.D. NEEDS TO KNOW WHAT THEY'RE UP TO.
I HATE TO ADMIT IT, BUT YOU'RE PROBABLY RIGHT.
WE'LL PHONE IN AN AIRSTRIKE ON THIS PLACE.

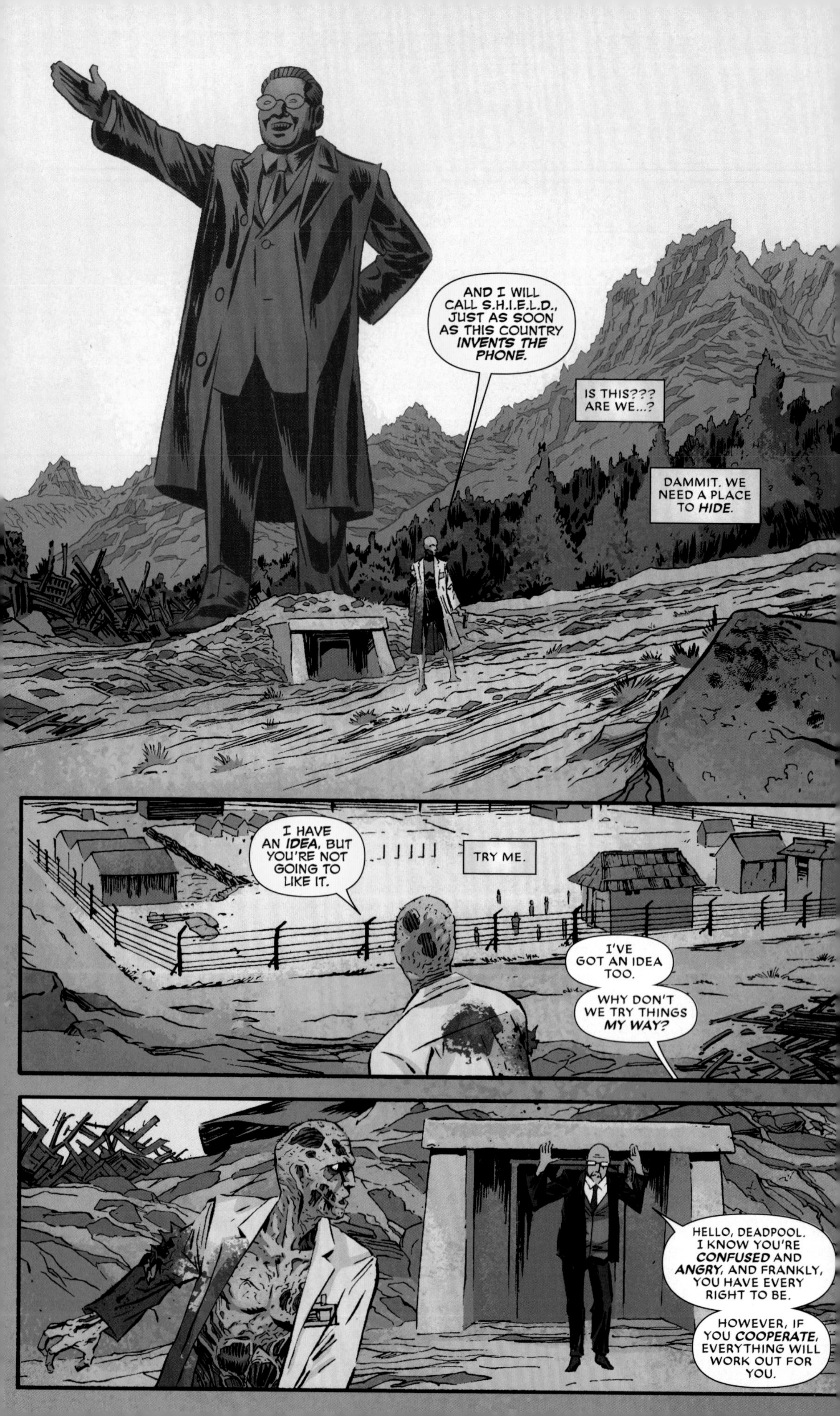
AND I WILL CALL S.H.I.E.L.D., JUST AS SOON AS THIS COUNTRY *INVENTS THE PHONE.*
IS THIS??? ARE WE...?
DAMMIT. WE NEED A PLACE TO *HIDE.*
I HAVE AN *IDEA,* BUT YOU'RE NOT GOING TO LIKE IT.
TRY ME.
I'VE GOT AN IDEA TOO.
WHY DON'T WE TRY THINGS *MY WAY?*
HELLO, DEADPOOL. I KNOW YOU'RE *CONFUSED* AND *ANGRY,* AND FRANKLY, YOU HAVE EVERY RIGHT TO BE.
HOWEVER, IF YOU *COOPERATE,* EVERYTHING WILL WORK OUT FOR YOU.

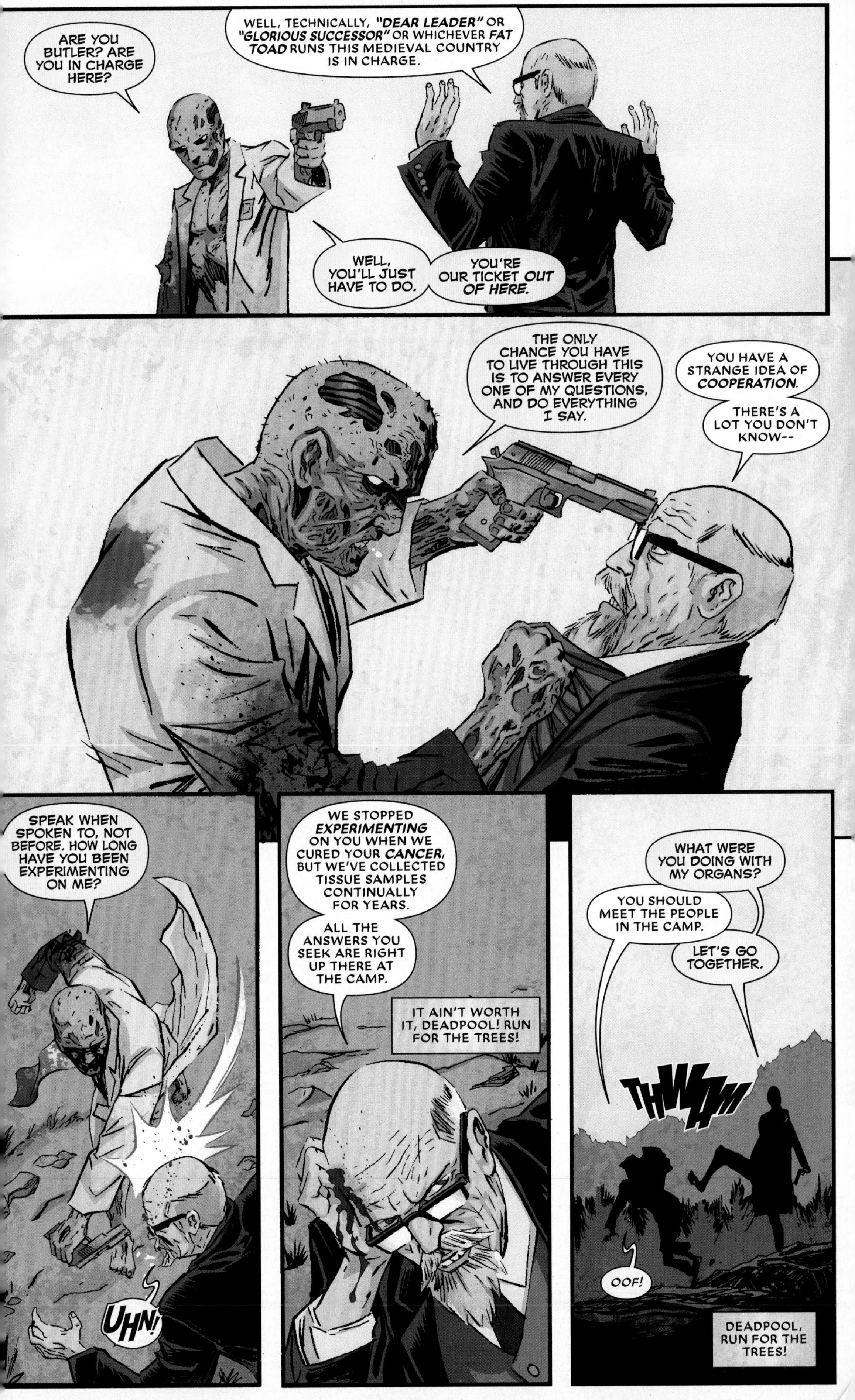
ARE YOU BUTLER? ARE YOU IN CHARGE HERE?
WELL, TECHNICALLY, "DEAR LEADER" OR "GLORIOUS SUCCESSOR" OR WHICHEVER FAT TOAD RUNS THIS MEDIEVAL COUNTRY IS IN CHARGE.
WELL, YOU'LL JUST HAVE TO DO.
YOU'RE OUR TICKET OUT OF HERE.
THE ONLY CHANCE YOU HAVE TO LIVE THROUGH THIS IS TO ANSWER EVERY ONE OF MY QUESTIONS, AND DO EVERYTHING I SAY.
YOU HAVE A STRANGE IDEA OF COOPERATION.
THERE'S A LOT YOU DON'T KNOW--
SPEAK WHEN SPOKEN TO, NOT BEFORE. HOW LONG HAVE YOU BEEN EXPERIMENTING ON ME?
UHN!
WE STOPPED EXPERIMENTING ON YOU WHEN WE CURED YOUR CANCER, BUT WE'VE COLLECTED TISSUE SAMPLES CONTINUALLY FOR YEARS.
ALL THE ANSWERS YOU SEEK ARE RIGHT UP THERE AT THE CAMP.
IT AIN'T WORTH IT, DEADPOOL! RUN FOR THE TREES!
WHAT WERE YOU DOING WITH MY ORGANS?
YOU SHOULD MEET THE PEOPLE IN THE CAMP.
LET'S GO TOGETHER.
THWOM
OOF!
DEADPOOL, RUN FOR THE TREES!

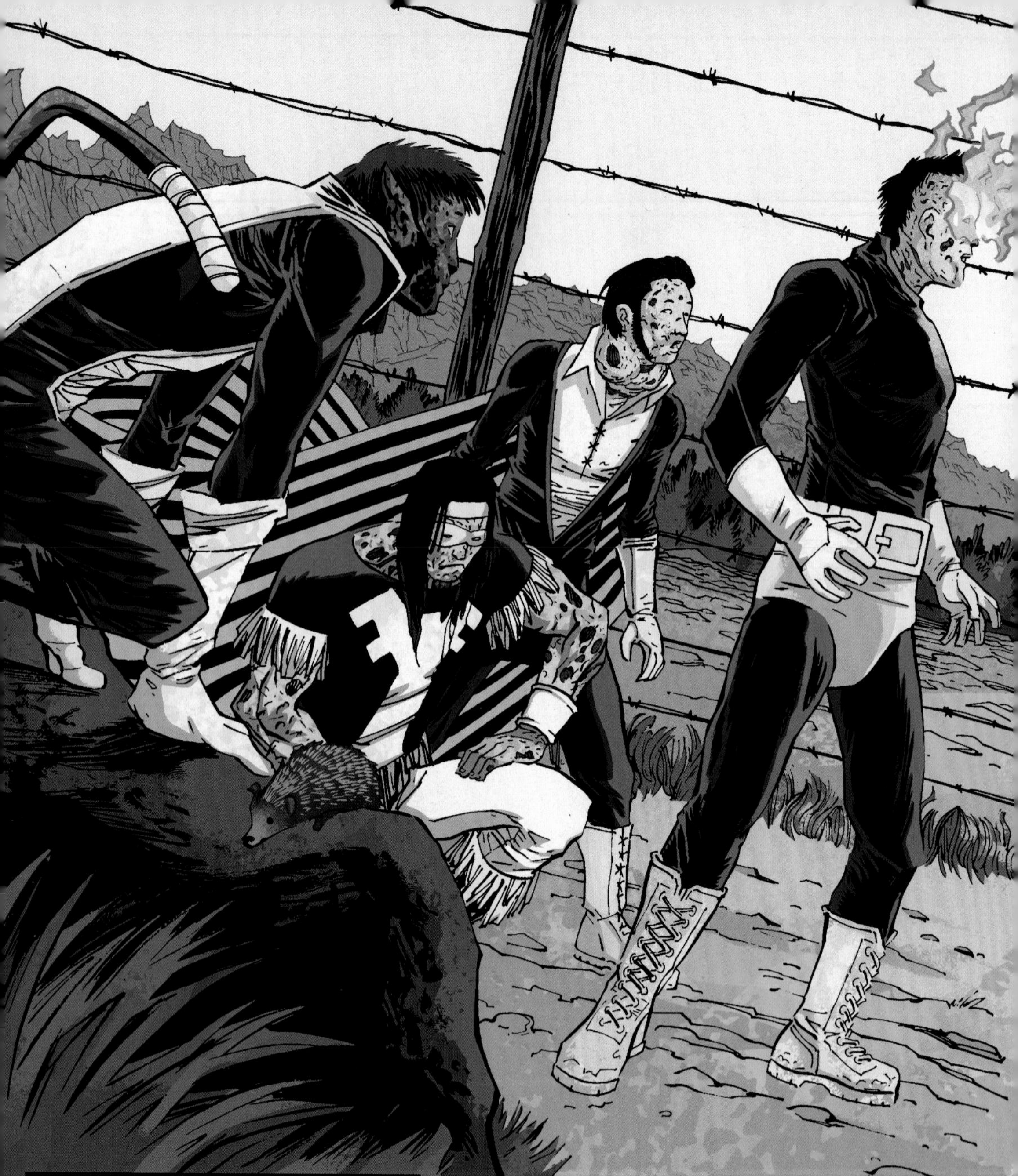

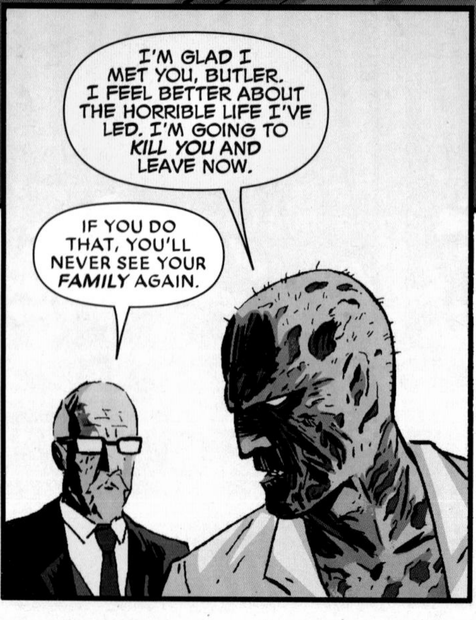

I'M GLAD I MET YOU, BUTLER. I FEEL BETTER ABOUT THE HORRIBLE LIFE I'VE LED. I'M GOING TO KILL YOU AND LEAVE NOW.
IF YOU DO THAT, YOU'LL NEVER SEE YOUR FAMILY AGAIN.

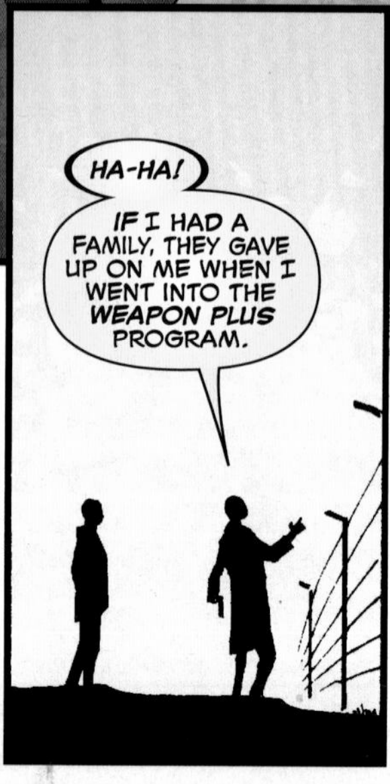

HA-HA!
IF I HAD A FAMILY, THEY GAVE UP ON ME WHEN I WENT INTO THE WEAPON PLUS PROGRAM.

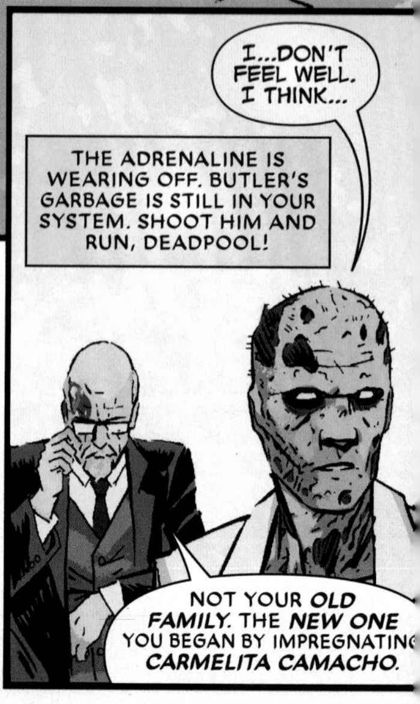

I...DON'T FEEL WELL. I THINK...
THE ADRENALINE IS WEARING OFF. BUTLER'S GARBAGE IS STILL IN YOUR SYSTEM. SHOOT HIM AND RUN, DEADPOOL!
NOT YOUR OLD FAMILY. THE NEW ONE YOU BEGAN BY IMPREGNATING CARMELITA CAMACHO.

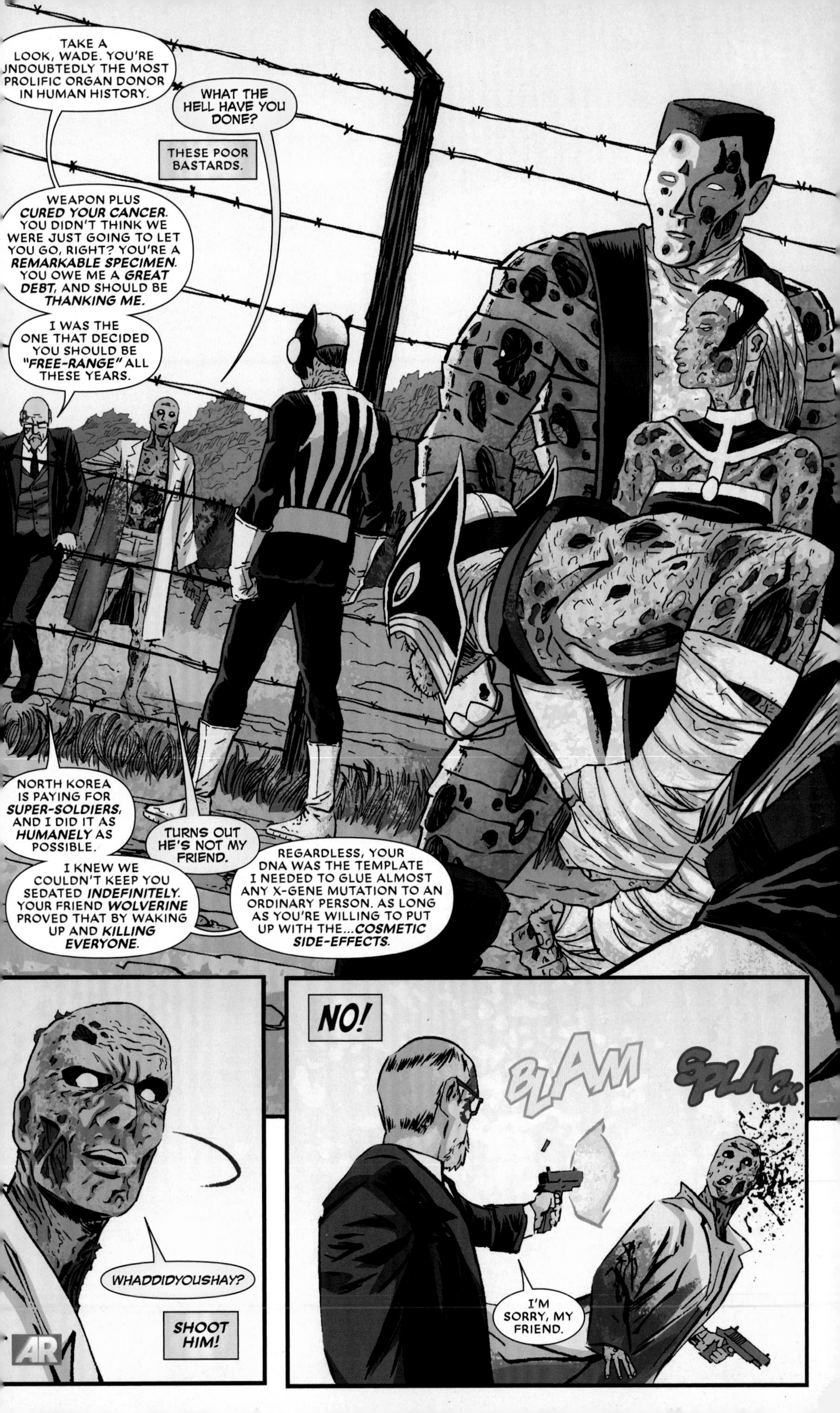
TAKE A LOOK, WADE. YOU'RE UNDOUBTEDLY THE MOST PROLIFIC ORGAN DONOR IN HUMAN HISTORY.
WHAT THE HELL HAVE YOU DONE?
THESE POOR BASTARDS.
WEAPON PLUS CURED YOUR CANCER. YOU DIDN'T THINK WE WERE JUST GOING TO LET YOU GO, RIGHT? YOU'RE A REMARKABLE SPECIMEN. YOU OWE ME A GREAT DEBT, AND SHOULD BE THANKING ME.
I WAS THE ONE THAT DECIDED YOU SHOULD BE "FREE-RANGE" ALL THESE YEARS.
NORTH KOREA IS PAYING FOR SUPER-SOLDIERS, AND I DID IT AS HUMANELY AS POSSIBLE.
I KNEW WE COULDN'T KEEP YOU SEDATED INDEFINITELY. YOUR FRIEND WOLVERINE PROVED THAT BY WAKING UP AND KILLING EVERYONE.
TURNS OUT HE'S NOT MY FRIEND.
REGARDLESS, YOUR DNA WAS THE TEMPLATE I NEEDED TO GLUE ALMOST ANY X-GENE MUTATION TO AN ORDINARY PERSON. AS LONG AS YOU'RE WILLING TO PUT UP WITH THE...COSMETIC SIDE-EFFECTS.
WHADDIDYOUSHAY?
SHOOT HIM!
NO!
BLAM
SPLACK
I'M SORRY, MY FRIEND.

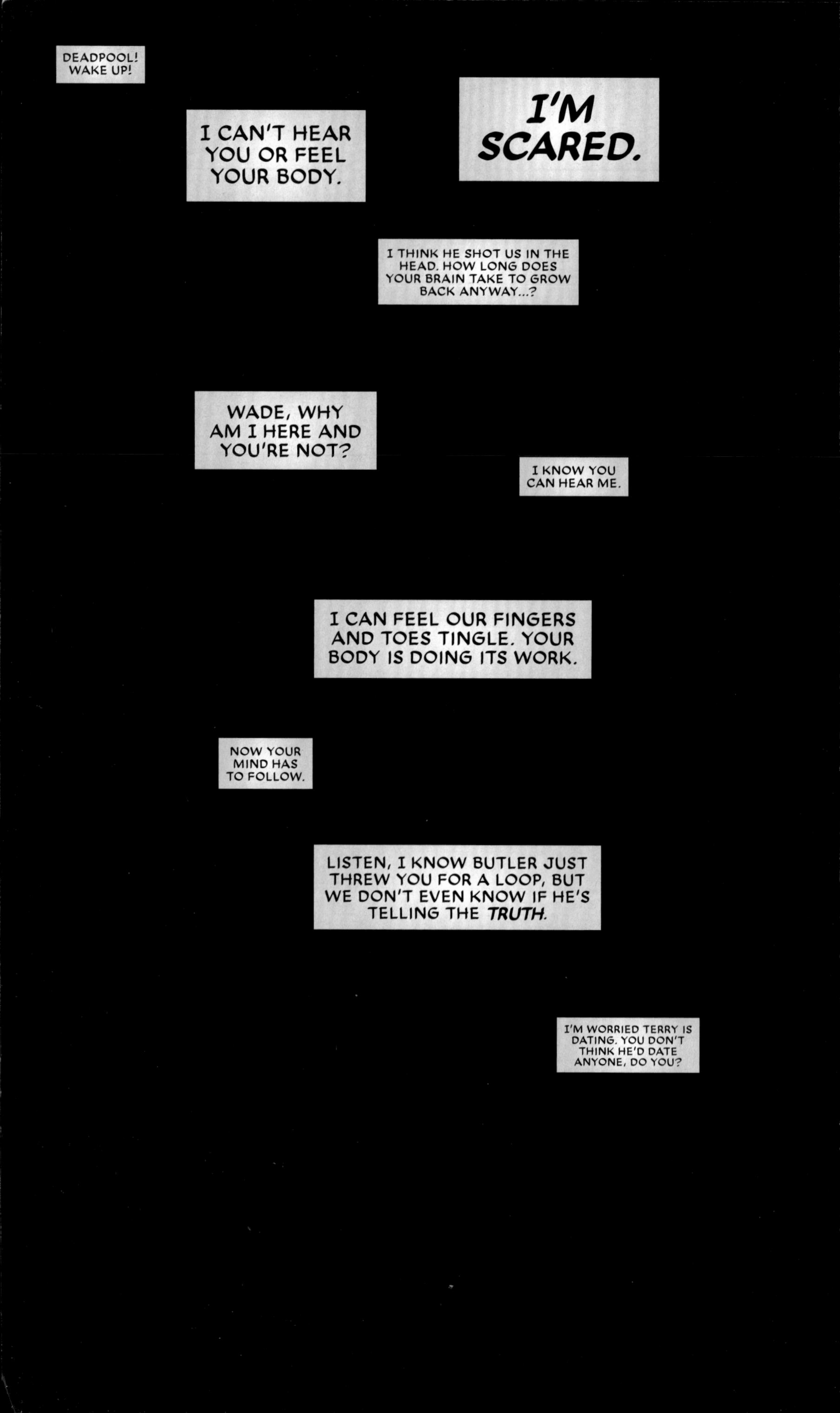
DEADPOOL! WAKE UP!
I CAN'T HEAR YOU OR FEEL YOUR BODY.
I'M SCARED.
I THINK HE SHOT US IN THE HEAD. HOW LONG DOES YOUR BRAIN TAKE TO GROW BACK ANYWAY...?
WADE, WHY AM I HERE AND YOU'RE NOT?
I KNOW YOU CAN HEAR ME.
I CAN FEEL OUR FINGERS AND TOES TINGLE. YOUR BODY IS DOING ITS WORK.
NOW YOUR MIND HAS TO FOLLOW.
LISTEN, I KNOW BUTLER JUST THREW YOU FOR A LOOP, BUT WE DON'T EVEN KNOW IF HE'S TELLING THE *TRUTH*.
I'M WORRIED TERRY IS DATING. YOU DON'T THINK HE'D DATE ANYONE, DO YOU?

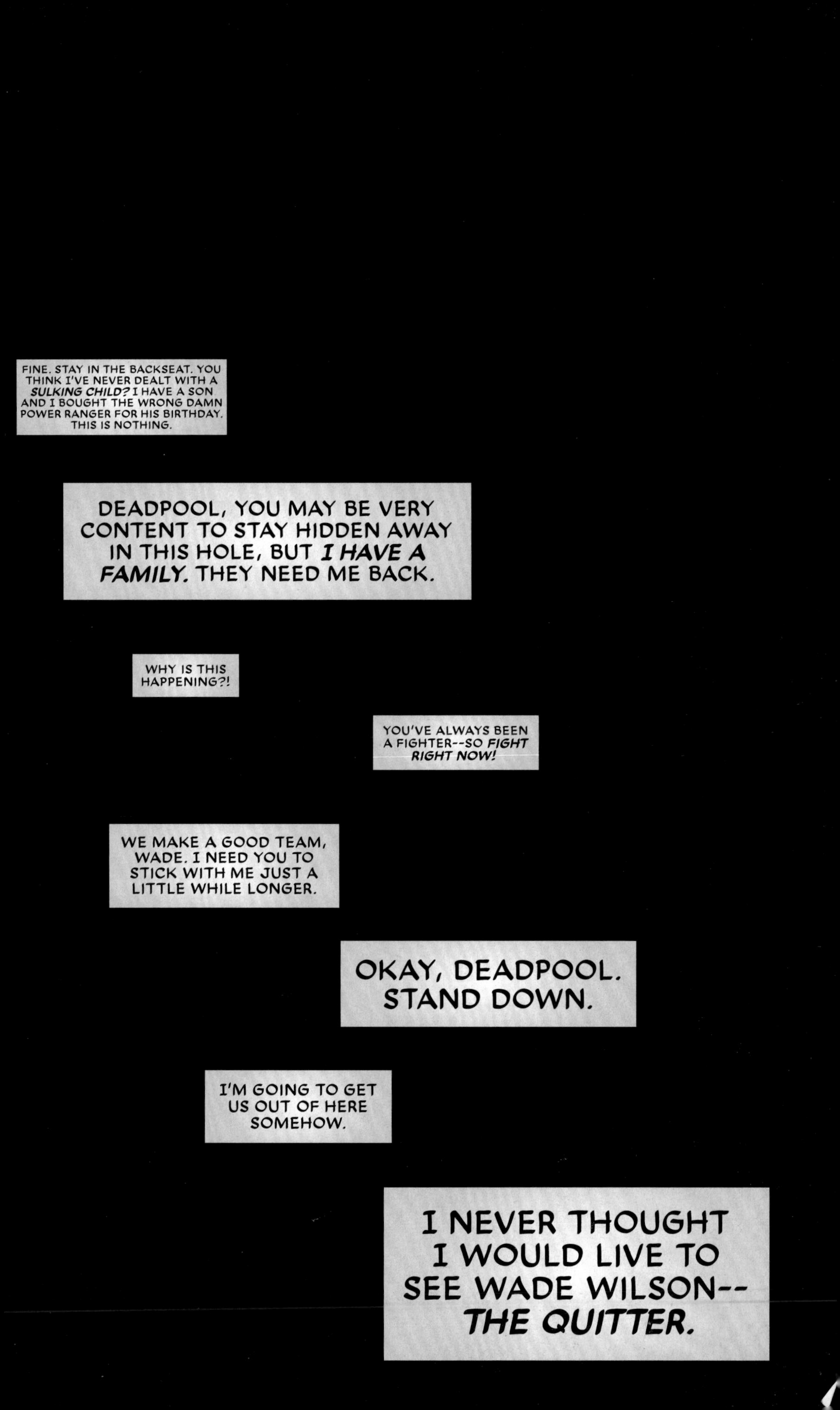
FINE. STAY IN THE BACKSEAT. YOU THINK I'VE NEVER DEALT WITH A *SULKING CHILD?* I HAVE A SON AND I BOUGHT THE WRONG DAMN POWER RANGER FOR HIS BIRTHDAY. THIS IS NOTHING.
DEADPOOL, YOU MAY BE VERY CONTENT TO STAY HIDDEN AWAY IN THIS HOLE, BUT *I HAVE A FAMILY.* THEY NEED ME BACK.
WHY IS THIS HAPPENING?!
YOU'VE ALWAYS BEEN A FIGHTER--SO *FIGHT RIGHT NOW!*
WE MAKE A GOOD TEAM, WADE. I NEED YOU TO STICK WITH ME JUST A LITTLE WHILE LONGER.
OKAY, DEADPOOL. STAND DOWN.
I'M GOING TO GET US OUT OF HERE SOMEHOW.
I NEVER THOUGHT I WOULD LIVE TO SEE WADE WILSON-- *THE QUITTER.*

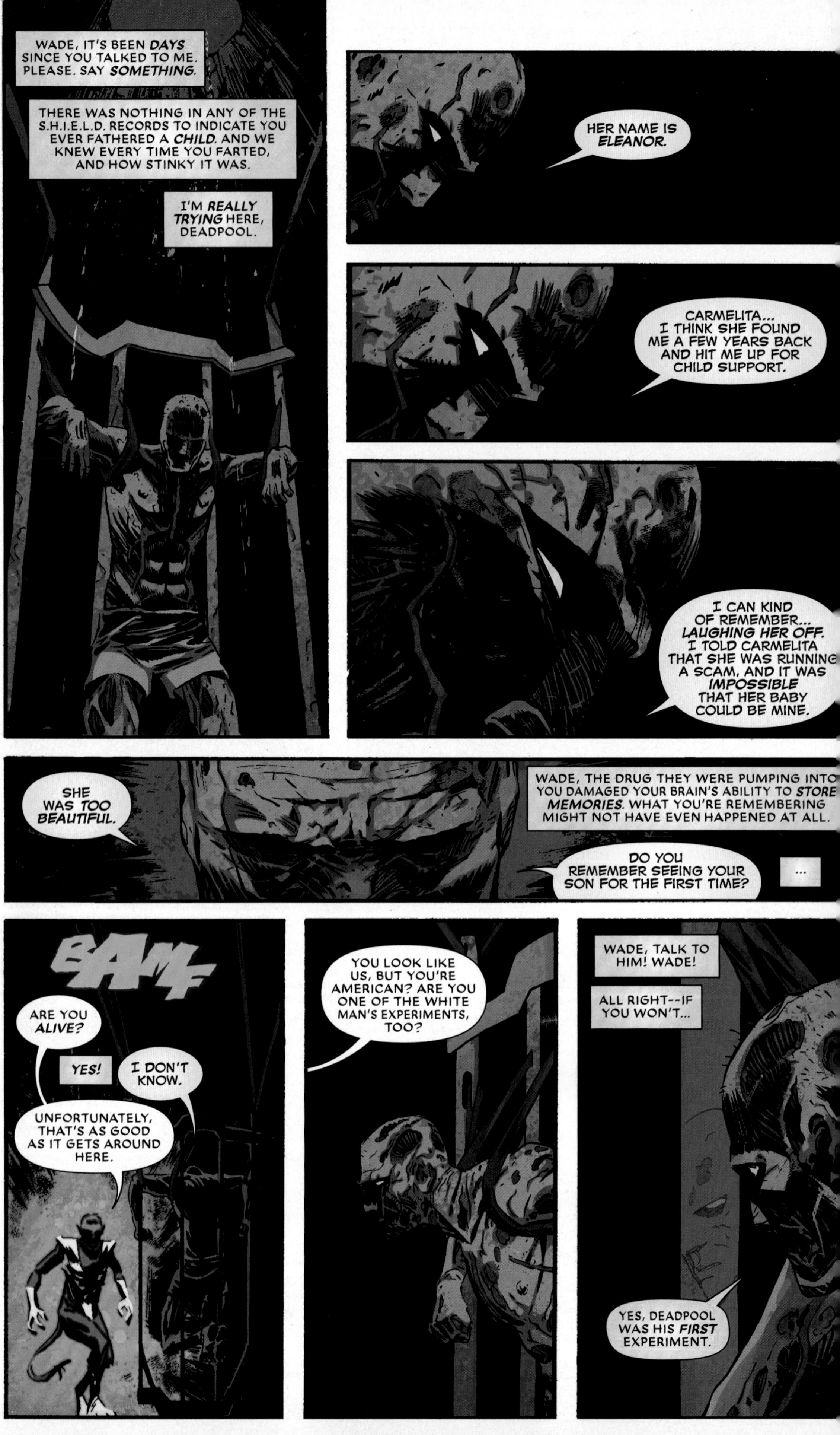
WADE, IT'S BEEN DAYS SINCE YOU TALKED TO ME. PLEASE. SAY SOMETHING.
THERE WAS NOTHING IN ANY OF THE S.H.I.E.L.D. RECORDS TO INDICATE YOU EVER FATHERED A CHILD. AND WE KNEW EVERY TIME YOU FARTED, AND HOW STINKY IT WAS.
I'M REALLY TRYING HERE, DEADPOOL.
HER NAME IS ELEANOR.
CARMELITA... I THINK SHE FOUND ME A FEW YEARS BACK AND HIT ME UP FOR CHILD SUPPORT.
I CAN KIND OF REMEMBER... LAUGHING HER OFF. I TOLD CARMELITA THAT SHE WAS RUNNING A SCAM, AND IT WAS IMPOSSIBLE THAT HER BABY COULD BE MINE.
SHE WAS TOO BEAUTIFUL.
WADE, THE DRUG THEY WERE PUMPING INTO YOU DAMAGED YOUR BRAIN'S ABILITY TO STORE MEMORIES. WHAT YOU'RE REMEMBERING MIGHT NOT HAVE EVEN HAPPENED AT ALL.
DO YOU REMEMBER SEEING YOUR SON FOR THE FIRST TIME?
...
BAMF
ARE YOU ALIVE?
YES!
I DON'T KNOW.
UNFORTUNATELY, THAT'S AS GOOD AS IT GETS AROUND HERE.
YOU LOOK LIKE US, BUT YOU'RE AMERICAN? ARE YOU ONE OF THE WHITE MAN'S EXPERIMENTS, TOO?
WADE, TALK TO HIM! WADE!
ALL RIGHT--IF YOU WON'T...
YES, DEADPOOL WAS HIS FIRST EXPERIMENT.

PERHAPS THIS WAS A MISTAKE.

NO! TAKE US WITH YOU! PLEASE.

MY NAME IS DEADPOOL.

I'M KIM. WE'RE ESCAPING TONIGHT.

THAT SHOULD BE NO PROBLEM WITH YOUR POWERS.

IT'S NOT THAT SIMPLE. OUR FAMILIES ARE BEING HELD HOSTAGE IN ANOTHER CAMP.

PRESTON, THIS COULD BE A *TRAP*.

WADE, I KNOW YOU WANT TO PROTECT THIS DAUGHTER YOU THINK YOU HAVE, BUT-- *WE CANNOT STAY HERE.*

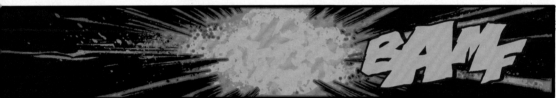

BAMF

WHY DO YOU AND I LOOK ALIKE?

YOU WERE MADE FROM PIECES OF A MAN THAT WAS BORN WITH YOUR POWERS AND PIECES OF ME.

THAT'S *FASCINATING.* I NEVER IMAGINED THAT THEIR EXPERIMENTS WERE BASED ON *ACTUAL PEOPLE.*

I WOULD LIKE TO MEET THIS *OTHER ME* SOMEDAY.

WHO TRAINED YOU TO USE YOUR STOLEN POWERS?

TRAINED?

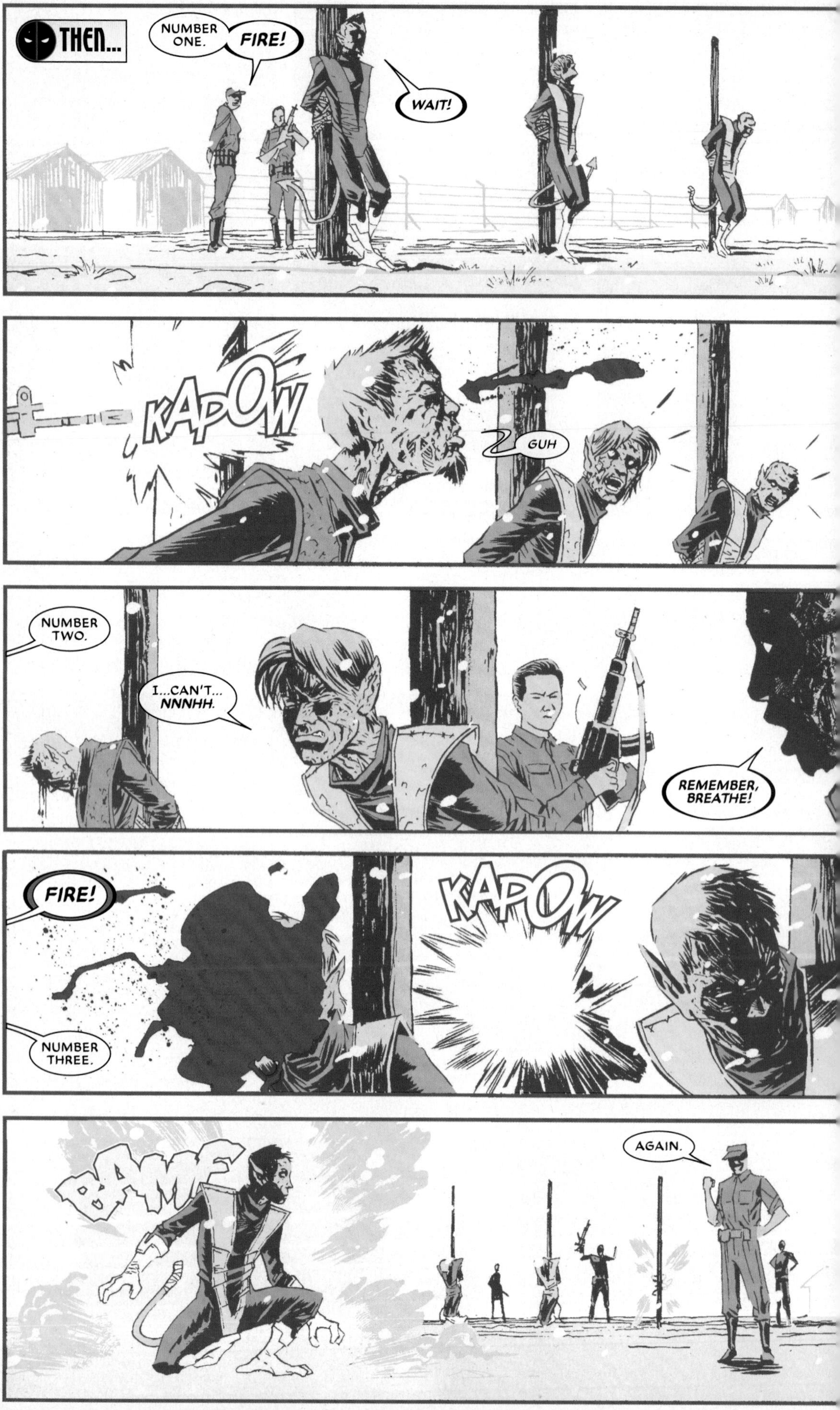
THEN...
NUMBER ONE.
FIRE!
WAIT!
KAPOW
GUH
NUMBER TWO.
I...CAN'T... NNNHH.
REMEMBER, BREATHE!
FIRE!
NUMBER THREE.
KAPOW
BAMF
AGAIN.

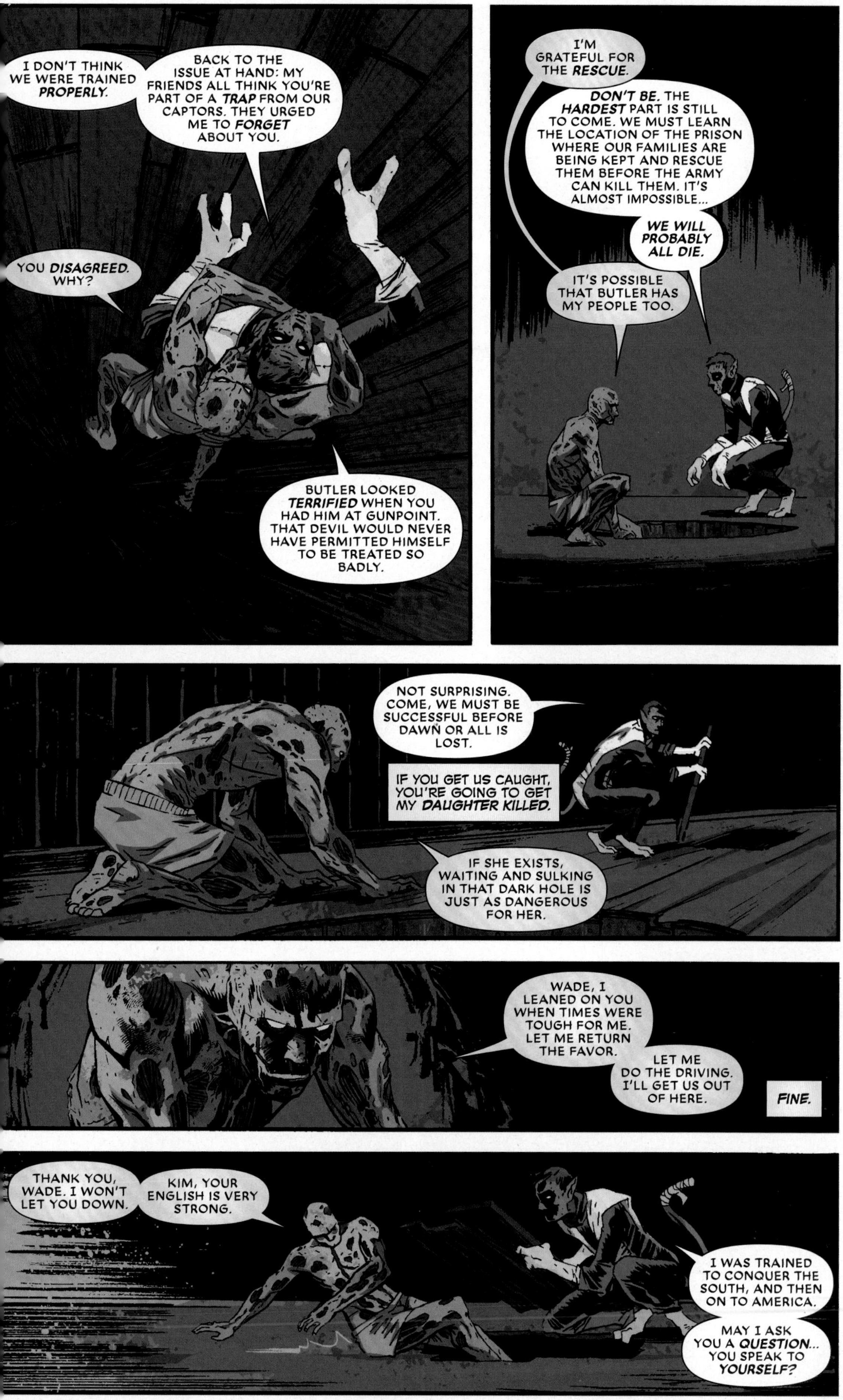
I DON'T THINK WE WERE TRAINED *PROPERLY.*
BACK TO THE ISSUE AT HAND: MY FRIENDS ALL THINK YOU'RE PART OF A *TRAP* FROM OUR CAPTORS. THEY URGED ME TO *FORGET* ABOUT YOU.
YOU *DISAGREED.* WHY?
BUTLER LOOKED *TERRIFIED* WHEN YOU HAD HIM AT GUNPOINT. THAT DEVIL WOULD NEVER HAVE PERMITTED HIMSELF TO BE TREATED SO BADLY.
I'M GRATEFUL FOR THE *RESCUE.*
DON'T BE. THE *HARDEST* PART IS STILL TO COME. WE MUST LEARN THE LOCATION OF THE PRISON WHERE OUR FAMILIES ARE BEING KEPT AND RESCUE THEM BEFORE THE ARMY CAN KILL THEM. IT'S ALMOST IMPOSSIBLE...
WE WILL PROBABLY ALL DIE.
IT'S POSSIBLE THAT BUTLER HAS MY PEOPLE TOO.
NOT SURPRISING. COME, WE MUST BE SUCCESSFUL BEFORE DAWN OR ALL IS LOST.
IF YOU GET US CAUGHT, YOU'RE GOING TO GET MY *DAUGHTER KILLED.*
IF SHE EXISTS, WAITING AND SULKING IN THAT DARK HOLE IS JUST AS DANGEROUS FOR HER.
WADE, I LEANED ON YOU WHEN TIMES WERE TOUGH FOR ME. LET ME RETURN THE FAVOR.
LET ME DO THE DRIVING. I'LL GET US OUT OF HERE.
FINE.
THANK YOU, WADE. I WON'T LET YOU DOWN.
KIM, YOUR ENGLISH IS VERY STRONG.
I WAS TRAINED TO CONQUER THE SOUTH, AND THEN ON TO AMERICA.
MAY I ASK YOU A *QUESTION*... YOU SPEAK TO *YOURSELF?*

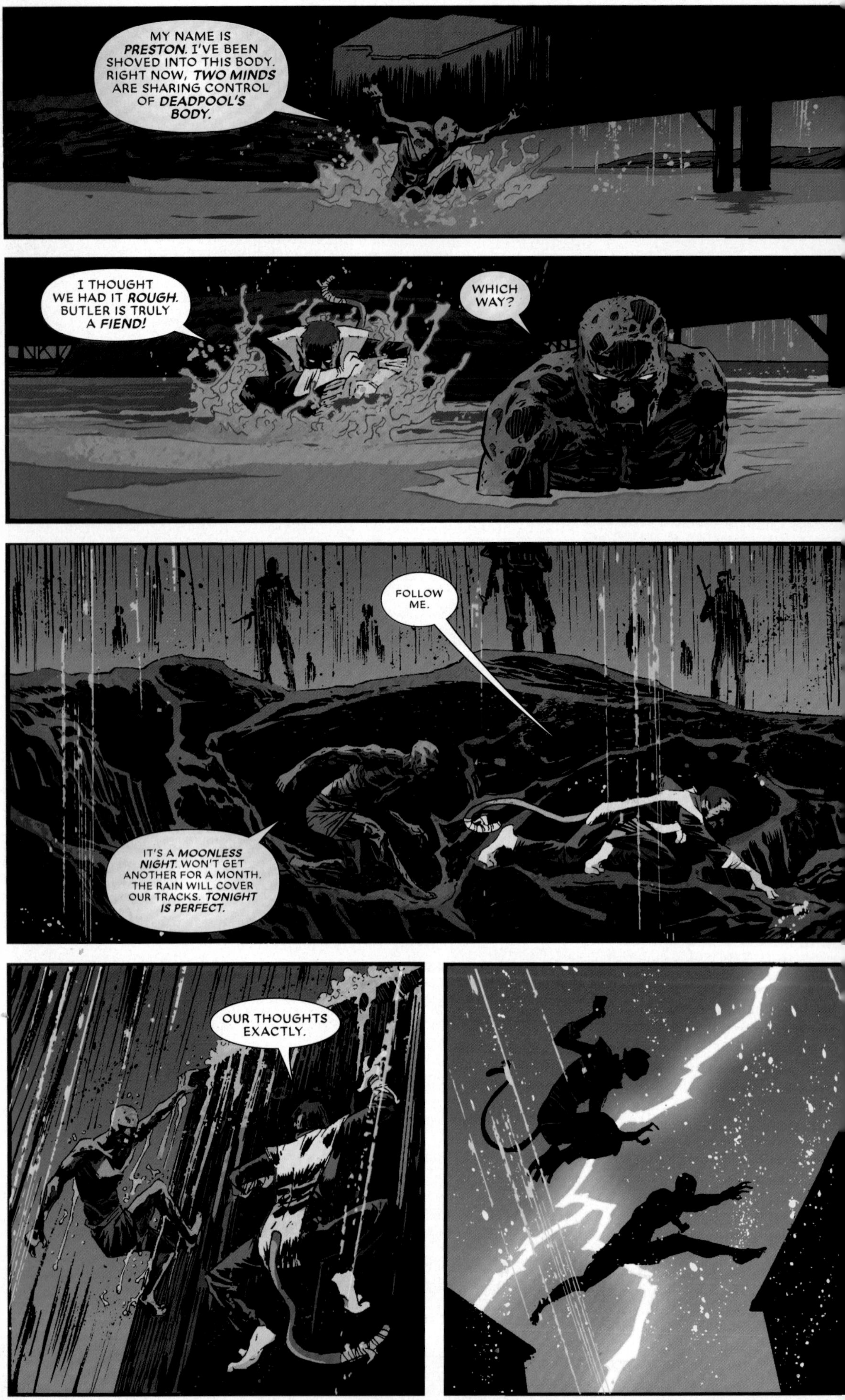
MY NAME IS PRESTON. I'VE BEEN SHOVED INTO THIS BODY. RIGHT NOW, TWO MINDS ARE SHARING CONTROL OF DEADPOOL'S BODY.
I THOUGHT WE HAD IT ROUGH. BUTLER IS TRULY A FIEND!
WHICH WAY?
FOLLOW ME.
IT'S A MOONLESS NIGHT. WON'T GET ANOTHER FOR A MONTH. THE RAIN WILL COVER OUR TRACKS. TONIGHT IS PERFECT.
OUR THOUGHTS EXACTLY.

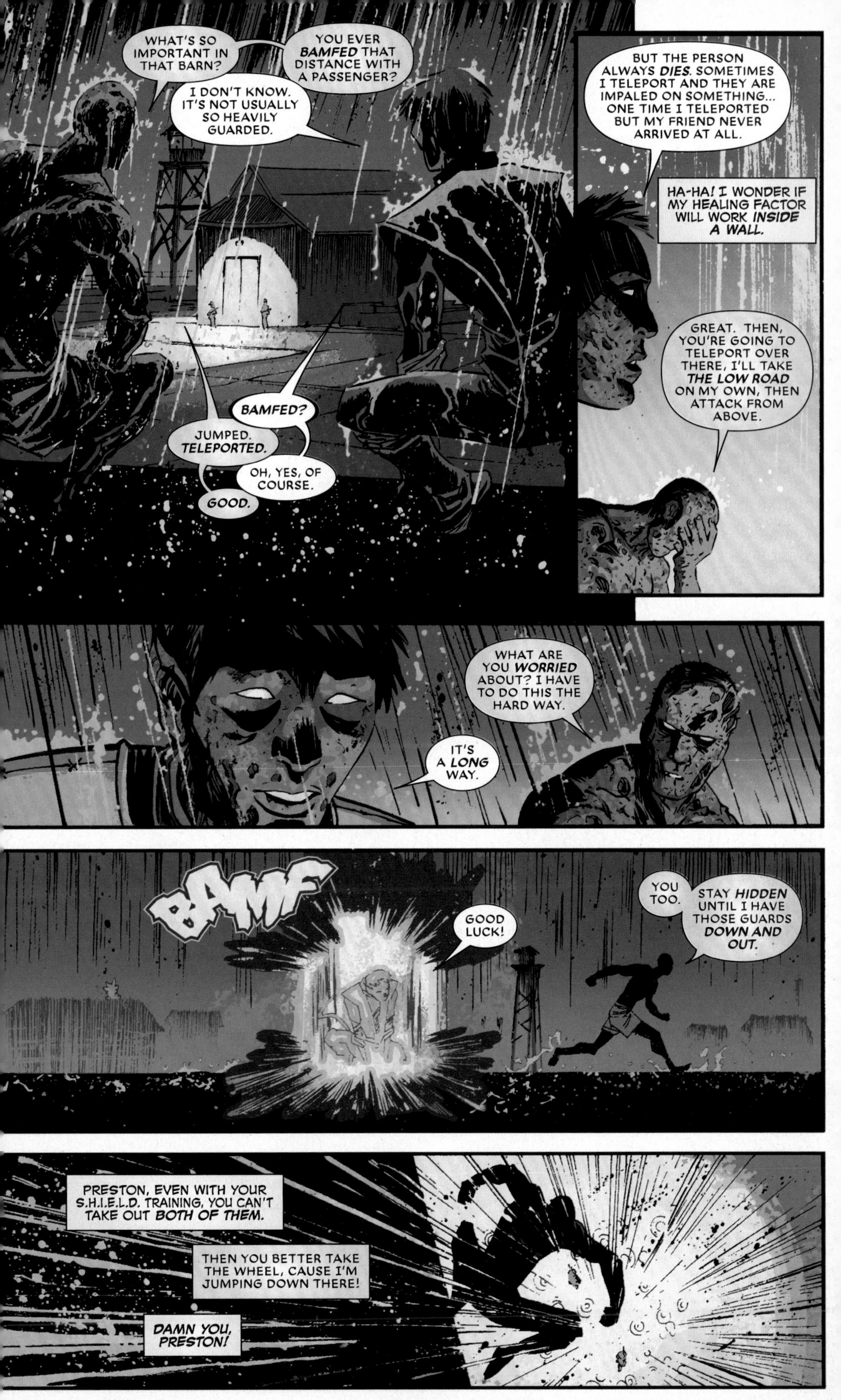
WHAT'S SO IMPORTANT IN THAT BARN?
YOU EVER BAMFED THAT DISTANCE WITH A PASSENGER?
I DON'T KNOW. IT'S NOT USUALLY SO HEAVILY GUARDED.
BAMFED?
JUMPED. TELEPORTED.
OH, YES, OF COURSE.
GOOD.
BUT THE PERSON ALWAYS DIES. SOMETIMES I TELEPORT AND THEY ARE IMPALED ON SOMETHING... ONE TIME I TELEPORTED BUT MY FRIEND NEVER ARRIVED AT ALL.
HA-HA! I WONDER IF MY HEALING FACTOR WILL WORK INSIDE A WALL.
GREAT. THEN, YOU'RE GOING TO TELEPORT OVER THERE, I'LL TAKE THE LOW ROAD ON MY OWN, THEN ATTACK FROM ABOVE.
WHAT ARE YOU WORRIED ABOUT? I HAVE TO DO THIS THE HARD WAY.
IT'S A LONG WAY.
BAMF
GOOD LUCK!
YOU TOO.
STAY HIDDEN UNTIL I HAVE THOSE GUARDS DOWN AND OUT.
PRESTON, EVEN WITH YOUR S.H.I.E.L.D. TRAINING, YOU CAN'T TAKE OUT BOTH OF THEM.
THEN YOU BETTER TAKE THE WHEEL, CAUSE I'M JUMPING DOWN THERE!
DAMN YOU, PRESTON!

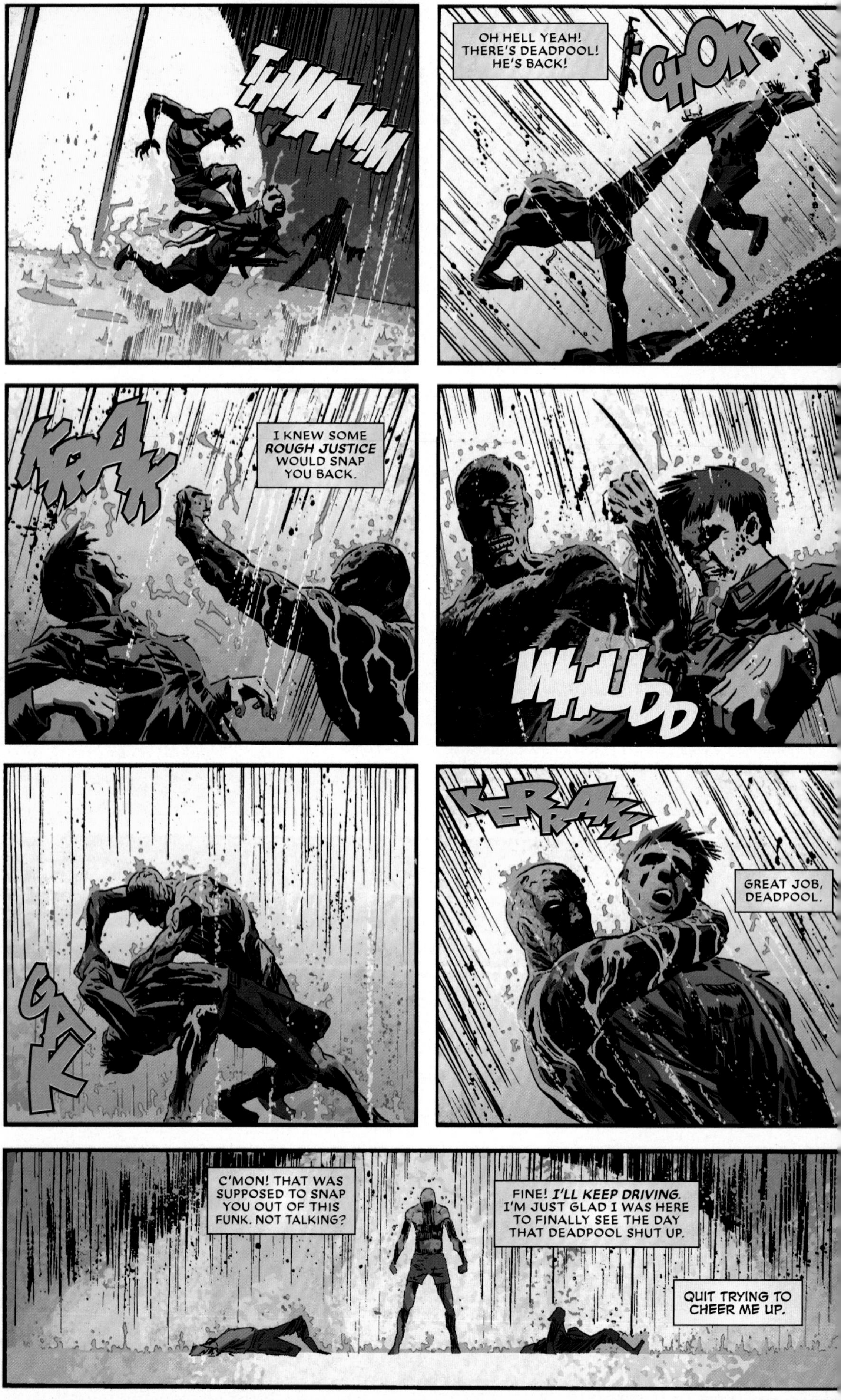
THWAMM
OH HELL YEAH! THERE'S DEADPOOL! HE'S BACK!
CHOK
KRAK
I KNEW SOME *ROUGH JUSTICE* WOULD SNAP YOU BACK.
WHUDD
GAK
KERRAK
GREAT JOB, DEADPOOL.
C'MON! THAT WAS SUPPOSED TO SNAP YOU OUT OF THIS FUNK. NOT TALKING?
FINE! *I'LL KEEP DRIVING.* I'M JUST GLAD I WAS HERE TO FINALLY SEE THE DAY THAT DEADPOOL SHUT UP.
QUIT TRYING TO CHEER ME UP.

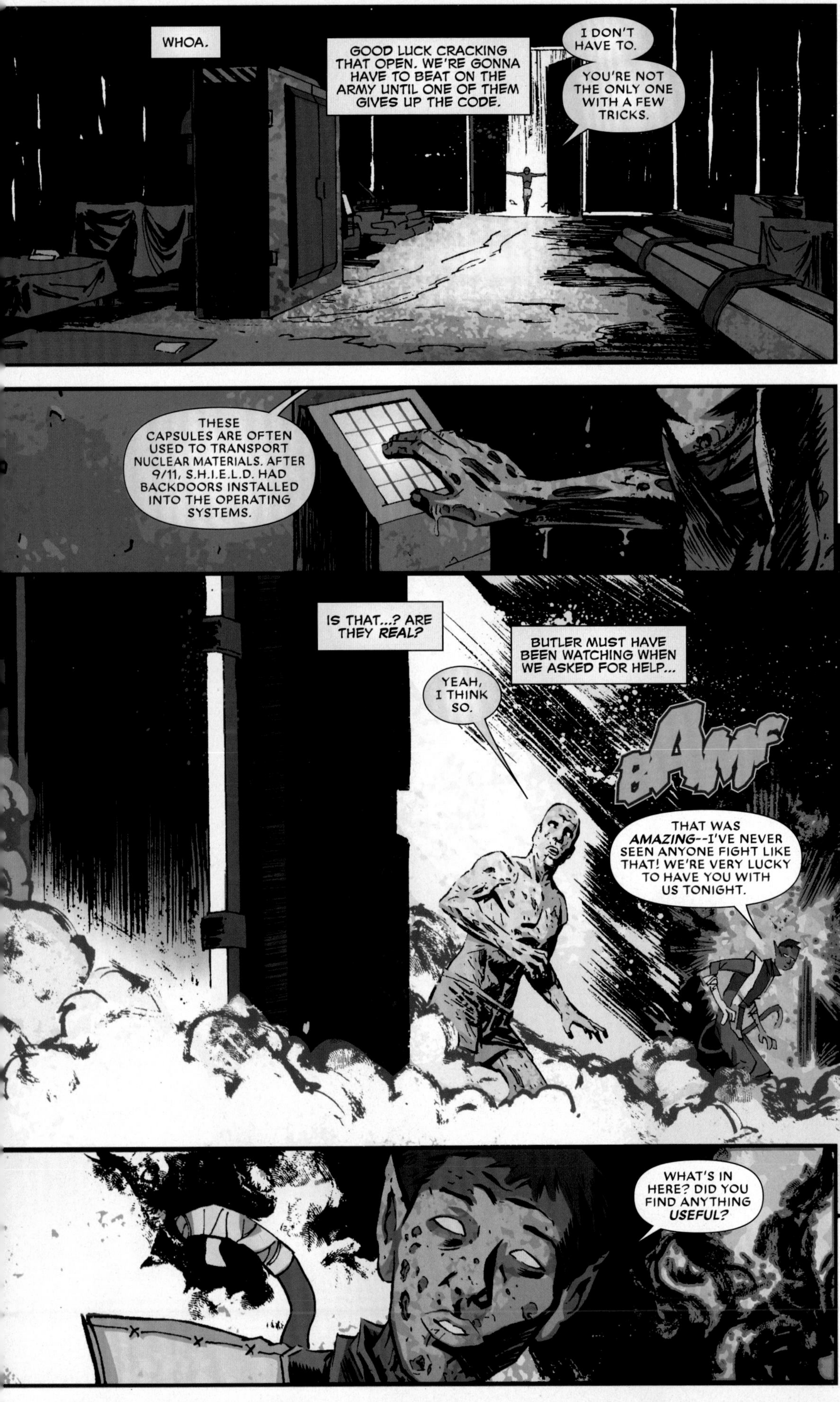
WHOA.
GOOD LUCK CRACKING THAT OPEN. WE'RE GONNA HAVE TO BEAT ON THE ARMY UNTIL ONE OF THEM GIVES UP THE CODE.
I DON'T HAVE TO.
YOU'RE NOT THE ONLY ONE WITH A FEW TRICKS.
THESE CAPSULES ARE OFTEN USED TO TRANSPORT NUCLEAR MATERIALS. AFTER 9/11, S.H.I.E.L.D. HAD BACKDOORS INSTALLED INTO THE OPERATING SYSTEMS.
IS THAT...? ARE THEY *REAL?*
BUTLER MUST HAVE BEEN WATCHING WHEN WE ASKED FOR HELP...
YEAH, I THINK SO.
BAMF
THAT WAS *AMAZING*--I'VE NEVER SEEN ANYONE FIGHT LIKE THAT! WE'RE VERY LUCKY TO HAVE YOU WITH US TONIGHT.
WHAT'S IN HERE? DID YOU FIND ANYTHING *USEFUL?*

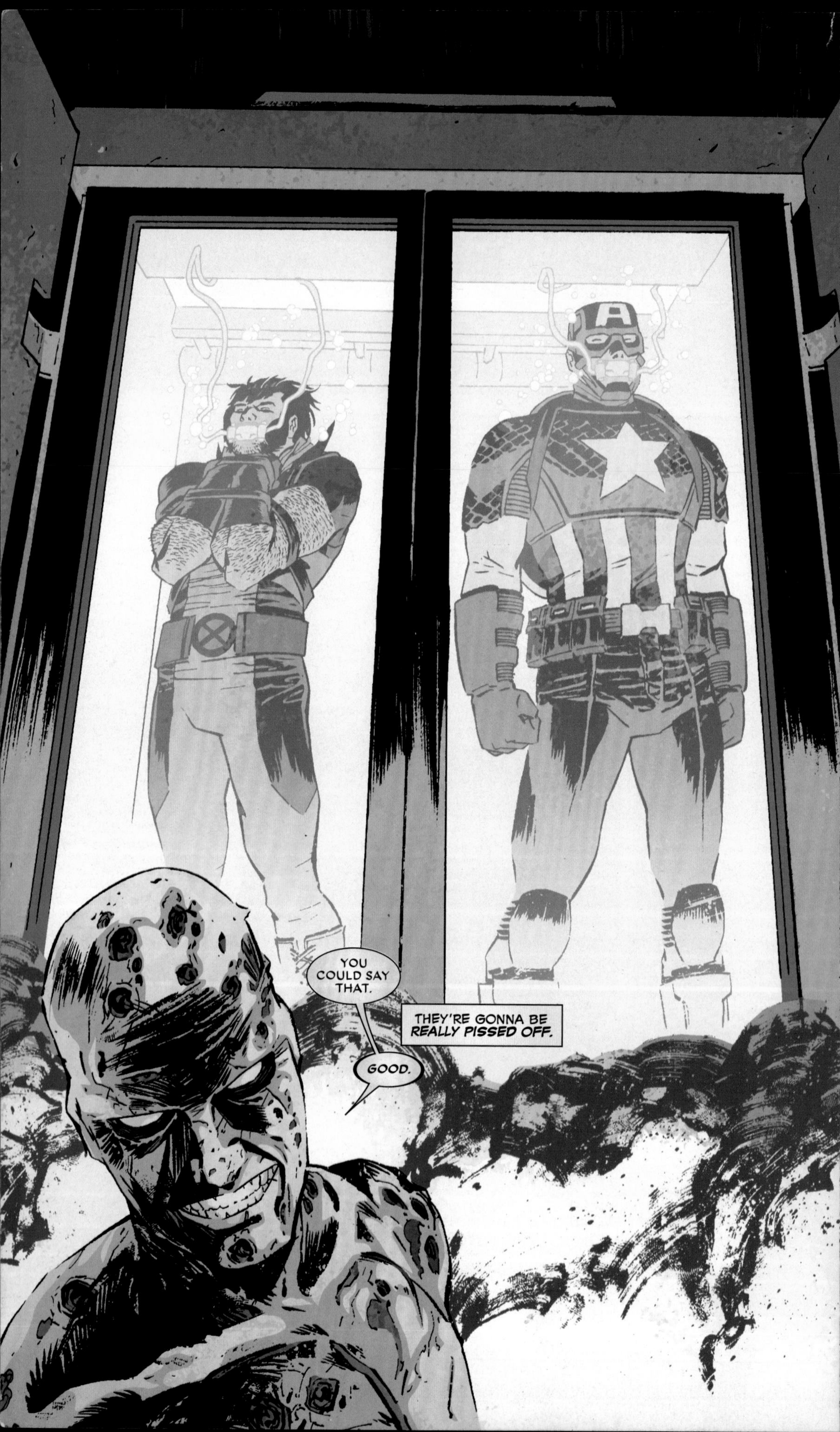
YOU COULD SAY THAT.
THEY'RE GONNA BE *REALLY PISSED OFF.*
GOOD.

17

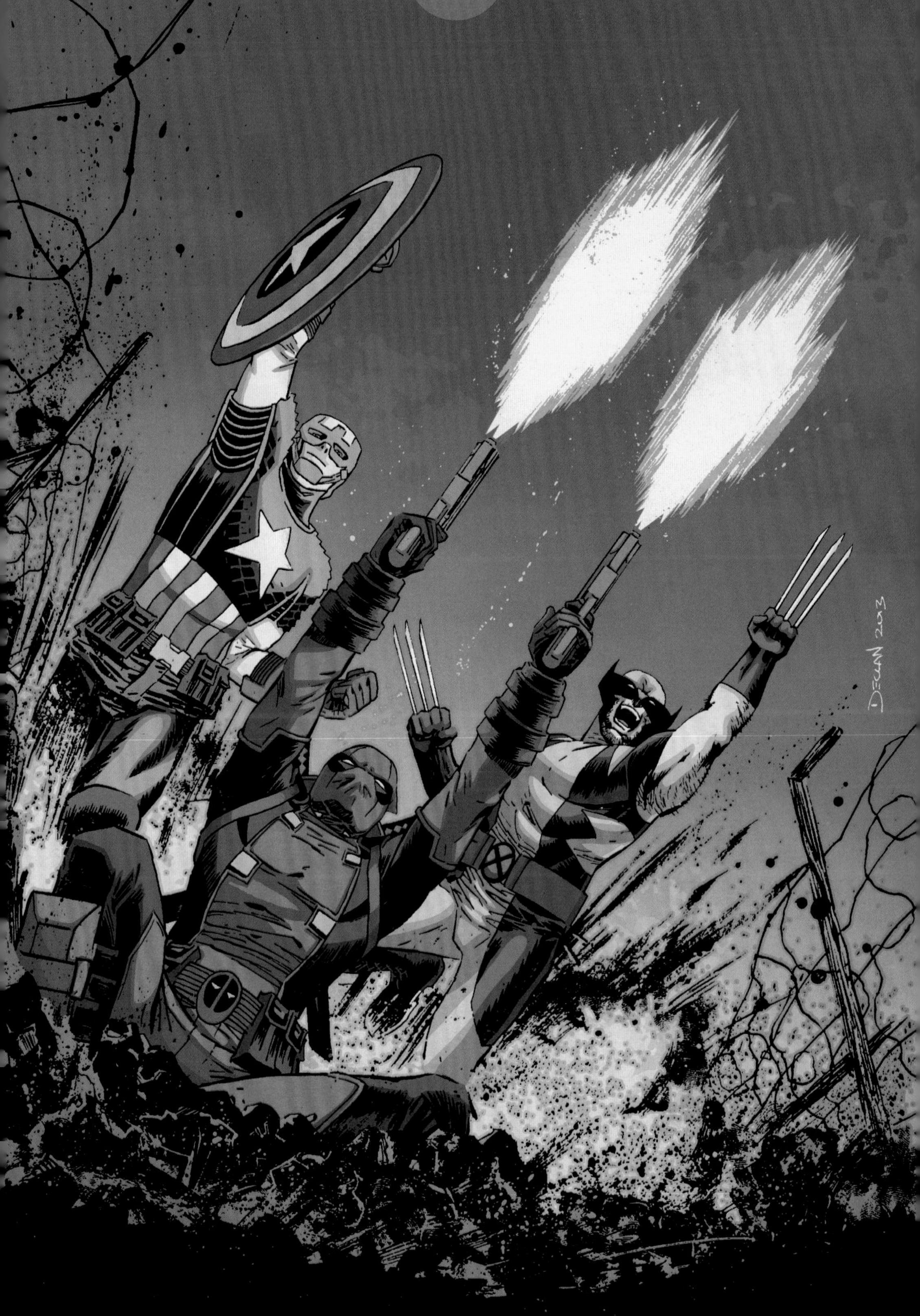
DECLAN 2013

THE GOOD, THE BAD AND THE UGLY PART THREE

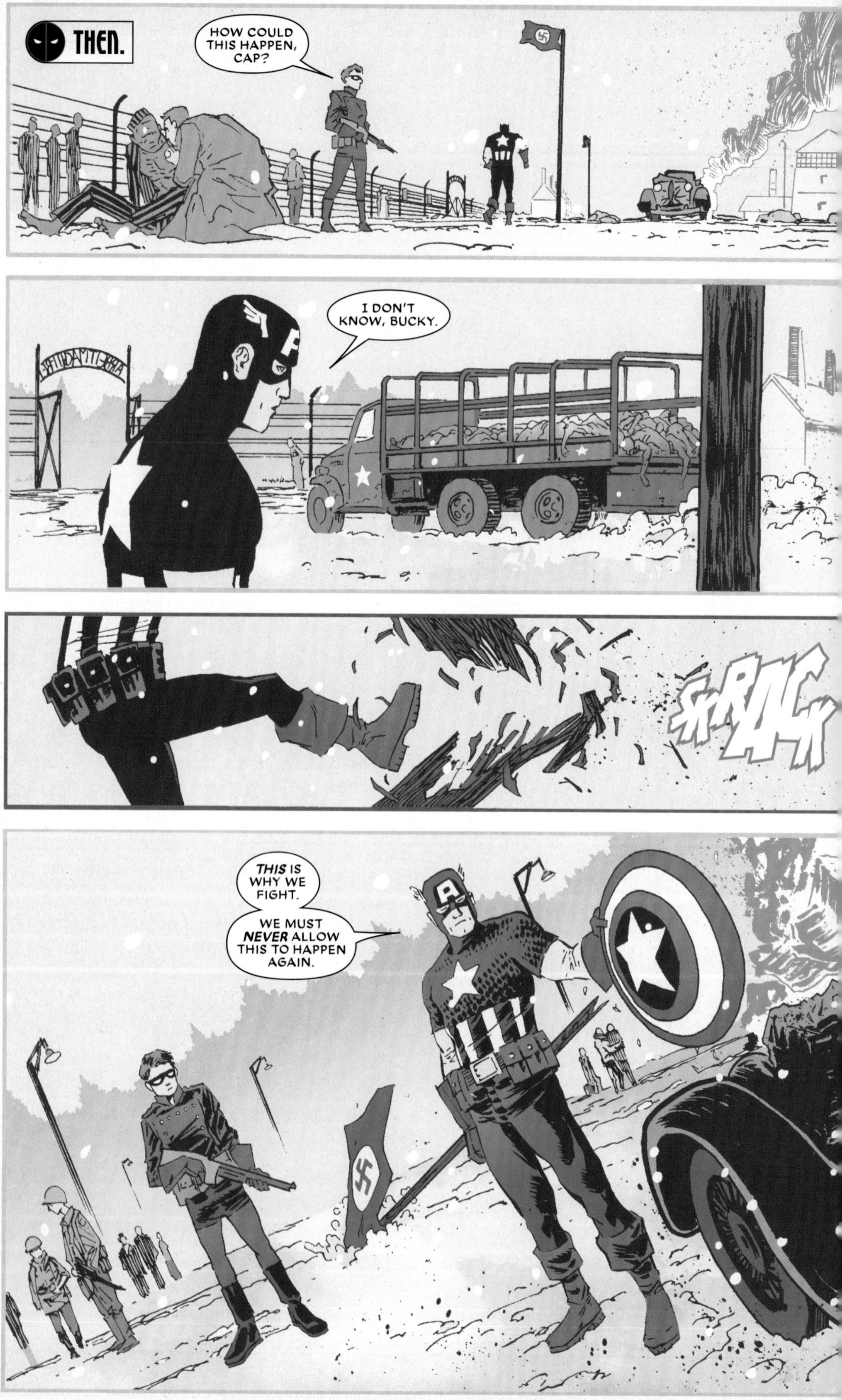
THEN.
HOW COULD THIS HAPPEN, CAP?
I DON'T KNOW, BUCKY.
SKRACK
THIS IS WHY WE FIGHT.
WE MUST NEVER ALLOW THIS TO HAPPEN AGAIN.

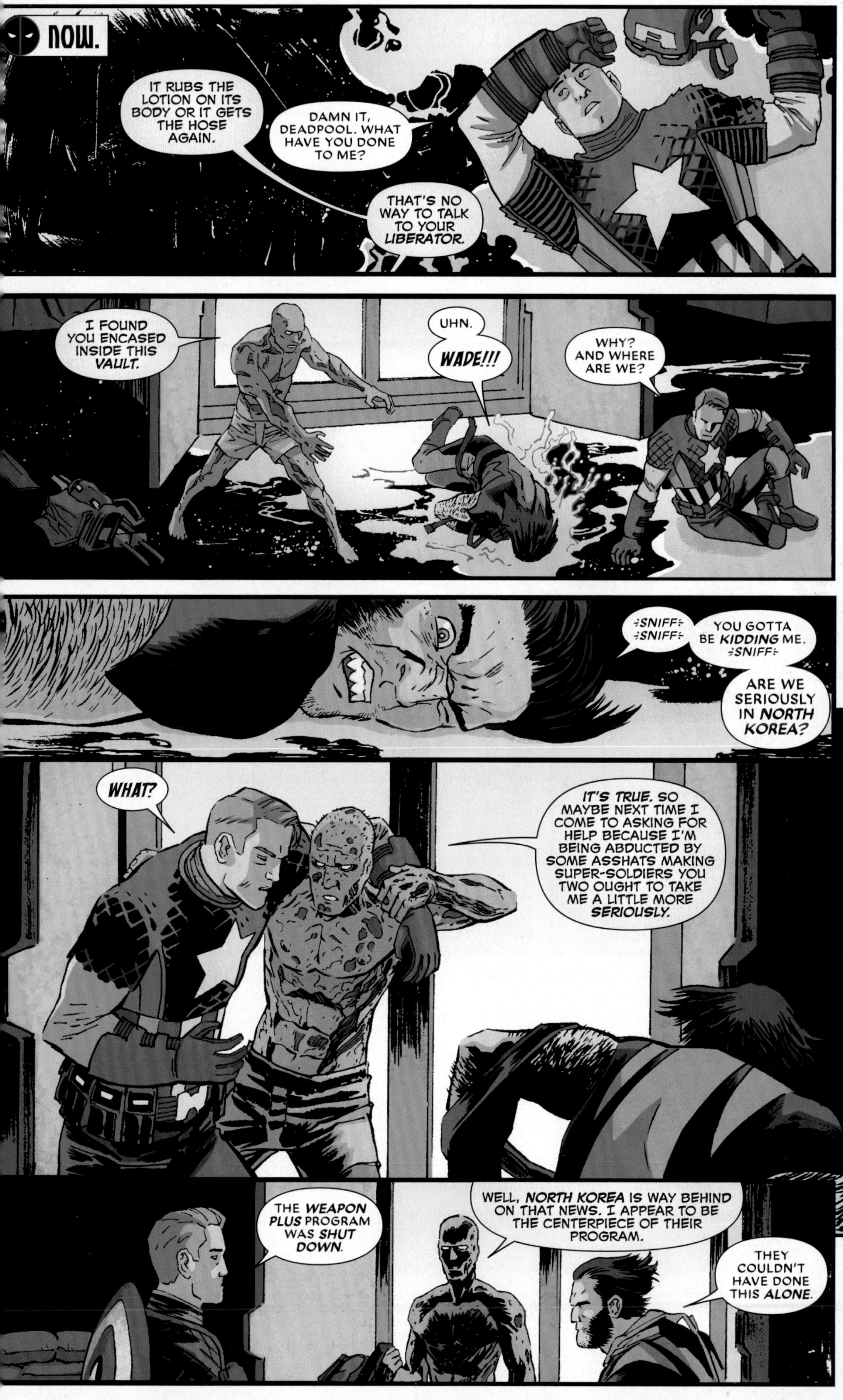
NOW.
IT RUBS THE LOTION ON ITS BODY OR IT GETS THE HOSE AGAIN.
DAMN IT, DEADPOOL. WHAT HAVE YOU DONE TO ME?
THAT'S NO WAY TO TALK TO YOUR LIBERATOR.
I FOUND YOU ENCASED INSIDE THIS VAULT.
UHN.
WADE!!!
WHY? AND WHERE ARE WE?
SNIFF SNIFF
YOU GOTTA BE KIDDING ME. SNIFF
ARE WE SERIOUSLY IN NORTH KOREA?
WHAT?
IT'S TRUE. SO MAYBE NEXT TIME I COME TO ASKING FOR HELP BECAUSE I'M BEING ABDUCTED BY SOME ASSHATS MAKING SUPER-SOLDIERS YOU TWO OUGHT TO TAKE ME A LITTLE MORE SERIOUSLY.
THE WEAPON PLUS PROGRAM WAS SHUT DOWN.
WELL, NORTH KOREA IS WAY BEHIND ON THAT NEWS. I APPEAR TO BE THE CENTERPIECE OF THEIR PROGRAM.
THEY COULDN'T HAVE DONE THIS ALONE.

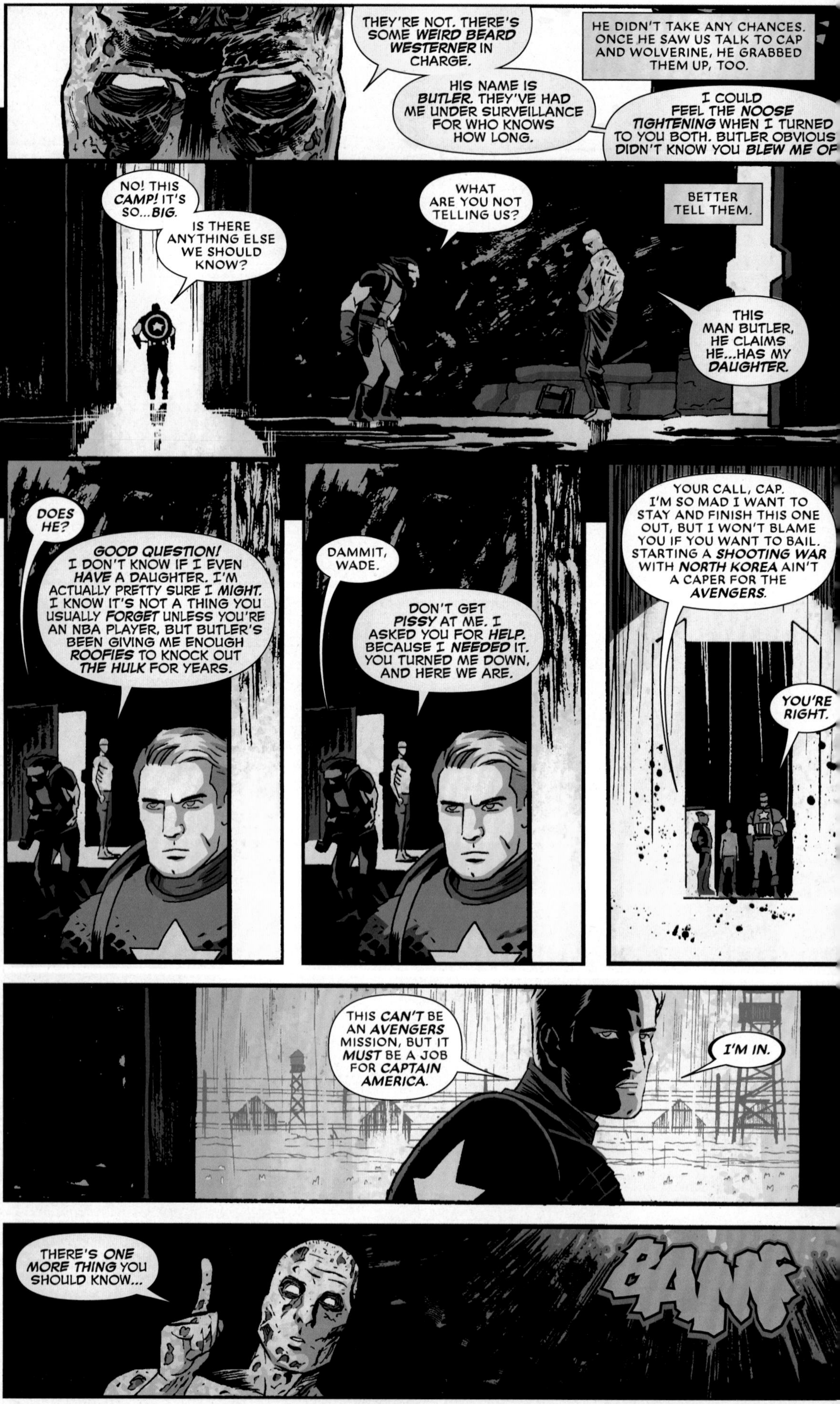

THEY'RE NOT. THERE'S SOME WEIRD BEARD WESTERNER IN CHARGE.
HIS NAME IS BUTLER. THEY'VE HAD ME UNDER SURVEILLANCE FOR WHO KNOWS HOW LONG.
HE DIDN'T TAKE ANY CHANCES. ONCE HE SAW US TALK TO CAP AND WOLVERINE, HE GRABBED THEM UP, TOO.
I COULD FEEL THE NOOSE TIGHTENING WHEN I TURNED TO YOU BOTH. BUTLER OBVIOUS DIDN'T KNOW YOU BLEW ME OF
NO! THIS CAMP! IT'S SO...BIG.
IS THERE ANYTHING ELSE WE SHOULD KNOW?
WHAT ARE YOU NOT TELLING US?
BETTER TELL THEM.
THIS MAN BUTLER, HE CLAIMS HE...HAS MY DAUGHTER.
DOES HE?
GOOD QUESTION! I DON'T KNOW IF I EVEN HAVE A DAUGHTER. I'M ACTUALLY PRETTY SURE I MIGHT. I KNOW IT'S NOT A THING YOU USUALLY FORGET UNLESS YOU'RE AN NBA PLAYER, BUT BUTLER'S BEEN GIVING ME ENOUGH ROOFIES TO KNOCK OUT THE HULK FOR YEARS.
DAMMIT, WADE.
DON'T GET PISSY AT ME. I ASKED YOU FOR HELP. BECAUSE I NEEDED IT. YOU TURNED ME DOWN, AND HERE WE ARE.
YOUR CALL, CAP. I'M SO MAD I WANT TO STAY AND FINISH THIS ONE OUT, BUT I WON'T BLAME YOU IF YOU WANT TO BAIL. STARTING A SHOOTING WAR WITH NORTH KOREA AIN'T A CAPER FOR THE AVENGERS.
YOU'RE RIGHT.
THIS CAN'T BE AN AVENGERS MISSION, BUT IT MUST BE A JOB FOR CAPTAIN AMERICA.
I'M IN.
THERE'S ONE MORE THING YOU SHOULD KNOW...
BAM

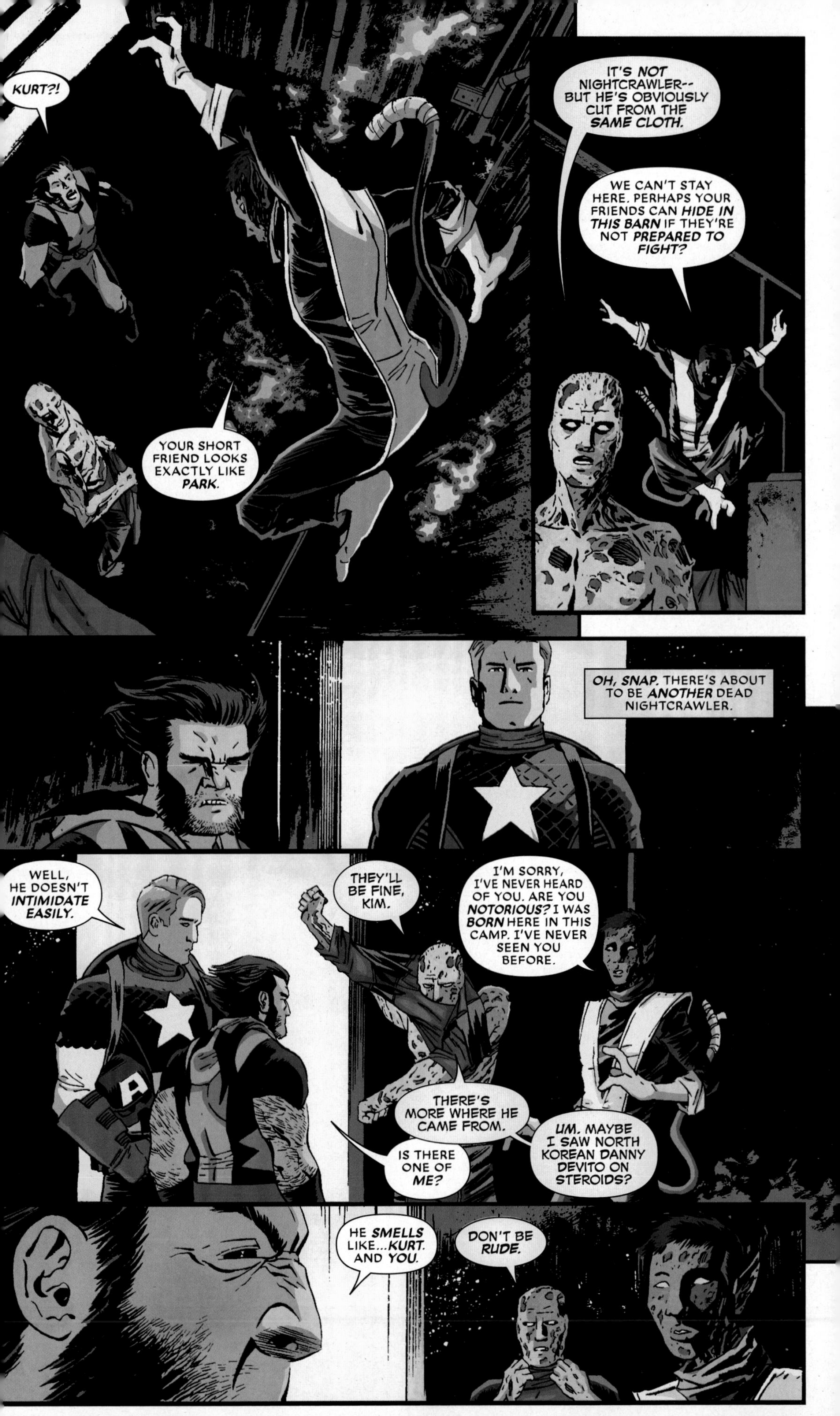
KURT?!
YOUR SHORT FRIEND LOOKS EXACTLY LIKE PARK.
IT'S NOT NIGHTCRAWLER-- BUT HE'S OBVIOUSLY CUT FROM THE SAME CLOTH.
WE CAN'T STAY HERE. PERHAPS YOUR FRIENDS CAN HIDE IN THIS BARN IF THEY'RE NOT PREPARED TO FIGHT?
OH, SNAP. THERE'S ABOUT TO BE ANOTHER DEAD NIGHTCRAWLER.
WELL, HE DOESN'T INTIMIDATE EASILY.
THEY'LL BE FINE, KIM.
I'M SORRY, I'VE NEVER HEARD OF YOU. ARE YOU NOTORIOUS? I WAS BORN HERE IN THIS CAMP. I'VE NEVER SEEN YOU BEFORE.
THERE'S MORE WHERE HE CAME FROM.
IS THERE ONE OF ME?
UM. MAYBE I SAW NORTH KOREAN DANNY DEVITO ON STEROIDS?
HE SMELLS LIKE...KURT. AND YOU.
DON'T BE RUDE.

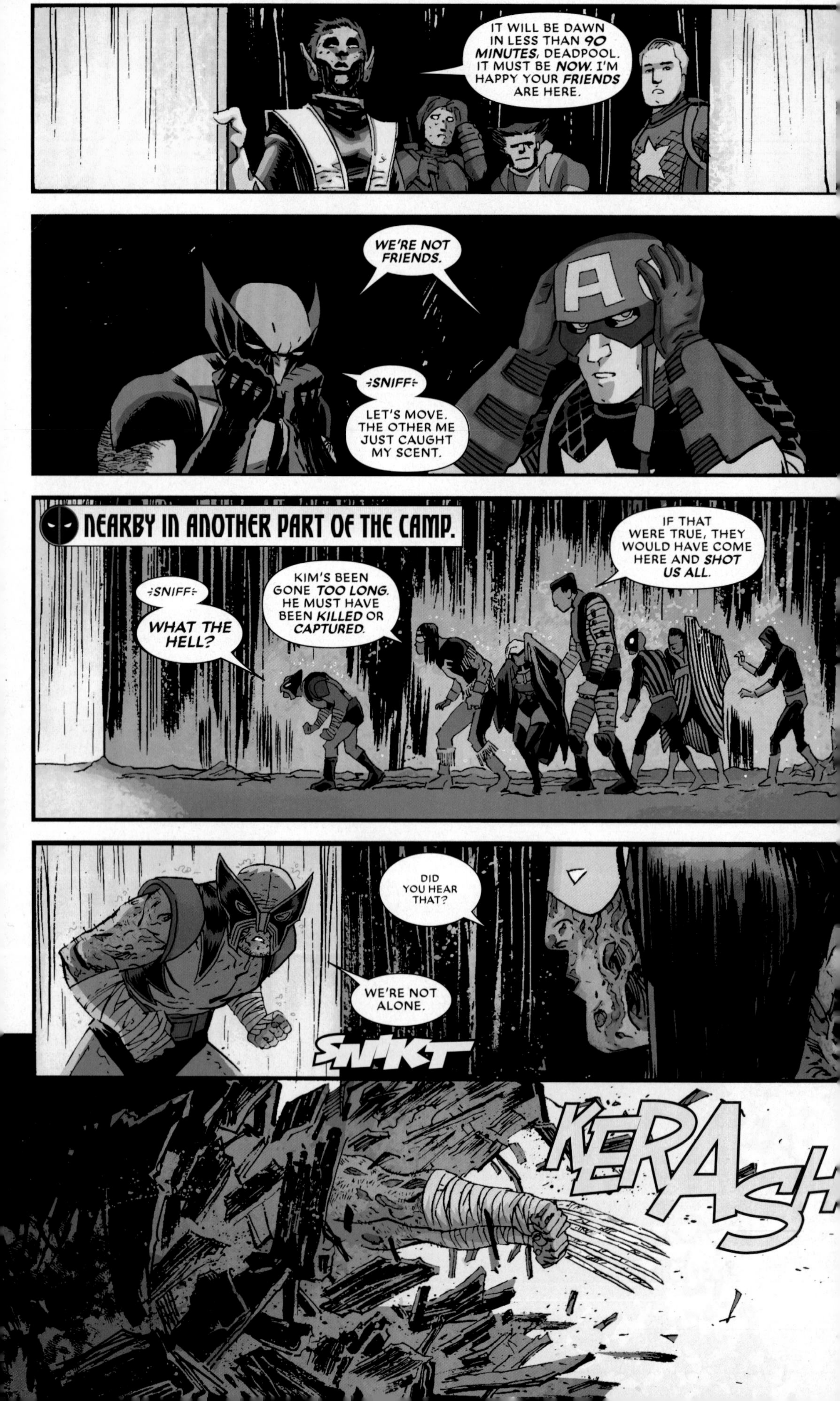
IT WILL BE DAWN IN LESS THAN 90 MINUTES, DEADPOOL. IT MUST BE NOW. I'M HAPPY YOUR FRIENDS ARE HERE.
WE'RE NOT FRIENDS.
=SNIFF=
LET'S MOVE. THE OTHER ME JUST CAUGHT MY SCENT.
NEARBY IN ANOTHER PART OF THE CAMP.
=SNIFF=
WHAT THE HELL?
KIM'S BEEN GONE TOO LONG. HE MUST HAVE BEEN KILLED OR CAPTURED.
IF THAT WERE TRUE, THEY WOULD HAVE COME HERE AND SHOT US ALL.
DID YOU HEAR THAT?
WE'RE NOT ALONE.
SNIKT
KERASH

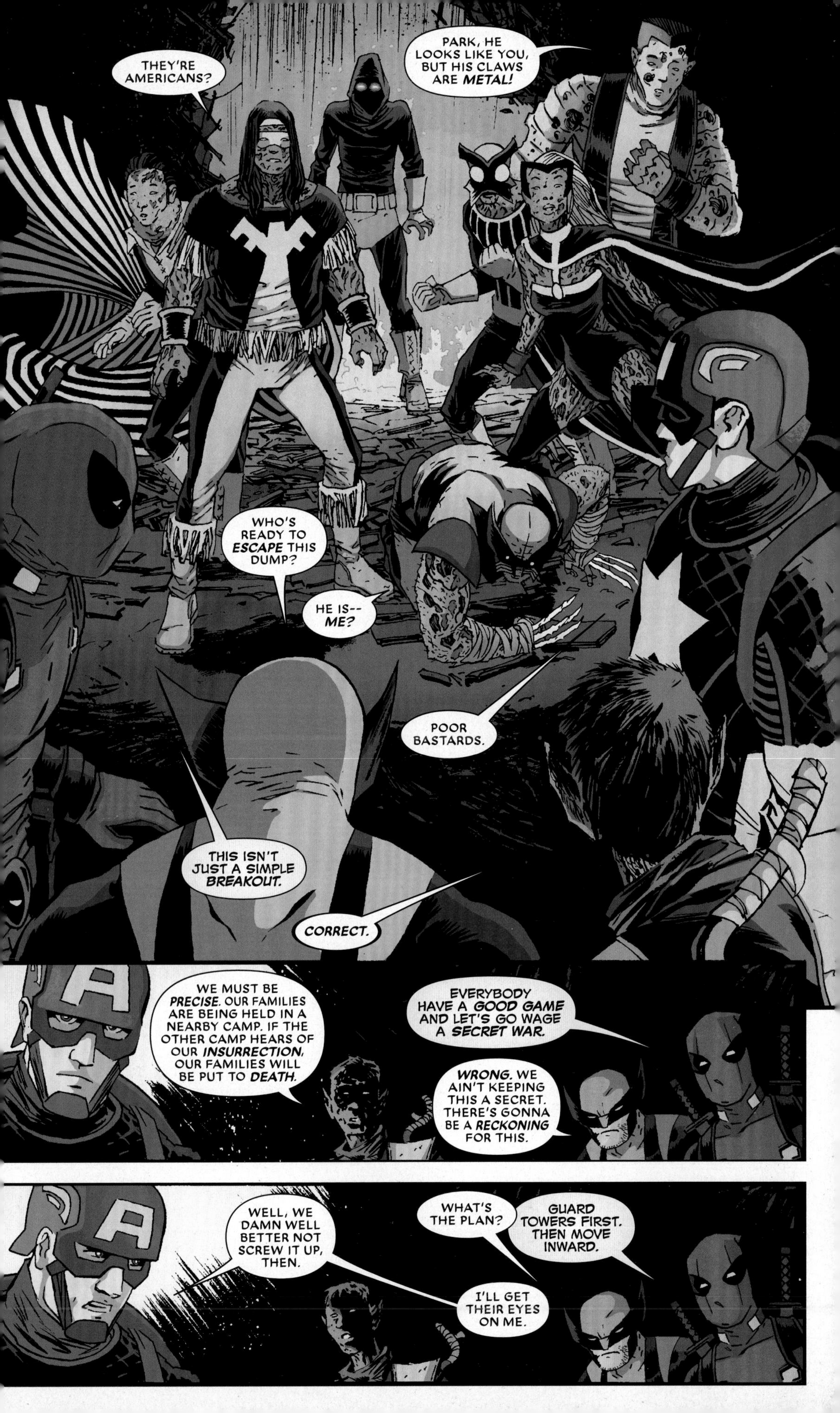
THEY'RE AMERICANS?
PARK, HE LOOKS LIKE YOU, BUT HIS CLAWS ARE METAL!
WHO'S READY TO ESCAPE THIS DUMP?
HE IS-- ME?
POOR BASTARDS.
THIS ISN'T JUST A SIMPLE BREAKOUT.
CORRECT.
WE MUST BE PRECISE. OUR FAMILIES ARE BEING HELD IN A NEARBY CAMP. IF THE OTHER CAMP HEARS OF OUR INSURRECTION, OUR FAMILIES WILL BE PUT TO DEATH.
EVERYBODY HAVE A GOOD GAME AND LET'S GO WAGE A SECRET WAR.
WRONG. WE AIN'T KEEPING THIS A SECRET. THERE'S GONNA BE A RECKONING FOR THIS.
WELL, WE DAMN WELL BETTER NOT SCREW IT UP, THEN.
WHAT'S THE PLAN?
GUARD TOWERS FIRST. THEN MOVE INWARD.
I'LL GET THEIR EYES ON ME.

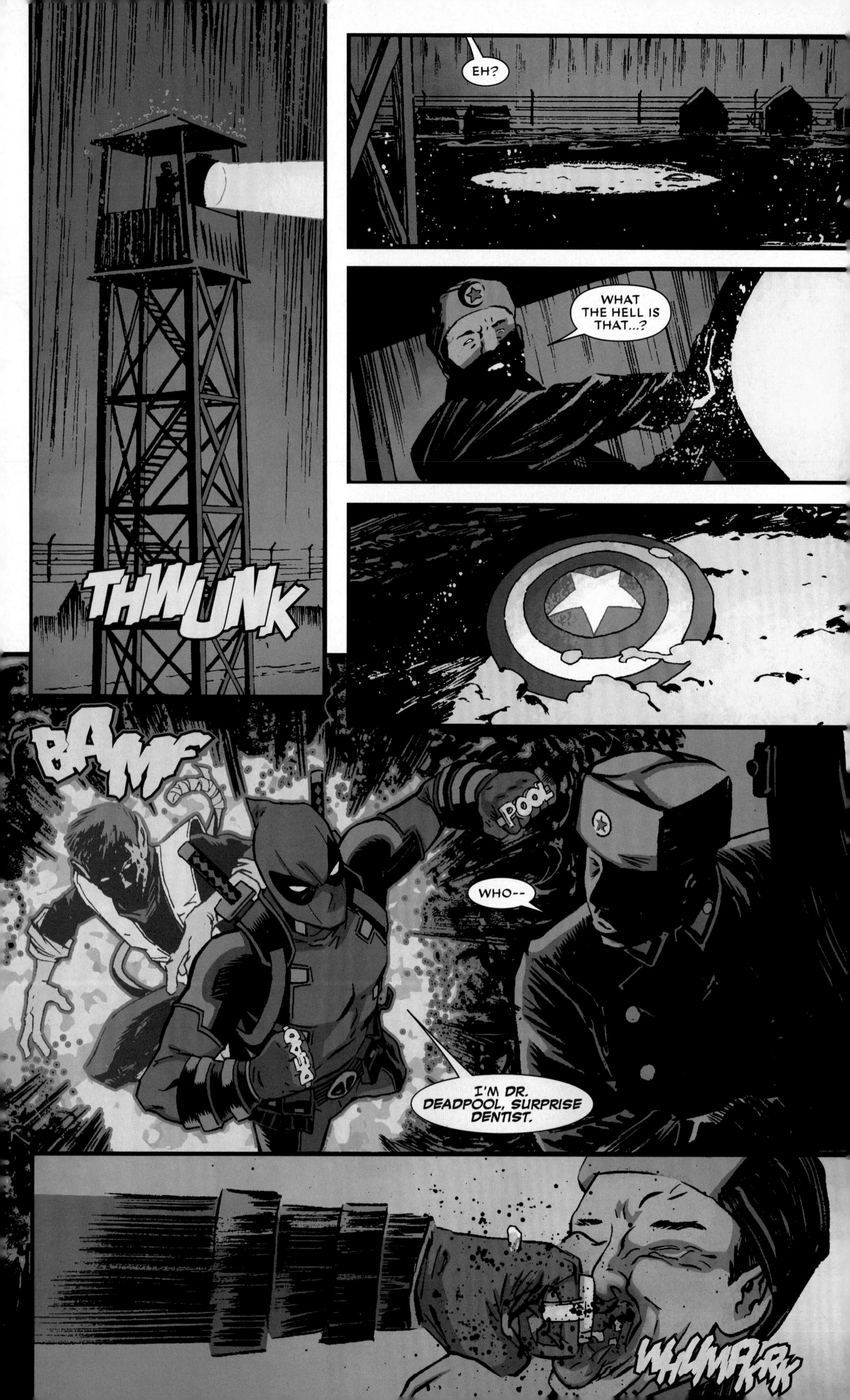
EH?
WHAT THE HELL IS THAT...?
THWUNK
BAMF
WHO--
I'M DR. DEADPOOL, SURPRISE DENTIST.
WHUMPKRK

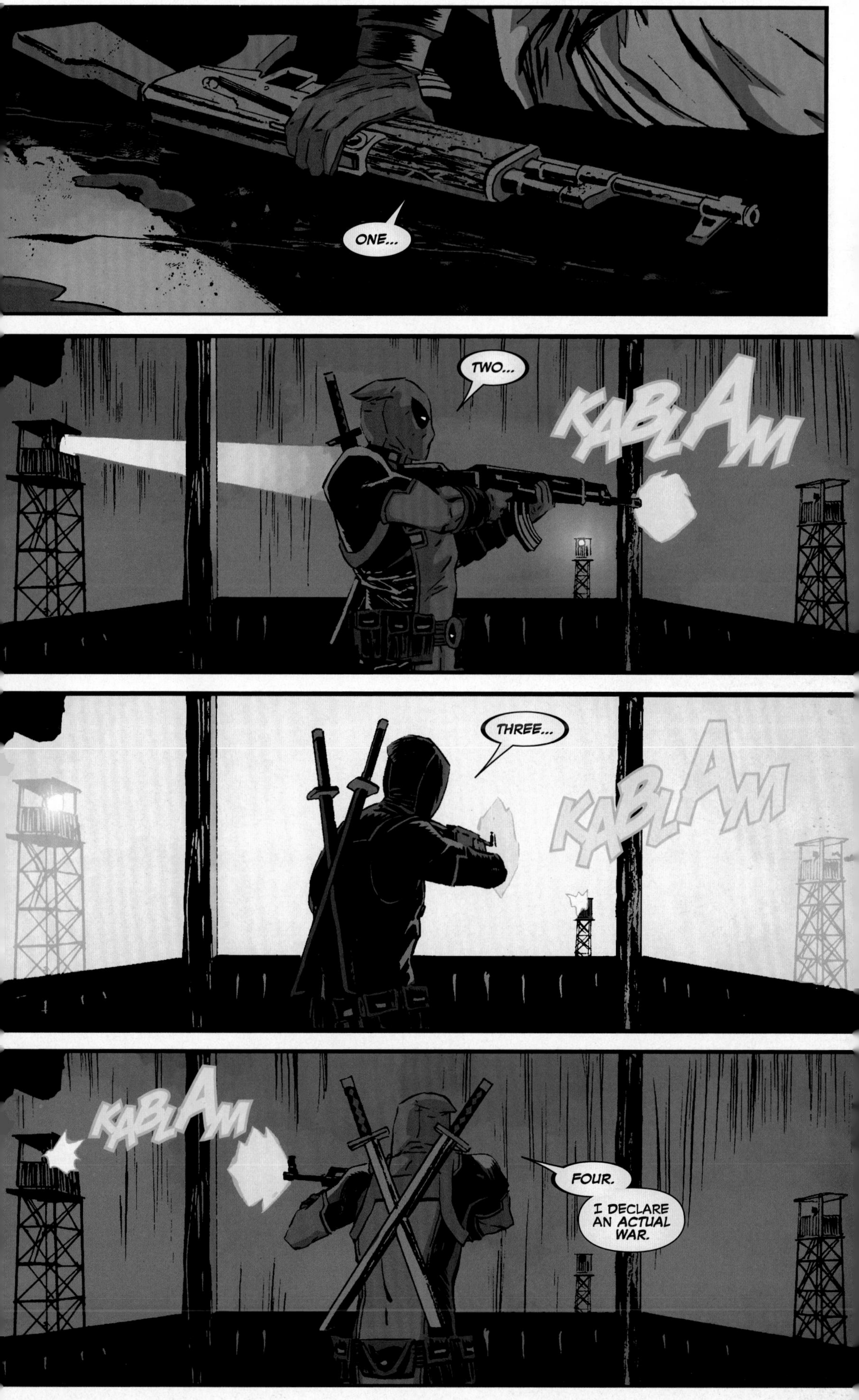
ONE...
TWO...
KABLAM
THREE...
KABLAM
KABLAM
FOUR.
I DECLARE AN ACTUAL WAR.

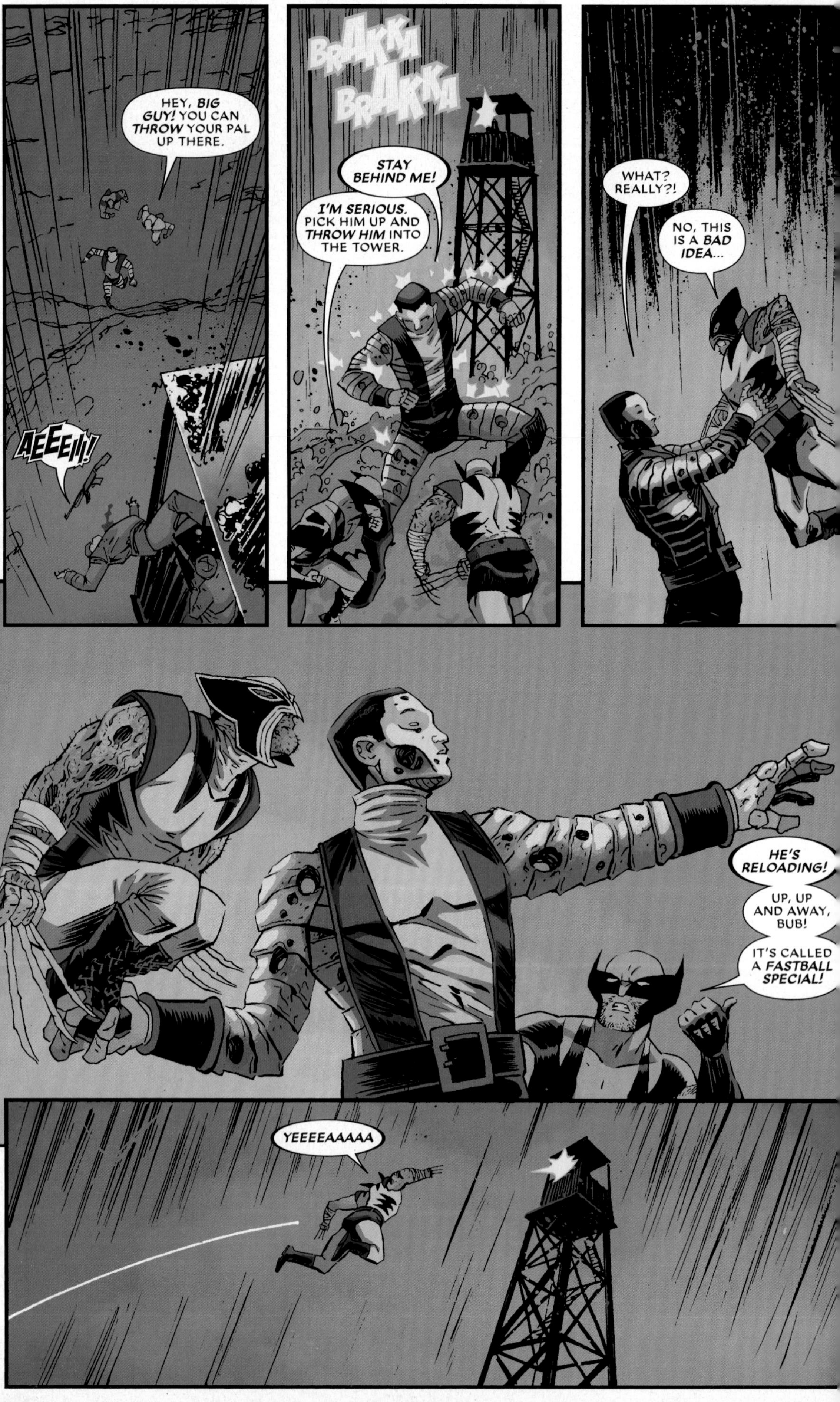
HEY, BIG GUY! YOU CAN THROW YOUR PAL UP THERE.
AEEEIII!
BRAKKA BRAKKA
STAY BEHIND ME!
I'M SERIOUS. PICK HIM UP AND THROW HIM INTO THE TOWER.
WHAT? REALLY?!
NO, THIS IS A BAD IDEA...
HE'S RELOADING!
UP, UP AND AWAY, BUB!
IT'S CALLED A FASTBALL SPECIAL!
YEEEEAAAAA

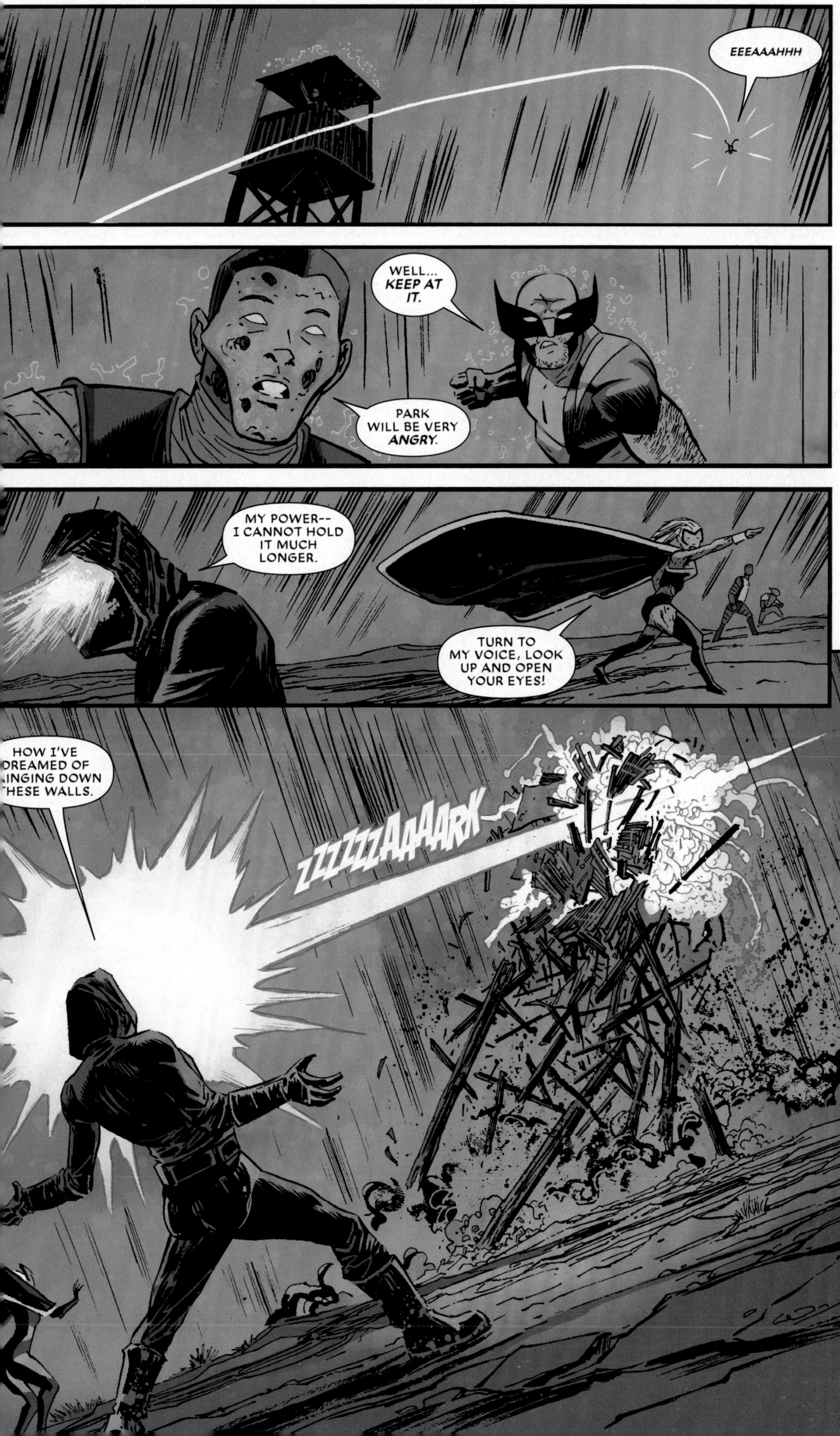

EEEAAAHHH
WELL... KEEP AT IT.
PARK WILL BE VERY ANGRY.
MY POWER-- I CANNOT HOLD IT MUCH LONGER.
TURN TO MY VOICE, LOOK UP AND OPEN YOUR EYES!
HOW I'VE DREAMED OF INGING DOWN THESE WALLS.
ZZZZZZAAAARK

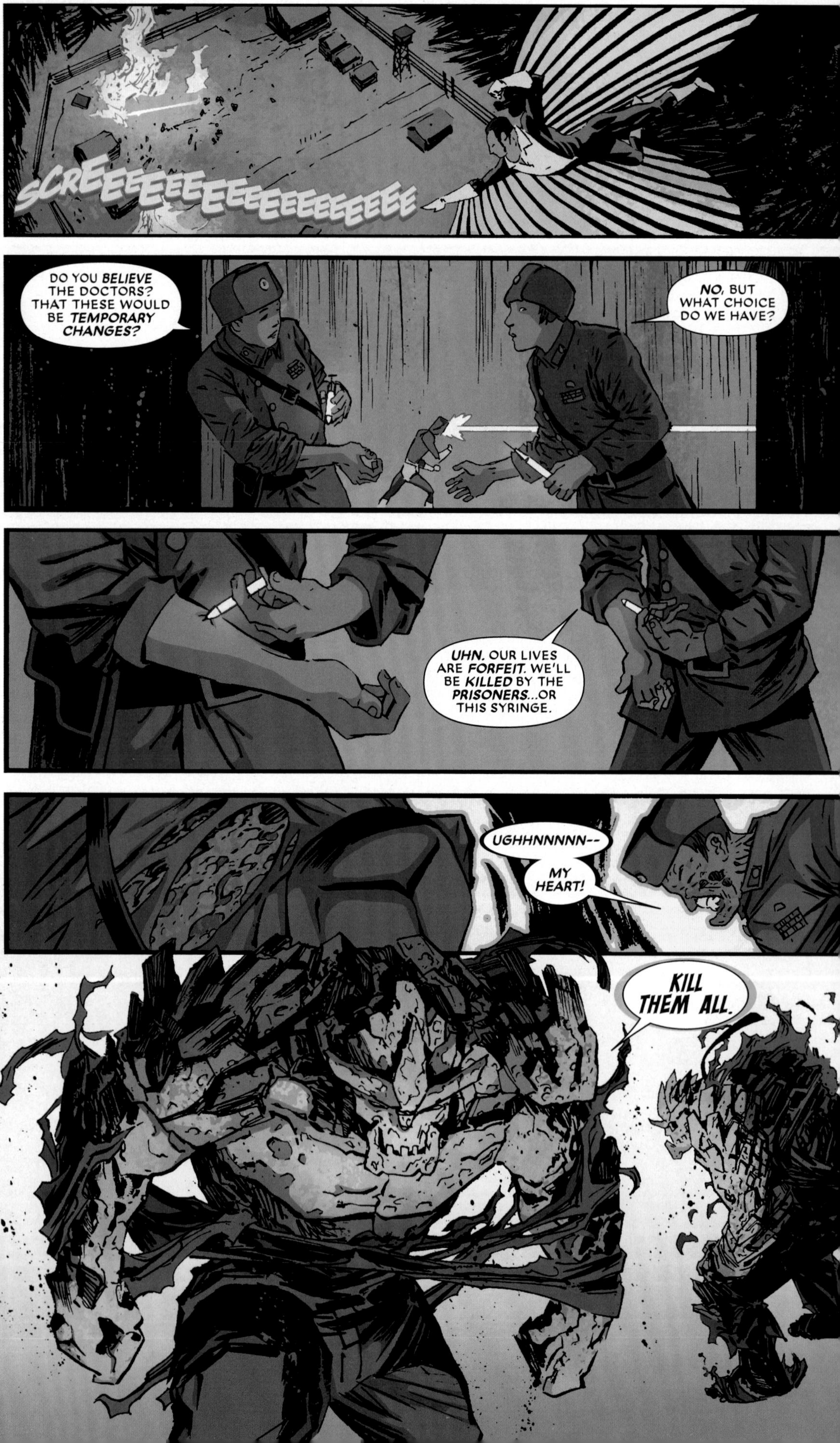
SCREEEEEEEEEEEEEEEEEEE
DO YOU *BELIEVE* THE DOCTORS? THAT THESE WOULD BE *TEMPORARY CHANGES?*
NO, BUT WHAT CHOICE DO WE HAVE?
UHN. OUR LIVES ARE *FORFEIT.* WE'LL BE *KILLED* BY THE *PRISONERS*...OR THIS SYRINGE.
UGHHNNNNN--
MY HEART!
KILL THEM ALL.

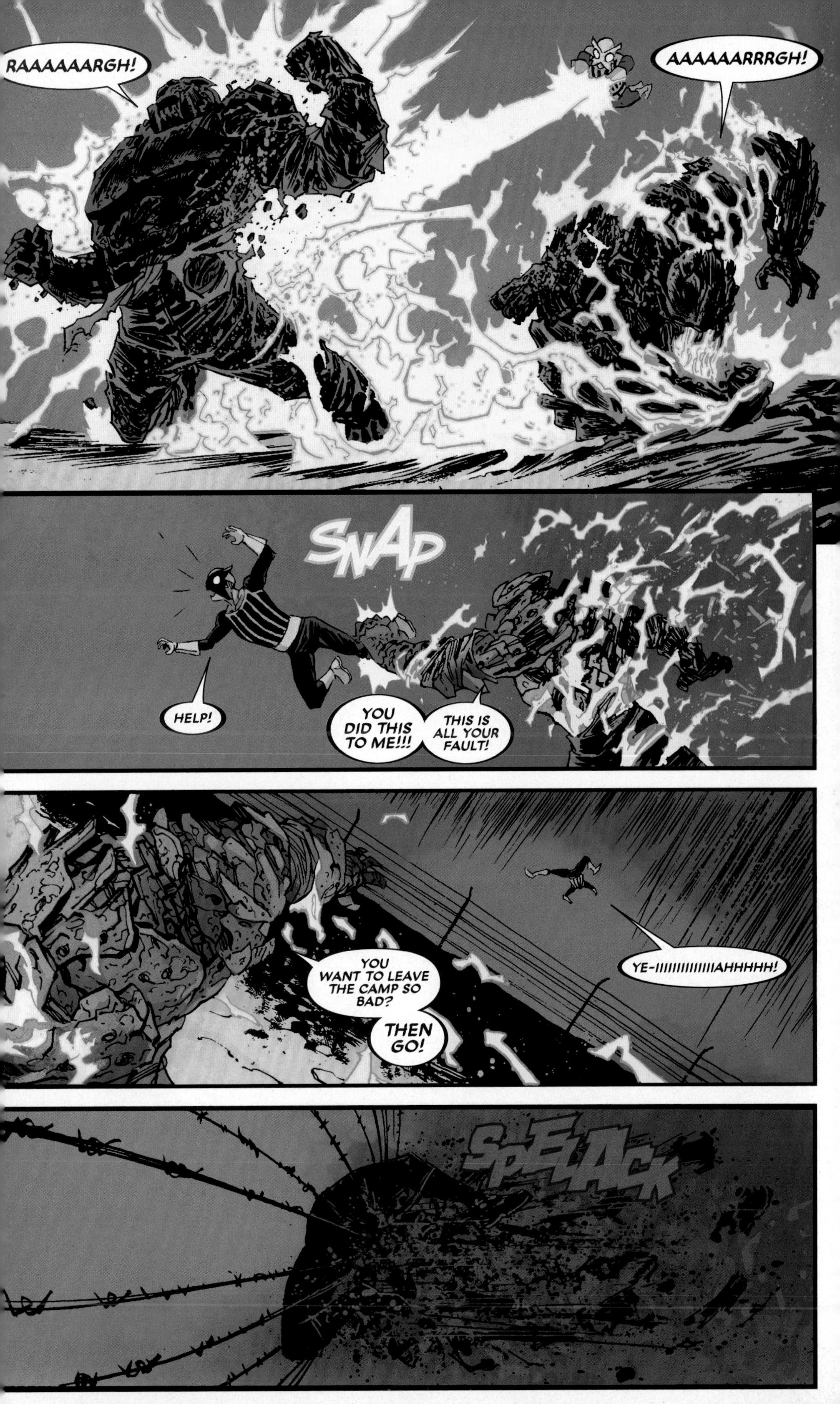
RAAAAAARGH!
AAAAAARRRGH!
SNAP
HELP!
YOU DID THIS TO ME!!!
THIS IS ALL YOUR FAULT!
YOU WANT TO LEAVE THE CAMP SO BAD?
THEN GO!
YE-IIIIIIIIIIIIIAHHHHH!
SPLACK

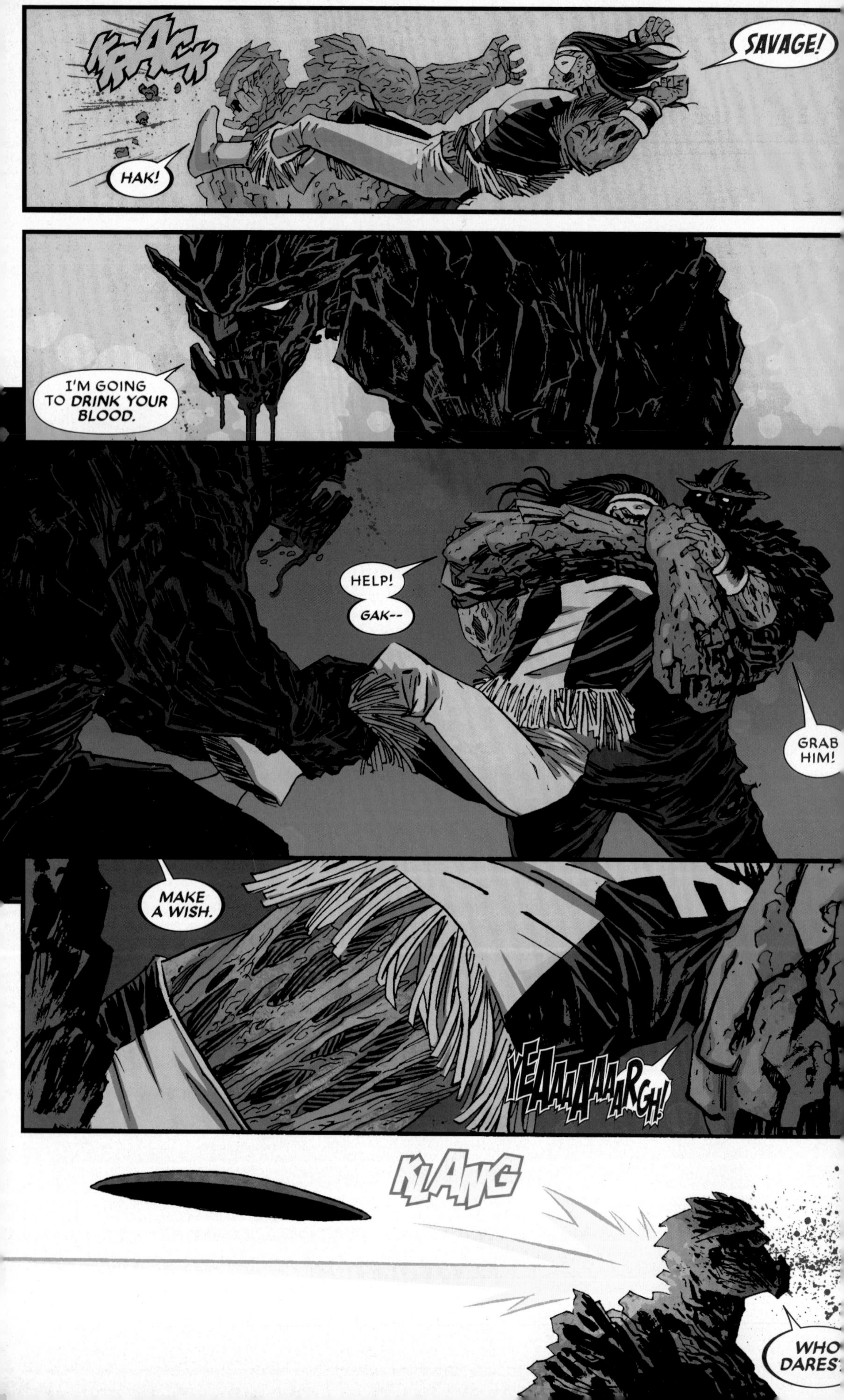
KRACK
SAVAGE!
HAK!
I'M GOING TO DRINK YOUR BLOOD.
HELP!
GAK--
GRAB HIM!
MAKE A WISH.
YEAAAAAAARGH!
KLANG
WHO DARES

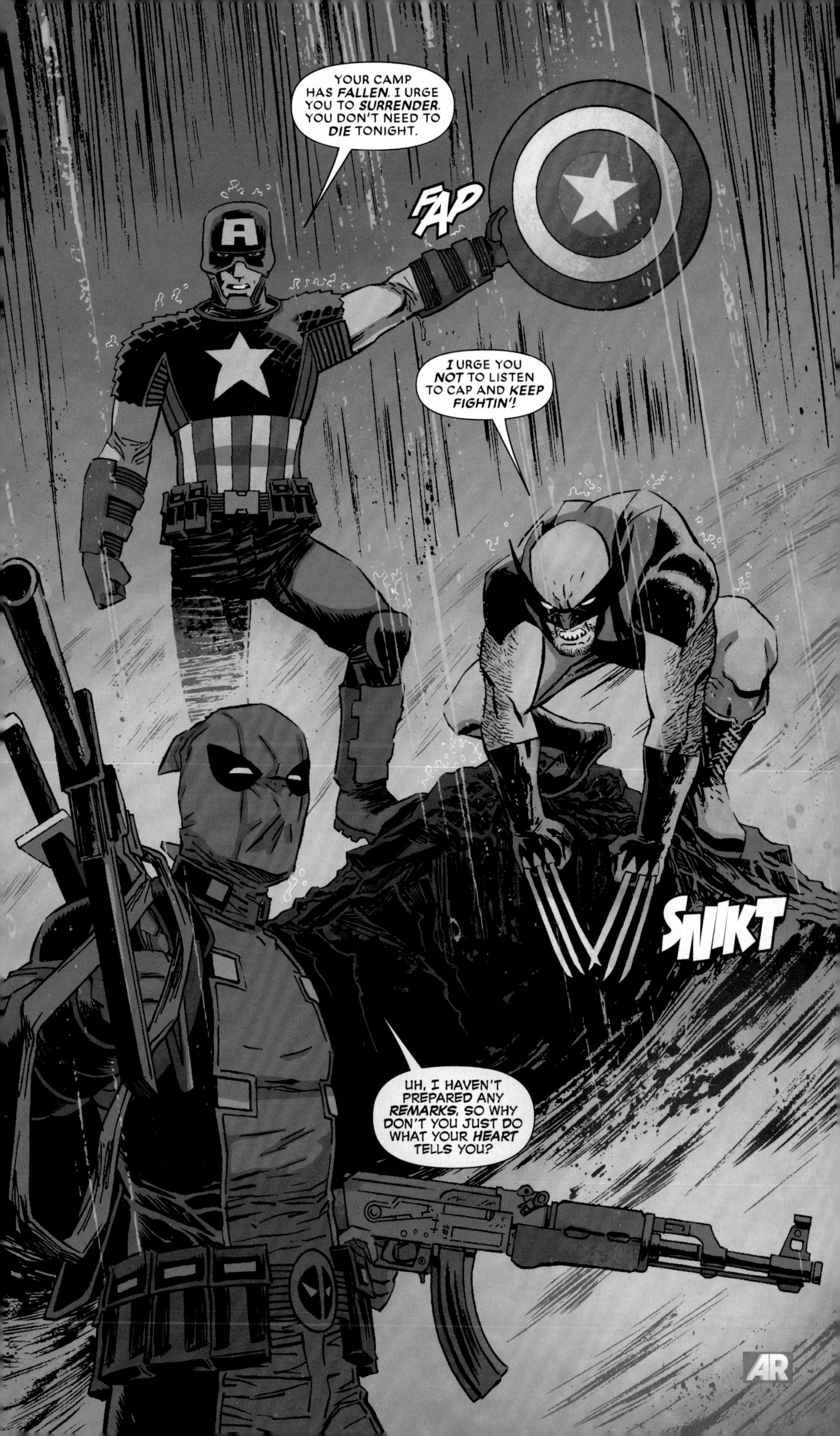
YOUR CAMP HAS FALLEN. I URGE YOU TO SURRENDER. YOU DON'T NEED TO DIE TONIGHT.
FAP
I URGE YOU NOT TO LISTEN TO CAP AND KEEP FIGHTIN'!
SNIKT
UH, I HAVEN'T PREPARED ANY REMARKS, SO WHY DON'T YOU JUST DO WHAT YOUR HEART TELLS YOU?
AR

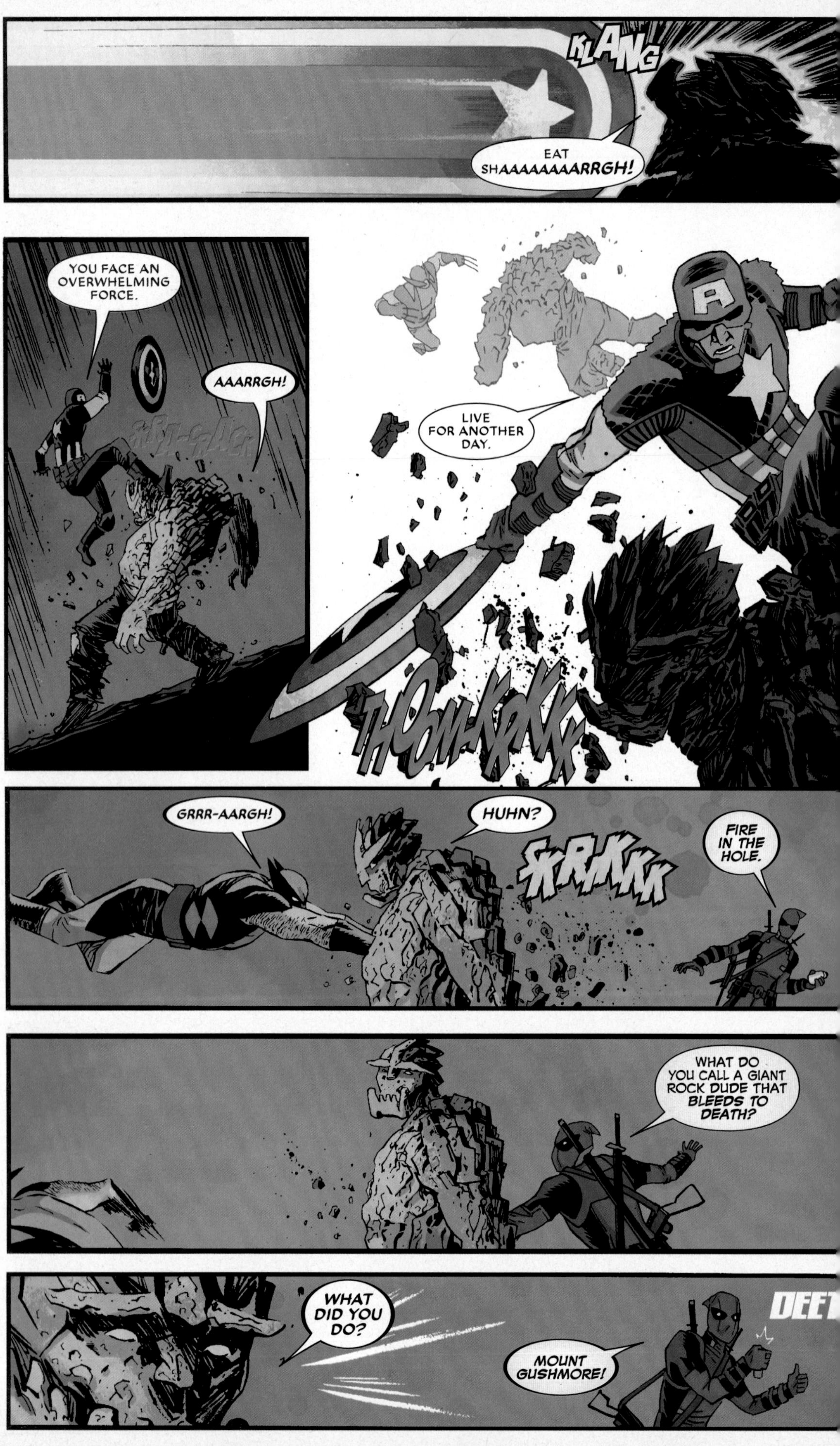
KLANG
EAT SHAAAAAAAARRGH!
YOU FACE AN OVERWHELMING FORCE.
AAARRGH!
LIVE FOR ANOTHER DAY.
THOM-KRKKK
GRRR-AARGH!
HUHN?
SKRAKKK
FIRE IN THE HOLE.
WHAT DO YOU CALL A GIANT ROCK DUDE THAT BLEEDS TO DEATH?
WHAT DID YOU DO?
MOUNT GUSHMORE!
DEET

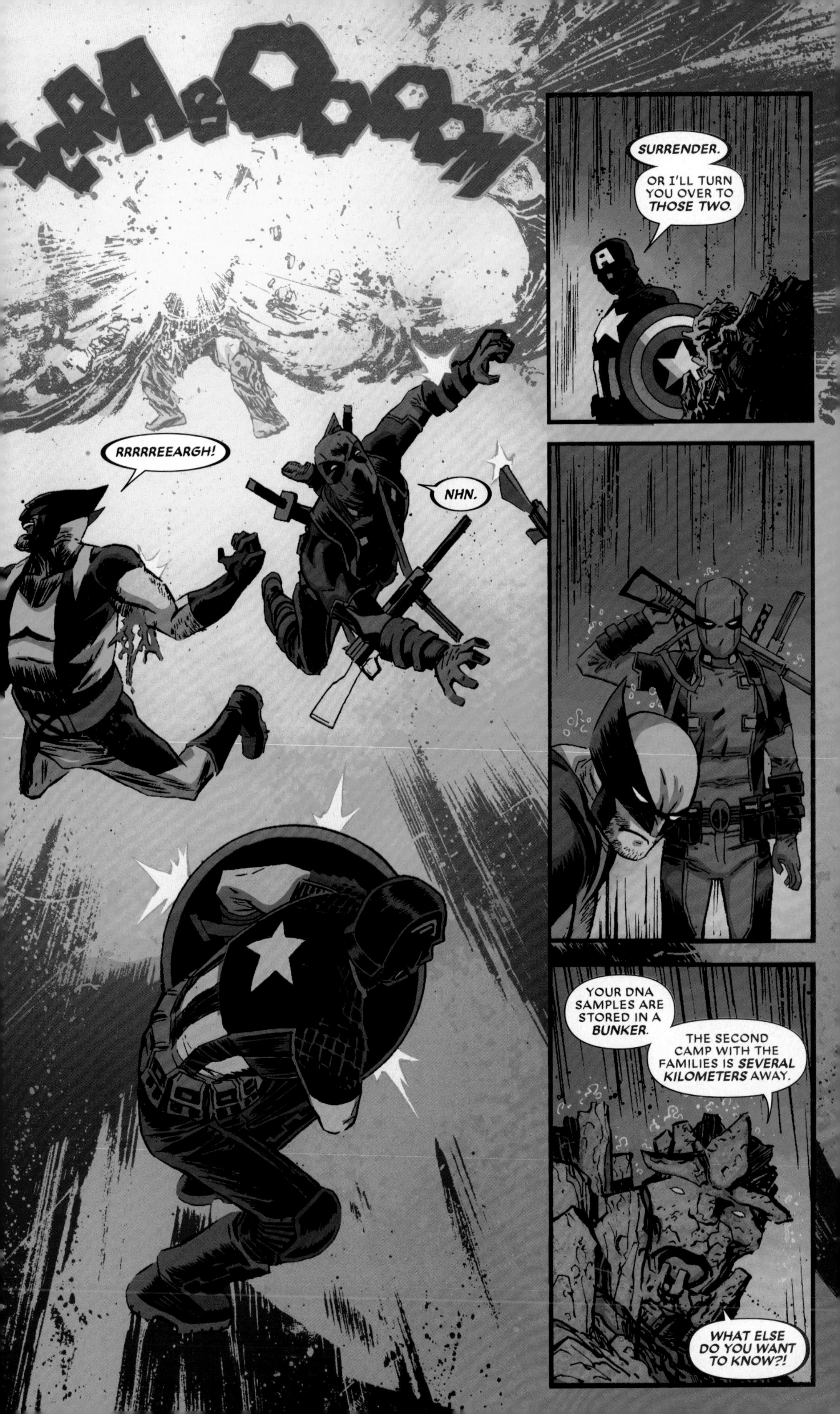
SKRABOOOOOM
RRRRRREEARGH!
NHN.
SURRENDER.
OR I'LL TURN YOU OVER TO THOSE TWO.
YOUR DNA SAMPLES ARE STORED IN A BUNKER.
THE SECOND CAMP WITH THE FAMILIES IS SEVERAL KILOMETERS AWAY.
WHAT ELSE DO YOU WANT TO KNOW?!

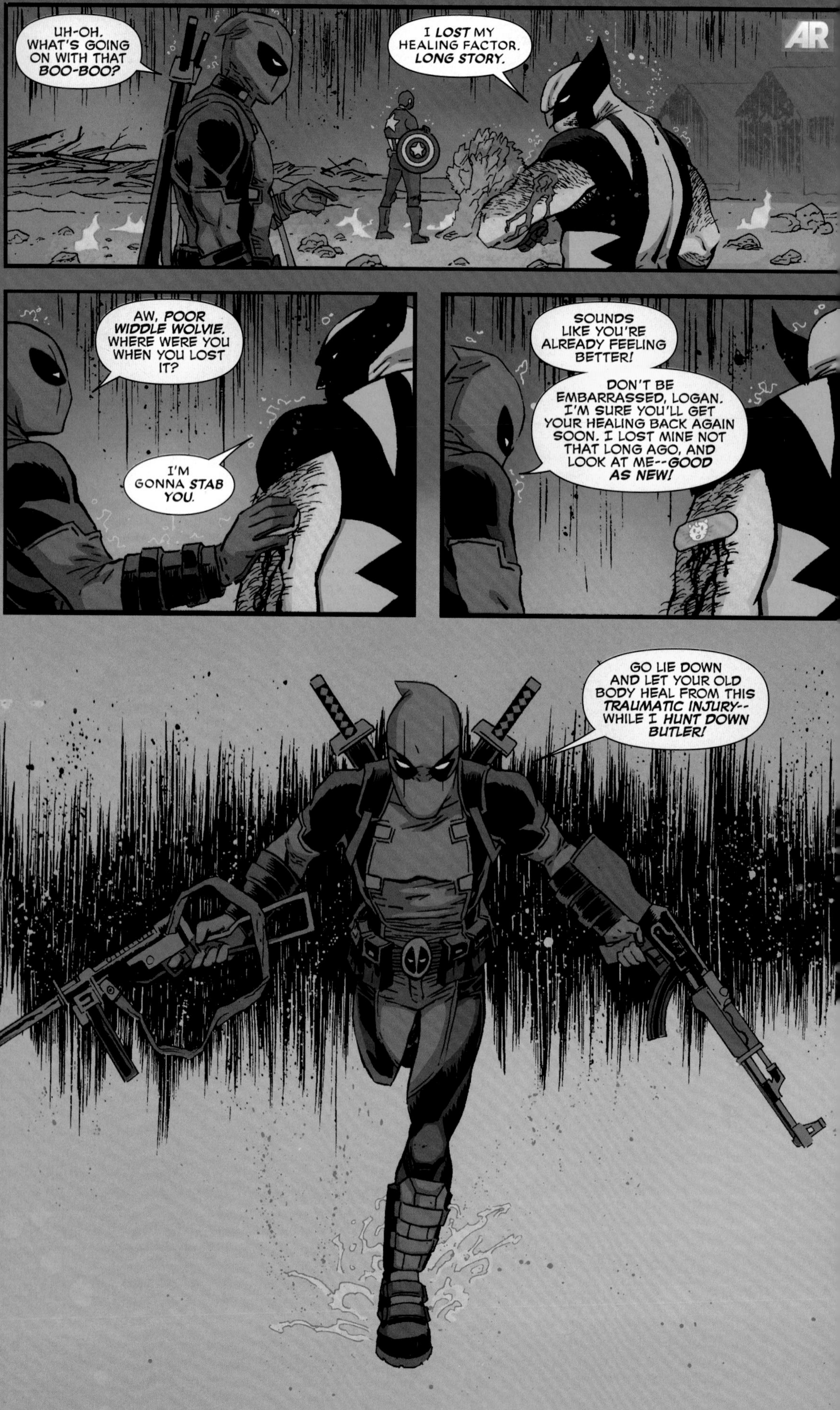
UH-OH. WHAT'S GOING ON WITH THAT BOO-BOO?
I LOST MY HEALING FACTOR. LONG STORY.
AW, POOR WIDDLE WOLVIE. WHERE WERE YOU WHEN YOU LOST IT?
I'M GONNA STAB YOU.
SOUNDS LIKE YOU'RE ALREADY FEELING BETTER!
DON'T BE EMBARRASSED, LOGAN. I'M SURE YOU'LL GET YOUR HEALING BACK AGAIN SOON. I LOST MINE NOT THAT LONG AGO, AND LOOK AT ME--GOOD AS NEW!
GO LIE DOWN AND LET YOUR OLD BODY HEAL FROM THIS TRAUMATIC INJURY--WHILE I HUNT DOWN BUTLER!

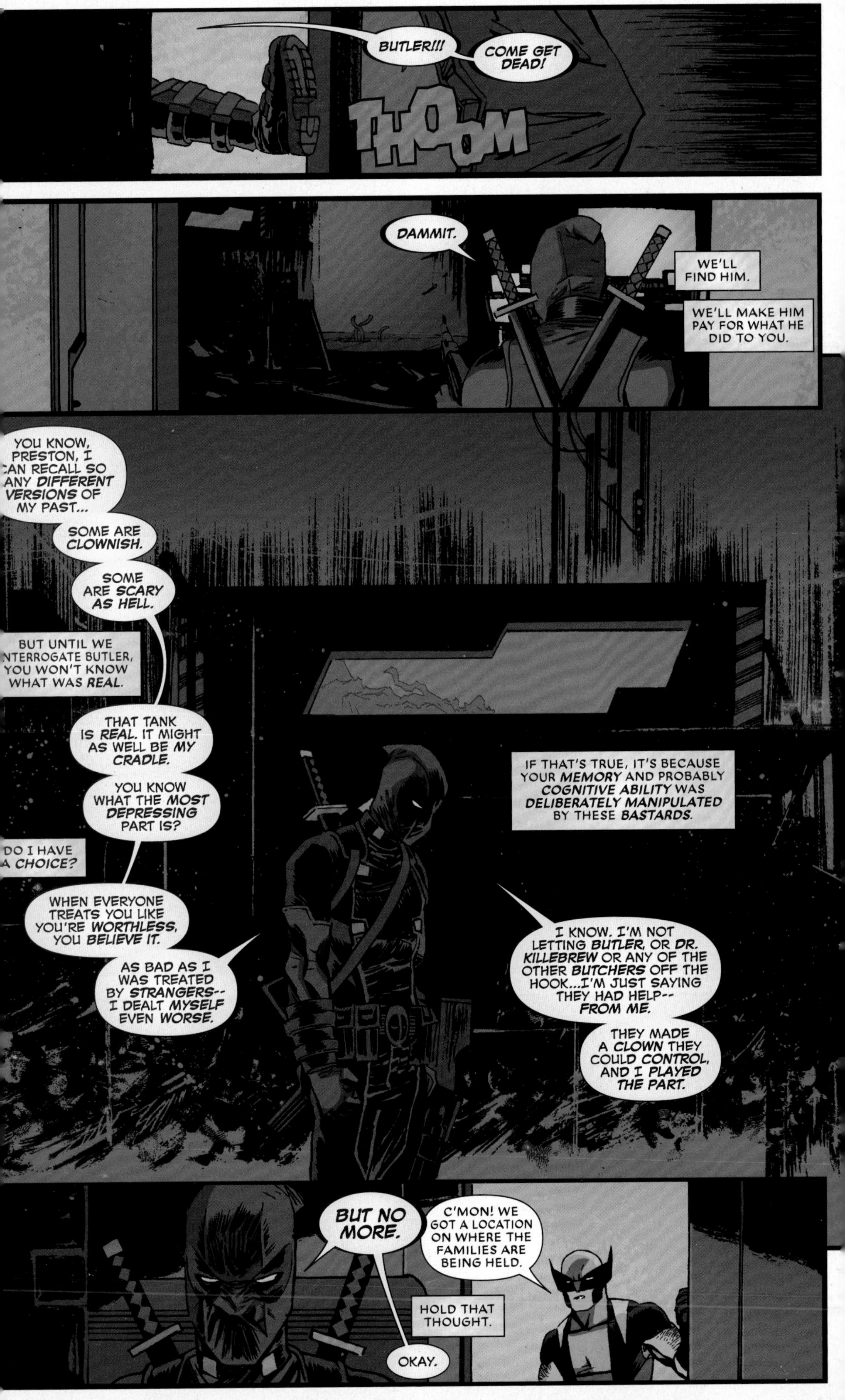
BUTLER!!!
COME GET DEAD!
THOOM
DAMMIT.
WE'LL FIND HIM.
WE'LL MAKE HIM PAY FOR WHAT HE DID TO YOU.
YOU KNOW, PRESTON, I CAN RECALL SO ANY DIFFERENT VERSIONS OF MY PAST...
SOME ARE CLOWNISH.
SOME ARE SCARY AS HELL.
BUT UNTIL WE NTERROGATE BUTLER, YOU WON'T KNOW WHAT WAS REAL.
THAT TANK IS REAL. IT MIGHT AS WELL BE MY CRADLE.
YOU KNOW WHAT THE MOST DEPRESSING PART IS?
DO I HAVE A CHOICE?
WHEN EVERYONE TREATS YOU LIKE YOU'RE WORTHLESS, YOU BELIEVE IT.
AS BAD AS I WAS TREATED BY STRANGERS-- I DEALT MYSELF EVEN WORSE.
IF THAT'S TRUE, IT'S BECAUSE YOUR MEMORY AND PROBABLY COGNITIVE ABILITY WAS DELIBERATELY MANIPULATED BY THESE BASTARDS.
I KNOW. I'M NOT LETTING BUTLER, OR DR. KILLEBREW OR ANY OF THE OTHER BUTCHERS OFF THE HOOK...I'M JUST SAYING THEY HAD HELP-- FROM ME.
THEY MADE A CLOWN THEY COULD CONTROL, AND I PLAYED THE PART.
BUT NO MORE.
C'MON! WE GOT A LOCATION ON WHERE THE FAMILIES ARE BEING HELD.
HOLD THAT THOUGHT.
OKAY.

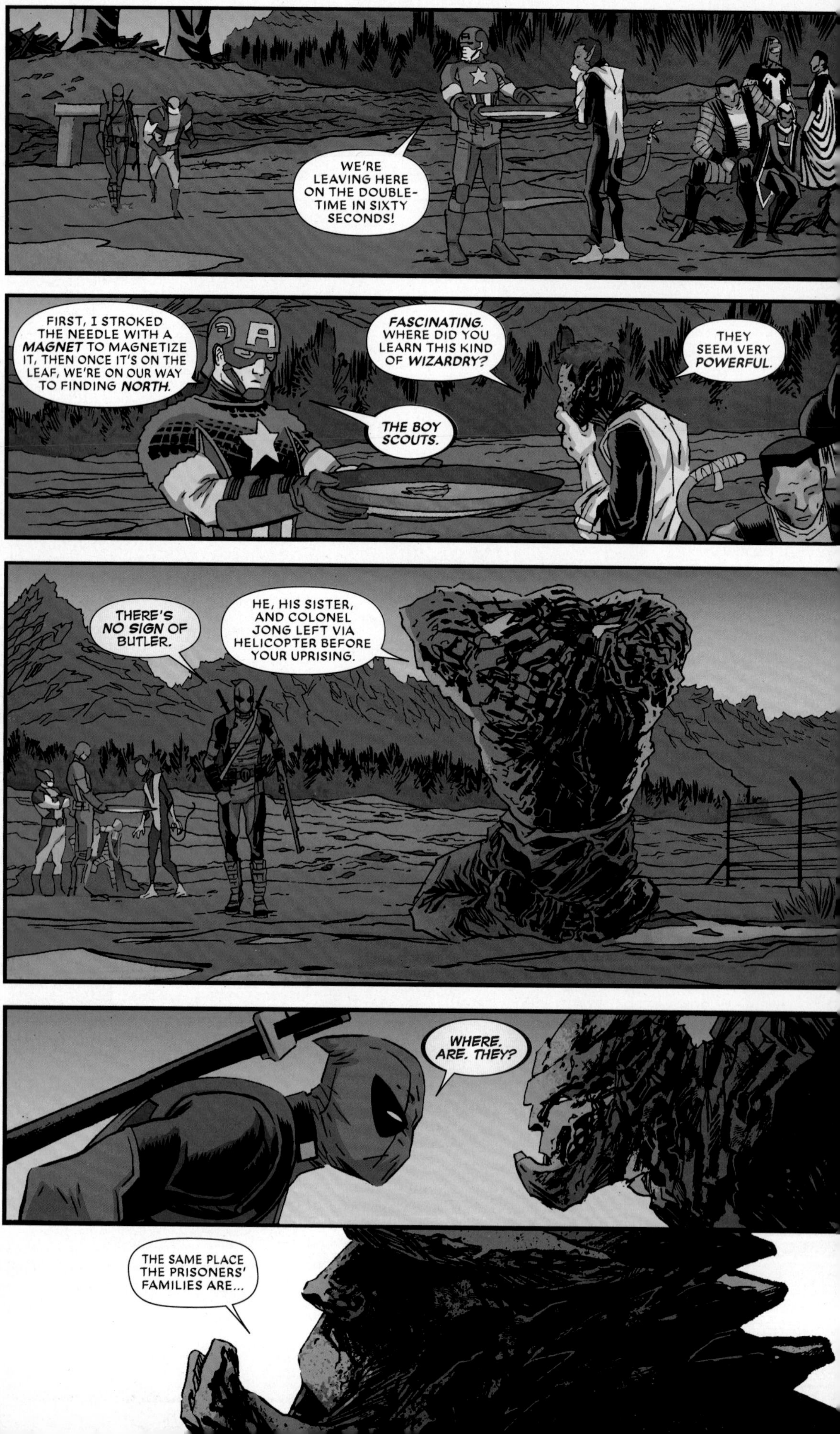
WE'RE LEAVING HERE ON THE DOUBLE-TIME IN SIXTY SECONDS!
FIRST, I STROKED THE NEEDLE WITH A MAGNET TO MAGNETIZE IT, THEN ONCE IT'S ON THE LEAF, WE'RE ON OUR WAY TO FINDING NORTH.
FASCINATING. WHERE DID YOU LEARN THIS KIND OF WIZARDRY?
THE BOY SCOUTS.
THEY SEEM VERY POWERFUL.
THERE'S NO SIGN OF BUTLER.
HE, HIS SISTER, AND COLONEL JONG LEFT VIA HELICOPTER BEFORE YOUR UPRISING.
WHERE. ARE. THEY?
THE SAME PLACE THE PRISONERS' FAMILIES ARE...

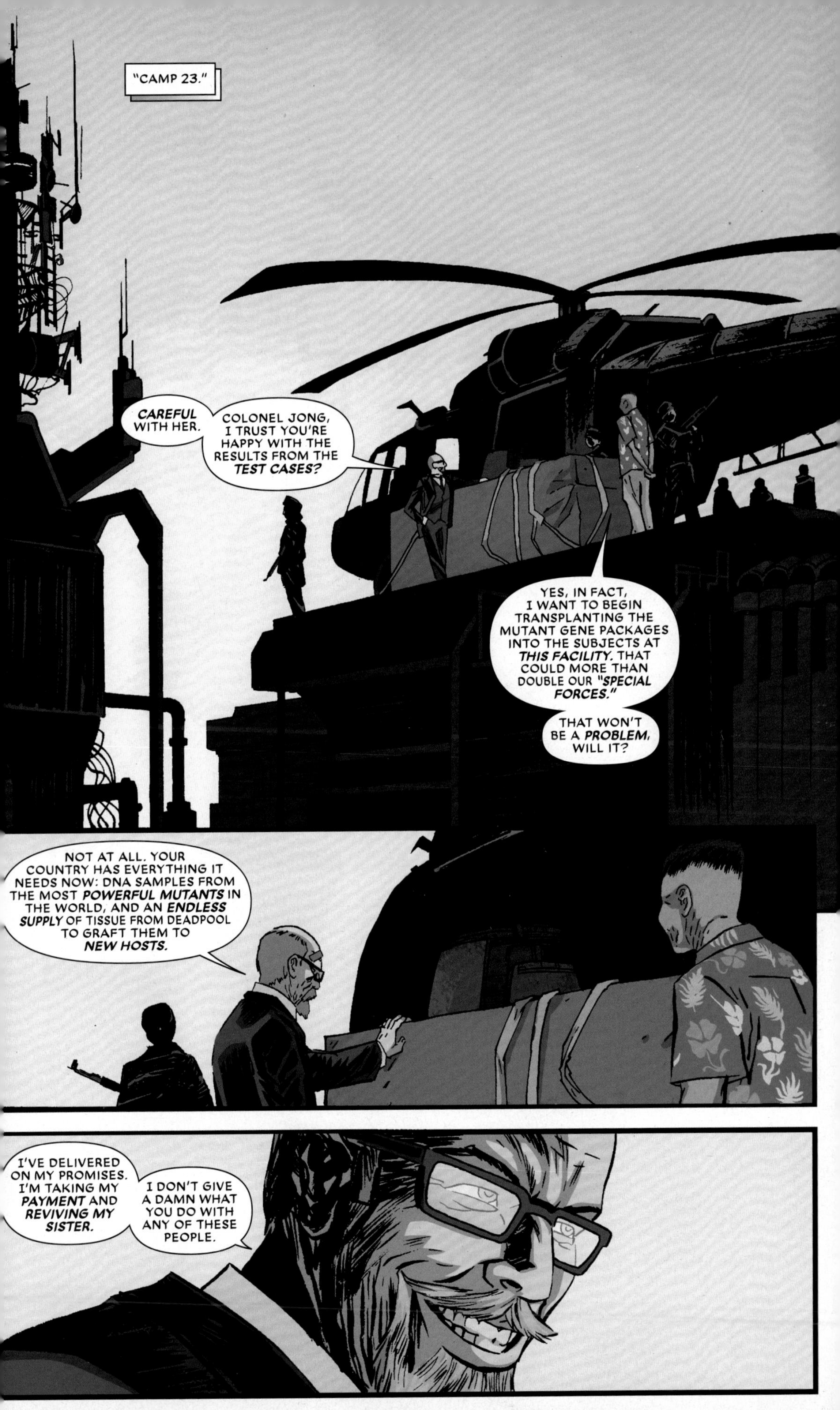
"CAMP 23."
CAREFUL WITH HER.
COLONEL JONG, I TRUST YOU'RE HAPPY WITH THE RESULTS FROM THE TEST CASES?
YES, IN FACT, I WANT TO BEGIN TRANSPLANTING THE MUTANT GENE PACKAGES INTO THE SUBJECTS AT THIS FACILITY. THAT COULD MORE THAN DOUBLE OUR "SPECIAL FORCES."
THAT WON'T BE A PROBLEM, WILL IT?
NOT AT ALL. YOUR COUNTRY HAS EVERYTHING IT NEEDS NOW: DNA SAMPLES FROM THE MOST POWERFUL MUTANTS IN THE WORLD, AND AN ENDLESS SUPPLY OF TISSUE FROM DEADPOOL TO GRAFT THEM TO NEW HOSTS.
I'VE DELIVERED ON MY PROMISES. I'M TAKING MY PAYMENT AND REVIVING MY SISTER.
I DON'T GIVE A DAMN WHAT YOU DO WITH ANY OF THESE PEOPLE.

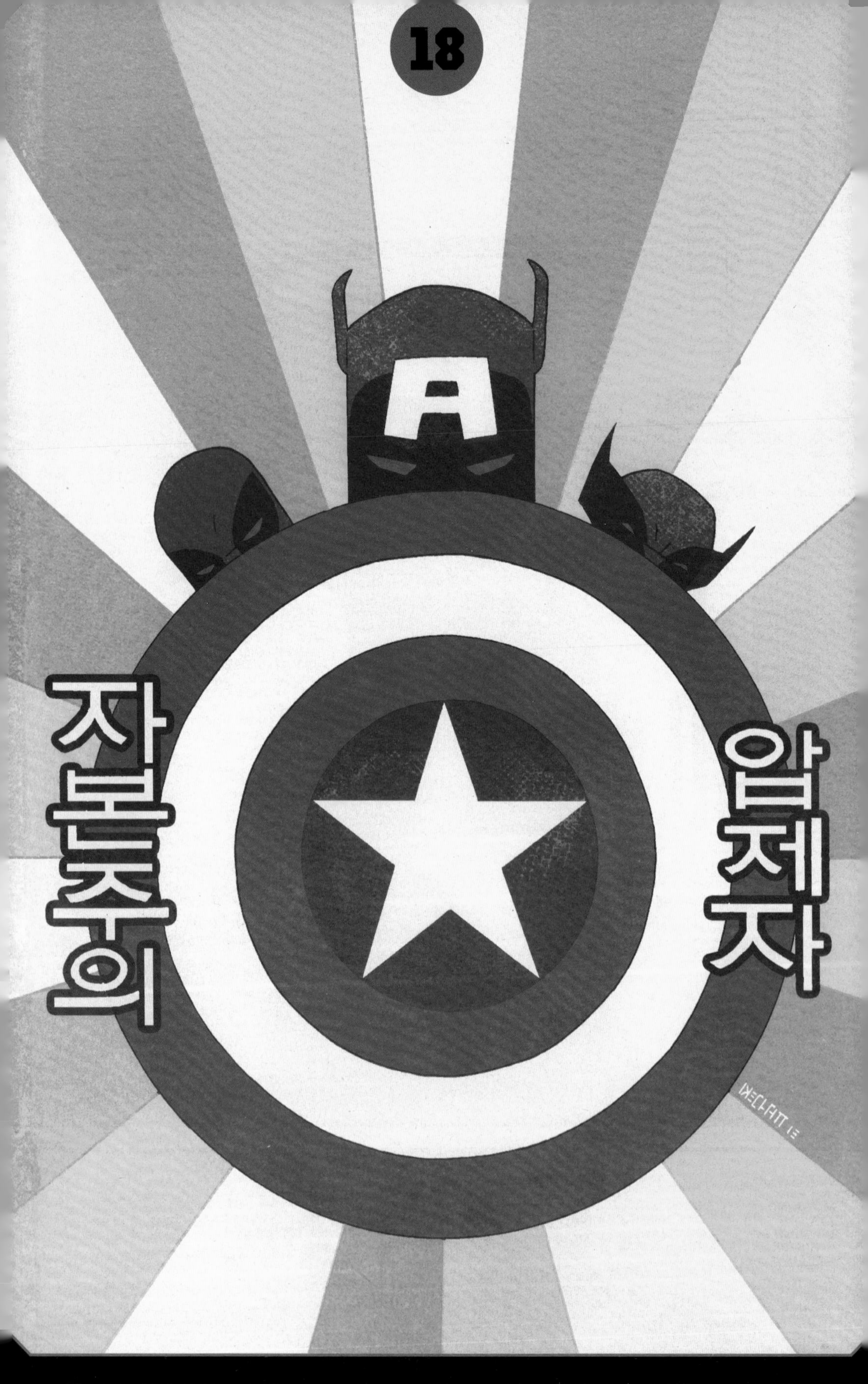

18
자본주의
압제자

THE GOOD, THE BAD AND THE UGLY PART FOUR

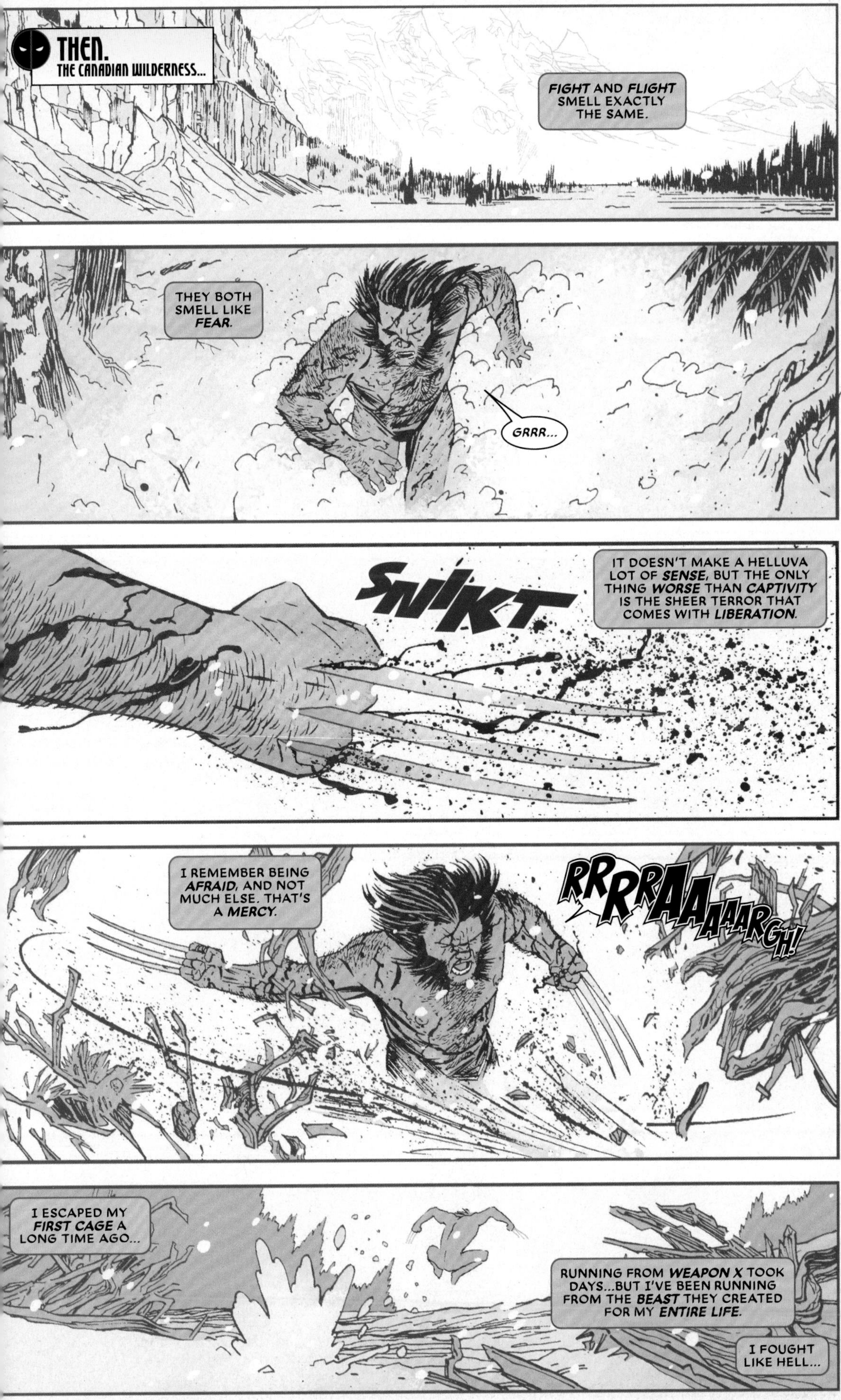
THEN.
THE CANADIAN WILDERNESS...
FIGHT AND FLIGHT SMELL EXACTLY THE SAME.
THEY BOTH SMELL LIKE FEAR.
GRRR...
SNIKT
IT DOESN'T MAKE A HELLUVA LOT OF SENSE, BUT THE ONLY THING WORSE THAN CAPTIVITY IS THE SHEER TERROR THAT COMES WITH LIBERATION.
I REMEMBER BEING AFRAID, AND NOT MUCH ELSE. THAT'S A MERCY.
RRRRAAAAARGH!
I ESCAPED MY FIRST CAGE A LONG TIME AGO...
RUNNING FROM WEAPON X TOOK DAYS...BUT I'VE BEEN RUNNING FROM THE BEAST THEY CREATED FOR MY ENTIRE LIFE.
I FOUGHT LIKE HELL...

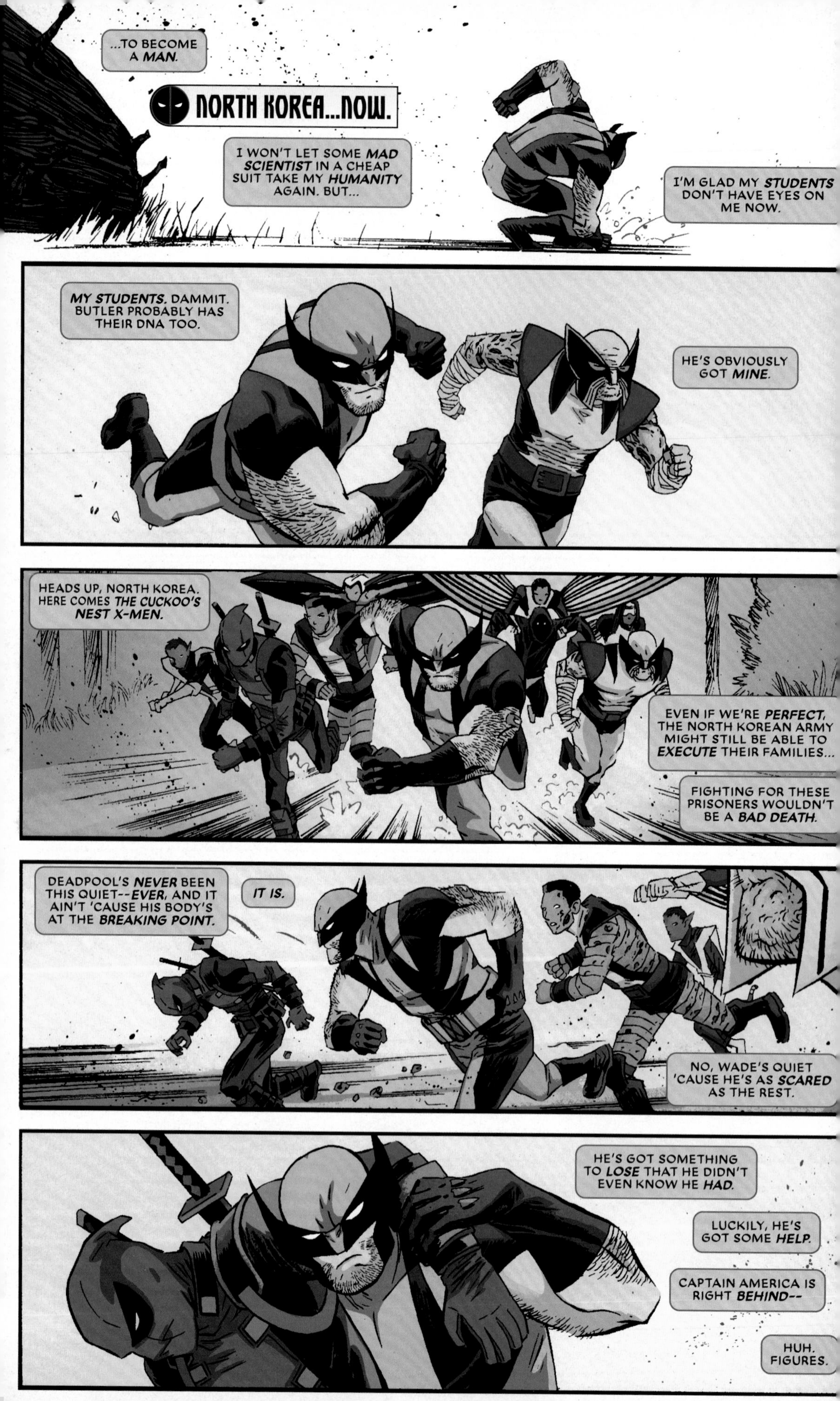
...TO BECOME A *MAN.*
NORTH KOREA...NOW.
I WON'T LET SOME *MAD SCIENTIST* IN A CHEAP SUIT TAKE MY *HUMANITY* AGAIN. BUT...
I'M GLAD MY *STUDENTS* DON'T HAVE EYES ON ME NOW.
MY STUDENTS. DAMMIT. BUTLER PROBABLY HAS THEIR DNA TOO.
HE'S OBVIOUSLY GOT *MINE.*
HEADS UP, NORTH KOREA. HERE COMES *THE CUCKOO'S NEST X-MEN.*
EVEN IF WE'RE *PERFECT,* THE NORTH KOREAN ARMY MIGHT STILL BE ABLE TO *EXECUTE* THEIR FAMILIES...
FIGHTING FOR THESE PRISONERS WOULDN'T BE A *BAD DEATH.*
DEADPOOL'S *NEVER* BEEN THIS QUIET--*EVER,* AND IT AIN'T 'CAUSE HIS BODY'S AT THE *BREAKING POINT.*
IT IS.
NO, WADE'S QUIET 'CAUSE HE'S AS *SCARED* AS THE REST.
HE'S GOT SOMETHING TO *LOSE* THAT HE DIDN'T EVEN KNOW HE *HAD.*
LUCKILY, HE'S GOT SOME *HELP.*
CAPTAIN AMERICA IS RIGHT *BEHIND--*
HUH. FIGURES.

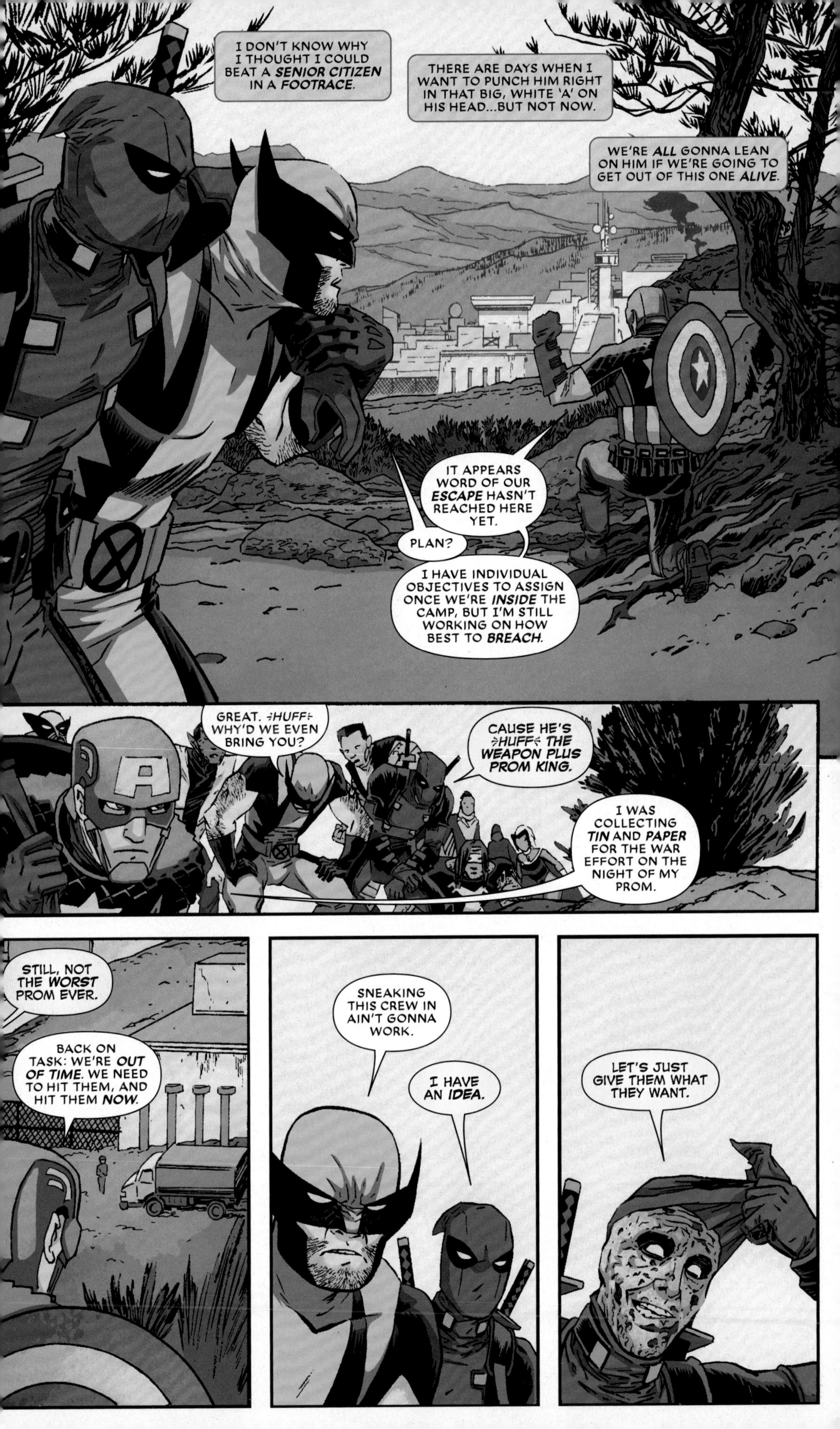
I DON'T KNOW WHY I THOUGHT I COULD BEAT A SENIOR CITIZEN IN A FOOTRACE.
THERE ARE DAYS WHEN I WANT TO PUNCH HIM RIGHT IN THAT BIG, WHITE 'A' ON HIS HEAD...BUT NOT NOW.
WE'RE ALL GONNA LEAN ON HIM IF WE'RE GOING TO GET OUT OF THIS ONE ALIVE.
IT APPEARS WORD OF OUR ESCAPE HASN'T REACHED HERE YET.
PLAN?
I HAVE INDIVIDUAL OBJECTIVES TO ASSIGN ONCE WE'RE INSIDE THE CAMP, BUT I'M STILL WORKING ON HOW BEST TO BREACH.
GREAT. ≠HUFF≠ WHY'D WE EVEN BRING YOU?
CAUSE HE'S ≠HUFF≠ THE WEAPON PLUS PROM KING.
I WAS COLLECTING TIN AND PAPER FOR THE WAR EFFORT ON THE NIGHT OF MY PROM.
STILL, NOT THE WORST PROM EVER.
BACK ON TASK: WE'RE OUT OF TIME. WE NEED TO HIT THEM, AND HIT THEM NOW.
SNEAKING THIS CREW IN AIN'T GONNA WORK.
I HAVE AN IDEA.
LET'S JUST GIVE THEM WHAT THEY WANT.

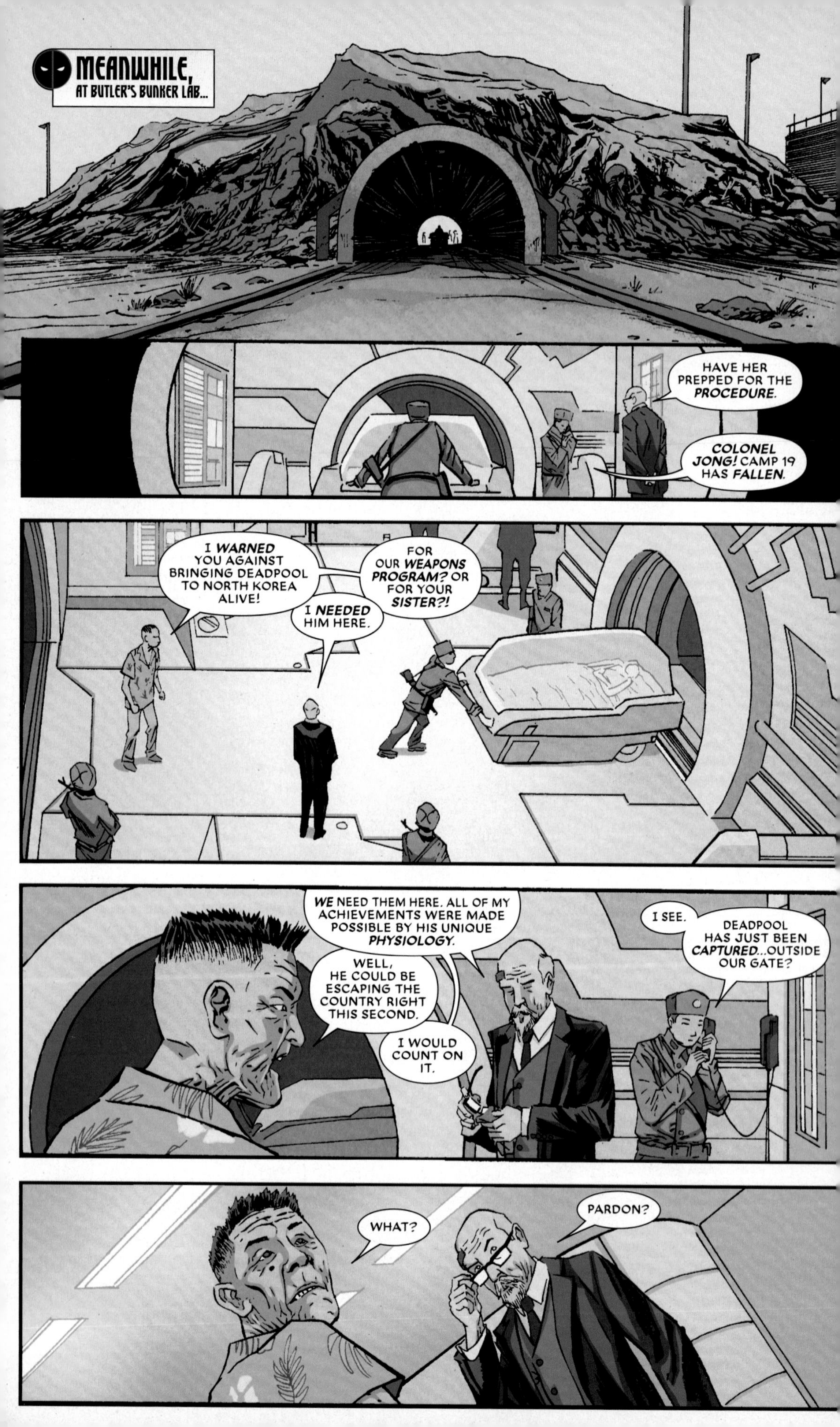
MEANWHILE, AT BUTLER'S BUNKER LAB...
HAVE HER PREPPED FOR THE PROCEDURE.
COLONEL JONG! CAMP 19 HAS FALLEN.
I WARNED YOU AGAINST BRINGING DEADPOOL TO NORTH KOREA ALIVE!
FOR OUR WEAPONS PROGRAM? OR FOR YOUR SISTER?!
I NEEDED HIM HERE.
WE NEED THEM HERE. ALL OF MY ACHIEVEMENTS WERE MADE POSSIBLE BY HIS UNIQUE PHYSIOLOGY.
WELL, HE COULD BE ESCAPING THE COUNTRY RIGHT THIS SECOND.
I WOULD COUNT ON IT.
I SEE.
DEADPOOL HAS JUST BEEN CAPTURED...OUTSIDE OUR GATE?
WHAT?
PARDON?

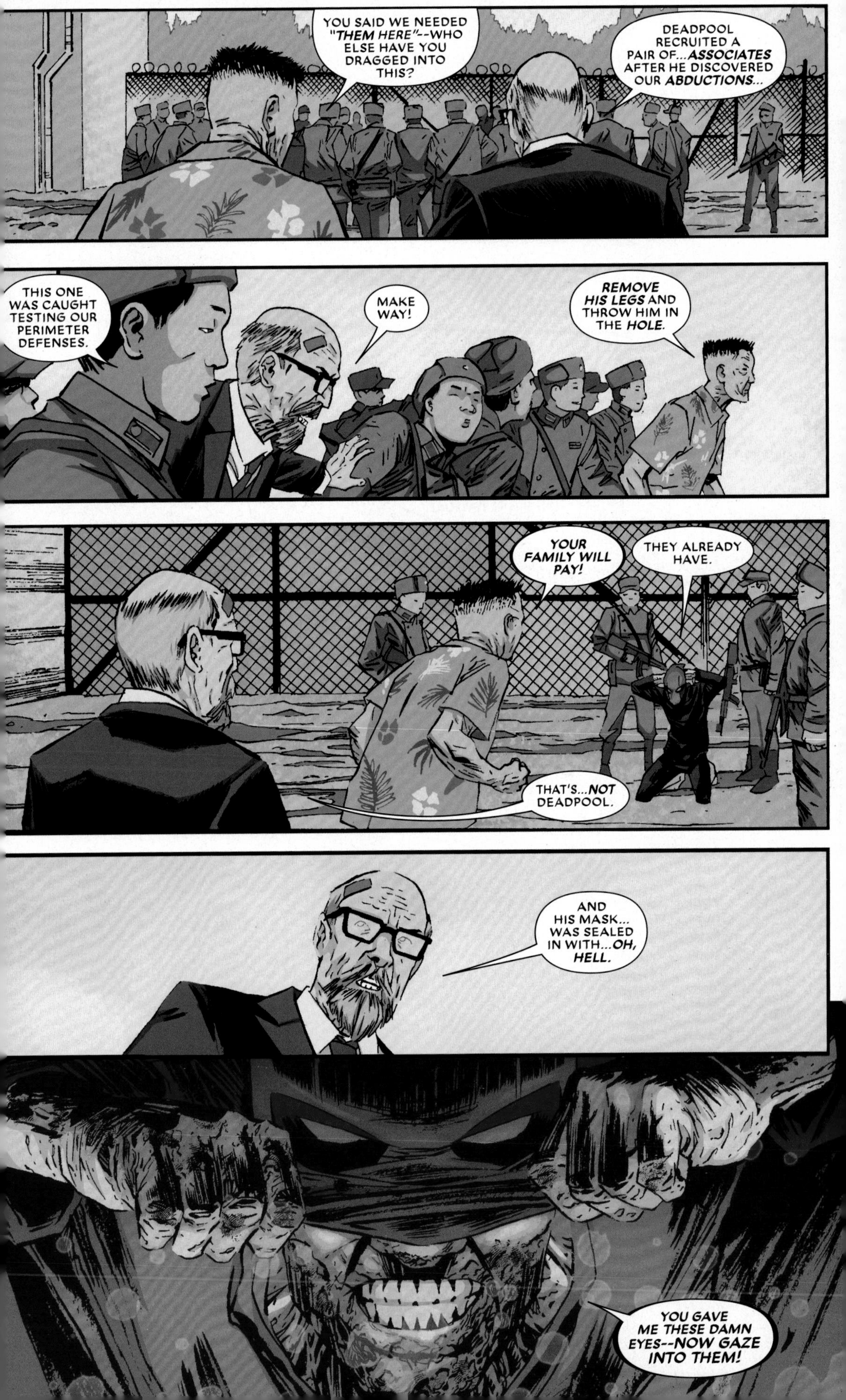

YOU SAID WE NEEDED "THEM HERE"--WHO ELSE HAVE YOU DRAGGED INTO THIS?
DEADPOOL RECRUITED A PAIR OF...ASSOCIATES AFTER HE DISCOVERED OUR ABDUCTIONS...
THIS ONE WAS CAUGHT TESTING OUR PERIMETER DEFENSES.
MAKE WAY!
REMOVE HIS LEGS AND THROW HIM IN THE HOLE.
YOUR FAMILY WILL PAY!
THEY ALREADY HAVE.
THAT'S...NOT DEADPOOL.
AND HIS MASK... WAS SEALED IN WITH...OH, HELL.
YOU GAVE ME THESE DAMN EYES--NOW GAZE INTO THEM!

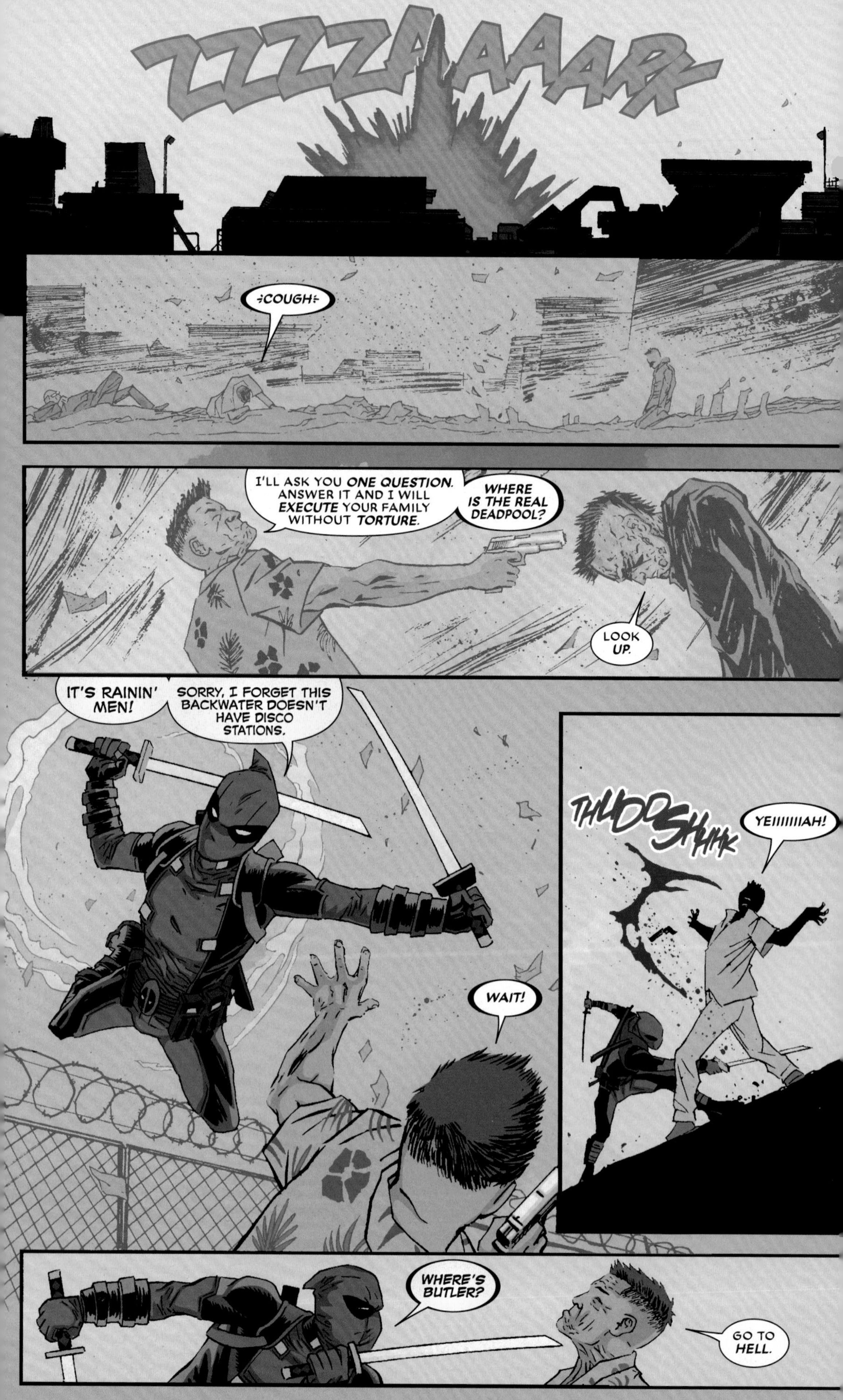
ZZZZAAAARR
COUGH
I'LL ASK YOU ONE QUESTION. ANSWER IT AND I WILL EXECUTE YOUR FAMILY WITHOUT TORTURE.
WHERE IS THE REAL DEADPOOL?
LOOK UP.
IT'S RAININ' MEN!
SORRY, I FORGET THIS BACKWATER DOESN'T HAVE DISCO STATIONS.
WAIT!
THUDDSHUNK
YEIIIIIIAH!
WHERE'S BUTLER?
GO TO HELL.

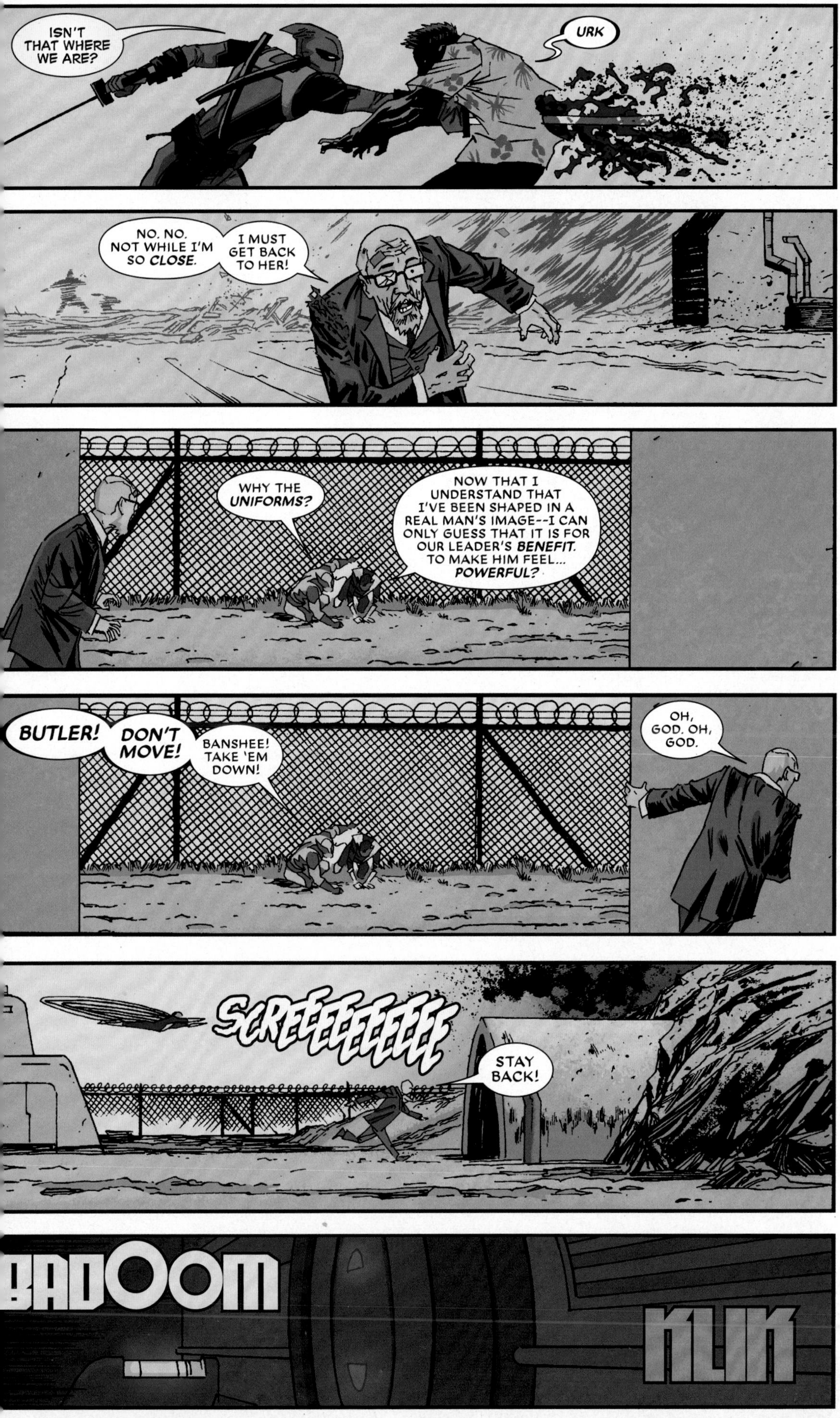
ISN'T THAT WHERE WE ARE?
URK
NO. NO. NOT WHILE I'M SO CLOSE.
I MUST GET BACK TO HER!
WHY THE UNIFORMS?
NOW THAT I UNDERSTAND THAT I'VE BEEN SHAPED IN A REAL MAN'S IMAGE--I CAN ONLY GUESS THAT IT IS FOR OUR LEADER'S BENEFIT. TO MAKE HIM FEEL... POWERFUL?
BUTLER!
DON'T MOVE!
BANSHEE! TAKE 'EM DOWN!
OH, GOD. OH, GOD.
SCREEEEEEEEEE
STAY BACK!
BADOOM
KLIK

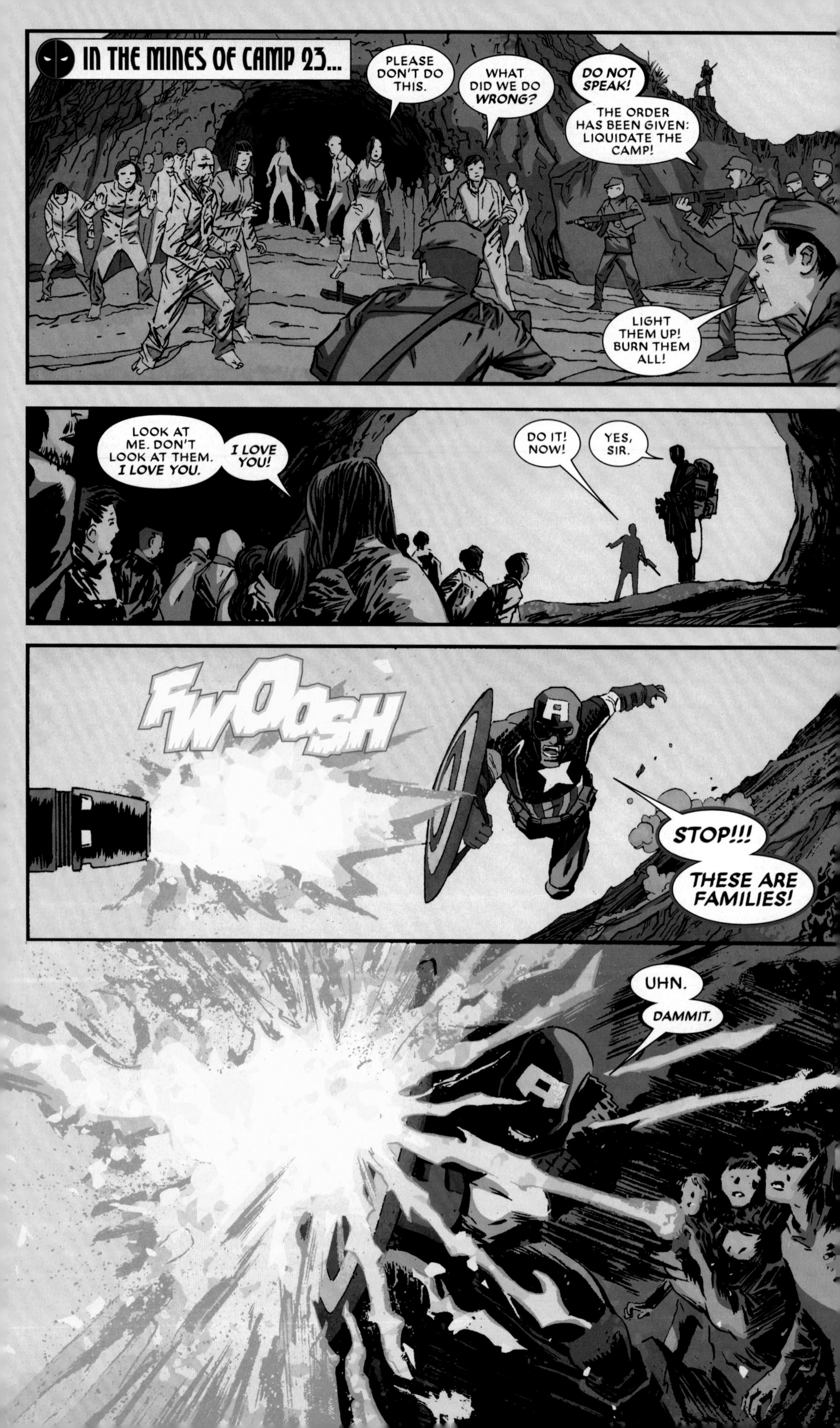
IN THE MINES OF CAMP 23...
PLEASE DON'T DO THIS.
WHAT DID WE DO WRONG?
DO NOT SPEAK!
THE ORDER HAS BEEN GIVEN: LIQUIDATE THE CAMP!
LIGHT THEM UP! BURN THEM ALL!
LOOK AT ME. DON'T LOOK AT THEM. I LOVE YOU.
I LOVE YOU!
DO IT! NOW!
YES, SIR.
FWOOSH
STOP!!!
THESE ARE FAMILIES!
UHN.
DAMMIT.

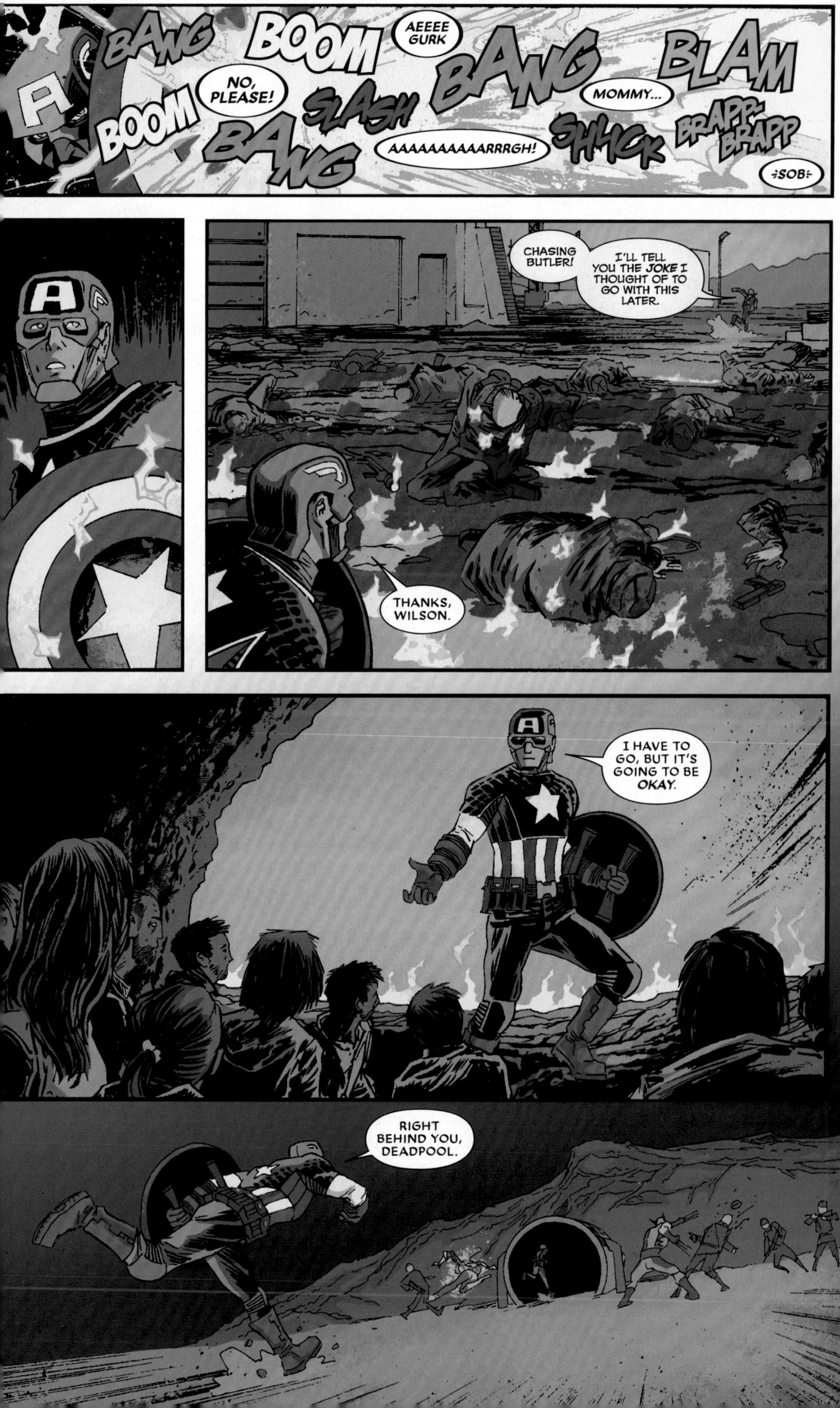
BANG
BOOM
AEEEE GURK
BOOM
NO, PLEASE!
SLASH
BANG
BANG
BLAM
MOMMY...
AAAAAAAAAARRRGH!
SHLICK
BRAPP-BRAPP
SOB
CHASING BUTLER!
I'LL TELL YOU THE JOKE I THOUGHT OF TO GO WITH THIS LATER.
THANKS, WILSON.
I HAVE TO GO, BUT IT'S GOING TO BE OKAY.
RIGHT BEHIND YOU, DEADPOOL.

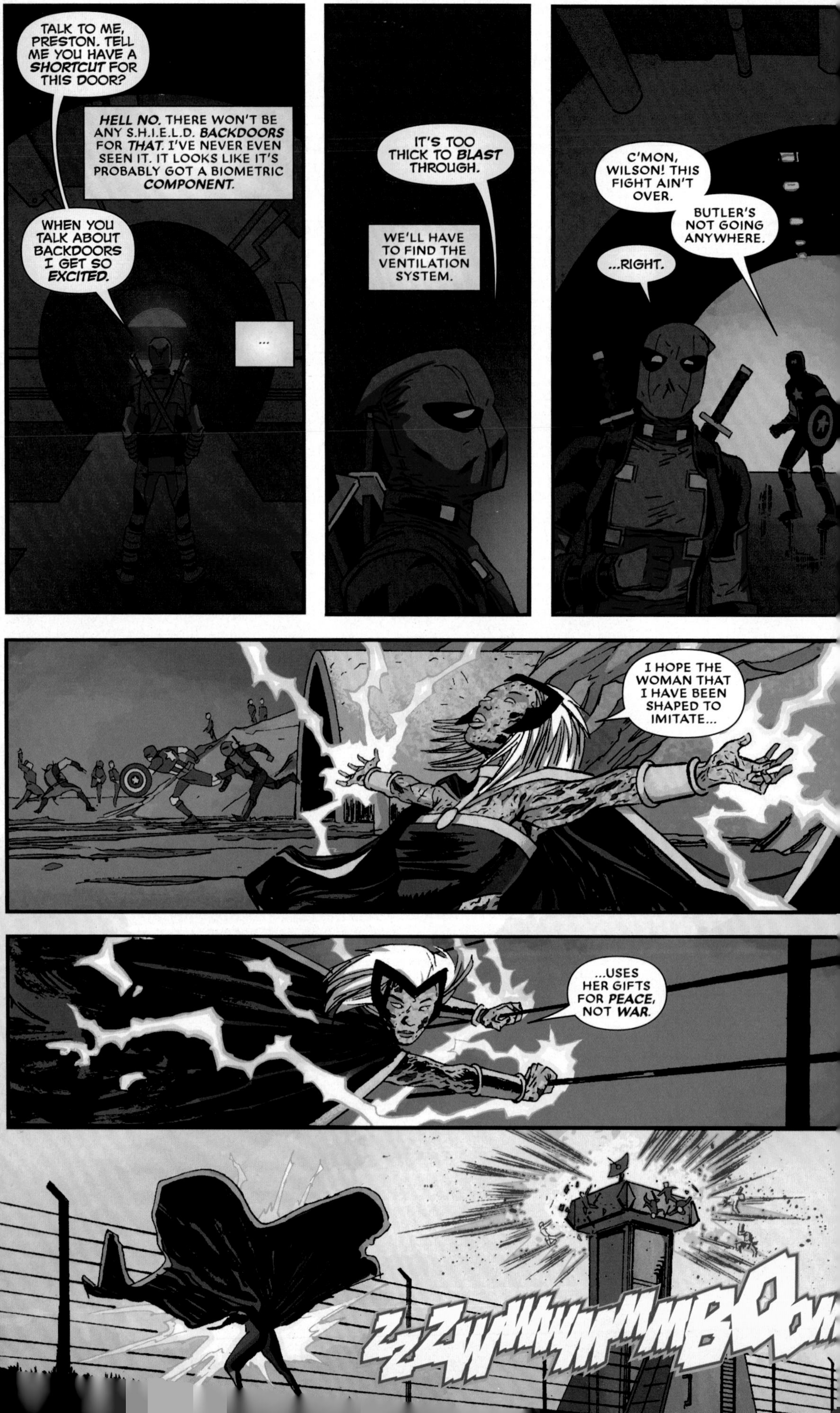

TALK TO ME, PRESTON. TELL ME YOU HAVE A SHORTCUT FOR THIS DOOR?
HELL NO. THERE WON'T BE ANY S.H.I.E.L.D. BACKDOORS FOR THAT. I'VE NEVER EVEN SEEN IT. IT LOOKS LIKE IT'S PROBABLY GOT A BIOMETRIC COMPONENT.
WHEN YOU TALK ABOUT BACKDOORS I GET SO EXCITED.
...
IT'S TOO THICK TO BLAST THROUGH.
WE'LL HAVE TO FIND THE VENTILATION SYSTEM.
C'MON, WILSON! THIS FIGHT AIN'T OVER.
BUTLER'S NOT GOING ANYWHERE.
...RIGHT.
I HOPE THE WOMAN THAT I HAVE BEEN SHAPED TO IMITATE...
...USES HER GIFTS FOR PEACE, NOT WAR.
ZZZWWWWWMMMBOOM

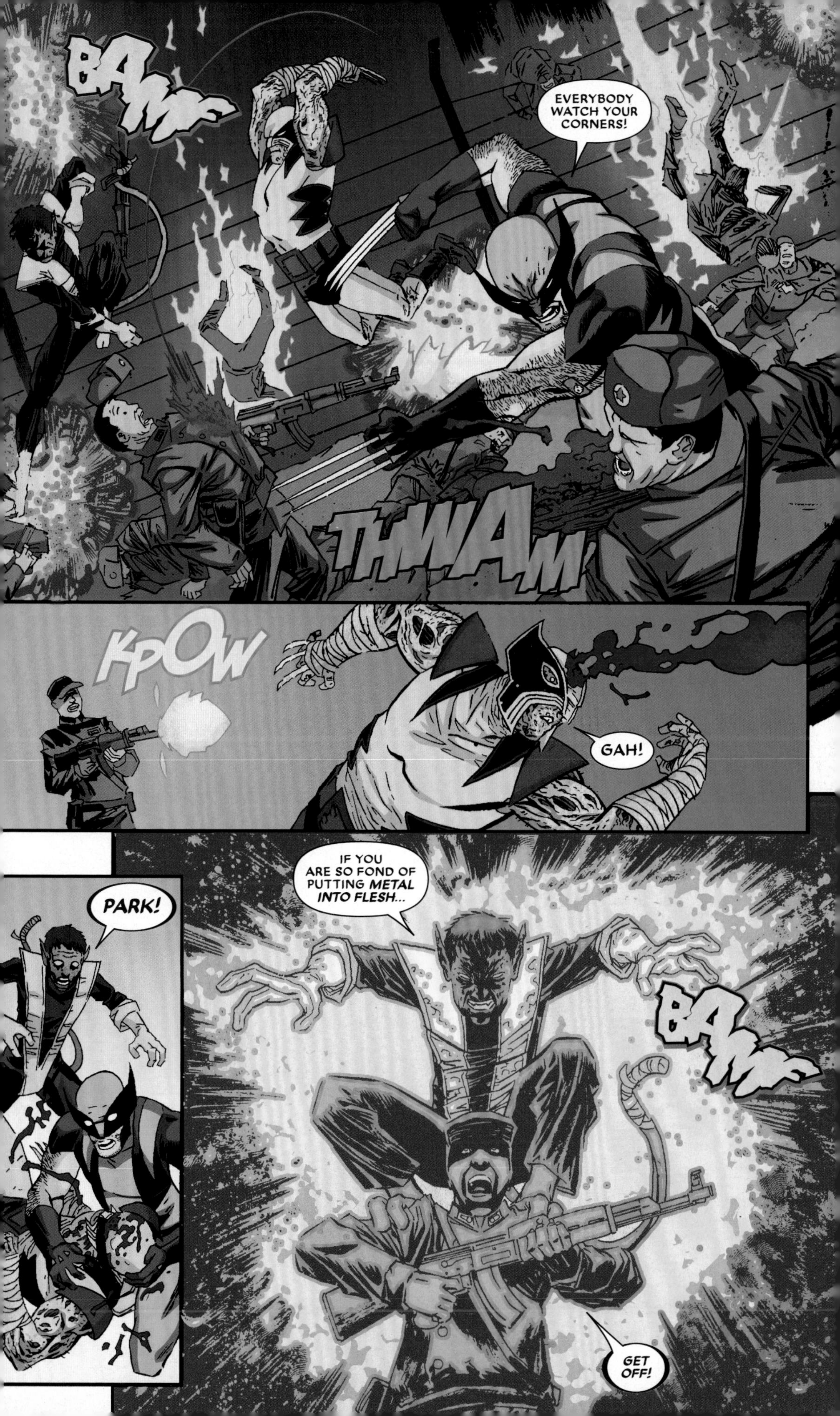
BAMF
EVERYBODY WATCH YOUR CORNERS!
THWAAM
KPOW
GAH!
PARK!
IF YOU ARE SO FOND OF PUTTING *METAL INTO FLESH*...
BAMF
GET OFF!

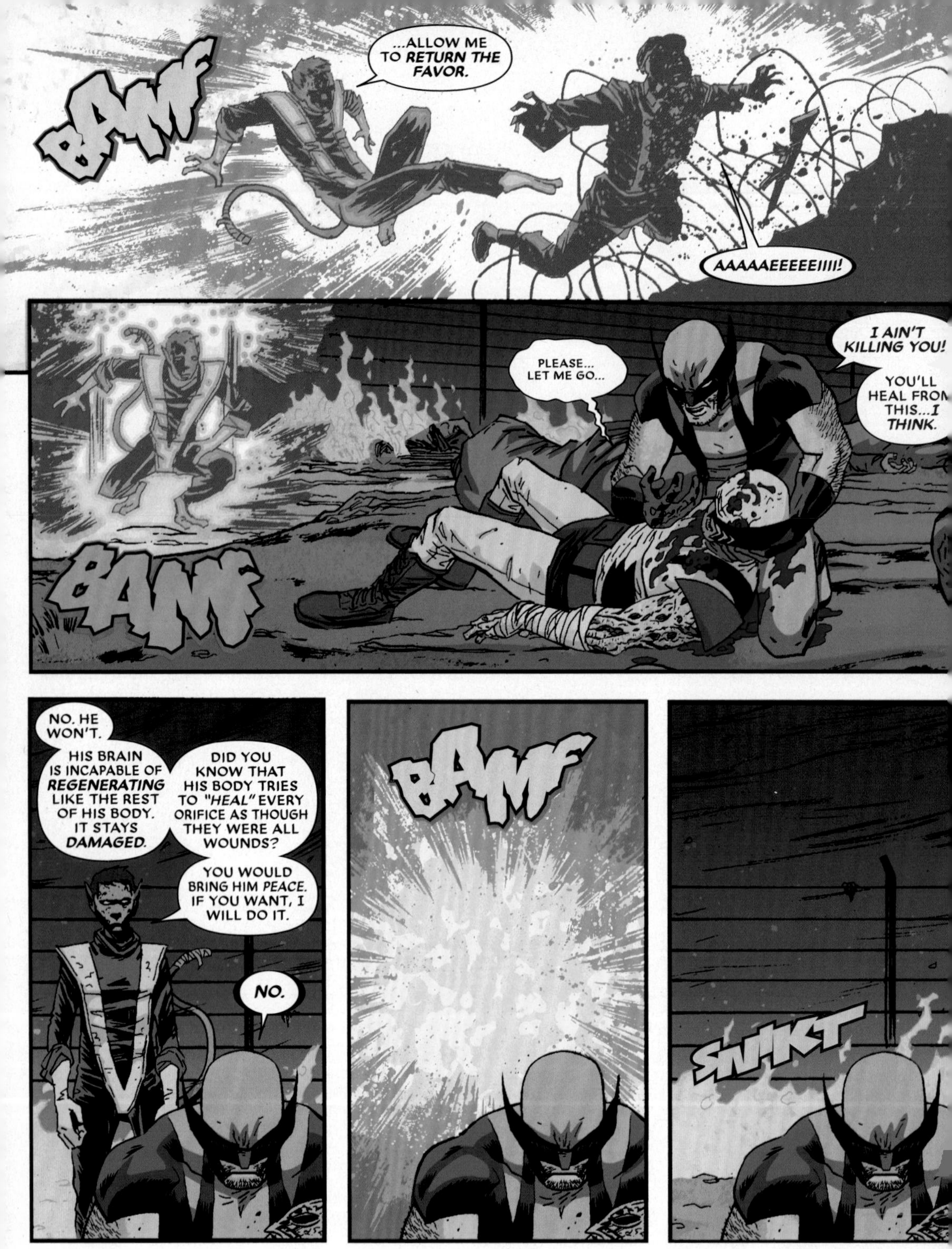
BAMF
...ALLOW ME TO RETURN THE FAVOR.
AAAAAEEEEEIIIII!
BAMF
PLEASE... LET ME GO...
I AIN'T KILLING YOU!
YOU'LL HEAL FROM THIS...I THINK.
NO. HE WON'T.
HIS BRAIN IS INCAPABLE OF REGENERATING LIKE THE REST OF HIS BODY. IT STAYS DAMAGED.
DID YOU KNOW THAT HIS BODY TRIES TO "HEAL" EVERY ORIFICE AS THOUGH THEY WERE ALL WOUNDS?
YOU WOULD BRING HIM PEACE. IF YOU WANT, I WILL DO IT.
NO.
BAMF
SNIKT

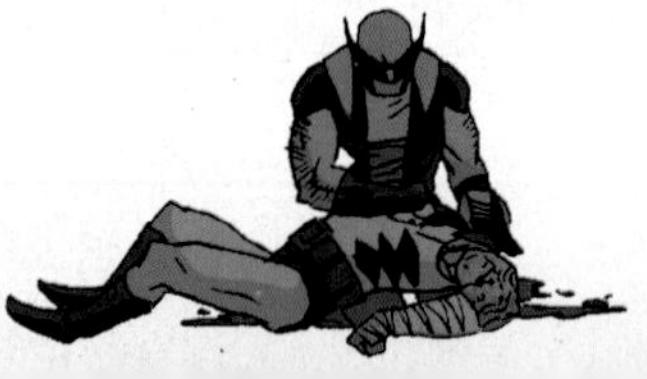

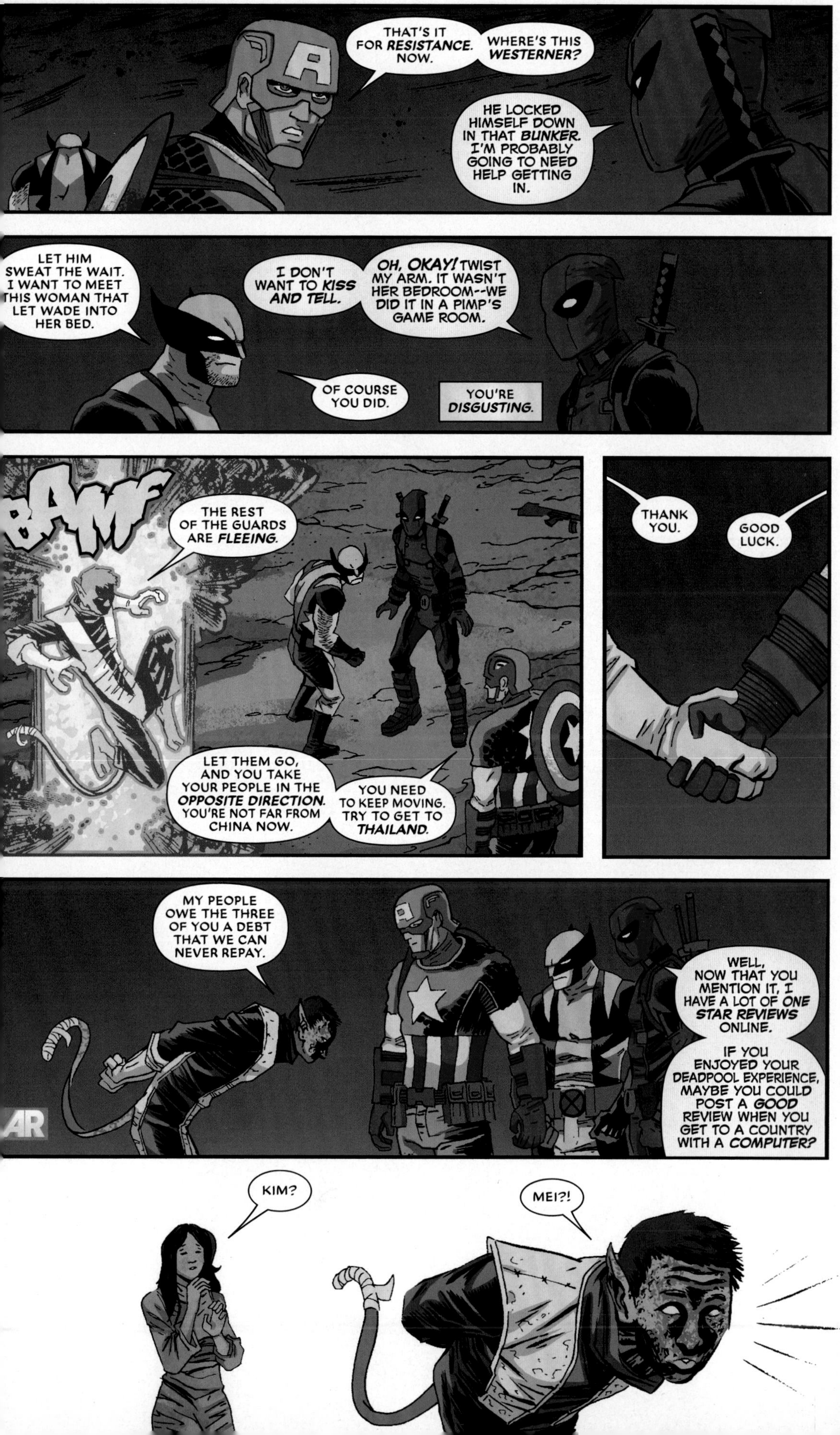
THAT'S IT FOR RESISTANCE. NOW.
WHERE'S THIS WESTERNER?
HE LOCKED HIMSELF DOWN IN THAT BUNKER. I'M PROBABLY GOING TO NEED HELP GETTING IN.
LET HIM SWEAT THE WAIT. I WANT TO MEET THIS WOMAN THAT LET WADE INTO HER BED.
I DON'T WANT TO KISS AND TELL.
OH, OKAY! TWIST MY ARM. IT WASN'T HER BEDROOM--WE DID IT IN A PIMP'S GAME ROOM.
OF COURSE YOU DID.
YOU'RE DISGUSTING.
BAMF
THE REST OF THE GUARDS ARE FLEEING.
LET THEM GO, AND YOU TAKE YOUR PEOPLE IN THE OPPOSITE DIRECTION. YOU'RE NOT FAR FROM CHINA NOW.
YOU NEED TO KEEP MOVING. TRY TO GET TO THAILAND.
THANK YOU.
GOOD LUCK.
MY PEOPLE OWE THE THREE OF YOU A DEBT THAT WE CAN NEVER REPAY.
WELL, NOW THAT YOU MENTION IT, I HAVE A LOT OF ONE STAR REVIEWS ONLINE.
IF YOU ENJOYED YOUR DEADPOOL EXPERIENCE, MAYBE YOU COULD POST A GOOD REVIEW WHEN YOU GET TO A COUNTRY WITH A COMPUTER?
KIM?
MEI?!

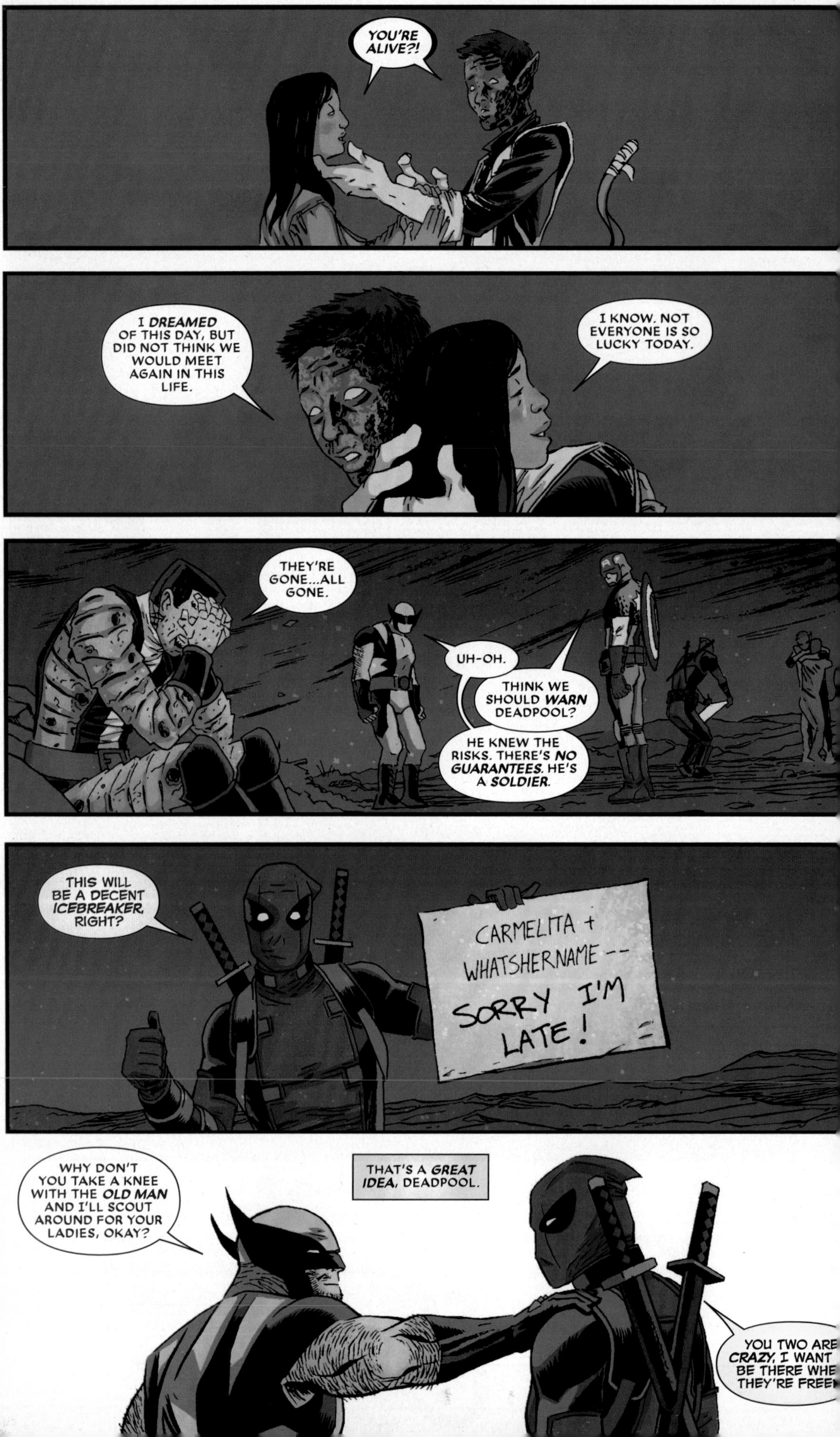
YOU'RE ALIVE?!
I DREAMED OF THIS DAY, BUT DID NOT THINK WE WOULD MEET AGAIN IN THIS LIFE.
I KNOW. NOT EVERYONE IS SO LUCKY TODAY.
THEY'RE GONE...ALL GONE.
UH-OH.
THINK WE SHOULD WARN DEADPOOL?
HE KNEW THE RISKS. THERE'S NO GUARANTEES. HE'S A SOLDIER.
THIS WILL BE A DECENT ICEBREAKER, RIGHT?
CARMELITA + WHATSHERNAME -- SORRY I'M LATE!
WHY DON'T YOU TAKE A KNEE WITH THE OLD MAN AND I'LL SCOUT AROUND FOR YOUR LADIES, OKAY?
THAT'S A GREAT IDEA, DEADPOOL.

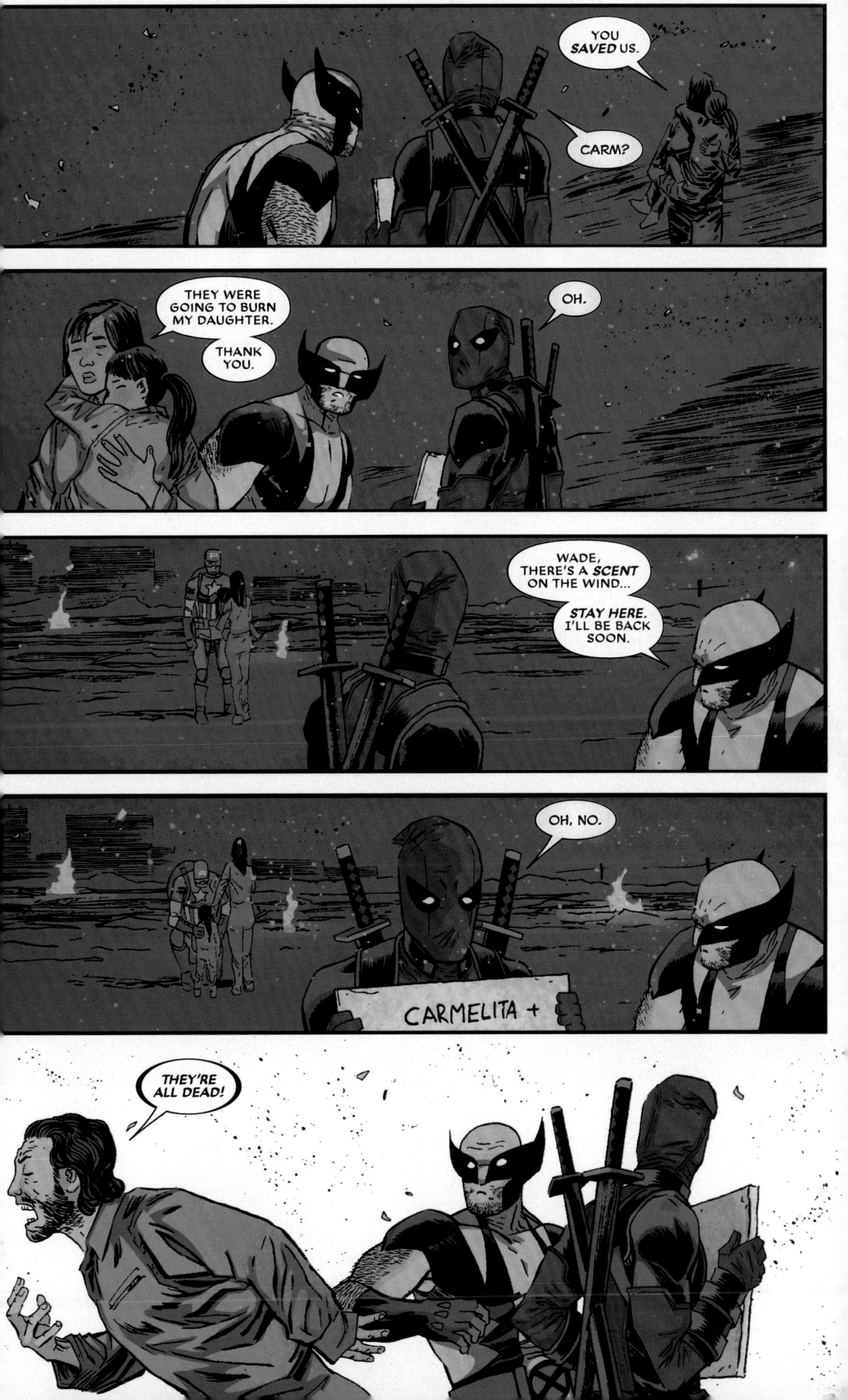
YOU SAVED US.
CARM?
THEY WERE GOING TO BURN MY DAUGHTER.
THANK YOU.
OH.
WADE, THERE'S A SCENT ON THE WIND...
STAY HERE. I'LL BE BACK SOON.
OH, NO.
CARMELITA +
THEY'RE ALL DEAD!

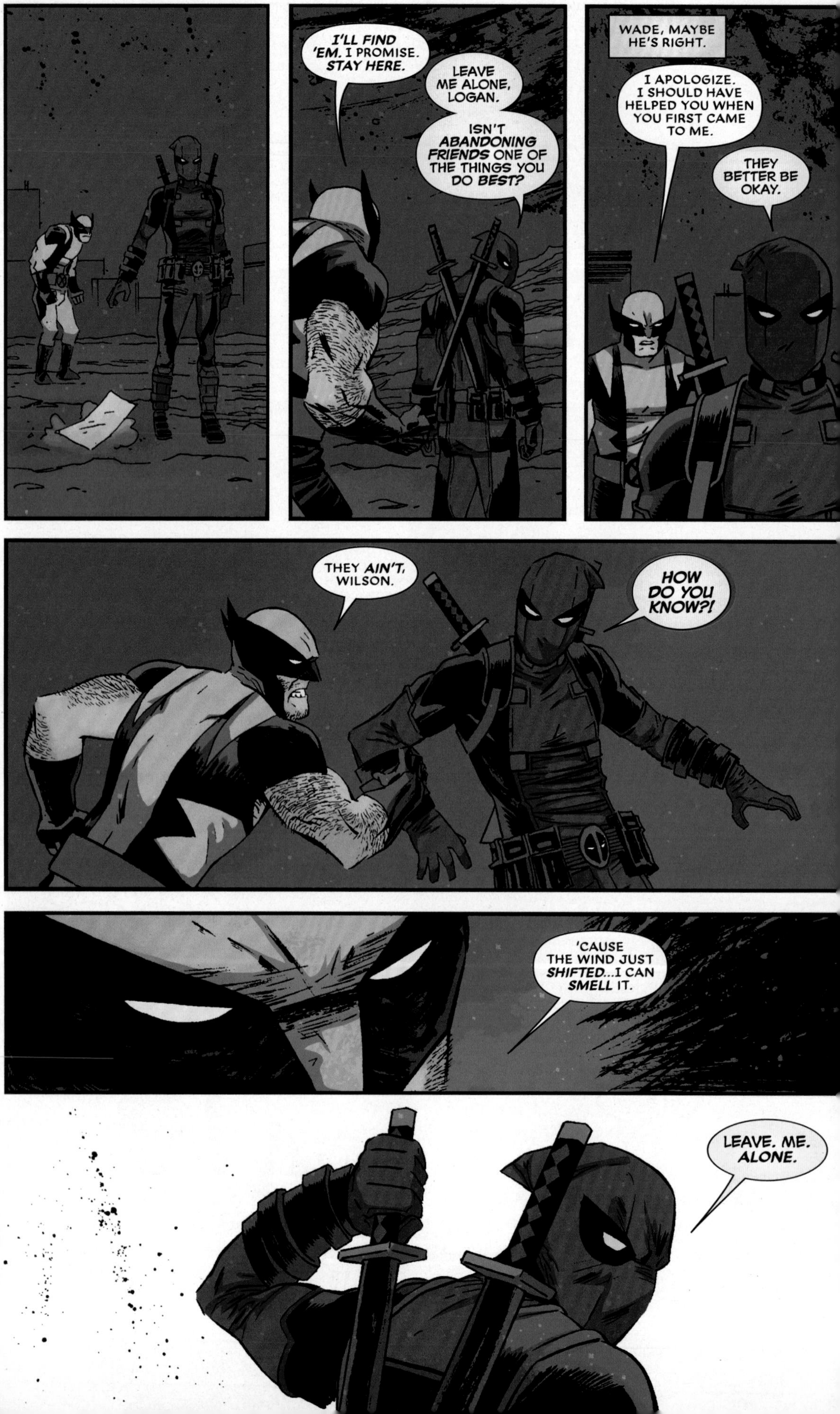
I'LL FIND 'EM. I PROMISE. STAY HERE.
LEAVE ME ALONE, LOGAN.
ISN'T ABANDONING FRIENDS ONE OF THE THINGS YOU DO BEST?
WADE, MAYBE HE'S RIGHT.
I APOLOGIZE. I SHOULD HAVE HELPED YOU WHEN YOU FIRST CAME TO ME.
THEY BETTER BE OKAY.
THEY AIN'T, WILSON.
HOW DO YOU KNOW?!
'CAUSE THE WIND JUST SHIFTED...I CAN SMELL IT.
LEAVE. ME. ALONE.

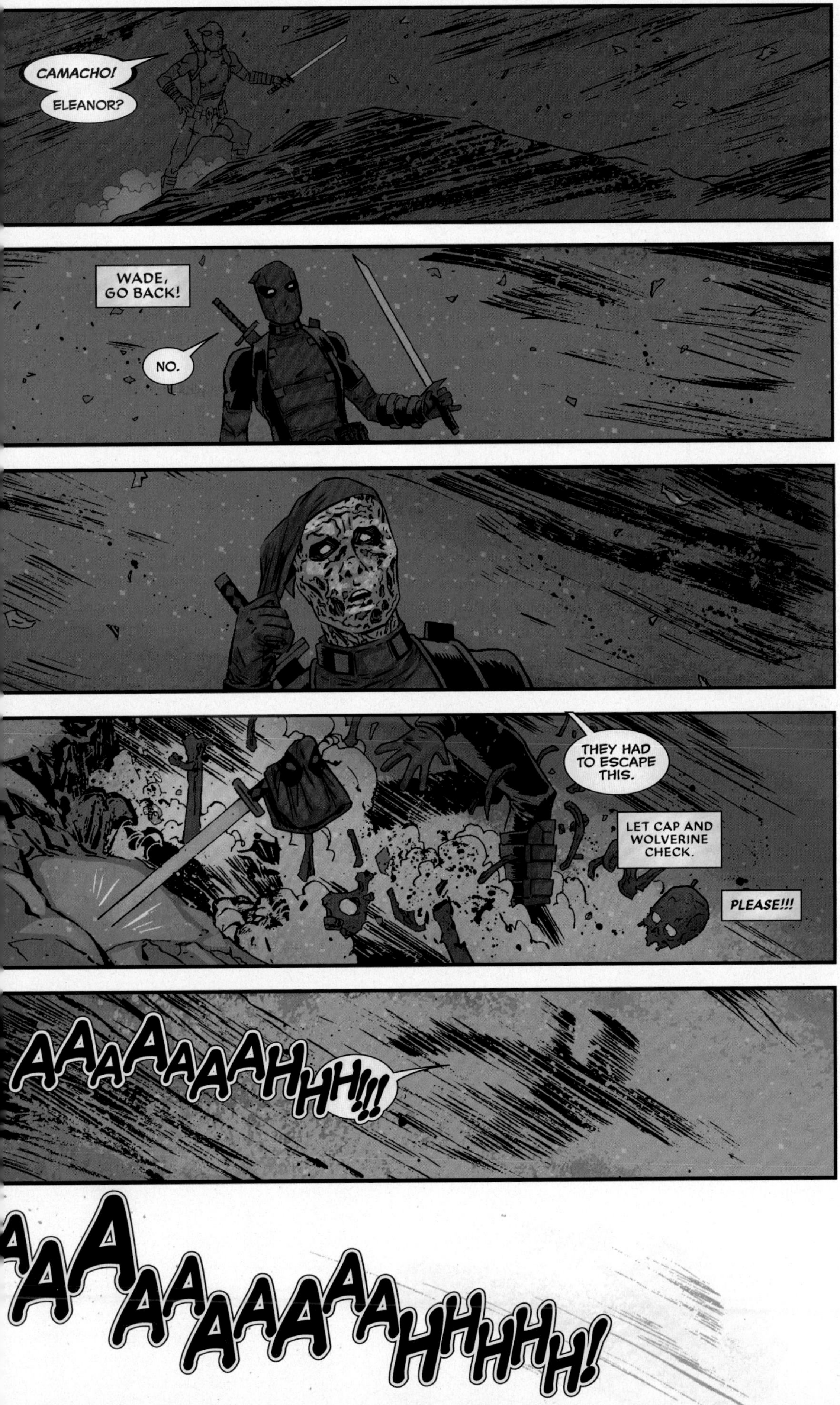
CAMACHO!
ELEANOR?
WADE, GO BACK!
NO.
THEY HAD TO ESCAPE THIS.
LET CAP AND WOLVERINE CHECK.
PLEASE!!!
AAAAAAAAHHHH!!!
AAAAAAAAAAAAHHHHHH!

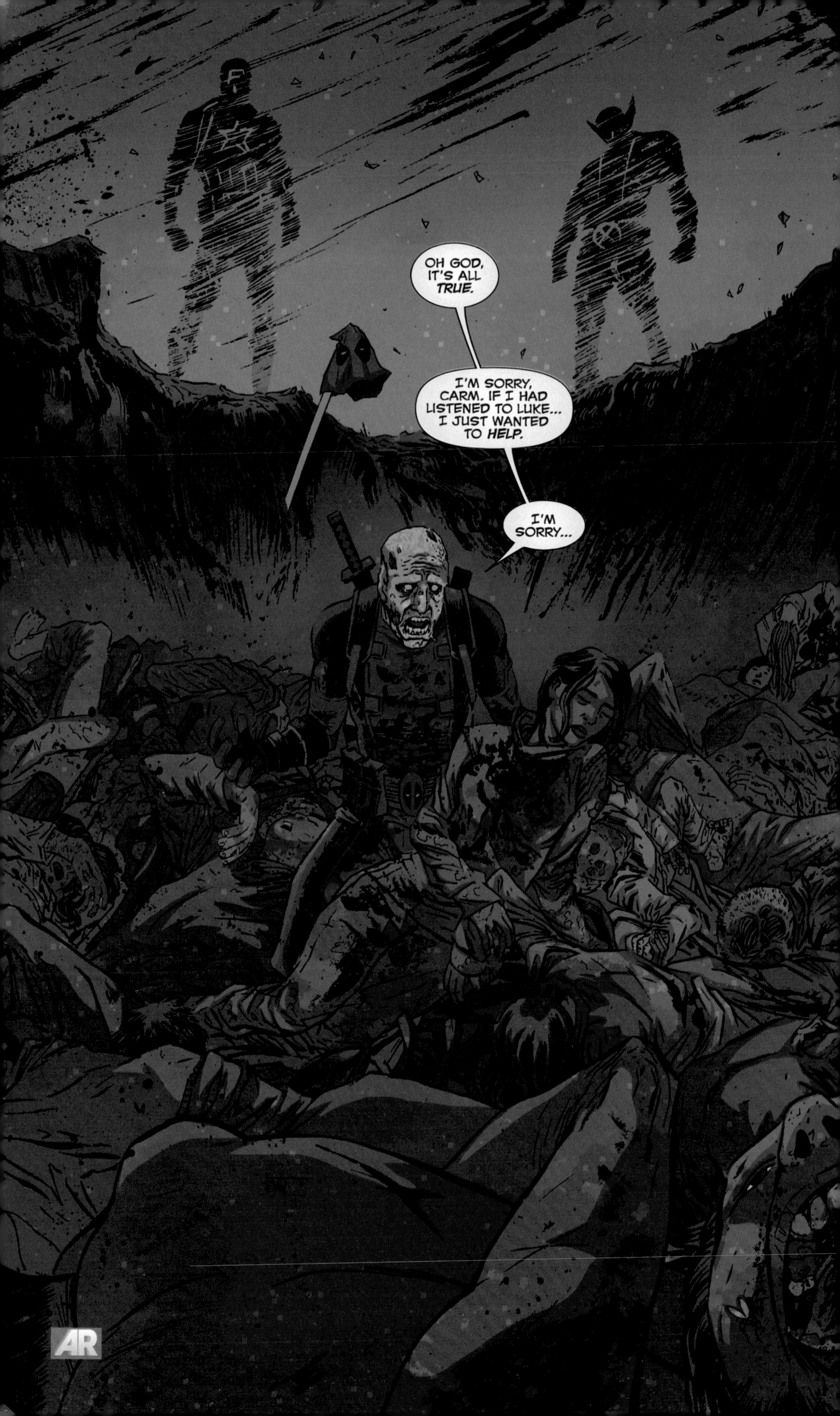
OH GOD, IT'S ALL *TRUE.*
I'M SORRY, CARM. IF I HAD LISTENED TO LUKE... I JUST WANTED TO *HELP.*
I'M SORRY...
AR

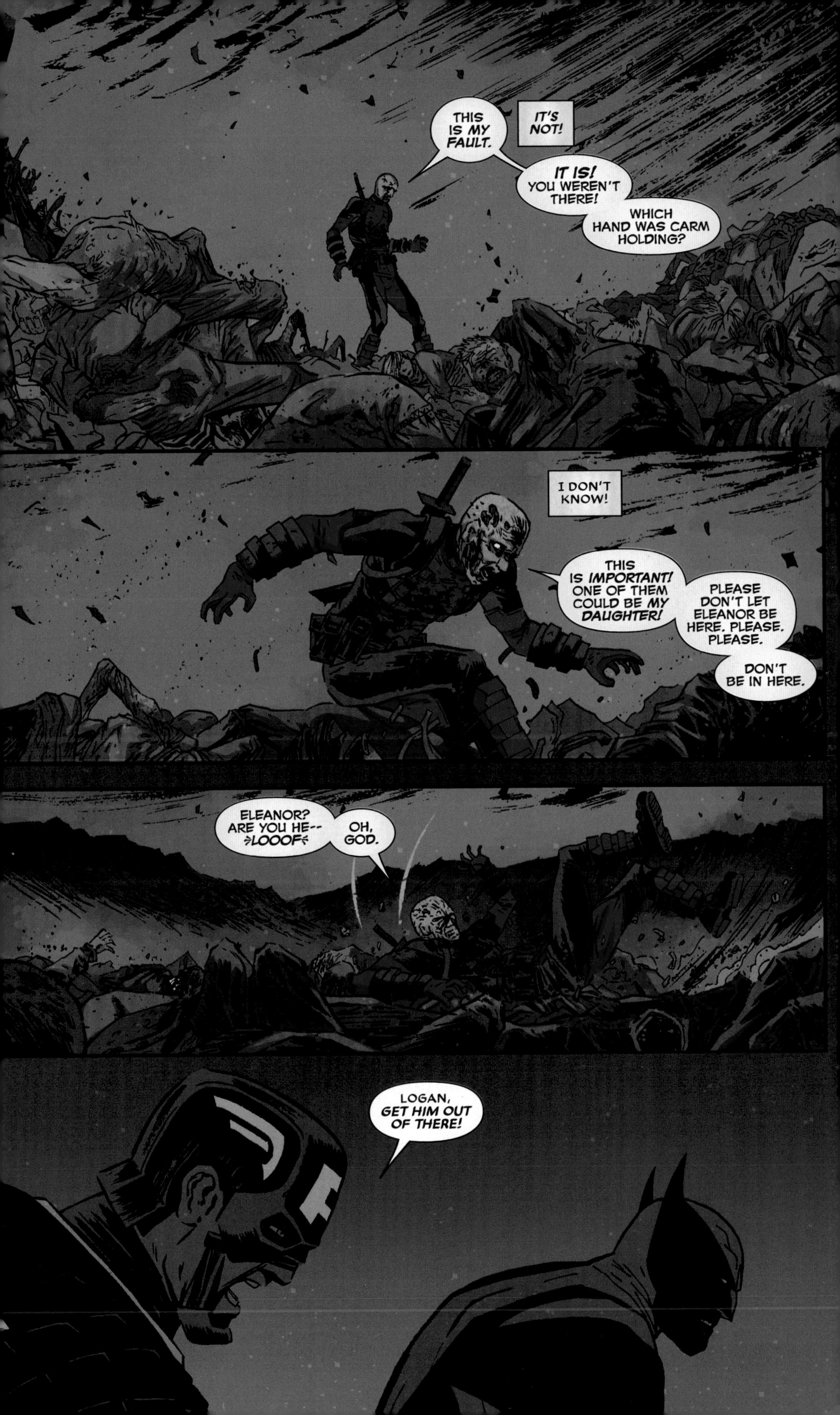
THIS IS MY FAULT.
IT'S NOT!
IT IS! YOU WEREN'T THERE!
WHICH HAND WAS CARM HOLDING?
I DON'T KNOW!
THIS IS IMPORTANT! ONE OF THEM COULD BE MY DAUGHTER!
PLEASE DON'T LET ELEANOR BE HERE. PLEASE. PLEASE.
DON'T BE IN HERE.
ELEANOR? ARE YOU HE-- LOOOF
OH, GOD.
LOGAN, GET HIM OUT OF THERE!

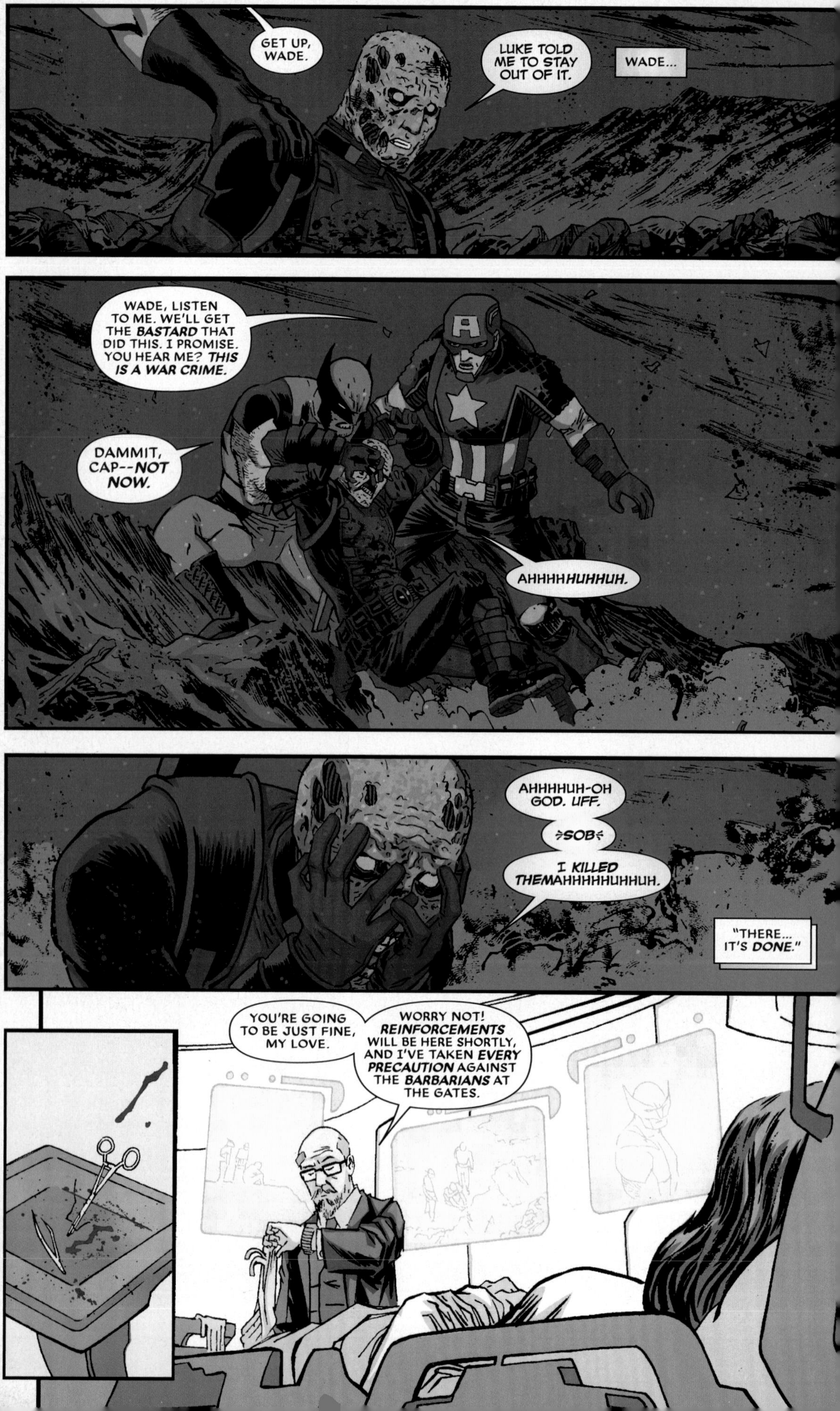
GET UP, WADE.
LUKE TOLD ME TO STAY OUT OF IT.
WADE...
WADE, LISTEN TO ME. WE'LL GET THE BASTARD THAT DID THIS. I PROMISE. YOU HEAR ME? THIS IS A WAR CRIME.
DAMMIT, CAP--NOT NOW.
AHHHHHUHHUH.
AHHHHUH-OH GOD. UFF.
SOB
I KILLED THEMAHHHHHUHHUH.
"THERE... IT'S DONE."
YOU'RE GOING TO BE JUST FINE, MY LOVE.
WORRY NOT! REINFORCEMENTS WILL BE HERE SHORTLY, AND I'VE TAKEN EVERY PRECAUTION AGAINST THE BARBARIANS AT THE GATES.

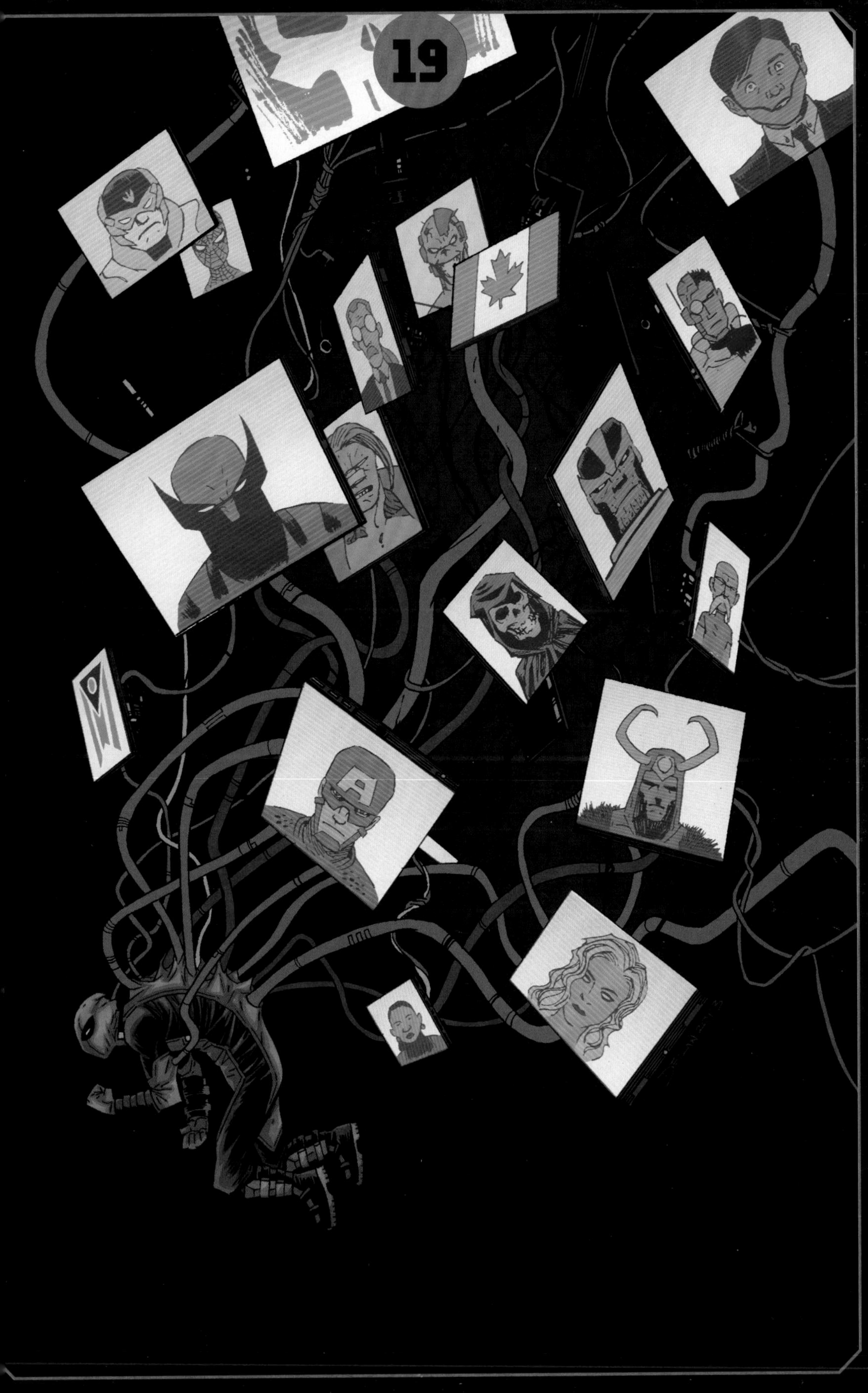
19

THE GOOD, THE BAD AND THE UGLY PART FIVE

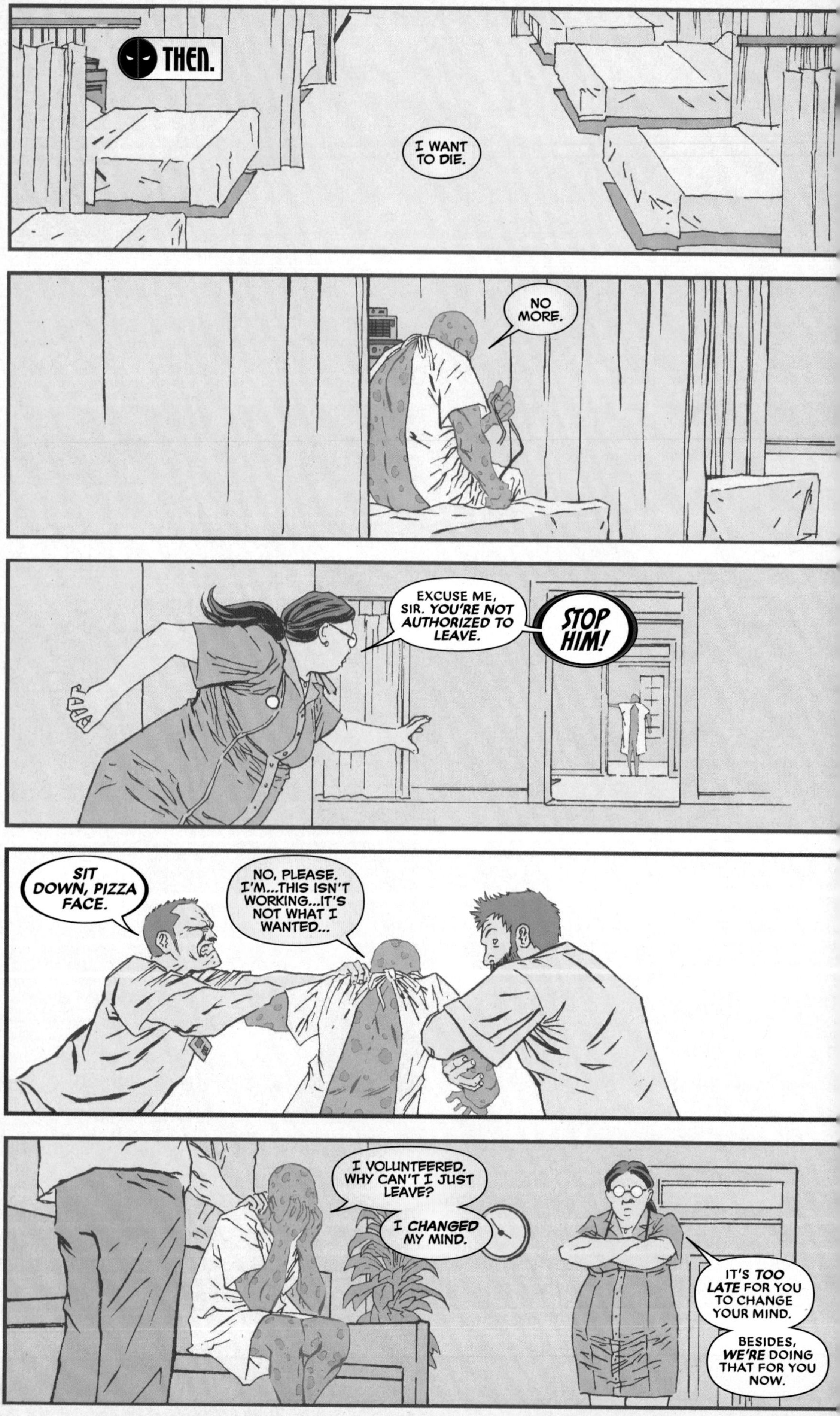
THEN.
I WANT TO DIE.
NO MORE.
EXCUSE ME, SIR. YOU'RE NOT AUTHORIZED TO LEAVE.
STOP HIM!
SIT DOWN, PIZZA FACE.
NO, PLEASE. I'M...THIS ISN'T WORKING...IT'S NOT WHAT I WANTED...
I VOLUNTEERED. WHY CAN'T I JUST LEAVE?
I CHANGED MY MIND.
IT'S TOO LATE FOR YOU TO CHANGE YOUR MIND.
BESIDES, WE'RE DOING THAT FOR YOU NOW.

HA.

YEAH, CAP. GOOD JOB. YOU *WATCH OUR BACKS* WHILE WE GO INTO THIS *HOLE* AND DO WHAT NEEDS TO BE DONE.

HE DOESN'T DESERVE THAT.

WHO CARES?

HE'S OBVIOUSLY GOT OUR FULL GENETIC MAKEUP IN PETRIE DISHES DOWN THERE.

WE GOTTA GET *INSIDE*.

AGREED.

I'LL STAY TOPSIDE. BUT, LOGAN--WE WON'T HAVE LONG.

SNIKT

WIRE THE PLACE TO BLOW, AND, LOGAN--KEEP HIM ON A *SHORT LEASH*.

I'LL TRY.

CAP'S NOT GOING TOPSIDE TO GET SOME *SUN*. HE'S PUTTING HIMSELF BETWEEN US AND THE *ENTIRE* NORTH KOREAN ARMY, SO DON'T BE SUCH A $#&%.

AND IF HE'S *UP THERE*...THEN HE NEVER HAS TO *LIE* ABOUT WHAT WE HAVE TO DO *DOWN HERE*.

NOW GET ON YOUR FEET AND GET TO WORK.

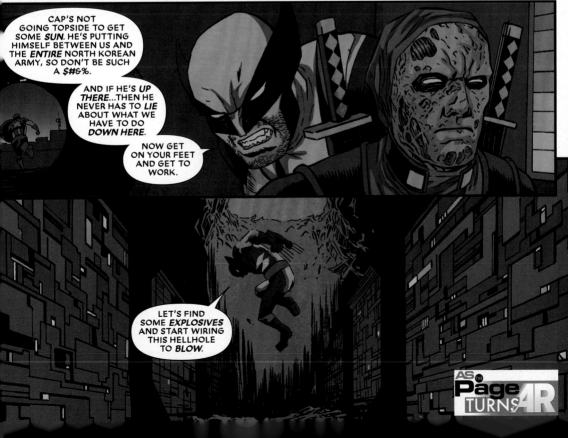

LET'S FIND SOME *EXPLOSIVES* AND START WIRING THIS HELLHOLE TO *BLOW*.

AS THE Page TURNS AR

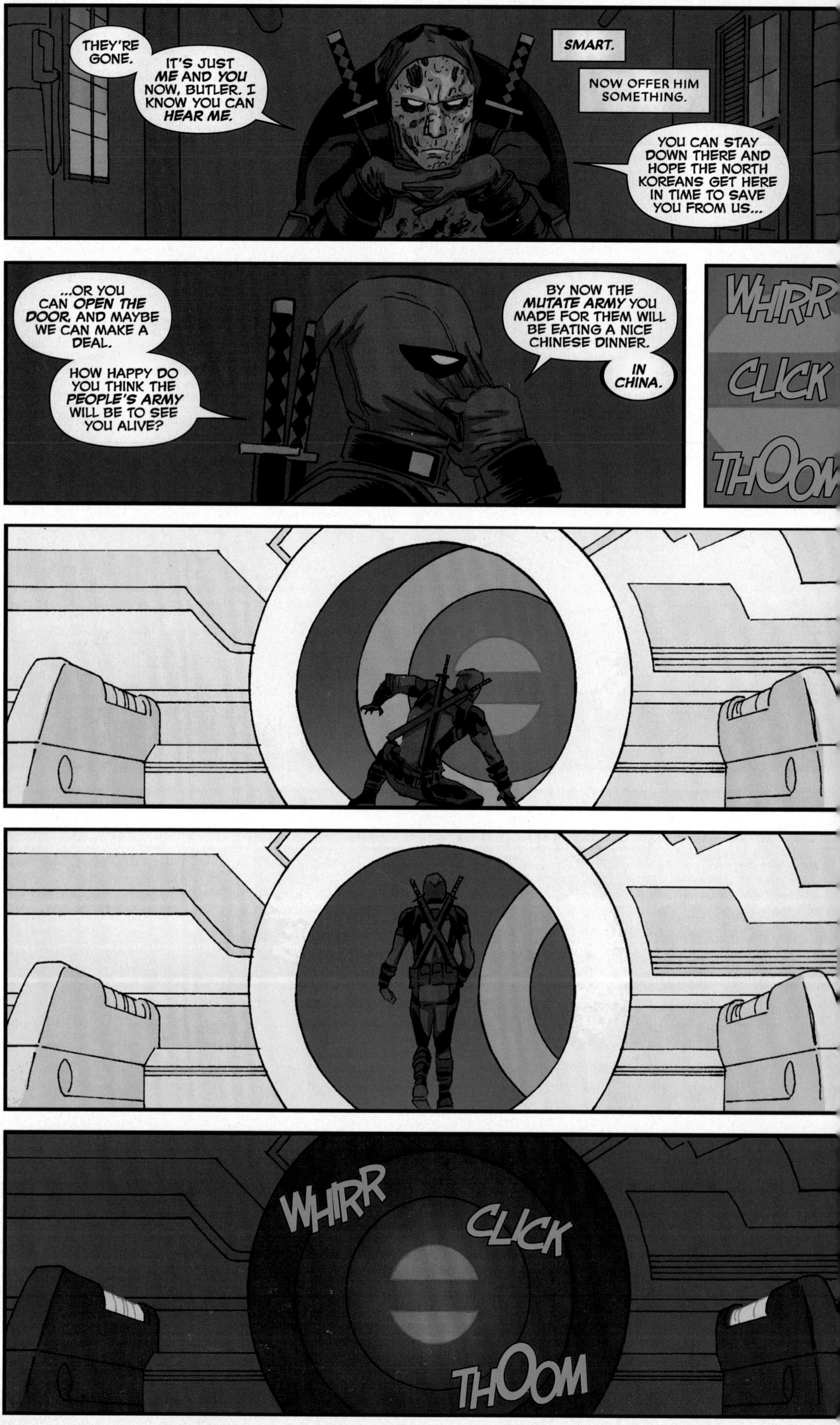
THEY'RE GONE.
IT'S JUST ME AND YOU NOW, BUTLER. I KNOW YOU CAN HEAR ME.
SMART.
NOW OFFER HIM SOMETHING.
YOU CAN STAY DOWN THERE AND HOPE THE NORTH KOREANS GET HERE IN TIME TO SAVE YOU FROM US...
...OR YOU CAN OPEN THE DOOR, AND MAYBE WE CAN MAKE A DEAL.
HOW HAPPY DO YOU THINK THE PEOPLE'S ARMY WILL BE TO SEE YOU ALIVE?
BY NOW THE MUTATE ARMY YOU MADE FOR THEM WILL BE EATING A NICE CHINESE DINNER.
IN CHINA.
WHIRR
CLICK
THOOM
WHIRR
CLICK
THOOM

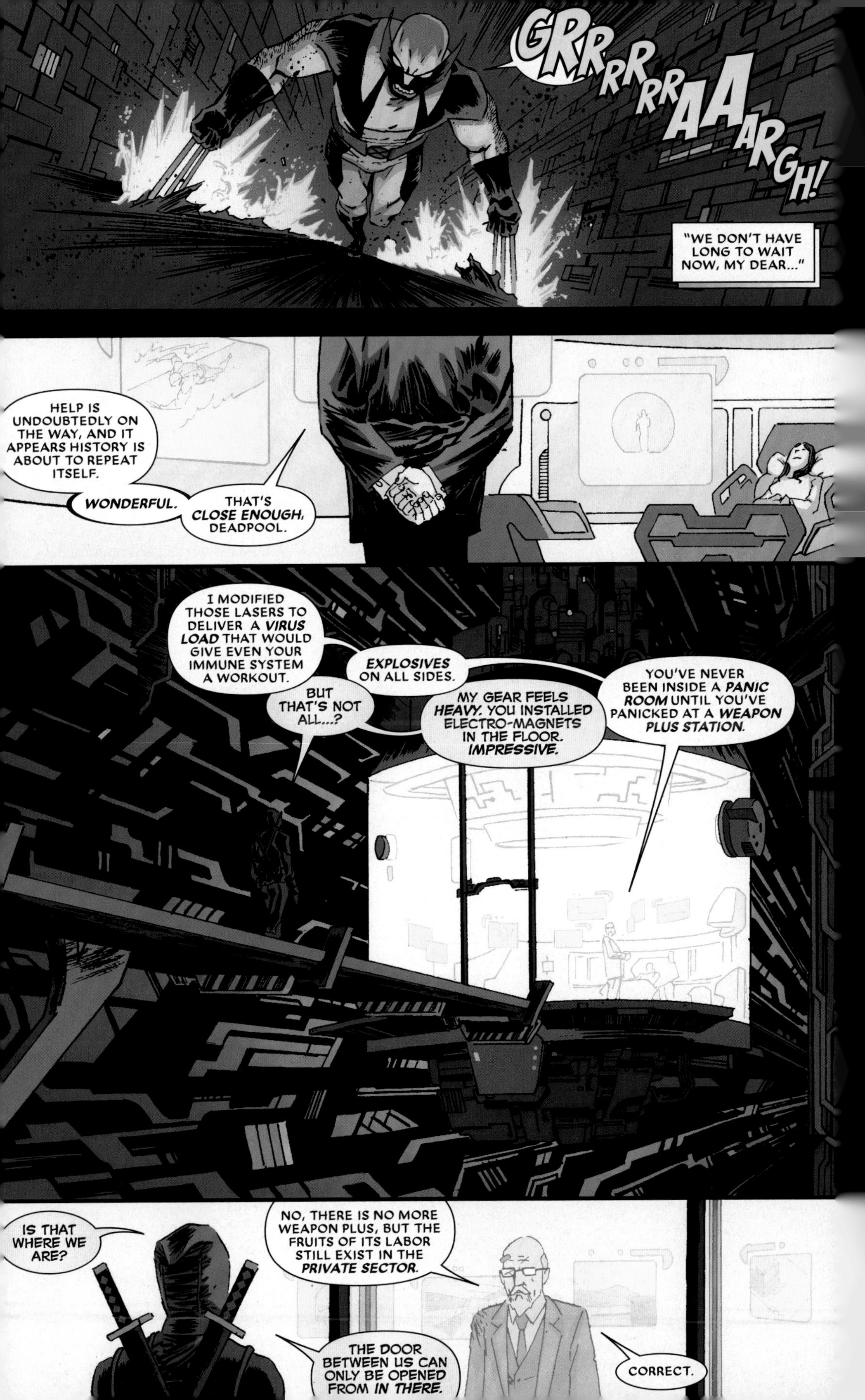
GRRRRRAAARGH!
"WE DON'T HAVE LONG TO WAIT NOW, MY DEAR..."
HELP IS UNDOUBTEDLY ON THE WAY, AND IT APPEARS HISTORY IS ABOUT TO REPEAT ITSELF.
WONDERFUL.
THAT'S CLOSE ENOUGH, DEADPOOL.
I MODIFIED THOSE LASERS TO DELIVER A VIRUS LOAD THAT WOULD GIVE EVEN YOUR IMMUNE SYSTEM A WORKOUT.
BUT THAT'S NOT ALL...?
EXPLOSIVES ON ALL SIDES.
MY GEAR FEELS HEAVY. YOU INSTALLED ELECTRO-MAGNETS IN THE FLOOR. IMPRESSIVE.
YOU'VE NEVER BEEN INSIDE A PANIC ROOM UNTIL YOU'VE PANICKED AT A WEAPON PLUS STATION.
IS THAT WHERE WE ARE?
NO, THERE IS NO MORE WEAPON PLUS, BUT THE FRUITS OF ITS LABOR STILL EXIST IN THE PRIVATE SECTOR.
THE DOOR BETWEEN US CAN ONLY BE OPENED FROM IN THERE.
CORRECT.

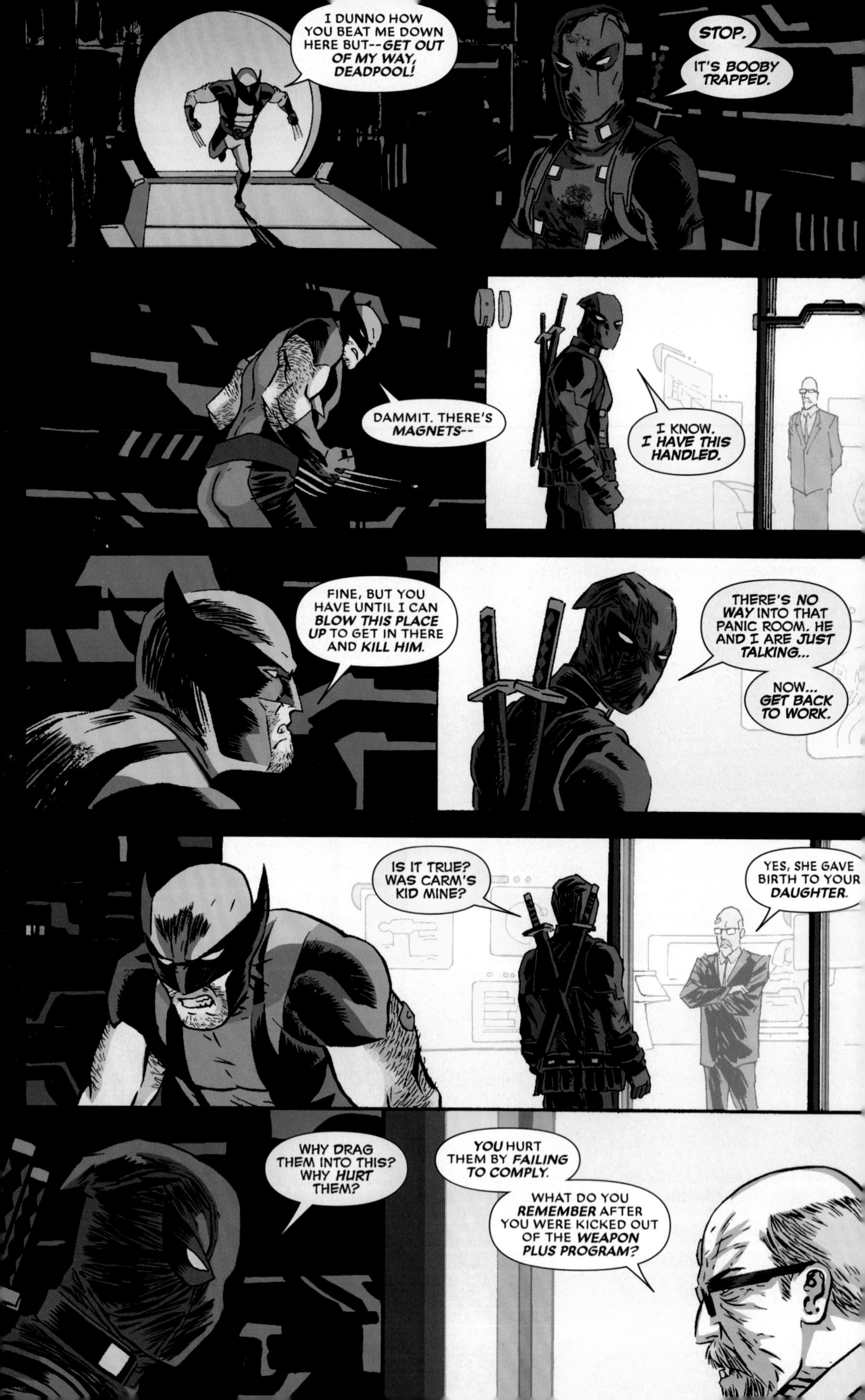
I DUNNO HOW YOU BEAT ME DOWN HERE BUT--GET OUT OF MY WAY, DEADPOOL!
STOP.
IT'S BOOBY TRAPPED.
DAMMIT. THERE'S MAGNETS--
I KNOW. I HAVE THIS HANDLED.
FINE, BUT YOU HAVE UNTIL I CAN BLOW THIS PLACE UP TO GET IN THERE AND KILL HIM.
THERE'S NO WAY INTO THAT PANIC ROOM. HE AND I ARE JUST TALKING...
NOW... GET BACK TO WORK.
IS IT TRUE? WAS CARM'S KID MINE?
YES, SHE GAVE BIRTH TO YOUR DAUGHTER.
WHY DRAG THEM INTO THIS? WHY HURT THEM?
YOU HURT THEM BY FAILING TO COMPLY.
WHAT DO YOU REMEMBER AFTER YOU WERE KICKED OUT OF THE WEAPON PLUS PROGRAM?

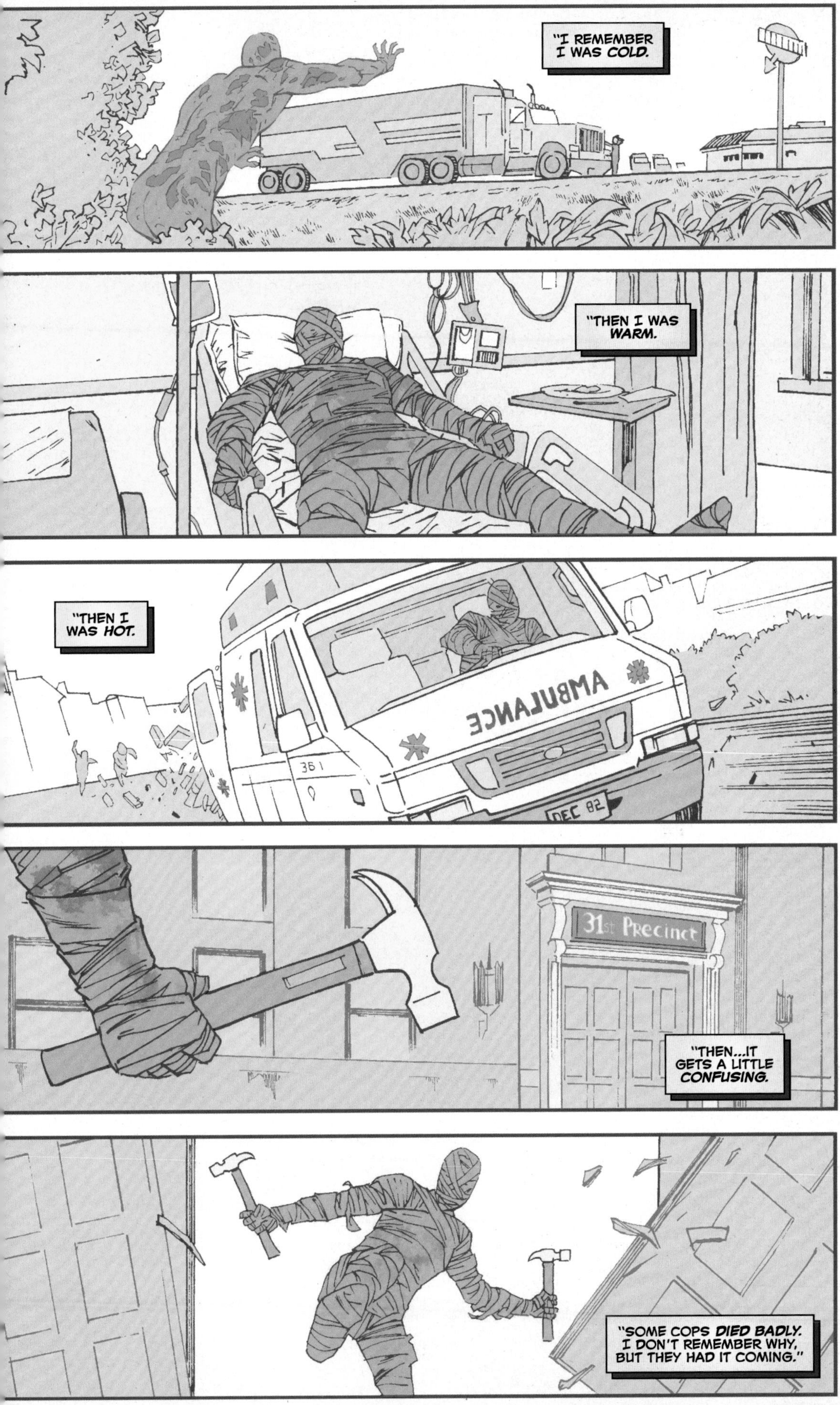
"I REMEMBER I WAS COLD.
"THEN I WAS WARM.
"THEN I WAS HOT.
AMBULANCE
361
DEC 82
31st Precinct
"THEN...IT GETS A LITTLE CONFUSING.
"SOME COPS DIED BADLY. I DON'T REMEMBER WHY, BUT THEY HAD IT COMING."

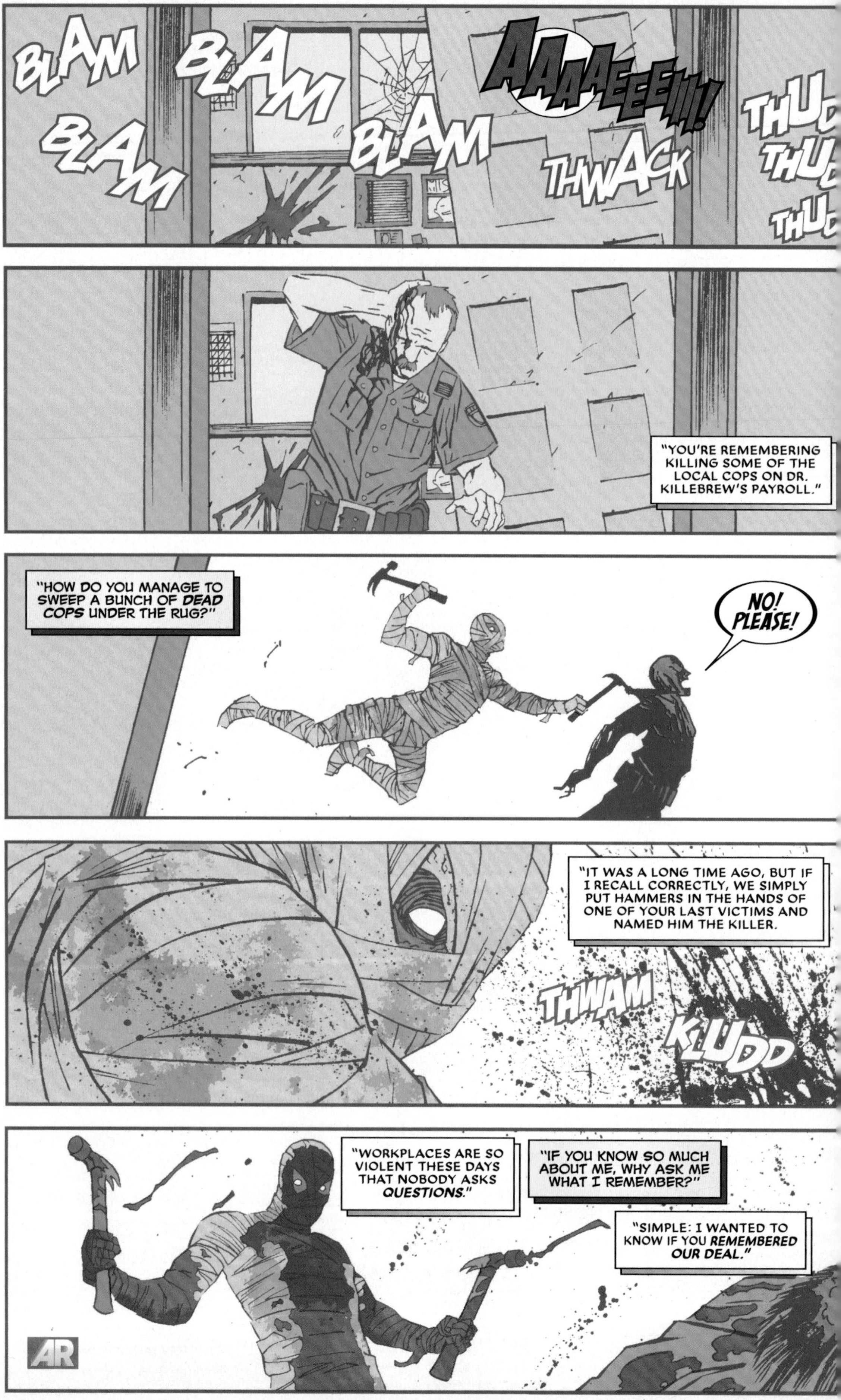

BLAM
BLAM
BLAM
BLAM
AAAAEEEIIII!
THWACK
THUD
THUD
THUD
"YOU'RE REMEMBERING KILLING SOME OF THE LOCAL COPS ON DR. KILLEBREW'S PAYROLL."
"HOW DO YOU MANAGE TO SWEEP A BUNCH OF *DEAD COPS* UNDER THE RUG?"
NO! PLEASE!
"IT WAS A LONG TIME AGO, BUT IF I RECALL CORRECTLY, WE SIMPLY PUT HAMMERS IN THE HANDS OF ONE OF YOUR LAST VICTIMS AND NAMED HIM THE KILLER.
THWAM
KLUDD
"WORKPLACES ARE SO VIOLENT THESE DAYS THAT NOBODY ASKS *QUESTIONS.*"
"IF YOU KNOW SO MUCH ABOUT ME, WHY ASK ME WHAT I REMEMBER?"
"SIMPLE: I WANTED TO KNOW IF YOU *REMEMBERED OUR DEAL.*"
AR

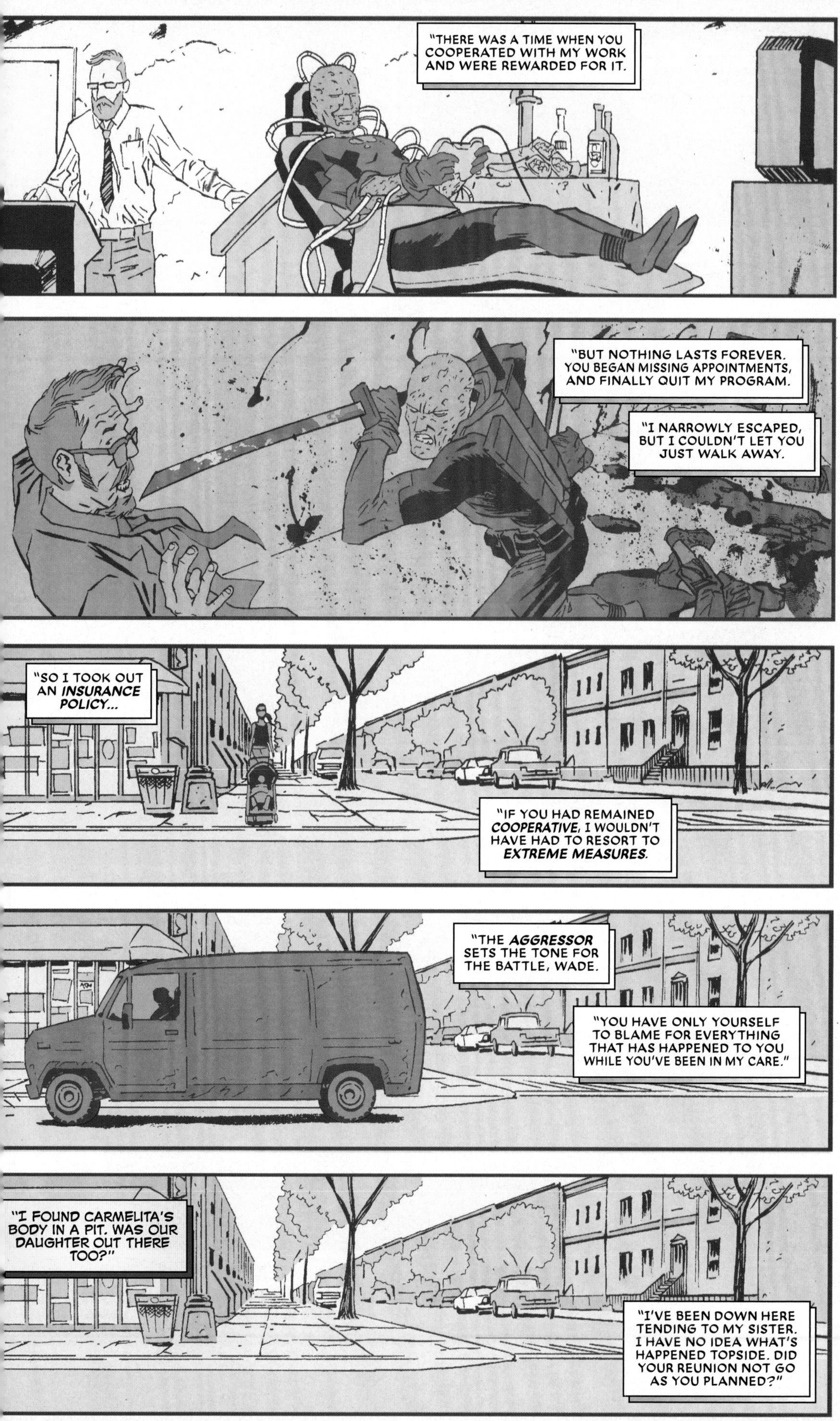
"THERE WAS A TIME WHEN YOU COOPERATED WITH MY WORK AND WERE REWARDED FOR IT.
"BUT NOTHING LASTS FOREVER. YOU BEGAN MISSING APPOINTMENTS, AND FINALLY QUIT MY PROGRAM.
"I NARROWLY ESCAPED, BUT I COULDN'T LET YOU JUST WALK AWAY.
"SO I TOOK OUT AN *INSURANCE POLICY*...
"IF YOU HAD REMAINED *COOPERATIVE*, I WOULDN'T HAVE HAD TO RESORT TO *EXTREME MEASURES*.
"THE *AGGRESSOR* SETS THE TONE FOR THE BATTLE, WADE.
"YOU HAVE ONLY YOURSELF TO BLAME FOR EVERYTHING THAT HAS HAPPENED TO YOU WHILE YOU'VE BEEN IN MY CARE."
"I FOUND CARMELITA'S BODY IN A PIT. WAS OUR DAUGHTER OUT THERE TOO?"
"I'VE BEEN DOWN HERE TENDING TO MY SISTER. I HAVE NO IDEA WHAT'S HAPPENED TOPSIDE. DID YOUR REUNION NOT GO AS YOU PLANNED?"

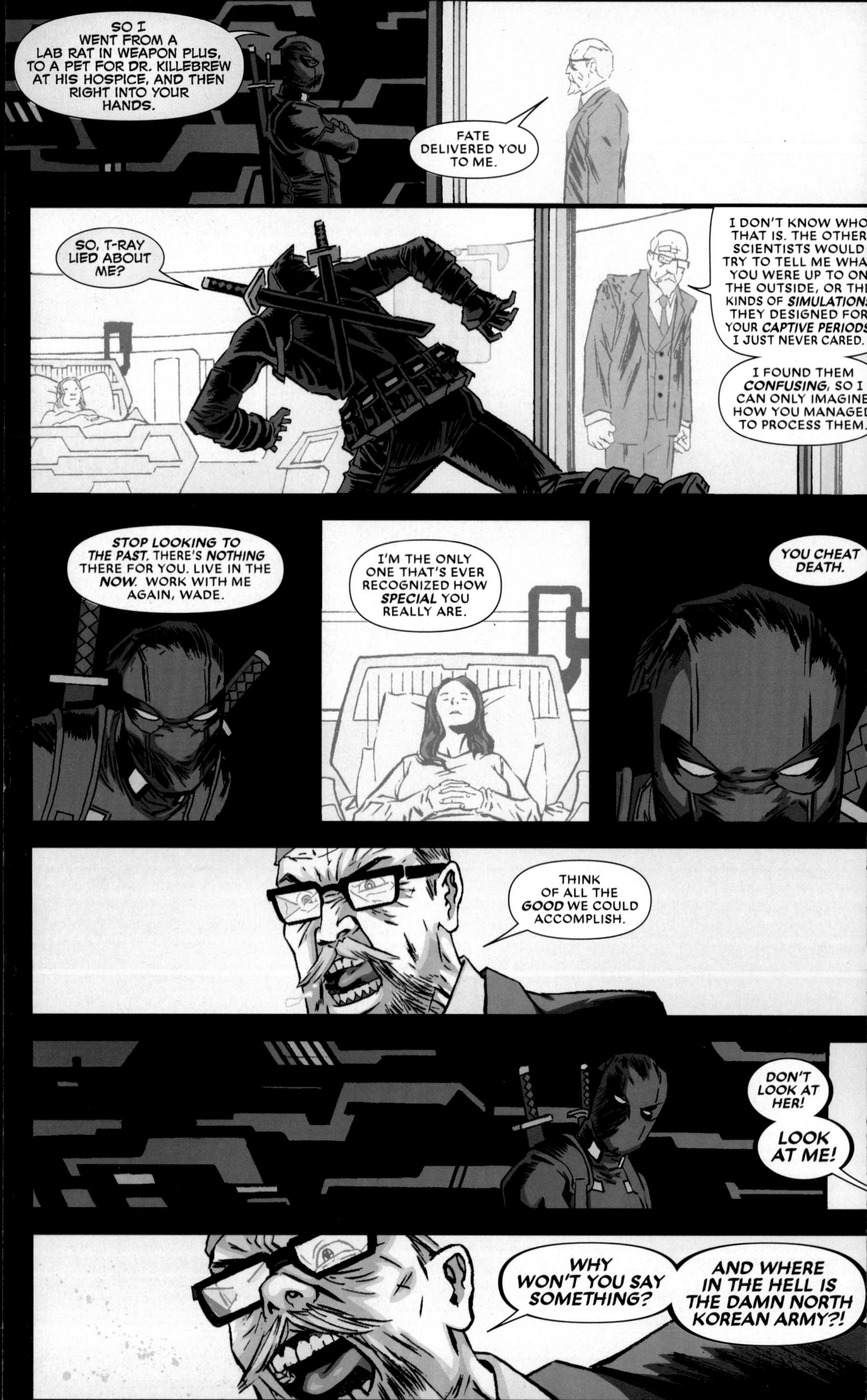
SO I WENT FROM A LAB RAT IN WEAPON PLUS, TO A PET FOR DR. KILLEBREW AT HIS HOSPICE, AND THEN RIGHT INTO YOUR HANDS.
FATE DELIVERED YOU TO ME.
SO, T-RAY LIED ABOUT ME?
I DON'T KNOW WHO THAT IS. THE OTHER SCIENTISTS WOULD TRY TO TELL ME WHA YOU WERE UP TO ON THE OUTSIDE, OR TH KINDS OF SIMULATION THEY DESIGNED FOR YOUR CAPTIVE PERIODS I JUST NEVER CARED.
I FOUND THEM CONFUSING, SO I CAN ONLY IMAGINE HOW YOU MANAGED TO PROCESS THEM.
STOP LOOKING TO THE PAST. THERE'S NOTHING THERE FOR YOU. LIVE IN THE NOW. WORK WITH ME AGAIN, WADE.
I'M THE ONLY ONE THAT'S EVER RECOGNIZED HOW SPECIAL YOU REALLY ARE.
YOU CHEAT DEATH.
THINK OF ALL THE GOOD WE COULD ACCOMPLISH.
DON'T LOOK AT HER!
LOOK AT ME!
WHY WON'T YOU SAY SOMETHING?
AND WHERE IN THE HELL IS THE DAMN NORTH KOREAN ARMY?!

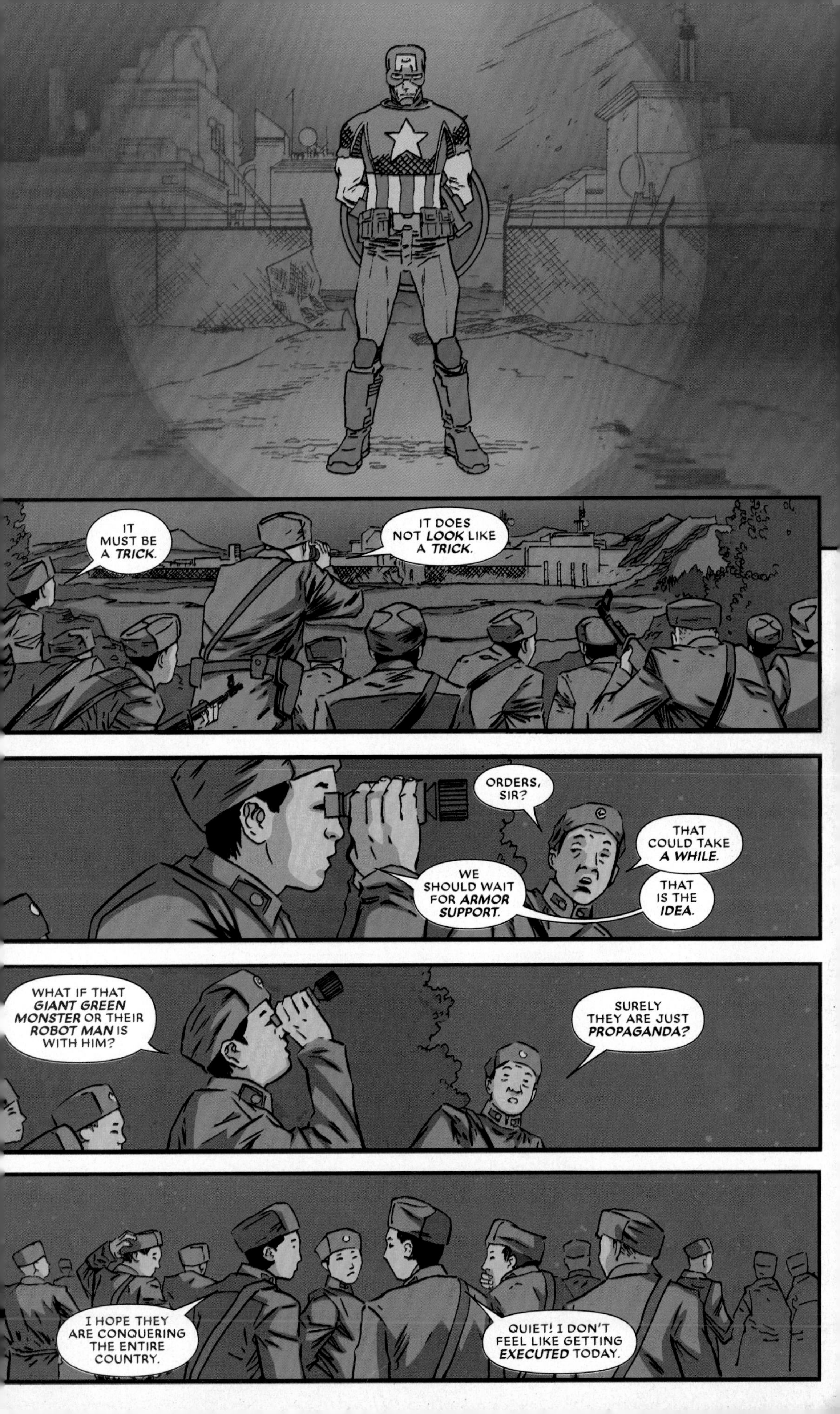

IT MUST BE A TRICK.
IT DOES NOT LOOK LIKE A TRICK.
ORDERS, SIR?
WE SHOULD WAIT FOR ARMOR SUPPORT.
THAT COULD TAKE A WHILE.
THAT IS THE IDEA.
WHAT IF THAT GIANT GREEN MONSTER OR THEIR ROBOT MAN IS WITH HIM?
SURELY THEY ARE JUST PROPAGANDA?
I HOPE THEY ARE CONQUERING THE ENTIRE COUNTRY.
QUIET! I DON'T FEEL LIKE GETTING EXECUTED TODAY.

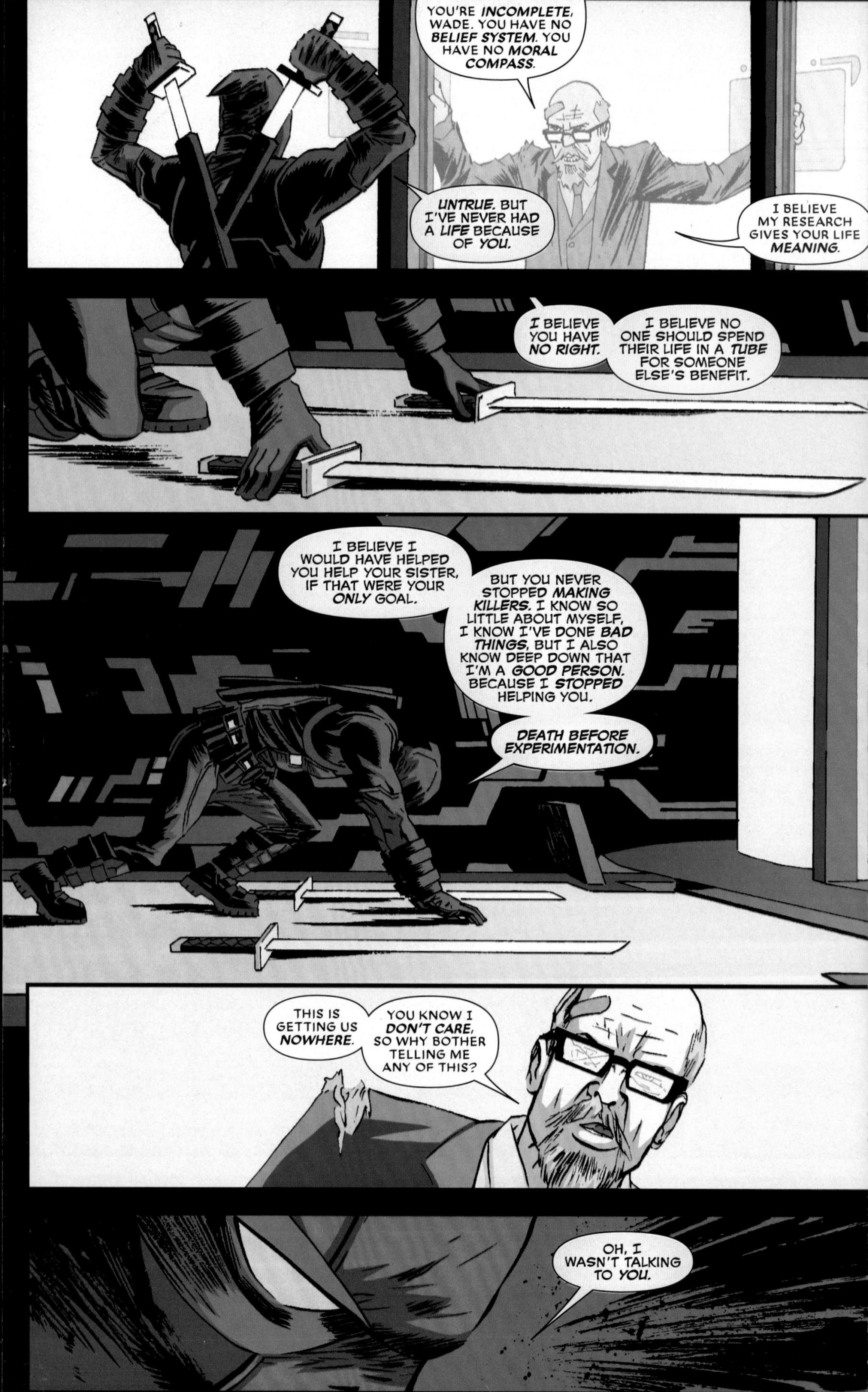
YOU'RE INCOMPLETE, WADE. YOU HAVE NO BELIEF SYSTEM. YOU HAVE NO MORAL COMPASS.
UNTRUE. BUT I'VE NEVER HAD A LIFE BECAUSE OF YOU.
I BELIEVE MY RESEARCH GIVES YOUR LIFE MEANING.
I BELIEVE YOU HAVE NO RIGHT.
I BELIEVE NO ONE SHOULD SPEND THEIR LIFE IN A TUBE FOR SOMEONE ELSE'S BENEFIT.
I BELIEVE I WOULD HAVE HELPED YOU HELP YOUR SISTER, IF THAT WERE YOUR ONLY GOAL.
BUT YOU NEVER STOPPED MAKING KILLERS. I KNOW SO LITTLE ABOUT MYSELF, I KNOW I'VE DONE BAD THINGS, BUT I ALSO KNOW DEEP DOWN THAT I'M A GOOD PERSON. BECAUSE I STOPPED HELPING YOU.
DEATH BEFORE EXPERIMENTATION.
THIS IS GETTING US NOWHERE.
YOU KNOW I DON'T CARE, SO WHY BOTHER TELLING ME ANY OF THIS?
OH, I WASN'T TALKING TO YOU.

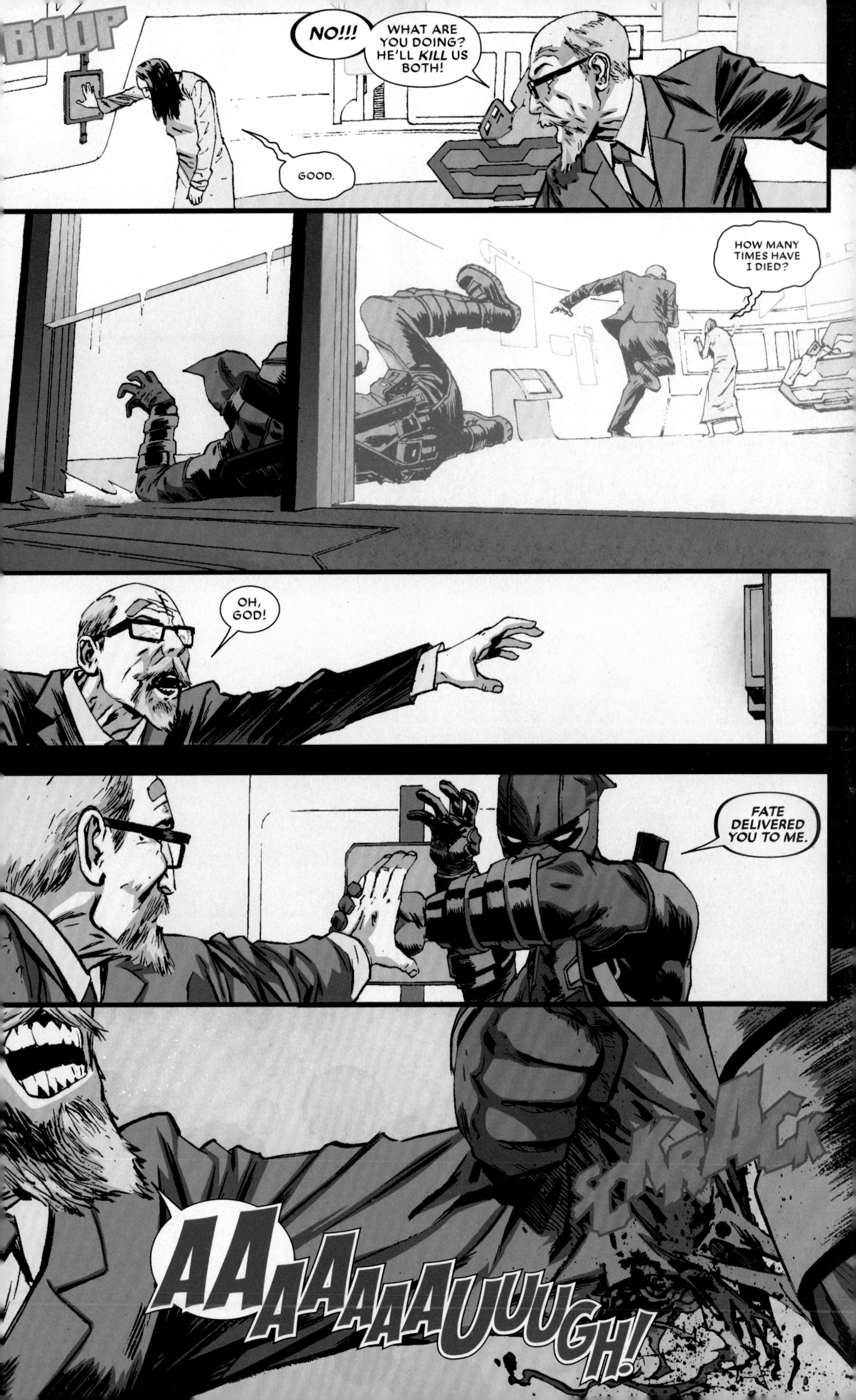
BOOP
NO!!!
WHAT ARE YOU DOING? HE'LL KILL US BOTH!
GOOD.
HOW MANY TIMES HAVE I DIED?
OH, GOD!
FATE DELIVERED YOU TO ME.
SCHRACK
AAAAAAAAUUUUGH!

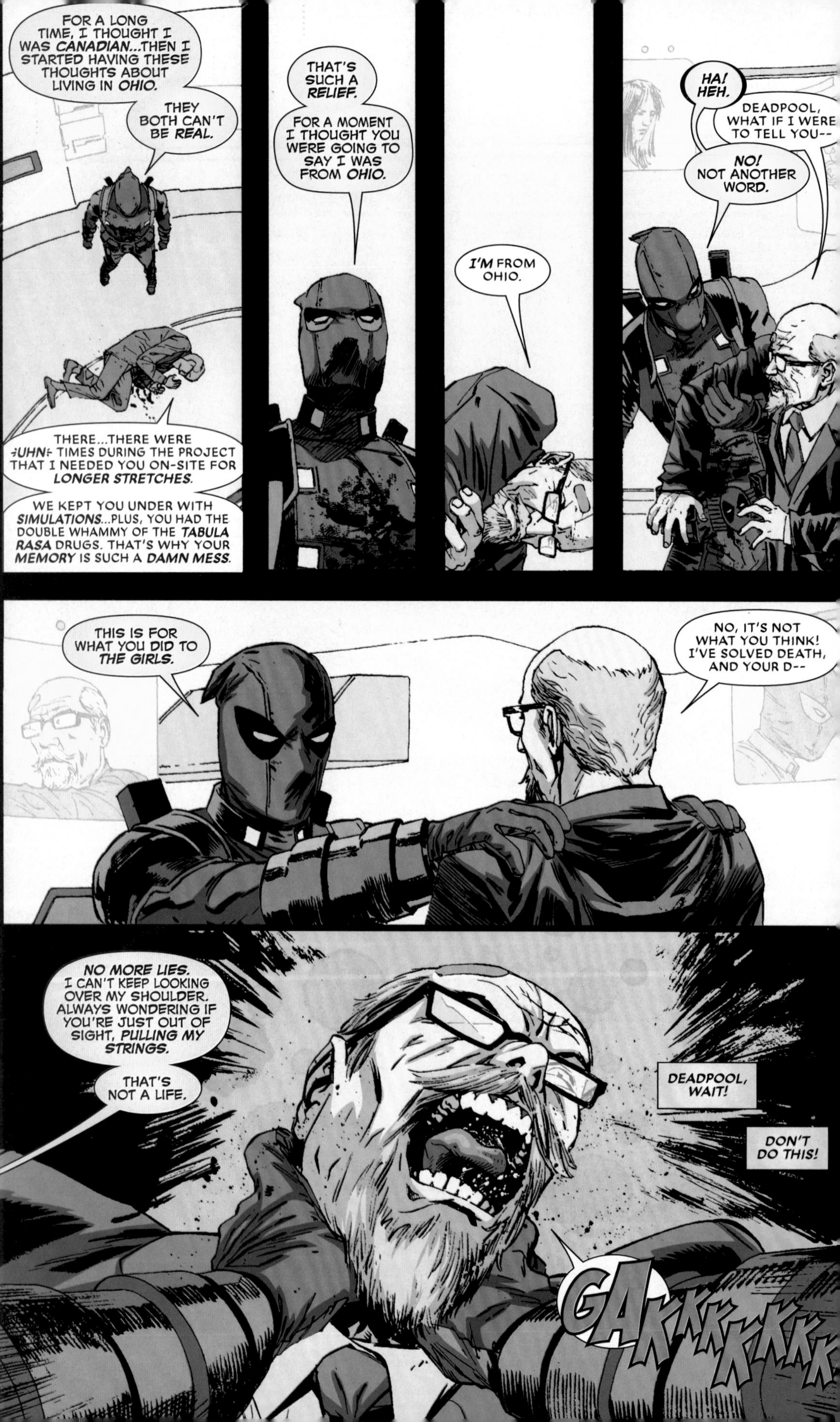

FOR A LONG TIME, I THOUGHT I WAS *CANADIAN*...THEN I STARTED HAVING THESE THOUGHTS ABOUT LIVING IN *OHIO.*
THEY BOTH CAN'T BE *REAL.*
THERE...THERE WERE ‡UHN‡ TIMES DURING THE PROJECT THAT I NEEDED YOU ON-SITE FOR *LONGER STRETCHES.*
WE KEPT YOU UNDER WITH *SIMULATIONS*...PLUS, YOU HAD THE DOUBLE WHAMMY OF THE *TABULA RASA* DRUGS. THAT'S WHY YOUR *MEMORY* IS SUCH A *DAMN MESS.*
THAT'S SUCH A *RELIEF.*
FOR A MOMENT I THOUGHT YOU WERE GOING TO SAY I WAS FROM *OHIO.*
I'M FROM OHIO.
HA! HEH.
DEADPOOL, WHAT IF I WERE TO TELL YOU--
NO! NOT ANOTHER *WORD.*
THIS IS FOR WHAT YOU *DID* TO *THE GIRLS.*
NO, IT'S NOT WHAT YOU THINK! I'VE SOLVED DEATH, AND YOUR D--
NO MORE LIES. I CAN'T KEEP LOOKING OVER MY SHOULDER. ALWAYS WONDERING IF YOU'RE JUST OUT OF SIGHT, *PULLING MY STRINGS.*
THAT'S NOT A LIFE.
DEADPOOL, WAIT!
DON'T DO THIS!
GAKKKKKK

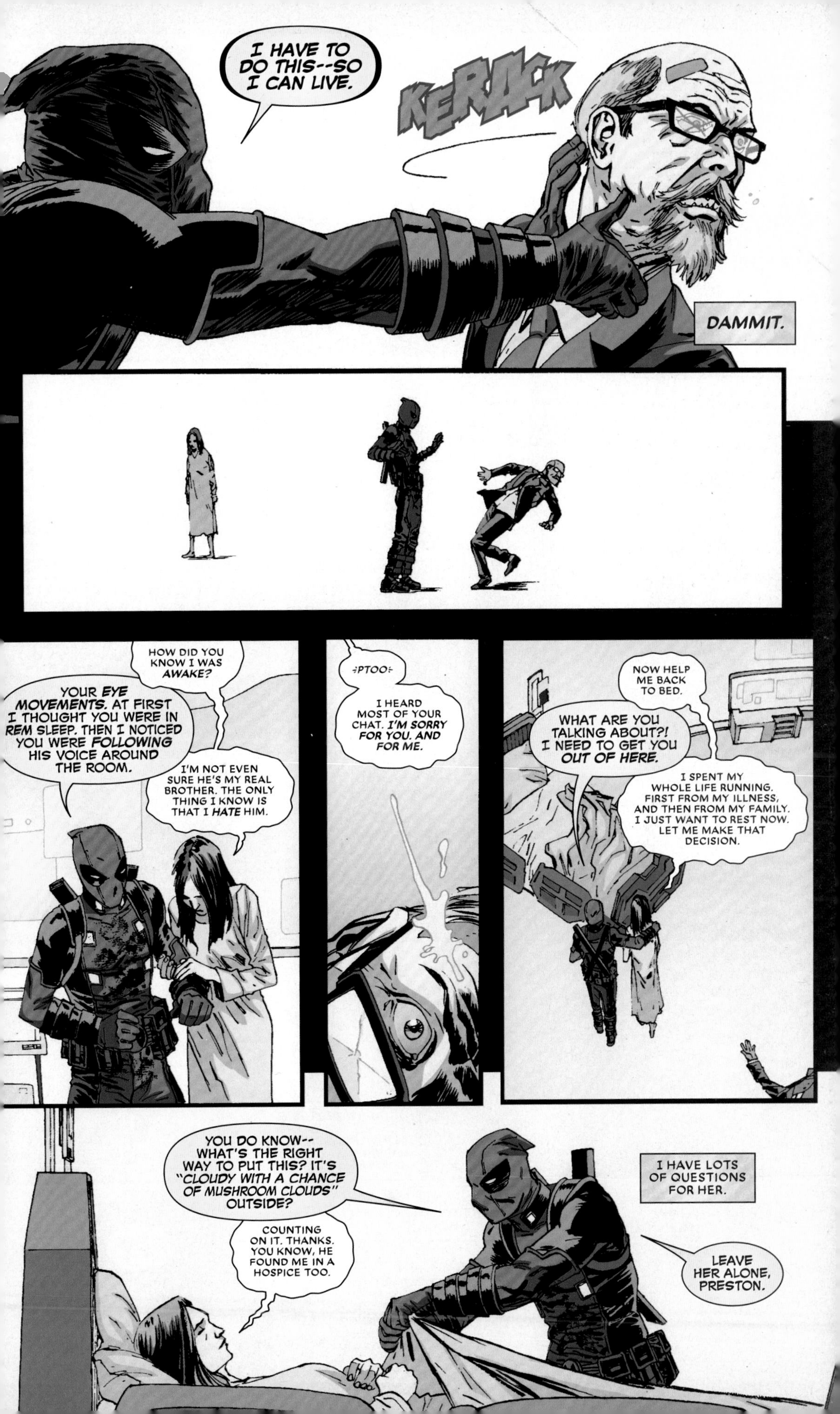

I HAVE TO DO THIS--SO I CAN LIVE.
KERACK
DAMMIT.
HOW DID YOU KNOW I WAS AWAKE?
YOUR EYE MOVEMENTS. AT FIRST I THOUGHT YOU WERE IN REM SLEEP. THEN I NOTICED YOU WERE FOLLOWING HIS VOICE AROUND THE ROOM.
I'M NOT EVEN SURE HE'S MY REAL BROTHER. THE ONLY THING I KNOW IS THAT I HATE HIM.
PTOO
I HEARD MOST OF YOUR CHAT. I'M SORRY FOR YOU. AND FOR ME.
NOW HELP ME BACK TO BED.
WHAT ARE YOU TALKING ABOUT?! I NEED TO GET YOU OUT OF HERE.
I SPENT MY WHOLE LIFE RUNNING. FIRST FROM MY ILLNESS, AND THEN FROM MY FAMILY. I JUST WANT TO REST NOW. LET ME MAKE THAT DECISION.
YOU DO KNOW--WHAT'S THE RIGHT WAY TO PUT THIS? IT'S "CLOUDY WITH A CHANCE OF MUSHROOM CLOUDS" OUTSIDE?
COUNTING ON IT. THANKS. YOU KNOW, HE FOUND ME IN A HOSPICE TOO.
I HAVE LOTS OF QUESTIONS FOR HER.
LEAVE HER ALONE, PRESTON.

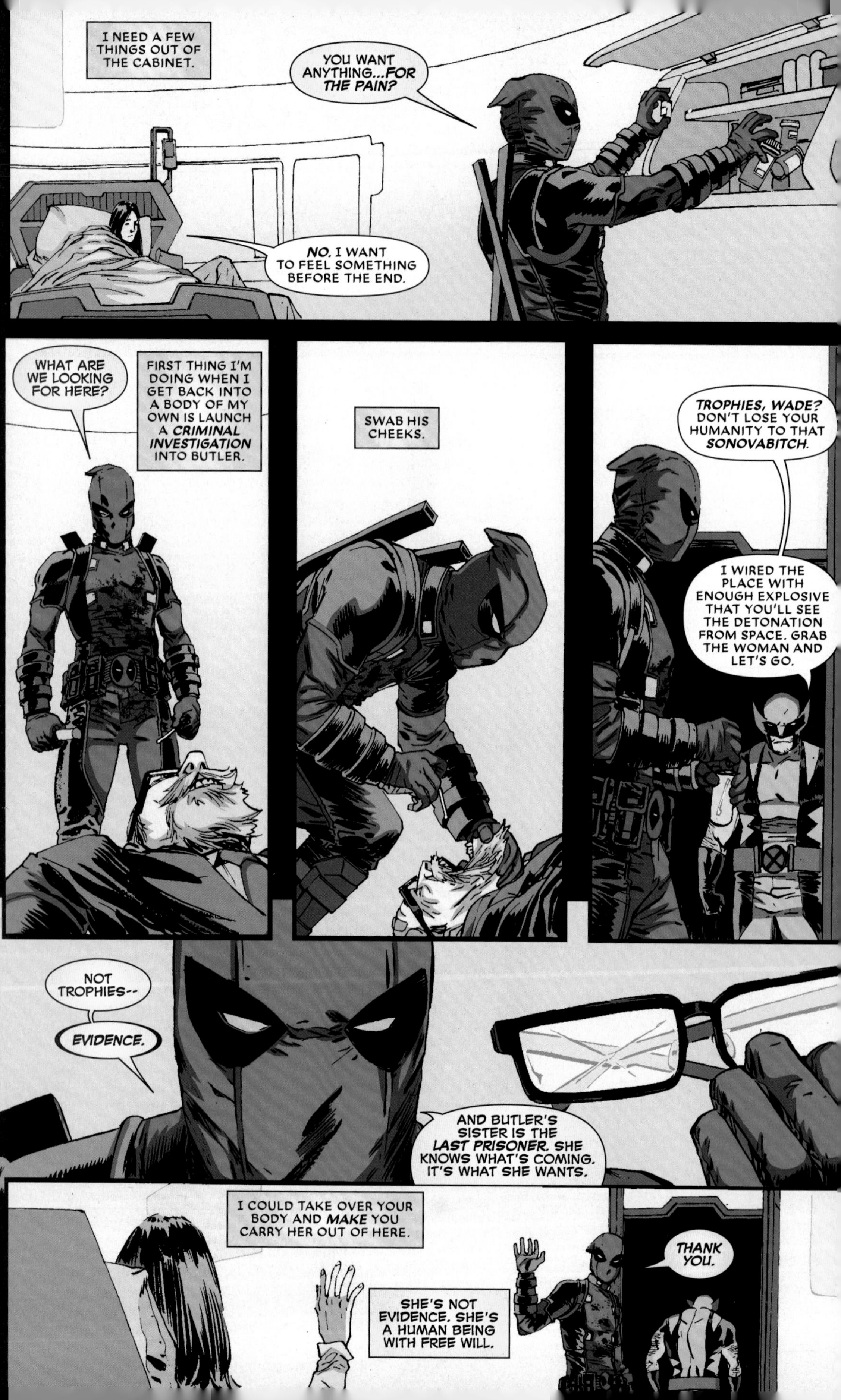
I NEED A FEW THINGS OUT OF THE CABINET.
YOU WANT ANYTHING...FOR THE PAIN?
NO. I WANT TO FEEL SOMETHING BEFORE THE END.
WHAT ARE WE LOOKING FOR HERE?
FIRST THING I'M DOING WHEN I GET BACK INTO A BODY OF MY OWN IS LAUNCH A CRIMINAL INVESTIGATION INTO BUTLER.
SWAB HIS CHEEKS.
TROPHIES, WADE? DON'T LOSE YOUR HUMANITY TO THAT SONOVABITCH.
I WIRED THE PLACE WITH ENOUGH EXPLOSIVE THAT YOU'LL SEE THE DETONATION FROM SPACE. GRAB THE WOMAN AND LET'S GO.
NOT TROPHIES--
EVIDENCE.
AND BUTLER'S SISTER IS THE LAST PRISONER. SHE KNOWS WHAT'S COMING. IT'S WHAT SHE WANTS.
I COULD TAKE OVER YOUR BODY AND MAKE YOU CARRY HER OUT OF HERE.
SHE'S NOT EVIDENCE. SHE'S A HUMAN BEING WITH FREE WILL.
THANK YOU.

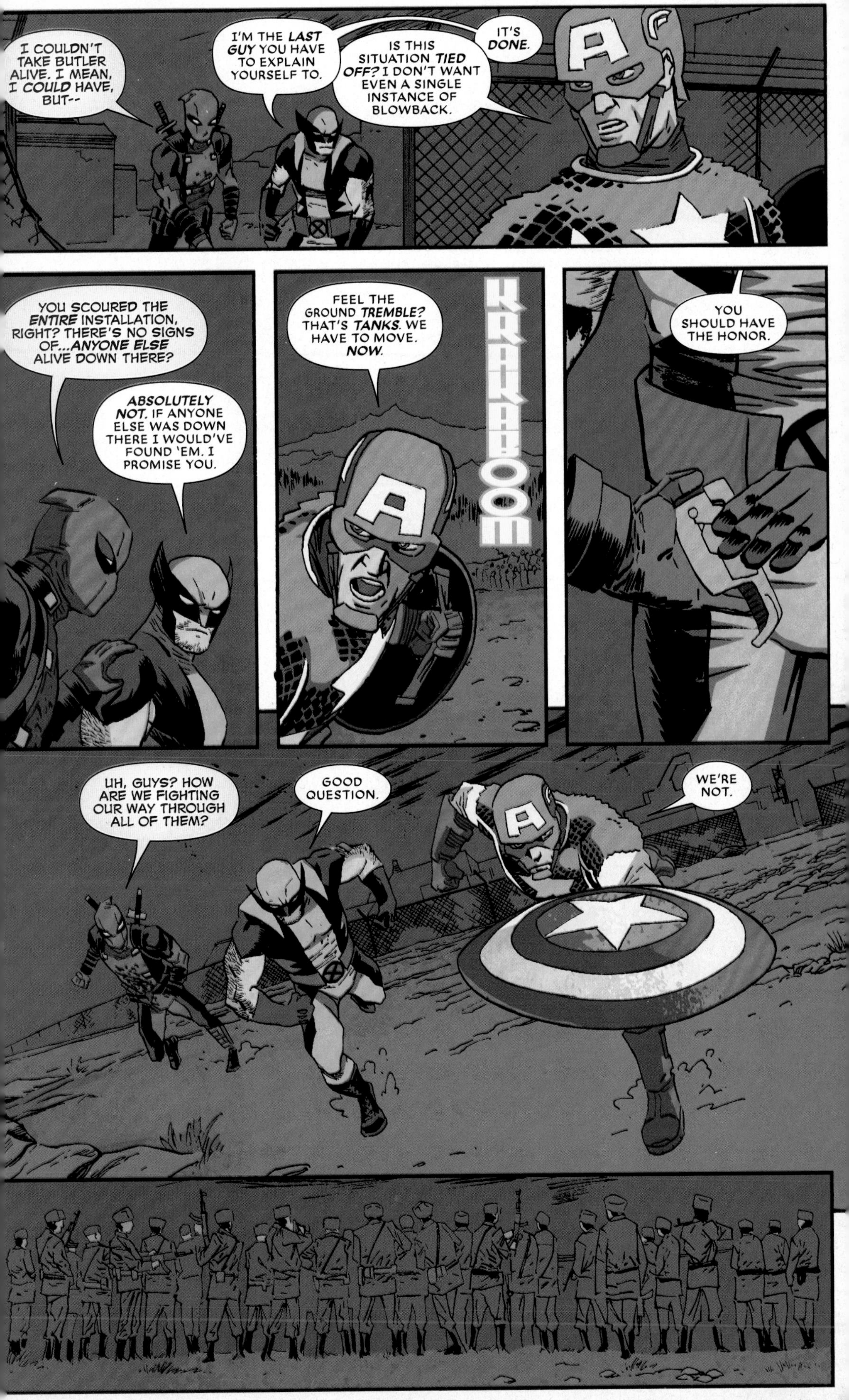
I COULDN'T TAKE BUTLER ALIVE. I MEAN, I COULD HAVE, BUT--
I'M THE LAST GUY YOU HAVE TO EXPLAIN YOURSELF TO.
IS THIS SITUATION TIED OFF? I DON'T WANT EVEN A SINGLE INSTANCE OF BLOWBACK.
IT'S DONE.
YOU SCOURED THE ENTIRE INSTALLATION, RIGHT? THERE'S NO SIGNS OF...ANYONE ELSE ALIVE DOWN THERE?
ABSOLUTELY NOT. IF ANYONE ELSE WAS DOWN THERE I WOULD'VE FOUND 'EM. I PROMISE YOU.
FEEL THE GROUND TREMBLE? THAT'S TANKS. WE HAVE TO MOVE. NOW.
KRAKABOOM
YOU SHOULD HAVE THE HONOR.
UH, GUYS? HOW ARE WE FIGHTING OUR WAY THROUGH ALL OF THEM?
GOOD QUESTION.
WE'RE NOT.

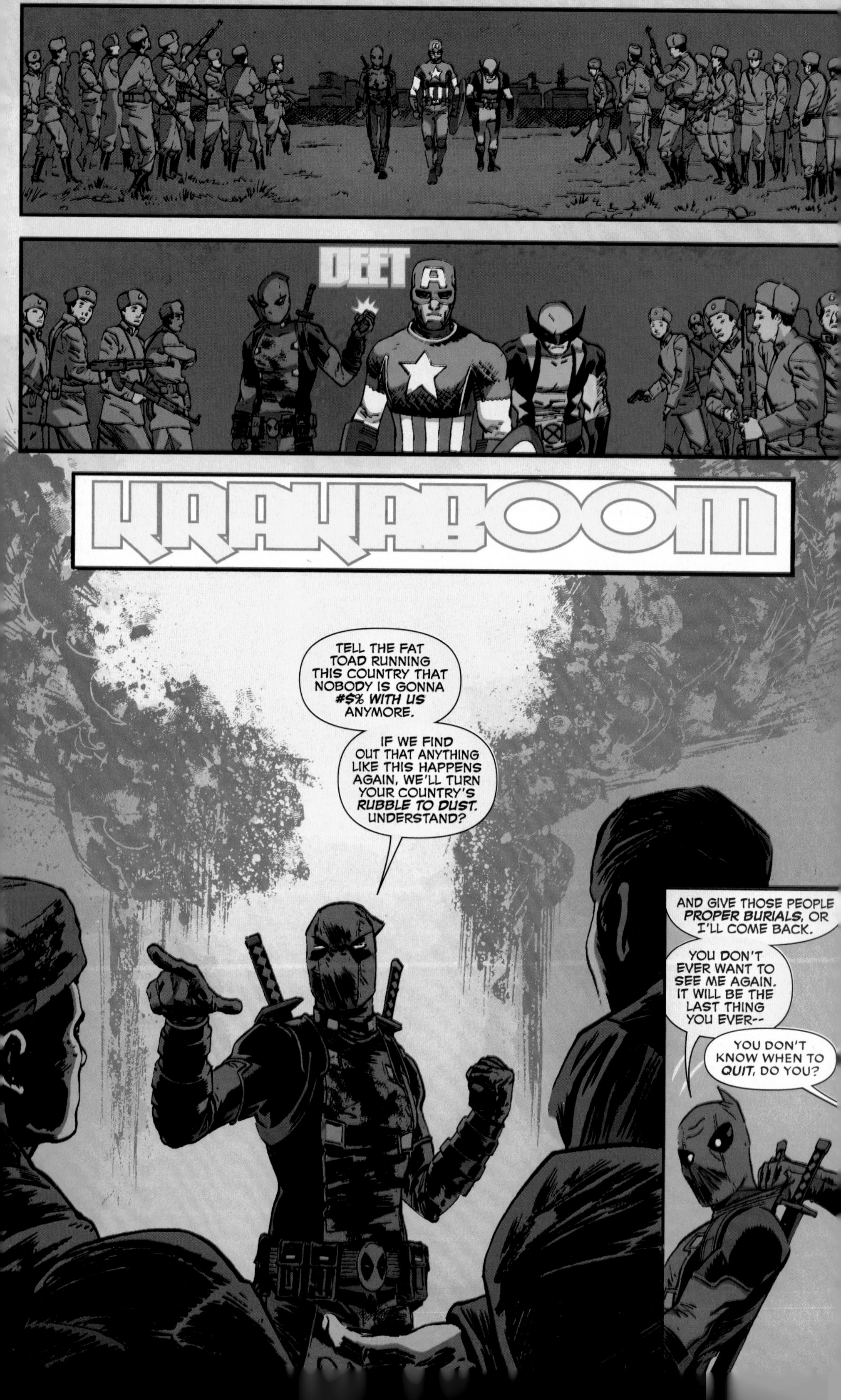
DEET
KRAKABOOM
TELL THE FAT TOAD RUNNING THIS COUNTRY THAT NOBODY IS GONNA #$% WITH US ANYMORE.
IF WE FIND OUT THAT ANYTHING LIKE THIS HAPPENS AGAIN, WE'LL TURN YOUR COUNTRY'S RUBBLE TO DUST. UNDERSTAND?
AND GIVE THOSE PEOPLE PROPER BURIALS, OR I'LL COME BACK.
YOU DON'T EVER WANT TO SEE ME AGAIN. IT WILL BE THE LAST THING YOU EVER--
YOU DON'T KNOW WHEN TO QUIT, DO YOU?

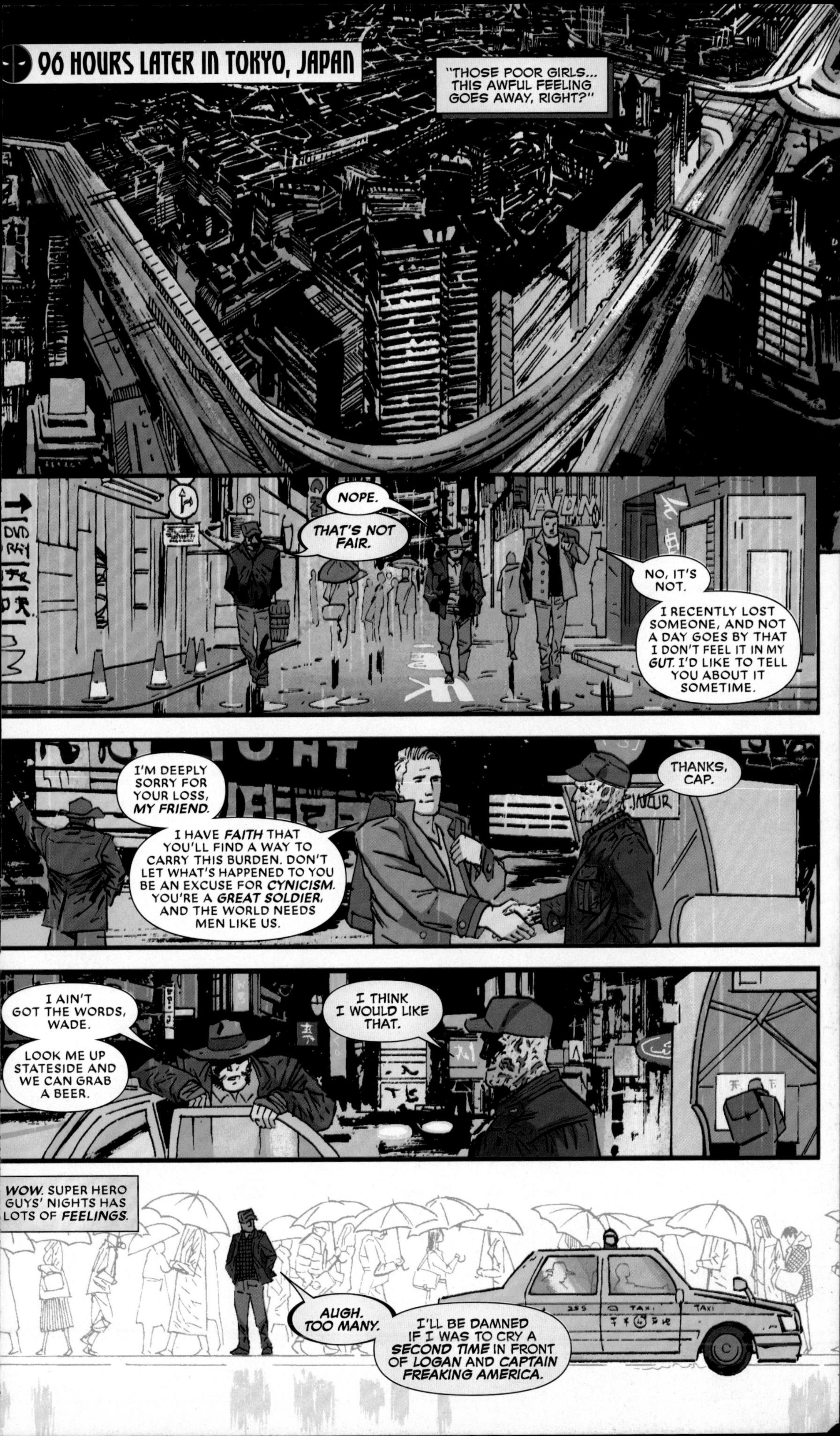

96 HOURS LATER IN TOKYO, JAPAN
"THOSE POOR GIRLS... THIS AWFUL FEELING GOES AWAY, RIGHT?"
NOPE.
THAT'S NOT FAIR.
NO, IT'S NOT.
I RECENTLY LOST SOMEONE, AND NOT A DAY GOES BY THAT I DON'T FEEL IT IN MY GUT. I'D LIKE TO TELL YOU ABOUT IT SOMETIME.
I'M DEEPLY SORRY FOR YOUR LOSS, MY FRIEND.
I HAVE FAITH THAT YOU'LL FIND A WAY TO CARRY THIS BURDEN. DON'T LET WHAT'S HAPPENED TO YOU BE AN EXCUSE FOR CYNICISM. YOU'RE A GREAT SOLDIER, AND THE WORLD NEEDS MEN LIKE US.
THANKS, CAP.
I AIN'T GOT THE WORDS, WADE.
LOOK ME UP STATESIDE AND WE CAN GRAB A BEER.
I THINK I WOULD LIKE THAT.
WOW. SUPER HERO GUYS' NIGHTS HAS LOTS OF FEELINGS.
AUGH. TOO MANY.
I'LL BE DAMNED IF I WAS TO CRY A SECOND TIME IN FRONT OF LOGAN AND CAPTAIN FREAKING AMERICA.

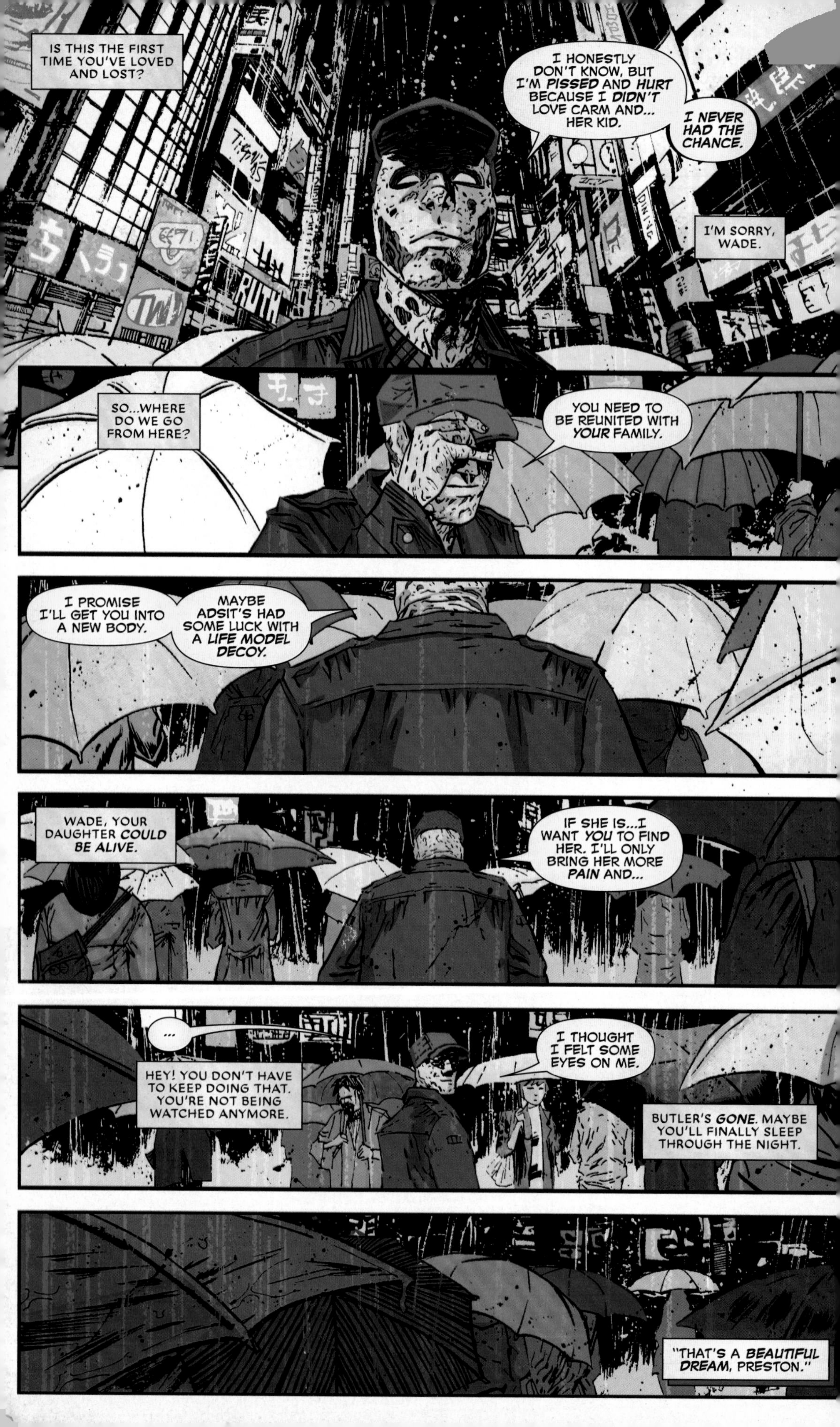
IS THIS THE FIRST TIME YOU'VE LOVED AND LOST?
I HONESTLY DON'T KNOW, BUT I'M PISSED AND HURT BECAUSE I DIDN'T LOVE CARM AND... HER KID.
I NEVER HAD THE CHANCE.
I'M SORRY, WADE.
SO...WHERE DO WE GO FROM HERE?
YOU NEED TO BE REUNITED WITH YOUR FAMILY.
I PROMISE I'LL GET YOU INTO A NEW BODY.
MAYBE ADSIT'S HAD SOME LUCK WITH A LIFE MODEL DECOY.
WADE, YOUR DAUGHTER COULD BE ALIVE.
IF SHE IS...I WANT YOU TO FIND HER. I'LL ONLY BRING HER MORE PAIN AND...
...
HEY! YOU DON'T HAVE TO KEEP DOING THAT. YOU'RE NOT BEING WATCHED ANYMORE.
I THOUGHT I FELT SOME EYES ON ME.
BUTLER'S GONE. MAYBE YOU'LL FINALLY SLEEP THROUGH THE NIGHT.
"THAT'S A BEAUTIFUL DREAM, PRESTON."

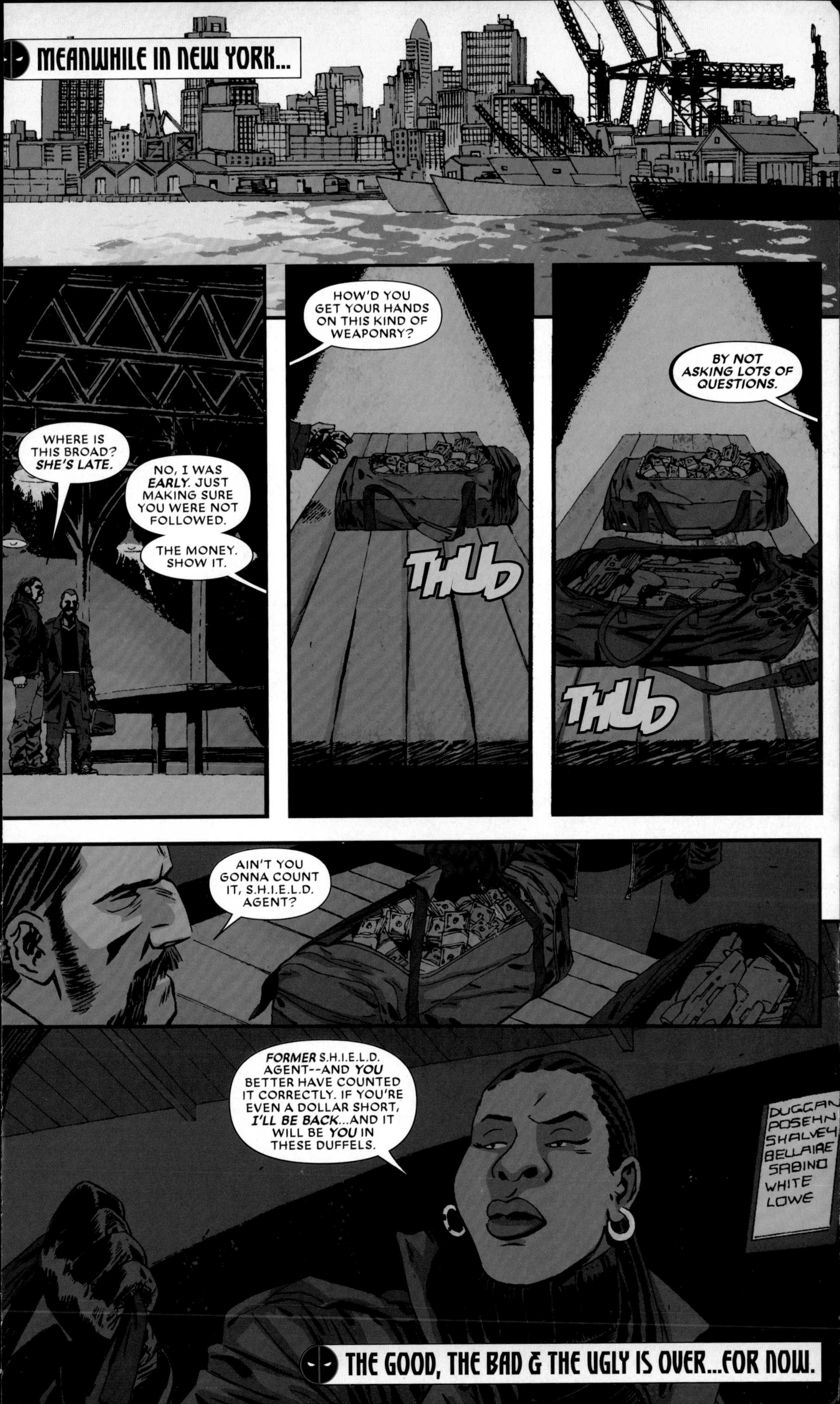
MEANWHILE IN NEW YORK...
WHERE IS THIS BROAD? *SHE'S LATE.*
NO, I WAS *EARLY*. JUST MAKING SURE YOU WERE NOT FOLLOWED.
THE MONEY. SHOW IT.
HOW'D YOU GET YOUR HANDS ON THIS KIND OF WEAPONRY?
THUD
BY NOT ASKING LOTS OF QUESTIONS.
THUD
AIN'T YOU GONNA COUNT IT, S.H.I.E.L.D. AGENT?
FORMER S.H.I.E.L.D. AGENT--AND *YOU* BETTER HAVE COUNTED IT CORRECTLY. IF YOU'RE EVEN A DOLLAR SHORT, *I'LL BE BACK*...AND IT WILL BE *YOU* IN THESE DUFFELS.
DUGGAN
POSEHN
SHALVEY
BELLAIRE
SABINO
WHITE
LOWE
THE GOOD, THE BAD & THE UGLY IS OVER...FOR NOW.

DECLAN SHALVEY SKETCHBOOK

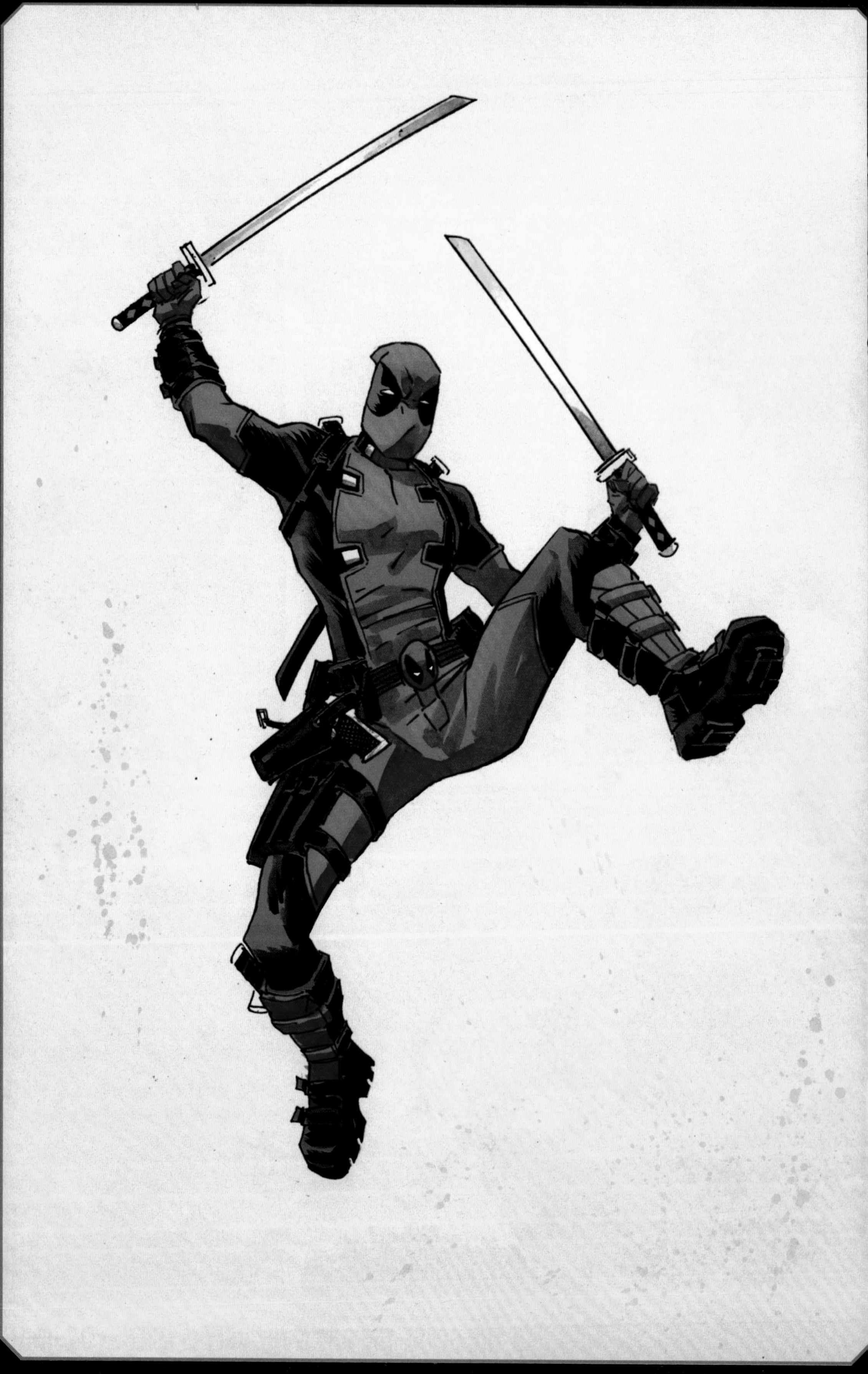

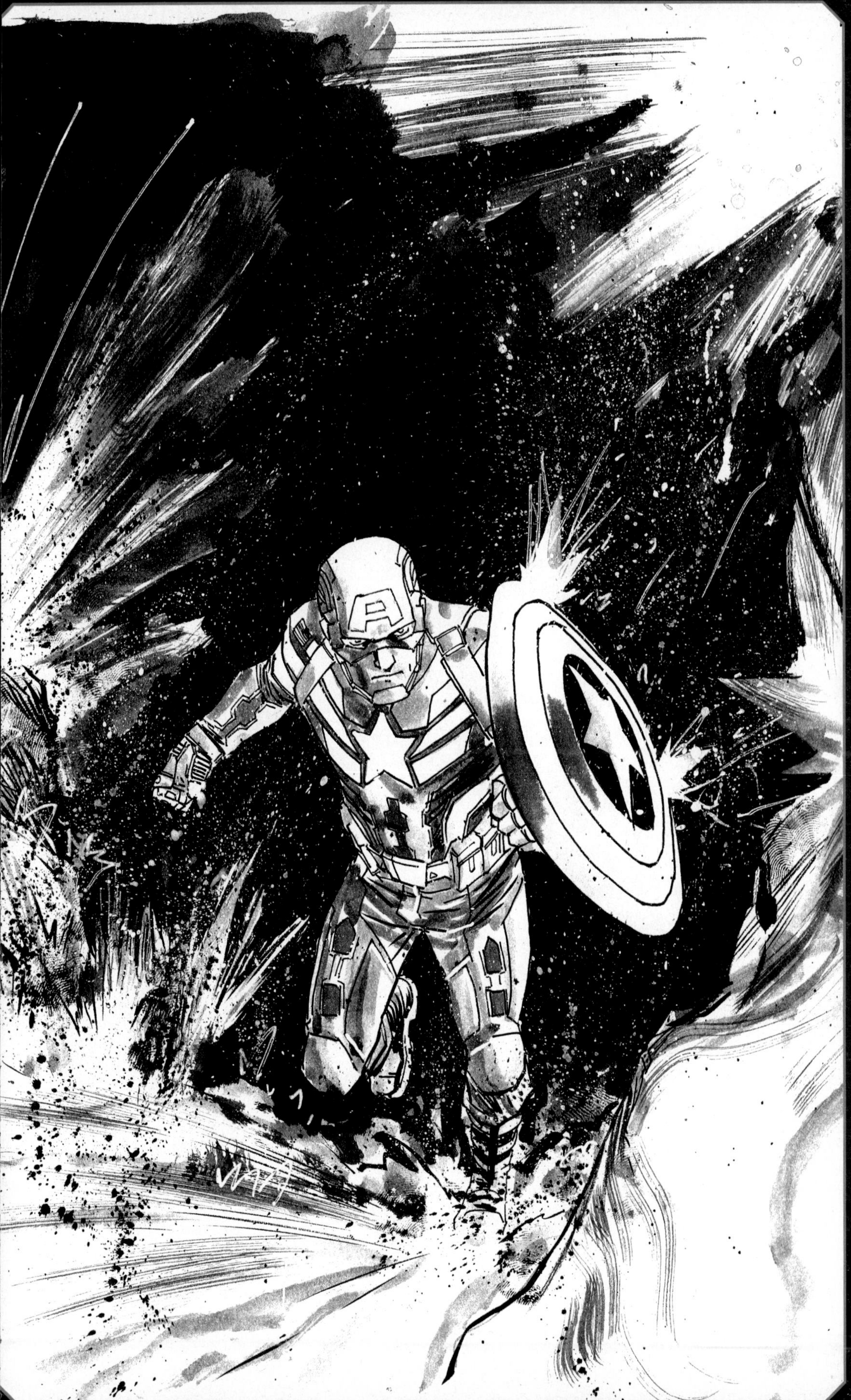

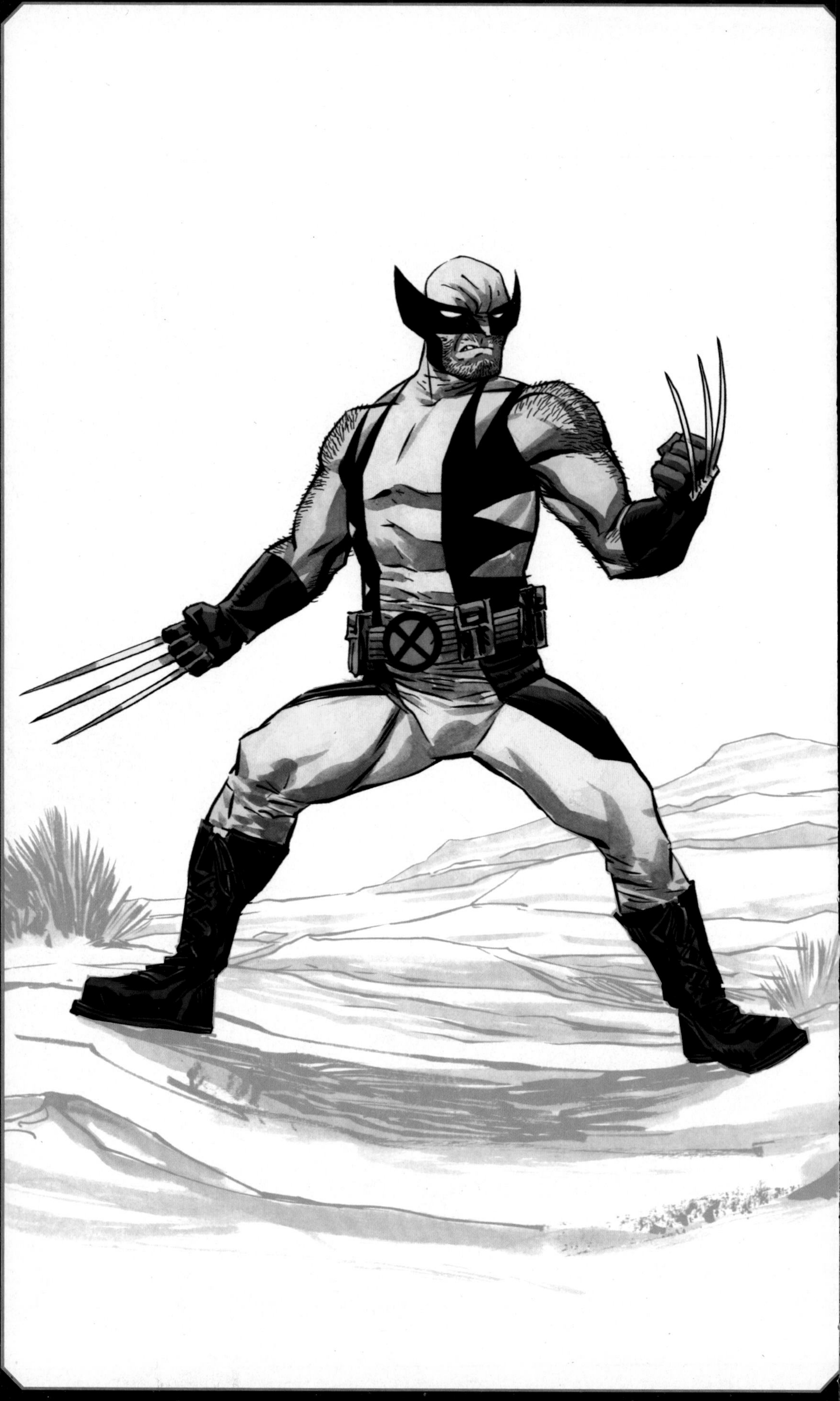

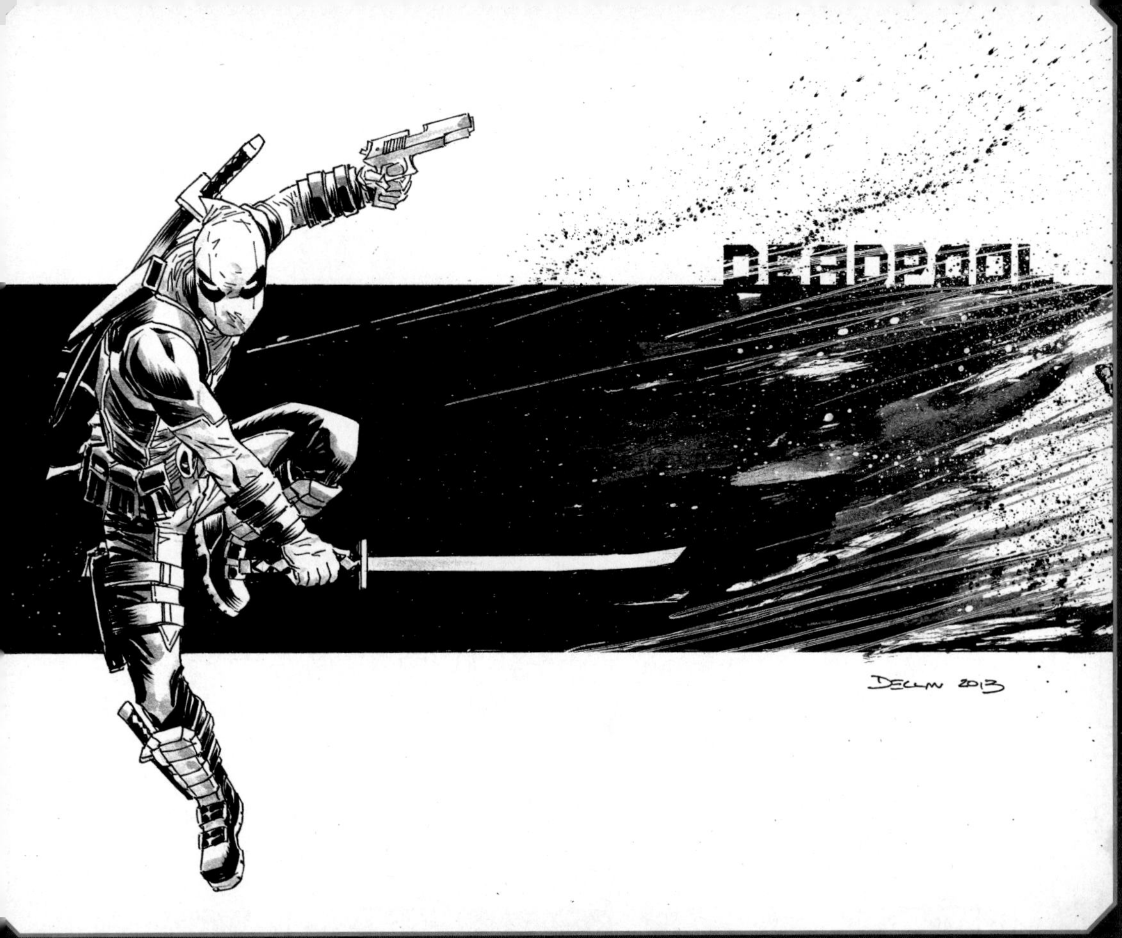
DEADPOOL
DECLAN 2013

COVER SKETCHES

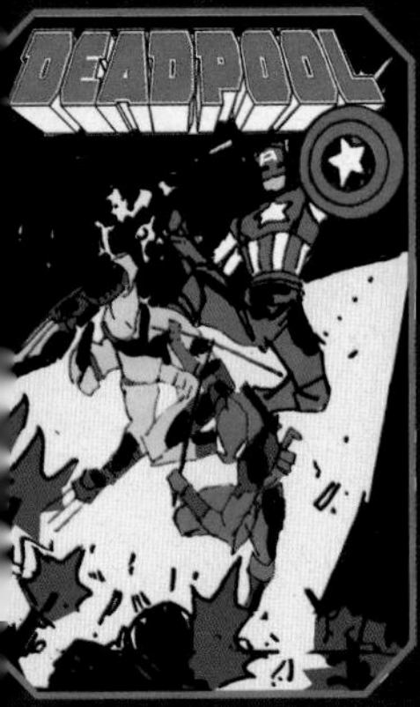
DEADPOOL

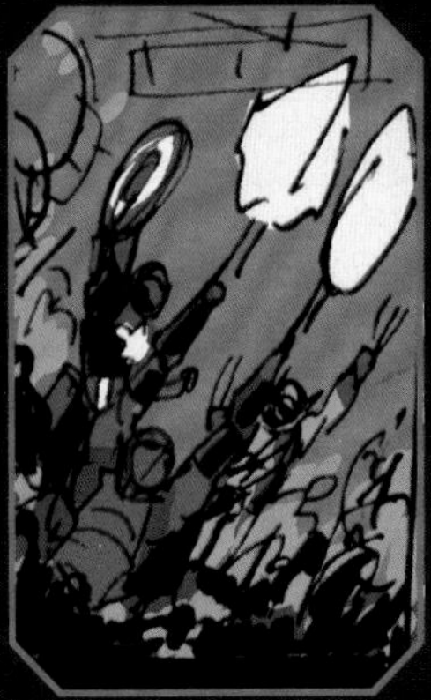

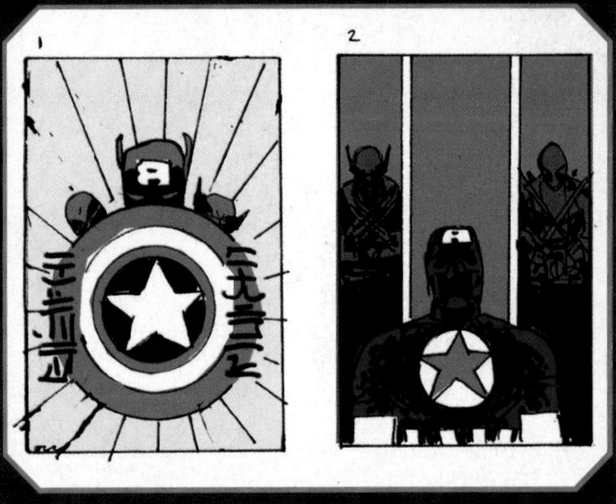
1
2

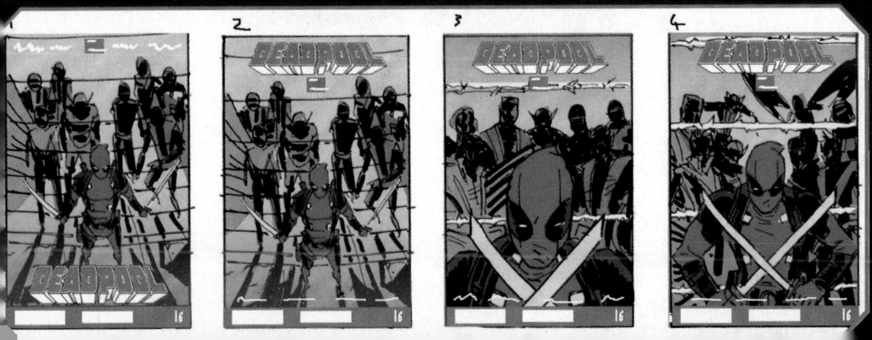
1
2
DEADPOOL
3
DEADPOOL
4
DEADPOOL
DEADPOOL

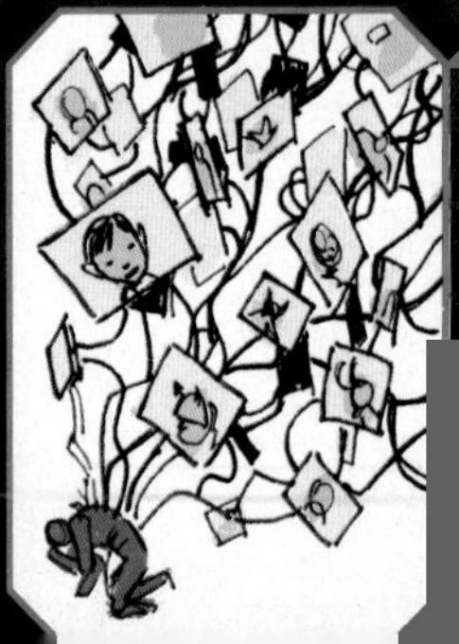

#15 & #16 LAYOUTS

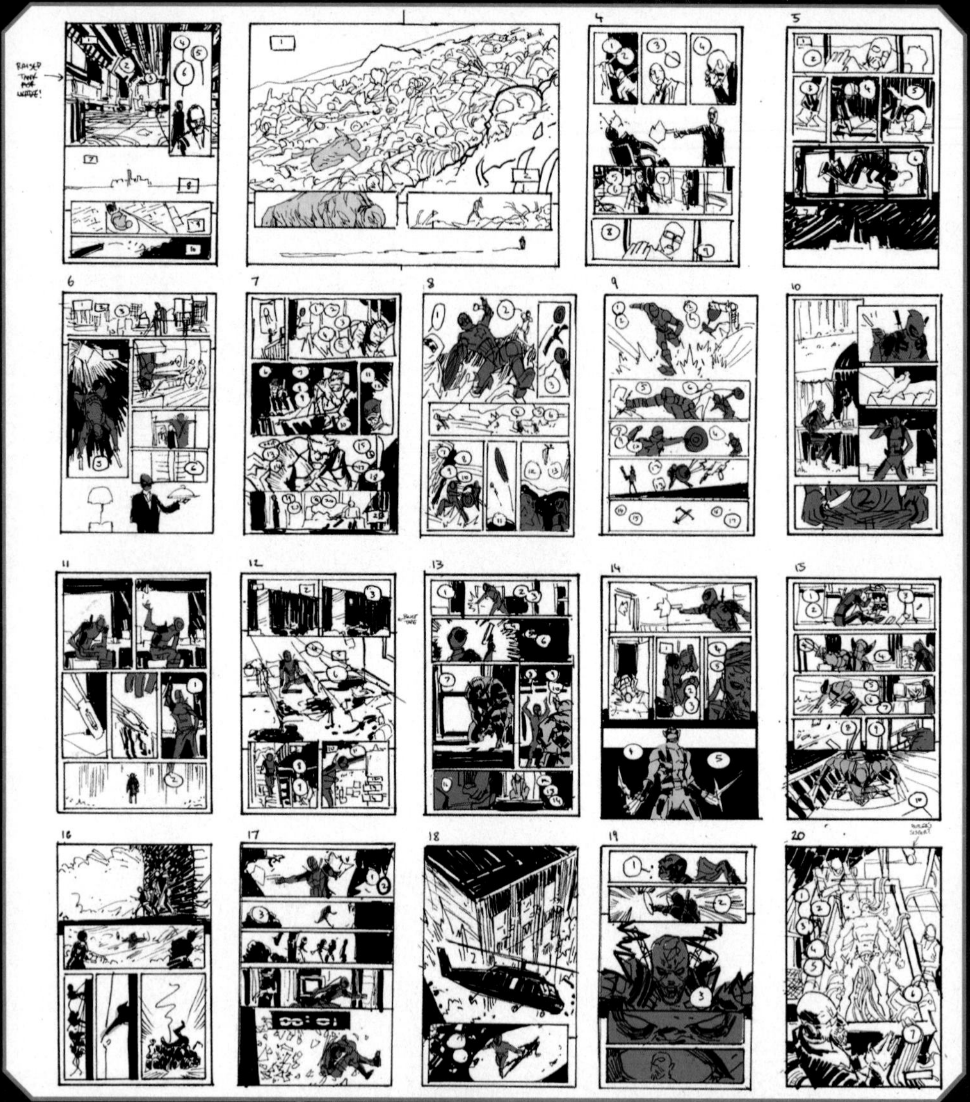

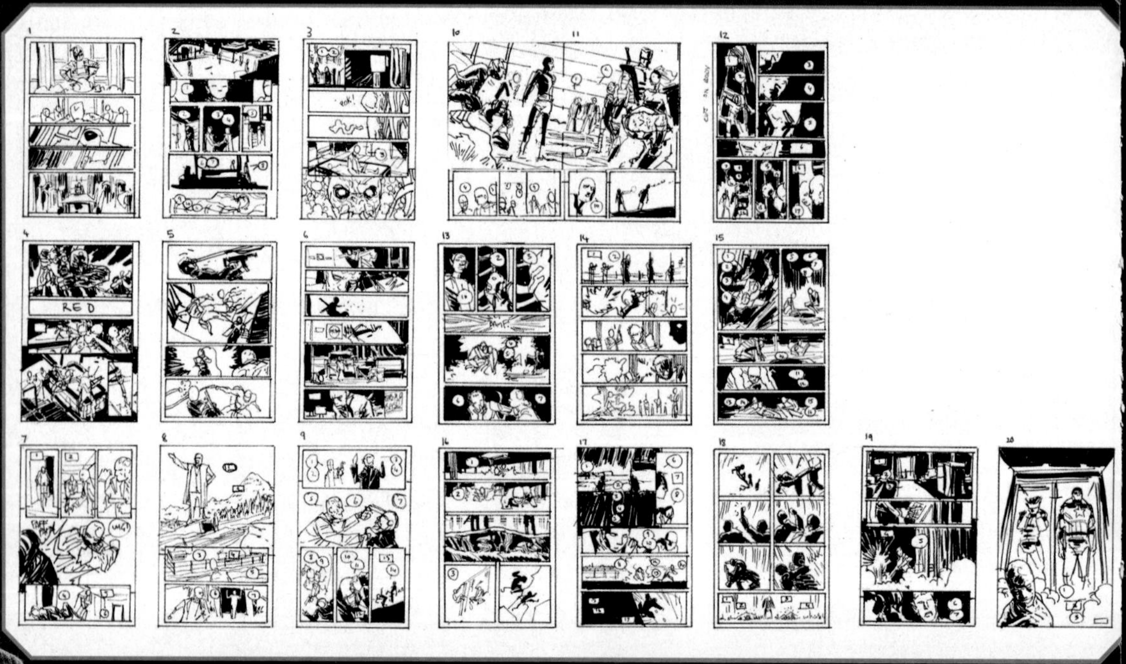
RED

"THIS STORY ALONE IS LIKELY TO MAKE IT ONE OF THE GREATS" - *CBR.com*

"This is a great start to a new chapter of Spider-Man, and you're not going to want to miss a second of it."
— *ComicVine.com*

SLOTT · STEGMAN · CAMUNCOLI
MY OWN WORST ENEMY

MARVEL NOW!

SUPERIOR SPIDER-MAN VOL. 1: MY OWN WORST ENEMY TPB
978-0-7851-6704-4 • MAR130724

"...THE NEW STATUS QUO HAS GIVEN THIS BOOK A BOOST IN MOMENTUM." – *AVClub.com*

MARVEL NOW!

© 2013 MARVEL

MARVEL AR AUGMENTED REALITY

MARVEL AUGMENTED REALITY (AR) ENHANCES AND CHANGES THE WAY YOU EXPERIENCE COMICS!

TO ACCESS THE FREE MARVEL AR CONTENT IN THIS BOOK*:

1. Locate the AR logo within the comic.
2. Go to Marvel.com/AR in your web browser.
3. Search by series title to find the corresponding AR.
4. Enjoy Marvel AR!

*All AR content that appears in this book has been archived and will be available only at Marvel.com/AR – no longer in the Marvel AR App. Content subject to change and availability.

DEADPOOL

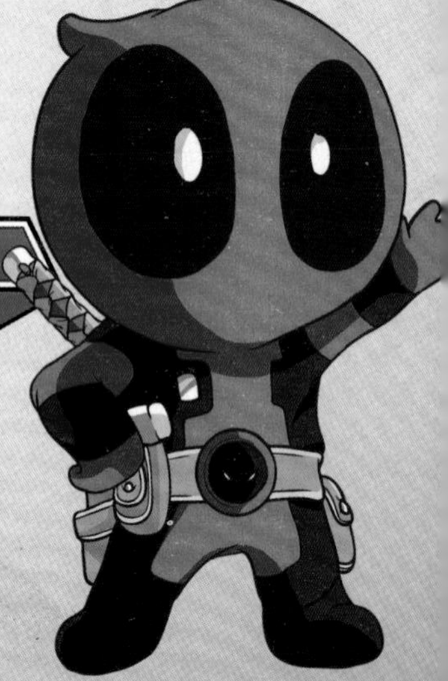

AR INDEX